Cosmopolitan Intimacies

Cosmopolitan Intimacies

Malay Film Music of the Independence Era

Adil Johan

NUS PRESS
SINGAPORE

© 2018 Adil Johan

Published by:
NUS Press
National University of Singapore
AS3-01-02, 3 Arts Link
Singapore 117569

Fax: (65) 6774-0652
E-mail: nusbooks@nus.edu.sg
Website: http://nuspress.nus.edu.sg

ISBN 978-981-4722-63-6 (paper)

National Library Board, Singapore Cataloguing in Publication Data

Name(s): Adil Johan.
Title: Cosmopolitan intimacies: Malay film music of the independence era / Adil
Johan.
Description: Singapore: NUS Press, [2018] | Includes bibliographical references
and index.
Identifier(s): OCN 993851926 | ISBN 978-981-4722-63-6 (paperback)
Subject(s): LCSH: Motion picture music–Singapore–20th century–History and
criticism. | Motion picture music–Malaysia–20th century–History and
criticism. | Malays (Asian people)–Singapore–Music–History and criticism. |
Malays (Asian people)–Malaysia–Music–History and criticism. | Motion
picture music–Social aspects–Singapore. | Motion picture music–Social
aspects–Malaysia.
Classification: DDC 781.542095957–dc23

Cover image: Illustration by Faris Ridzwan

Typeset by: Janice Cheong
Printed by: Vinlin Press Sdn Bhd

For
Nabilah and Asha

Contents

Figures

Abbreviations and Acronyms

A&R	artists and repertoire
ASAS '50	Angkatan Sasterawan '50 (Literary Generation of 1950)
ASWARA	Akademi Seni Budaya dan Warisan Kebangsaan (National Academy of Arts, Culture and Heritage)
BBM	BlackBerry Messenger
BN	Barisan Nasional (National Front, Malaysia)
CD	compact disc
DIY	do-it-yourself
EMI	Electric and Musical Industries
HMV	His Master's Voice
ISEAS	Institute of Southeast Asian Studies (Singapore)
KMM	Kesatuan Melayu Muda (Young Malays Union)
KRIS	Kesatuan Rakyat Indonesia Semenanjung (Indonesian Peoples of the Peninsula Organisation)
MCA	Malayan (Malaysian) Chinese Association
MCP	Malayan Communist Party
MFP	Malay Film Productions (Singapore)
MIC	Malayan (Malaysian) Indian Congress
MPAJA	Malayan People's Anti-Japanese Army
NEP	New Economic Policy (Malaysia)
NHB	National Heritage Board (Singapore)
PKMM	Partai Kebangsaan Melayu Malaya (Malay Nationalist Party of Malaya)
UMNO	United Malays National Organisation (Malaysia)
XFM	XFresh FM (Malaysia)

Note to the Reader

Film and Song Citations

I have used the author–title style of referencing for all printed sources. However, I have used in-text citations for films and songs. For films, I have included in parentheses the film's English translation (for initial citations), followed by the year and the director: for example, *Ibu Mertua-ku* (My Mother-in-law, 1962, dir. P. Ramlee). Films that do not include an English title translation are those that feature a protagonist's name, for example *Dang Anom* (1962, dir. Hussein Haniff) and *Hang Tuah* (1958, dir. Phani Majumdar).

Song titles are indicated in the standard way by single quotation marks, with English translations in parentheses and, if not indicated elsewhere, followed by the name of the composer: for example, 'Tunggu Sekejap' (Wait for a While, comp. P. Ramlee) and 'Sayang di Sayang' (Sweetheart Is Loved, comp. Zubir Said). If the lyrics for a song are not credited to the composer, I include the lyricist's name listed in Appendix A or in the footnotes.

In addition, for the films analysed in detail I have sought versions that are easily accessible on YouTube, with English subtitles where available, for the benefit of the reader. A selection of the films listed in the filmography includes references to the YouTube videos that were used for my analyses. While many of these films are broadcast on Malaysian national television and are still available in VCD and DVD formats in Malaysia and Singapore, their longevity and continued remembrance are now largely attributed to fans who have devoted entire YouTube channels to preserving such films. In addition, there is a wealth of YouTube videos that feature specific songs from these films.

Malay Names

Since Malay names employ a patronymic naming convention, in which the father's name is used in place of a surname, I have not abbreviated Malay names in the bibliography, in footnote references and throughout the book. For example, Zubir Said, Rohana Zubir and Ahmad Sarji are not shortened to their last names, which are in fact the names of their fathers. Many Malay female recording artists and actors are also referred to by their widely known screen or stage names, for instance Siput Sarawak, Saadiah, Zaiton and Normadiah. The shortening of Malay artists' names was a common practice in the 1950s and 1960s film and music industry, and P. Ramlee was known for adapting many of these abbreviated names including that of his third wife, Salmah Ismail, who is widely known as Saloma.

Language and Translation

The Malay language has spelling conventions that have changed drastically from their earliest introduction to romanised text to the present. Malaysian Malay spelling and vocabulary also vary significantly compared to Indonesian (*Bahasa Indonesia*). When citing Malay-language sources from the 1950s and 1960s, I reproduce verbatim the spellings of the source texts. These include the use of the '2' symbol for 'doubled' or plural words such as '*kesalahan2*' (faults), common in the 1950s and 1960s, which in contemporary (post-1980s) Malay is spelt out and hyphenated as '*kesalahan-kesalahan*'. In my transcriptions of 1950s and 1960s Malay film dialogue, I employ the latter, contemporary spelling conventions. Another example of old versus new Malay spelling is the replacement of 'o' with 'u' and the omission the letter 'h', for instance '*mabok*' (drunk) is spelt '*mabuk*' and '*chita2*' (aspirations) is now spelt '*cita-cita*'.

In addition, the reader will notice that many of the interview excerpts in Malay actually contain some English words. This is due to the inherently cosmopolitan nature of Malaysian and Singaporean Malay culture, in which English words are commonly interspersed in conversation. As such, I have only italicised the words in Malay. While any translation is ultimately a form of interpretation, I have nonetheless tried to adhere to the intended meaning of the interlocutors and texts. The same applies to my translation of Malay film titles as some words in Malay express nuanced meanings that cannot be conveyed with a literal translation.

Appendices

The appendices contain lyrics for the Malay songs that are analysed and their English translations; and the original Malay texts of longer citations that are translated into English in the text. Finally, there is a selection of musical transcriptions for some of the songs that are analysed.

Preface

This is a book about Malay film music from the 1950s and 1960s and its intertwined and culturally intimate relationship with postcolonial nation-making in the Malay Peninsula. Malay films produced in Singapore during this era were made during a period animated by Malaya's drive to independence and its aftermath, during which sentiments of anti-imperialist self-determination reverberated throughout what was then termed the Third World. While much has been written about the films, politics, history and nation-making movements in the region, there is a dearth of scholarship that addresses the importance of film music in articulating the cultural and political context of Malayan nation-making. I propose that a discussion of the *cosmopolitan intimacies* expressed in the music of these films is valuable in extending our understanding of nation-making in the region. Malay music and film are particularly potent art forms. They expressed in the popular culture of the period ideas of national independence and self-determination. This film music continues to be rearticulated in a nostalgic mode in present-day Malaysia and Singapore, thus referencing that liberating spirit of national independence in contemporary contexts.

The films and music of P. Ramlee, the omnipresent icon of 1950s and 1960s Malay film and music, continue to be broadcast on national television and radio stations, especially in Malaysia. His films and music are also shared for online streaming on YouTube by Malay-speaking fans from Malaysia and Indonesia. Reinterpretations of his films and music still abound. In fact, his iconicity as a national arts legend has been appropriated by state institutions, film-makers, musicians and global corporations for different political agendas, artistic goals and marketing purposes.

Across the Causeway, the musician and film composer Zubir Said has re-emerged as a symbol of Singapore's multicultural diversity. He is also mobilised by the Malay-minority community to assert the importance of Malay contributions to the Chinese-dominated island state. While this book is heavily weighted on the works and impact of P. Ramlee, Zubir Said offers an important counter-narrative to the development of Malay ethnonationalism in the Malay Peninsula. The recent re-emergence of Zubir Said as a Singaporean arts icon provides a mirror to the ubiquitous impact of P. Ramlee in Malaysia. Zubir Said was P. Ramlee's predecessor in the Singaporean music and film industry, and was also a vocal exponent of Malay nationalism in the arts prior to Singapore's expulsion from the Federation of Malaysia in 1965. He also retained his Indonesian citizenship until officially becoming Singaporean in the 1970s.

P. Ramlee, by contrast, while producing most of his best films in Singapore, was quick to leave the island for Kuala Lumpur in 1964. In Malaysia, P. Ramlee would experience a rapid decline in popularity and considerable obstacles to producing films right up to his death in 1973. Zubir Said, while residing in comparative obscurity in Singapore, lived a stable life until his death. Being the composer of Singapore's national anthem was a highlight among his numerous artistic contributions that immortalised him as one of very few ethnic Malay Singaporean national icons. In 2012, while I was conducting field research for this book, the memorialising of Zubir Said's contributions appeared in a detailed biography written by his daughter Rohana Zubir, a film festival showcasing his music held at the National Museum of Singapore and a tribute concert held at the Esplanade concert hall.

In Malaysia, the posthumous recognition of P. Ramlee's work that was ignited in the late 1980s continues to be articulated in street names, national monuments, state institutions, shopping malls, documentary and fictional films, theatrical productions and the online media. I am particularly interested in the lifespan of his music and national cultural iconicity that have recently been appropriated, refashioned, reinterpreted and consumed in artistic and commercial contexts. P. Ramlee's musical and cinematic legacy has become a space for contestation between state-sanctioned narratives and actors 'independent' of the state. I highlight indie music interpretations of P. Ramlee's songs that are ultimately co-opted by corporations to appeal to the local youth market.

I draw attention to the development of Malay nationalism through film music specifically within the Malay Peninsula. While the larger Malay-speaking nation of Indonesia intersects at various junctures with the discussion, I do not delve into Indonesian nation-making in the context of Malay film music. However, it is impossible to overlook the implicit role of Indonesia, especially when considering Zubir Said's Indonesian origins, P. Ramlee's Acehnese father, the numerous film actors and personnel with Indonesian origins, and the consumption of Singapore-made Malay films across Indonesia in the post-war period. For example, the first commercially successful Malay-language film, *Terang Boelan* (Bright Moon, 1937, dir. A. Balink), helped to circulate the popular film song of the film's title across the region (and beyond). The melody of 'Terang Boelan' would become the melody for Malaya's (and then Malaysia's) national anthem. In light of this, a detailed study ought to be undertaken to uncover the history of film music and Indonesian nationalism, and it is hoped that this book may form a launching pad for such work.

Another deliberate limitation of this book is to only analyse films produced in Singapore in the 1950s and 1960s. I do this because most Malaysian film scholars and fans argue that P. Ramlee's best work was produced in Singapore. While this is an issue of critical interpretation, it fits well with the narrative that P. Ramlee experienced a decline in both quality and reception once he made his move to Malaysia. It is interesting to note, however, the ways in which P. Ramlee's Singaporean-made films and music have now become symbols of Malaysian artistic greatness, simply by virtue of being the works of P. Ramlee, a citizen *par excellence* of Malaysia. This, then, presents an overarching paradox that recurs throughout the book. P. Ramlee is not only a Malaysian icon, but even more so an ethnic Malay icon of artistic greatness in the Malay world. However, it was the Chinese-owned Shaw Brothers' Malay Film Productions studio in post-war Singapore that enabled P. Ramlee to produce his so-called best works. Conversely, because of his return to Malaysia, the current nation state of Singapore has little official claim over P. Ramlee's films and music.

The book narrates how the national cultures of Singapore and Malaysia are poetically and intimately intertwined through the history of film music from the independence era of the Malay Peninsula. It also unravels how the 'golden era' of Malay film continues to be referenced, appropriated and rearticulated in diverging ways across present-day Malaysia and Singapore. There are still lacunae regarding the formation of these nation states, and I hope that a focus on film and music brings to light and amplifies new ideas about postcolonial nation-making, cosmopolitanism and cultural intimacy in the Southeast Asian region.

* * *

Being of mixed parentage—half Malay, quarter Chinese and quarter Sri Lankan Tamil—has provided me with a culturally unique upbringing in Malaysia. The everyday language of the household was English, and I grew up among many non-Malay, English-speaking friends. While this has never happened to me personally, Malays could refer to me as '*Melayu celup*' in a derogatory way, that is a 'dunked' Malay 'biscuit', only partially 'dipped', as it were, in authentic Malayness. This derision also implies a 'fakeness' in adopting the language of the (colonial) English other—of not being true to one's Malay roots. Nonetheless, there is no denying that I am culturally Malay and Muslim, growing up and congregating with Malay relatives and friends during the festive Aidilfitri (Eid ul-Fitr) or Hari Raya season that marks the end of the Muslim fasting month of Ramadan.

Concomitantly, growing up in mid-1980s to late-1990s Penang, Malaysia, I was never interested in learning 'traditional' Malay or Malaysian music. The lure of playing the saxophone and jazz enveloped me throughout my early teens, and grunge rock and heavy metal would soon intermingle with my musical interests in my later teen years. For my undergraduate studies, I went to Toronto, Canada, in the early 2000s, and was adamant in pursuing my passion for being a professional saxophonist, majoring in jazz performance. Then, while at university, my study of jazz would be complemented by a burgeoning attraction to electronic music and hip-hop.

Returning to Malaysia after six years of studying abroad, I taught contemporary music performance at a local private university and performed Western popular music, particularly jazz, rock and R & B.

In my years as a professional musician in Kuala Lumpur, I played a range of popular music, predominantly from the Western, English-speaking world. On the rare occasions that I would be asked to perform something Malaysian, I would inevitably play P. Ramlee's 'Getaran Jiwa' (Vibrations of the Soul), largely because it was one of the few Malay songs I knew. I understood it to be a jazzy, bossa nova-ish type of song composed by the most famous of Malaysian musicians.[1] I remembered watching his films on national television and hearing his songs during Hari Raya while growing up as a child, long before I started playing the saxophone. Despite my cosmopolitan upbringing and extremely Western or, even more so, African-American-inspired musical interests, P. Ramlee's music and films had somehow worked their way into my identity as a Malaysian musician. In retrospect, P. Ramlee's music was always a part of my musical subconsciousness as a Malaysian.

However, I was also self-conscious that I hardly knew anything about him, his music or his films. In my years as a professional musician, mostly performing in non-ethnically Malay contexts (English-language jazz and club bands, Chinese wedding functions), I noticed that few musicians in my circle knew much about P. Ramlee either. It was this realisation and deeply rooted embarrassment that became the initial impetus for the research of which this book is the outcome—feeling that I had spent most of my musical life looking outwards as it were, but ignoring what was part of my own culture. Of course, after gaining further knowledge about the cultural study of music (ethnomusicology), I came to realise that jazz, rock and hip-hop are as much a part of my identity as the film music of P. Ramlee. Further, I began to notice that Malay musicians such as P. Ramlee had very cosmopolitan backgrounds and diverse musical interests themselves.

Singapore, the de facto capital of the Malay Peninsula during the 1950s and 1960s, was a lively and vibrant hub for artists and entrepreneurs of all kinds from across the region and the world. While most Malay musicians from this era did not have the same opportunity

---

[1]   I would later learn that the underlying rhythm was a Latin American beguine.

to travel and learn music from outside Asia,[2] they had the privilege of creating music to call their own during an exciting yet ambiguous period of postcolonial nation-making. When P. Ramlee and Zubir Said started their musical careers, there were no clearly defined independent nation states to speak of, though the project of postcolonial autonomy through nation-making was the predominant sentiment throughout Southeast Asia at the time.[3] As cosmopolitan artists, P. Ramlee and Zubir Said had a unique opportunity to shape modern Malay artistic culture definitively through their music and films, and they did indeed do so by drawing from the rich local and foreign musical practices that circulated in their world. Their music also resonated with their own emotionally charged sentiments for an independent nation-in-the-making. Interestingly, this imagined nation would be unalterably divided into two, further reflecting the underlying racialised and postcolonial politics that underscored this period. Many of the romantic film narratives that featured their music intimated both the joys and troubles of their entangled protagonists, parallel to the dramatic and fraught formation of Malaysia and Singapore in 1965.

✳✳✳

Despite the minor struggles and heartaches encountered in any research project, this book was ultimately an immense pleasure to produce due to the much appreciated support from key individuals and institutions.

---

[2]   At the peak of his career P. Ramlee travelled to Asian countries such as Hong Kong and Japan for gatherings of the Asian Film Festival. P. Ramlee and Saloma also shot a scene in the Shaw Brothers' Mandarin film *Love Parade* (1961, dir. Ching Doe), in which the couple performed the popular Indonesian *keroncong* song 'Bengawan Solo' (comp. Gesang Martohartano, 1940). Zubir Said travelled frequently throughout Indonesia and the Malay Peninsula. Parallel to this, for a remarkable account of the Filipino jazz pianist Borromeo Lou, who spent six years performing in the United States in the early 1900s, see Peter Keppy, 'Southeast Asia in the age of jazz: Locating popular culture in the colonial Philippines and Indonesia', *Journal of Southeast Asian Studies* 44, 3 (2013): 450.

[3]   For an insightful edited volume on the films produced in the Commonwealth nations at the twilight of British colonial rule, see Lee Grieveson and Colin MacCabe, eds. *Film and the End of Empire*. London: British Film Institute, 2011.

Research conducted for this book was supported with funding from the King's College London Continuation Scholarship from the academic year 2012/13 to 2013/14, and the King's Partnership Grant funded a period of fieldwork and archival research in Singapore, hosted by the National University of Singapore.

Research was undertaken in libraries and archival resource centres in London, Singapore and Kuala Lumpur. I am especially thankful to Annabel Teh Gallop of the British Library, London, who introduced me to its vast collection of Malay film magazines from the 1940s to 1960s. I am grateful to Juffri Supa'at of the National Library, Singapore, for his enthusiastic support and intriguing conversations on Malay music and Singaporean nationalism. I am also thankful for the kind assistance of Farizam bt. Mustapha at the P. Ramlee Memorial Museum (Pustaka Peringatan P. Ramlee), who offered many resources and permitted me to take photographs at the museum. The staff of the Esplanade Library in Singapore, who allowed me to take photographs of the Malay Popular Music exhibition and the staff of the National Archives of Singapore, which contains recordings of the Singapore Oral History Project, were generous in their kind assistance. I am also thankful to the staff of the ISEAS-Yusof Ishak Institute Library in Singapore, as well as the National Archives of Malaysia (Arkib Negara Malaysia) and the Tunku Abdul Rahman Archive in Kuala Lumpur.

Katherine Butler Schofield has been a constant source of positive encouragement and indispensable scholarly advice. Andy Fry has always offered the most lucid advice for the most complicated situations, both personal and scholarly. The kind, encouraging and incisive advice of Martin Stokes, as well as his seminal scholarship, has left a significant impression on my own academic endeavours. Jim Sykes was a big brother-like academic presence and guided me accordingly during the initial years of the research. David Irving has been an inspiration in his pioneering research on music in Southeast Asia and the Malay world. I am very grateful for the mentorship of Frederick Moehn and the many early mornings and late evenings of first-year course planning, grading, emailing and straight-up musicking. I am also thankful for the radical perspectives offered by Zeynep Bulut and her class on experimentalism in popular music. Heather Wiebe was indispensible in her insightful comments and advice on my work. Richard Lund provided some very encouraging and candid comments on the state of Malaysian music research. Julia Byl has been inspiring in both her research on music in the Malay world and her energising presence. I am also thankful to both Ben Murtagh and Mulaika Hijjas of the School of Oriental and African Studies, University of London, who offered me the opportunity to screen a Malay film and present my research in their Jawi summer course in 2014. Anna Morcom pointed out the importance of my 'insider perspective' to this work, and I have done my best to be accordingly reflexive in this ethnography.

On the Malaysian and Singaporean side, I am indebted to Tan Sooi Beng who was the first ethnomusicologist I ever met. She encouraged me to pursue music performance and later ethnomusicology. The field of Malaysian (and Singaporean) music research is small and I hope to build on her enduring contributions to this growing area of study. During the early stages of my research, she alerted me to the work of Timothy P. Barnard, who became my mentor during the fieldwork period in Singapore. His work on Malay film history has been at the forefront of scholarship in this area of study and portions of this book are a musical expansion of the ideas proposed by his research. I am also very thankful to the energetic and encouraging guidance of Bart Barendregt who offered me the opportunity to publish a chapter in his edited volume.[4] A modified and expanded version of that piece is now Chapter Five of this book. In addition, Margaret Sarkissian has been very encouraging and supportive, sharing much enthusiasm regarding my study.

I was fortunate to meet Juffri Supa'at and Azlan Mohamed Said who recently wrote a biographical book on Malay Singaporean musicians from the 1900s to 1960s. My late-night conversation with them was instrumental to the ideas formulated here. I am indebted to Eddin Khoo for sharing his thoughts on Malay music as well as his father's copy of the compiled volume of working papers presented at the National Culture

---

[4] Adil Johan, 'Disquieting degeneracy: Policing Malaysian and Singaporean popular music culture from the mid-1960s to early-1970s', in *Sonic Modernities in the Malay World: A History of Popular Music, Social Distinction and Novel Lifestyles (1930s–2000s)*, ed. Bart Barendregt. Leiden: Brill, 2014, pp. 135–61.

Congress, Kuala Lumpur, in 1971. Syed Muhd Khairudin Aljunied took the time to meet me and share his historical passion for Malay films. Mohamad Jamal Mohamad, the programme manager of Taman Warisan Melayu (Malay Heritage Centre), Singapore, obliged with a lucid and highly insightful interview with me in his busy schedule.

I am also thankful for the support of my academic peers: Jenny McCallum, Richard Williams, Raja Iskandar @ Abang Is, David Marquiss, Lawrence Davies, Tamara Turner, Yvonne Liao, Alicia Izharuddin, Nazry Bahrawi and Patricia Hardwick.

My friend, Juan Pablo DeZubiria, reminded me that just because one performs music, it does not deny it from being an 'academic' endeavour. As such, I am thankful to all the non-scholarly musicians, from Australia, Britain, Canada, Indonesia, Malaysia and Singapore, whom I have performed and interacted with, as well as the musicians featured in this book who are scholars in their own right. In particular, I would like to acknowledge my band members, collaborators and musical co-conspirators: Nadir and the Azmyl Yunor Orkes Padu collective. I am also very grateful for the support, patience and understanding of my closest friends from Malaysia who have put up with my absence due to pursuing an academic career. In truth, my friendships and experiences of social life and music in Malaysia have been the source of inspiration for this study.

I had many interlocutors in Malaysia and Singapore whose interviews provided invaluable insights for this thesis. At the early stages of this research, Amir Muhammad, author of *120 Malay Movies*,[5] provided important insights and rightly reminded me to watch contemporary Malaysian films too. James Lochhead and Paul Augustin very kindly inspired me with their groundbreaking historical research on music in Penang and graciously connected me with very important informants. Ben Liew and Alif Omar Mahfix of *Juice* magazine gave me the low-down on the Malaysian indie scene—its complexities, contradictions and paradoxes were all discussed in the span of an afternoon in Kuala Lumpur. My interviews with Ahmad Nawab, Ahmad Merican, Low Zu

---

[5]   Amir Muhammad, *120 Malay Movies*. Petaling Jaya: Matahari Books, 2010.

Boon, Joseph Clement Pereira, Adly Syairi Ramly and the late Kassim Masdor were integral to this research. I am deeply indebted to all of them. I was very fortunate to meet Puan Sri Dr Rohana Zubir, and am thankful for her kind permission to reproduce a photo of her father from her book (Figure 3.8).[6] I am also indebted to Saidah Rastam who facilitated this meeting and whose detailed research and publication on Malayan popular music history have invigorated this field of study.[7]

The later stages of writing this book were completed while working at Sunway University's Department of Performance and Media and the Institute of Ethnic Studies (KITA) at Universiti Kebangsaan Malaysia. I am especially thankful for the diverse insights on Malaysia, music, film and performing arts provided by Azmyl Yusof, Rajeshkumar Subramaniam, Keith Hennigan, Imri Nasution, Mark Teh, Anne James, Brenda Danker, Sanjit Randhawa and Azrain Ariffin. Sharmila Subramaniam kept the department and its students in much needed order! The students of my World Cinema course illuminated my research with their impassioned debate over whether P. Ramlee 'belonged' to Singapore or Malaysia. I am indebted to Shamsul Amri Baharuddin, who helms KITA, for providing me with the opportunity to pursue my research full time. All my colleagues at KITA have added more depth to this research with their diverse insights and I am very thankful to be a member of the KITA family. Importantly, this book would not be possible without the professional support of the NUS Press team, Lena Qua, Christine Chong, Paul Kratoska and Peter Schoppert, and the impeccable editorial work of Gareth Richards, ably assisted by Helena Dodge-Wan and Siti Aishah Kamarudin. I am also thankful for the indispensable suggestions offered by two anonymous reviewers. Faris Ridzwan created the acrylic painting used on the front cover of the book—an impression of a well-known scene from P. Ramlee's film *Ibu Mertua-ku*—and I am grateful to him for this.

---

[6]   Rohana Zubir, *Zubir Said, the Composer of Majulah Singapura*. Singapore: ISEAS Publishing, 2012.

[7]   Saidah Rastam, *Rosalie and Other Love Songs*. 2nd ed., Petaling Jaya: Strategic Information and Research Development Centre, 2017.

Most of all, I would like to thank my family for their most consistent and irreplaceable support. My sister Rosa has been ever supportive in reminding me to stay grounded, and my parents, who provided my sister and I with a very cosmopolitan upbringing, have never failed to provide their invaluable encouragement and advice. Their dedication as parents and scholars is truly inspirational.

Over the course of this research, I was fortunate to join a new family. For that I am very thankful for the acceptance and generosity offered by my parents-in-law, Dato' Muhamad Mustapha Jantan and Datin Danila Daud. I am also thankful for three new brothers, two sisters and two nieces, Rania and Ines, who have enriched my life with their precocious energy.

Last, and certainly not least, I am deeply grateful for the support and encouragement of my life partner, Nabilah Hanim. She was by my side through all the emotional and intellectual challenges of this process, and, in doing so, has come to understand my journey in writing this book more than anyone else. Inseparably, she remains the melody to my rhythm and the music to my narrative.

This book is dedicated to the memory of my late paternal grandmother, Bobby Saravanamuttu @ Teng Ah Soo, my late maternal grandfather, Allahyarham Dato' Mohamad Yeop Mohamad Raof, and Allahyarham Kassim Masdor.

Adil Johan
Kuala Lumpur, January 2018

Chapter 1

Introduction

Malay [film] aesthetics are an eclectic thing. Ours is a crazy mixture of Indian, Chinese, Arab, Indonesian, Portuguese, and English cultures.[1]

The Javanese phrase '*Niat ingsun matek'aji Semar ngising!*' was used in the comedy film *Ali Baba Bujang Lapok* (1961, dir. P. Ramlee), a parody of the orientalised tale of *Ali Baba and the Forty Thieves*.[2] The chief thief (*ketua penyamun*) played by P. Ramlee sings the phrase in a *pelog* scale—commonly used in Javanese gamelan music—to open his secret cave of stolen riches. This phrase is a localised replacement of the well-known 'Open Sesame' of the story told in English.[3] Most Malaysians, Singaporeans and Indonesians who are fans of films from this era would be able to recall this famously humorous scene.[4] However, finding

---

[1]   Tilman Baumgärtel, "'I want you to forget about the race of the protagonists half an hour into the film". Interview with Yasmin Ahmad', in *Southeast Asian Independent Cinema: Essays, Documents, Interviews,* ed. Tilman Baumgärtel. Singapore: NUS Press, 2012, p. 252.
[2]   This comical phrase is sung in refined Javanese (*Jawa halus*).
[3]   Nazry Bahrawi, 'A thousand and one rewrites: Translating modernity in the *Arabian Nights*', *Journal of World Literature* 1, 3 (2016): 357–58 provides a brief description of the anachronism found in *Ali Baba Bujang Lapok* to initiate his discussion about the 'cross-cultural translatability' of rewritten tales from *A Thousand and One Nights* in three renditions of world literature.
[4]   James Harding and Ahmad Sarji, *P. Ramlee: The Bright Star.* 2nd ed., Petaling Jaya: MPH, 2011, p. 116. Jane Sunshine claims that 'any Malaysian ... will tell you that [the phrase] is a famous line from a movie made by the legendary filmmaker, P. Ramlee', adding that the phrase 'doesn't really mean anything, really'. Jane Sunshine, 'My language is mine: Ya in sing mata kaji', The Splendid Chronicles, 30 August 2005. Available at http://splenderfulchronicles.blogspot.my/2005/08/my-language-is-mine-ya-in-sing-mata.html [accessed 18 December 2017].

1

direct translations of the phrase requires some deeper digging on the internet, which led me to an interesting exchange between Malaysians and Indonesians who speak Javanese. On the Malaysian blog W.E. Chronicles, a post translates the phrase as '*Niat insan, dengan tekad hingga Semar terberak!*' (This mortal's will is so resolute that Semar will defecate!) A blog comment on this post from a Javanese speaker corrects the translation of the refined Javanese word '*ingsun*' to '*saya/aku*' (me), not having any other issues with the rest of the phrase's translation.[5]

There are different ways of glossing this phrase, and I propose two translations. The comic potency of the phrase lies in its manifold and irreverent interpretations. Of my two translations, one is more vulgar than the other. More commonly understood, the phrase can be read as a will so great that the mystical deity Semar would defecate: 'My wish is so resolute that even the deity Semar will be forced to defecate!' Such is the strength of will required to open the cave's hidden door. My second version relates to the local ritual of asking an unspecified deity or ancestral spirit (that is, a *datuk* or *nenek-moyang* in Malay) for permission to urinate or defecate outdoors in natural environs: 'My need is so great [deity] Semar, I wish to relieve myself!' This is a common superstitious practice that has been passed down from the region's pre-Islamic Hindu-Buddhist and animist practices.[6]

Beyond these translations or interpretations, it is salient to highlight that the phrase's reference to the Javanese shadow puppet theatre (*wayang kulit*) deity (*tokoh*) named Semar is an intertextual one, linking the film's comedic text to a regional lineage of 'screened' entertainment.[7]

---

5 'AliBaba', W.E. Chronicles, 23 December 2010. Available at https://niwtode.wordpress. com/2010/12/23/e-lol-alibaba/ [accessed 18 December 2017]. Harding and Ahmad, *P. Ramlee*, p. 116 'very roughly' translate it as 'Please open up, I really have to go [to the lavatory].'

6 Growing up in Malaysia from the 1980s to 2000s, I remember being told by my elders to ask for permission from an unknown spirit deity to relieve myself when outdoors.

7 The manifestation of Semar is further complicated in the corpus of *wayang* mythology and narrative interpretations. In eastern Java, Semar exists as a complex symbol of fertility and life; see Wisma Nugraha Christianto, 'Peran dan fungsi tokoh Semar-Bagong dalam pergelaran lakon wayang kulit gaya Jawa Timuran', *Humaniora* 15, 3 (2003): 285–301. But it is also described as a 'hermaphroditic clown-servant of wayang' in other interpretations; see Matthew Isaac Cohen, *The Komedie Stamboel:*

This musical Javanese phrase, then, is a potent example of a culturally intimate expression that is employed as a form of irreverent humour in P. Ramlee's film. The cross-cultural use of Javanese (instead of Malay) was also conveniently strategic in its evasion of British colonial censorship. *Ali Baba Bujang Lapok* was subjected to a temporary ban due to the excessive use of Arabised Malay accents that British censors felt would insult Singapore's Middle Eastern population.[8] Prior to the film's release, one of its female stars, Normadiah, related the difficulty of maintaining an 'Arabic accent' (*telor Arab*) in her dialogue.[9] The solution was to overdub most of the spoken dialogue into more *neutral* Malay accents.[10]

Nonetheless, when screened across the Malay world in the 1960s, an intimate acquaintance with ritual practices that acknowledged (or mocked) the supernatural Javanese phrases and melodies—of local profanities converging with a Western/cosmopolitan, Middle Eastern/

Popular Theatre in Colonial Indonesia, 1891–1903. Leiden: KITLV Press, 2006, p. 341. It has been interpreted by the Australian novelist C.J. Koch as 'a dwarf who serves Arjuna. But he's also a god in disguise—the old Javanese god Ismaja', cited in Felicia Campbell, 'Silver screen, shadow play: The tradition of the wayang kulit in *The Year of Living Dangerously*', *Journal of Popular Culture* 28, 1 (1994): 165. These are but a small selection of interpretations of the *tokoh*. Patricia Matusky, *Malaysian Shadow Play and Music: Continuity of an Oral Tradition*. Kuala Lumpur: The Asian Centre, 1997 provides an important ethnomusicological study on Malaysian shadow puppet theatre.

8 Rohayati Paseng Barnard and Timothy P. Barnard, 'The ambivalence of P. Ramlee: *Penarek Beca* and *Bujang Lapok* in perspective', *Asian Cinema* 13, 2 (2002): 26; Ahmad Sarji, *P. Ramlee: Erti Yang Sakti* [P. Ramlee: The Sacred Reality]. 2nd ed., Petaling Jaya: MPH, 2011, p. 16. The issue of the use of Arab accents and overdubbing is well known among P. Ramlee film enthusiasts. One blog sources this information to a conversation the blogger had with the actor Aziz Sattar who played Ali Baba in the film; '10+ Info tentang P Ramlee yang belum anda tahu', OtaiCerita, 10 December 2014. Available at http://otaicerita.blogspot.com/2014/12/10-info-tentang-p-ramlee-yang-belum.html#ixzz51cj8U2sE [accessed 18 December 2017].

9 In the magazine article, Normadiah is quoted as saying '*Memang tak mudah berlakun dalam filem arahan P. Ramlee, lebeh2 lagi saya di-kehendaki-nya berchakap dalam gaya dan telor Arab*' (It is definitely not easy to act in a P. Ramlee film, moreover, he wants me to speak in an Arabic manner and accent), *Majallah Filem*, 7 October 1960, p. 6.

10 U-Wei Haji Saari refers to the form of interregional Malay accent—the 'Jalan Ampas Malay'—that afforded Shaw Brothers' Malay Film Productions universality across different accents of the language in the region. U-Wei Haji Saari, 'Zubir Said, semoga bahagia' [Zubir Said, may you achieve happiness], in *Majulah! The Film Music of Zubir Said*. Singapore: National Museum of Singapore, 2012, p. 5.

orientalist narrative—elicits both unforgettable humour and intricately linked semiotic commonalities. Retrospectively, amid increasingly conservative and state-enforced Islam in Malaysia, any acknowledgement of this pre-Islamic superstitious practice would be considered problematic in public discourse. However, the irreverent hilarity of the phrase has allowed it to exist in Malay and Malaysian discourse about films and music. It has become a private inside joke for the Malay world's transnational network and history of popular culture. The expression and circulation of this musical phrase thus provides an example of the *cosmopolitan intimacy* of Malay film music from the 1950s and 1960s that resonates, albeit discreetly, in the present.

The period of film and music that is the focus of this book has been dubbed the Malay studio film era in line with mass production practices of the global post-war film industry.[11] Such films are also considered to belong to the independence (*merdeka*) era in the Malay Peninsula, and thus concomitant with an extensive period of postcolonial nation-making around the world.[12] In the contemporary Malay world, in the nationalist and populist discourse, this period has been recognised nostalgically as the 'golden era' of Malay film. My aim in this book is to provide a historical ethnography, through an analysis of film and music, of the nostalgic sentiments and cosmopolitan intimacies of nation-making in the Malay Peninsula.

The musical compositions of P. Ramlee—a director, actor, singer and composer of Malay-language films in the 1950s and 1960s—have remained omnipresent markers of Malaysian and, to some extent, Singaporean national cultural identity up to today. His numerous films and musical output from this era are regularly screened on Malaysian and Singaporean national television and heard on radio stations and are easily accessible online via websites such as YouTube.[13] Since the 1980s

---

[11] Amir Muhammad, *120 Malay Movies*. Petaling Jaya: Matahari Books, 2010, pp. 14–16.

[12] Timothy P. Barnard, 'Decolonization and the nation in Malay film, 1955–1965', *South East Asia Research* 17, 1 (2009): 65–86.

[13] Most of the films viewed for this book were accessed on YouTube; see Filmography. The online community of P. Ramlee and Malay film fandom is worthy of its own separate study.

his film songs have been the subject of innumerable interpretations in various styles, from orchestral arrangements to rock renditions to hip-hop remixes. Since 2007 a Broadway-style musical of his life, featuring his compositions, has been staged in sold-out theatres across Malaysia and Singapore.[14] An online mini-series titled *The Road to Ramlee*, about young Malaysians forming a rock band, was released on YouTube in 2015 to promote Samsung's Galaxy Note 4 mobile phone. And more recently, the National Academy of Arts, Culture and Heritage (Akademi Seni Budaya dan Warisan Kebangsaan, ASWARA) is awaiting an upgrade to university status and will be tentatively named Universiti P. Ramlee. In Malaysia, P. Ramlee's iconic presence is ubiquitous and inescapable.

Historically, P. Ramlee's films and music projected the aspirational sentiments of postcolonial nationhood alongside the social anxieties of rapid urbanisation and modernisation. There were also other film composers such as Zubir Said and Kassim Masdor whose music for films contributed similarly to these cultural constructions of nationhood in both Singapore and Malaysia.[15] Despite the enduring impact of these composers and their music on national culture in the Malay Peninsula, there has been a dearth of published research on them and the music of Malay films of the 1950s and 1960s. This book seeks to provide a much-needed in-depth study on this neglected area of historical, cultural and musicological scholarship by analysing the musical practices and cultural intimations expressed in commercially produced vernacular Malay films made in Singapore during this period. While I explore the potency of such films and music as intimate expressions of a national culture, I also consider the commercial context of Malay film and music production. Since the 1930s the vernacular film and music industries of the Malay Peninsula had consisted of private enterprises seeking to profit from a

---

[14] While I do not discuss this musical in detail, a brief analysis is available in Andrew Clay McGraw, 'Music and meaning in the independence-era Malaysian films of P. Ramlee', *Asian Cinema* 20, 1 (2009): 53–55. There is also a detailed publication about the production; see Karen J. Tan, Faridah Stephens and Najua Ismail, *Behind the Scenes at P. Ramlee—The Musical*. Petaling Jaya: MPH, 2008.

[15] A brief biography of Zubir Said is contained in Chapter Three. A more comprehensive biography is presented in Rohana Zubir, *Zubir Said, the Composer of Majulah Singapura*. Singapore: ISEAS Publishing, 2012.

growing market of Malay-speaking consumers. I thus aim to uncover the relevance of screened music in articulating the complexities and paradoxes of a cosmopolitan Malay identity in transition, within the context of mid-twentieth-century capitalism, late colonialism, and Malaysian and Singaporean independence.

My research also aims to advance analytical techniques for understanding the interactive links between postcolonial musical, film and cultural productions, while developing ideas about cultural intimacy and cosmopolitan nation-making. In doing so, it contributes methodologically to the field of ethnomusicology for studying such relationships. I hope to provide new perspectives for the field of Malay studies, in which music has long been neglected. Music provides new insights into how the concept of Malayness is affectively practised, performed and embodied in contemporary Singapore and Malaysia. I unravel how ideas and icons associated with Malay film music of the 1950s and 1960s have, in some cases, become static symbols of nostalgia. Yet, in other cases, they have allowed for a contestation of such rigid references to national culture. This study sets out to answer important questions about the impact and meaning of Malay film music and nation-making. Specifically, how has Malay film music made such a lasting impact on the historical narrative of nation-making in Malaysia and Singapore? Why has this music endured as a ubiquitous marker of a modern Malay ethnic identity in the Malay Peninsula? More importantly, how have such potent ethnonational associations been derived from a musical repertoire that is overtly cosmopolitan in style, diverse in cultural influences, yet resonant with the intimate expressions of Malay culture? Why has this music and its attendant icons (P. Ramlee and Zubir Said) played such an important role in the nostalgic imaginings, reimaginings and rearticulations of an idealistic period of nation-making?

I argue that film music produced in the 1950s and 1960s articulates, through cosmopolitan practices, the cultural intimacies of postcolonial nation-making based on a conception of Malay ethnonationalism that was initially fluid, but eventually became homogenised as 'national' culture. While the music of Malay films derived from a highly multiethnic and diverse local musical culture, the structural limitations of a profit-driven film industry have in turn defined and delineated the boundaries of ethnicity in order to suit a vernacular *Malay* market. In this period English-language films from the United States and Britain, Hindi films from India and Mandarin films from China and Hong Kong were all widely consumed. The Malay-speaking population of Southeast Asia, however, was considered an untapped market with lucrative potential. Due to the strict linguistic boundaries that defined film industries, a homogeneous Malay film industry was developed, perhaps even contrived, to reflect the perceived taste and culture of a Malay-speaking consumer market.

The 1950s and 1960s were also a time of great social change in the Malay Peninsula. It is no coincidence that the golden age of Malay film corresponded with the independence era. The possibility of an autonomous Asian nationhood that was suggested by the Japanese during their occupation of the region provided the spark for Malay nationalism after the Second World War. That sentiment of self-determination was expressed in the cosmopolitan activism of young Malay journalists and writers who largely populated the creative staff of the emerging Malay film industry as directors, scriptwriters, composers and lyricists. Their aim was to promote a modern conception of Malay nationalism through the extensive use of the Malay language.[16] Film and music were widely accessible to the general public as they were entertaining and did not require literacy, yet were effective in articulating progressive sentiments about postcolonial national autonomy to the masses. The intimate and cosmopolitan musical articulations of the golden age were thus integral to the project of Malay independence and nation-making.

The construction of homogeneous national music cultures from pluralistic cultural practices has been studied extensively in other countries such as Zimbabwe, Trinidad and Tobago and India.[17] This

---

[16] Timothy P. Barnard and Jan van der Putten, 'Malay cosmopolitan activism in post-war Singapore', in *Paths Not Taken: Political Pluralism in Post-War Singapore*, ed. Michael D. Barr and Carl A. Trocki. Singapore: NUS Press, 2008, p. 140.

[17] Thomas Turino, *Nationalists, Cosmopolitans, and Popular Music in Zimbabwe*. Chicago: University of Chicago Press, 2000; Jocelyne Guilbault, *Governing Sound: The Cultural Politics of Trinidad's Carnival Music*. Chicago: University of Chicago Press, 2007; Janaki Bakhle, *Two Men and Music: Nationalism in the Making of an Indian Classical Tradition*. Oxford: Oxford University Press, 2005; Amanda J. Weidman,

book is thus situated within an understanding of modernist reformism in musical culture as a global phenomenon, not exclusive to the Malay world. Nonetheless, there are issues of ethnicity, social agency and nation-making that are evidently particular to the case of film music in the Malay Peninsula. One unique aspect was the ethnicised social and economic structure of the post-war film industry that afforded considerable creative autonomy to Malays in the area of music. In the early period of the film studio industry screenwriters and directors of Malay films were predominantly non-Malays and rigorous censorship laws were enforced in particular by the British colonial administration.[18] But the musical authorship of such films was predominantly in the hands of Malay composers such as P. Ramlee, Zubir Said, Yusof B., Osman Ahmad, Ahmad Jaafar, Wandly Yazid and Kassim Masdor. The social-structural relationships of race, class and power in post-war Malaya can be revealed through an intertextual reading of Malay films and music against the historical context of postcolonial nation-making in the region.

Malay film songs were an important part of a pluralistic Malay nationalist narrative. Using a conceptual framework of modernity, cosmopolitanism and cultural intimacy helps explain how internal/indigenous practices were adapted to external/foreign ideas by creative individuals to express modern notions of national culture. By considering how cosmopolitan practices are intimated and produced within discursive and structural contexts, I proceed to analyse how

---

Singing the Classical, Voicing the Modern: The Postcolonial Politics of Music in South India. London: Duke University Press, 2006; Lakshmi Subramanian, 'The reinvention of tradition: Nationalism, Carnatic music and the Madras Music Academy, 1900–1947', *Indian Economic and Social History Review* 36, 2 (1999): 131–63. These studies are discussed in greater detail in Chapter Six.

[18] Despite the granting of Malayan independence in 1957, Malay films released after independence were made in Singapore, which was still a British Crown colony. Thus, films produced in Singapore were subject to British scrutiny before being shown in cinemas across the Malay Peninsula and Indonesia. For more on Malay film censorship and independence see Barnard, 'Decolonization and the nation'; Hassan Abdul Muthalib, '"Winning hearts and minds": Representations of Malays and their milieu in the films of British Malaya', *South East Asia Research* 17, 1 (2009): 47–63; and Hassan Abdul Muthalib, 'The end of empire: The films of the Malayan Film Unit in 1950s British Malaya', in *Film and the End of Empire*, ed. Lee Grieveson and Colin MacCabe. London: British Film Institute, 2011, pp. 177–96.

Malay film music articulates creative agency by covertly expressing radical ideas. This was the case despite being produced within a commercial film industry that subjected local film-makers, music composers and performers to budgetary constraints and official censorship. Towards the end of the book, I examine the potency of culturally intimate discourses linked to icons of film music. Such films, music and icons are frequently recalled, nostalgically, to articulate the sentiments of national culture that are instrumentalised by state institutions, individual actors and, increasingly, corporations.

Musical Cosmopolitanism

A cosmopolitan cultural practice is one that can be distinguished as articulating two or more contrasting identities simultaneously. These identities are not necessarily divergent, but can be interactive, and in the case of artistic practices are often the result of active *aesthetic agency*. Musical cosmopolitanism is therefore a process in which individuals or cultural collectives create a musical aesthetic that is dialogical of contrasting local and supralocal ideas or approaches. In Thomas Turino's words, cosmopolitan practices must be seen as 'simultaneously local and translocal'.[19] Before delving into the notion of agency I discuss how social conceptions of cosmopolitan practices may be understood sociologically in relation to modernity.

Central to the understanding of cosmopolitan practices is the acknowledgement of a discursive relationship between the past and the present, the internal to the external, the indigenous to the foreign. In ethnomusicological research, a fundamental discursive dichotomy that has emerged is that of the 'modern' in opposition to the 'traditional'. Exemplified throughout this study are cultural practices, ideas and processes that reflect hierarchical discourses that view the 'modern' as a progression from the 'traditional'.[20] In the historical context of

---

19 Turino, *Nationalists, Cosmopolitans, and Popular Music*, p. 7.
20 Christopher A. Waterman, '"Our tradition is a very modern tradition": Popular music and the construction of a pan-Yoruba identity', *Ethnomusicology* 34, 3 (1990): 367–79. See also Margaret Sarkissian, *D'Albuquerque's Children: Performing Tradition in Malaysia's Portuguese Settlement*. London: University of Chicago Press, 2000.

Malaysia, Singapore and many postcolonial states in the 1950s and 1960s, it is common to find cultural productions articulating ideologies of modernity that 'militated against the so-called traditional—that is, the various indigenous alternatives to modernity and capitalism—precisely by redundantly projecting them as a primitive past'.[21]

Malay film and music have expressed ideas about modernity in aesthetic ways such that 'modern' practices replace or are rearticulated as 'traditional' practices. Aesthetic practices are integral to the creation of new or renewed national and cultural identities in the wake of cosmopolitan postcoloniality and modernity. Motti Regev views cosmopolitanism at a sociological level, in which the production and consumption of film and music are understood within the aesthetic framework of the nation state. He suggests that 'aesthetic cosmopolitanism' is initially the result of a local, nationally bounded, ethnically defined self that consumes 'cultural products or art works that unequivocally "belong" to a nation or ethnicity other than their own'.[22] In the period of 'early to high modernity', this is further complicated by the construction of a 'national culture' that is characterised by an essentialist and purist conception of the 'ethnonational' self, which in the process represses and conceals 'exterior influences and sources of' that culture 'in order to glorify its authenticity' as 'fully indigenous'.[23] Following that, in the period of 'late modernity', cultural actors seek unique expressions to transcend such rigid ethnonational confines through 'fluid' understandings of local identity, wilfully implementing 'stylistic innovations in art and culture from different parts of the world'.[24] Regev effectively discounts the possibility for cultural agency conceiving aesthetic cosmopolitanism as a normative social condition.[25]

Crucially, though, Regev explains how cosmopolitanism as an aesthetic exists structurally in the form of cultural technologies, global

---

[21]   Turino, *Nationalists, Cosmopolitans, and Popular Music*, p. 7.
[22]   Motti Regev, 'Cultural uniqueness and aesthetic cosmopolitanism', *European Journal of Social Theory* 10, 1 (2007): 125.
[23]   Ibid.
[24]   Ibid.
[25]   Ibid., p. 126.

industries, nation states and musical fields of taste. This is an important observation, as it helps to contextualise and explain how cultural practices that are seen as foreign may be adopted and adapted by individuals as local artistic expressions. The indigenous past is adapted to the modern present, and local elements converge with foreign influences. Beyond this neat structural dichotomy of the internal and external, however, there is still the possibility of uniqueness, creativity and novelty in an artist's active embrace of a cosmopolitan attitude.

David Hesmondhalgh (2013) critiques Regev's pervasive theory of aesthetic cosmopolitanism.[26] He is unconvinced by Ulrich Beck's theory of 'second modernity', as applied in Regev's study on aesthetic cosmopolitanism in rock music.[27] Hesmondhalgh argues that the idea of aesthetic cosmopolitanism in rock music, in which foreign elements are mixed with local elements (derived from the 'first stage' of modernity), does not consider the ethical aspects of musical cosmopolitanism— the ability for such cosmopolitanism to contribute to the flourishing of commonalities 'on equal moral standing' of social agents across nation state-defined boundaries.[28] Hesmondhalgh thus highlights the cold and ambiguous empiricism of Regev's approach that implies a top-down transfer of musical and ideological innovation, when in fact the process is much more complex and varies from one geographical and cultural context to another. A further issue with Regev's aesthetic cosmopolitanism is that it is easily interchangeable with 'cultural hybridity' and more grievously does not consider how social class is embedded into these cultural practices.[29]

Where does this intersect with the development of Malay film music? The transition from Malay film music styles of the 1950s and early 1960s to *pop yeh yeh* youth music culture from the mid-1960s best demonstrates how aesthetic cosmopolitanism may be problematised

---

[26] David Hesmondhalgh, *Why Music Matters*. Chichester: Wiley-Blackwell, 2013, pp. 153–54.

[27] Ulrich Beck and Natan Sznaider, 'Unpacking cosmopolitanism for the social sciences: A research agenda', *British Journal of Sociology* 57, 1 (2006): 1–23.

[28] Hesmondhalgh, *Why Music Matters*, p. 154.

[29] Ibid.

(Chapter Five). It would be contentious to claim that the golden era of Malay film was an entirely conscious effort to seek a pure or essentialised form of Malay music. While this may fit with the intellectual aesthetic goals of Zubir Said, in his use of traditional Malay musical themes in Cathay-Keris films, it was definitely not the case in the music of P. Ramlee's Malay Film Productions' songs. Kassim Masdor, for one, explicitly indicates the diametrically opposed approaches to music of each studio: Malay Film Productions had more of a 'commercial touch', while Cathay-Keris was 'excessively Malay'.[30]

The history of Malay film music indicates how Zubir Said's and even more so P. Ramlee's pursuit of a national or ethnic Malay sound in music was not always clear. This stage of so-called early modernity was fraught with discrepancies in the formulation of national culture. While there may have been early attempts at creating an essentialised or 'pure' national(ist) music,

> [t]here was sometimes more hybridity and cross-cultural communication at work in some projects of nation formation than we may assume in looking back from our supposedly more hybridized twenty-first-century world. This is important in the present context, because it suggests that the role of musical experience in creating dynamics of collectivity in modern nations may be more complex than at first appears.[31]

Thus, aside from ignoring complexities particular to specific cultural contexts, Regev's argument of aesthetic cosmopolitanism as 'normal and routine' does not account for the individual actors who went against the grain to create novel cultural productions in a cosmopolitan vein. While such productions may have eventually been normalised into the fabric of ethnonationalist discourses and practices, it is impossible to ignore the creative agency that existed during the period and place of production. For example, in Singapore in the 1950s, P. Ramlee sang film songs with a 'universal' cosmopolitan aesthetic but did not sing the same way that

---

[30] Kassim Masdor, Oral History Interviews, Reel/Disc 6, Accession Number 002141, National Archives of Singapore, 1 May 1999.

[31] Hesmondhalgh, *Why Music Matters*, p. 155.

Abd al-Halim Hafiz did in the musical films of Egypt in the same period. P. Ramlee's voice remained uniquely and unequivocally his own.

Cosmopolitan musical practice in its complex negotiation of two or more divergent cultures—whether Western music against local practices or colonial rule against postcolonial autonomy—is best understood as an expression of artistic agency. This was a process born out of an awareness of active human agents of a rooted cultural identity in ongoing contact with foreign elements, ideas or practices. The agent finds creative ways to negotiate these cultural diversities within a holistic artistic expression or aesthetic format. The notion of 'musical cosmopolitanism' thus explains how people situated in specific cultural spaces connect to cultural ideas and practices from exogenous spaces and periods to form unique musical expressions that are distinctly local interpretations of globally distributed musical styles. Turino's study of music and cosmopolitanism in Zimbabwe considers local uniqueness at the centre of cosmopolitan cultural practices. Cosmopolitan cultural practices simultaneously draw from translocal elements while emphasising a sense of rootedness in the 'constitution of habitus'.[32] In music and other cultural practices, new local forms of expression are realised in the active interaction of the external and internal.

There is an active process of agency that is crucial to understanding musical practices in the context of political-economic structures and cultural discourses of 'globalism' or 'universality' in music. Martin Stokes proposes that musical cosmopolitanism allows for the observance and analysis of 'creativities' or uniqueness in cultural practitioners who are active agents in the process of making musical 'worlds' or aesthetic paradigms. These musical worlds are not entirely subjugated to structural hegemonies.[33] In saying this, Stokes does not intend to provide an altruistic vision of cosmopolitanism in music. Further, he rightly suggests that musical cosmopolitanism should be approached as

---

[32] Turino, *Nationalists, Cosmopolitans, and Popular Music*, p. 7.

[33] Martin Stokes, 'On musical cosmopolitanism', *The Macalester International Roundtable 2007*, Paper 3, 2007, p. 6. Available at http://digitalcommons.macalester.edu/intlrdtable/3 [accessed 18 December 2017].

'a set of questions and problems'.[34] In the same vein, my own theoretical application of cosmopolitanism to the study of Malay film music is critical and reflexive. I read the agency of local actors against processes of contestation and contradiction that are concomitant with postcolonial nation-making.

While there are contradictions brought about by an idealistic reading of cosmopolitanism in music that ignores sociological-structural hegemonies, it is equally problematic to discount the musical agency of individuals.[35] Such agents were instrumental in crafting a unique musical aesthetic of self-determination. Ingrid Monson understands aesthetic agency as a musically cosmopolitan process that emerges from the discursive and structural limitations of a given society. She views jazz aesthetics in the 1960s as a cosmopolitan musical practice resulting from an 'active musical self-fashioning' process in which African-American musicians articulated music that was different from the hegemonic structures and discourse of white America.[36] Aesthetics, therefore, provide a flexible conceptual space that accommodates fluid identities and plural cultures. The fluidity of aesthetic agency can also be read across time.

In applying this notion of aesthetic agency to understand Malay film music, composers like P. Ramlee and Zubir Said articulated a cosmopolitan aesthetic agency. Malay film songs expressed an indigenous Malayness using Western media and musical structures such as notated scores, non-indigenous instrumentation and harmony. Moreover, Indian film music styles and formats were also extensively adopted and practised.[37] Hence, divergent cultural ideas converging on an interactive

[34] Ibid.

[35] Differing from my approach to cosmopolitanism, though notable for its contribution to the concept, is Kwame Anthony Appiah's philosophical monograph on the potential of cosmopolitanism as an ethical ideology. See Kwame Anthony Appiah, *Cosmopolitanism: Ethics in a World of Strangers*. London: Penguin, 2006.

[36] Ingrid Monson, *Freedom Sounds: Civil Rights Call Out to Jazz and Africa*. Oxford: Oxford University Press, 2007, p. 74.

[37] Malay film histories frequently indicate the dominant presence and influence of Indian films and music in the 1950s. See the chapter on 'The Malay movie industry' in Mohd Anis Md Nor, *Zapin: Folk Dance of the Malay World*. Singapore: Oxford University Press, 1993, pp. 51–60; and the chapter on 'Film in Malaysia' in William

aesthetic space are observable in Malay film songs, facilitated by creative individuals who perceived and utilised exogenous or global universal elements as unique local indigenous expressions. It is erroneous to describe Zubir Said's and P. Ramlee's music as 'authentically' Malay as much as it is dangerously reductive to see it as 'inauthentic' and thus Western. What is apparent in the music of cultural actors such as Zubir Said and P. Ramlee is the deep internalisation of 'foreign ideas and practices'.[38] The diverse international music used by Malay film song composers was not imitated but *internalised*, indicative of 'internally generated cultural creativity, practices, and identities'.[39]

Cosmopolitan Modernity and the Agency of Nation-making

In addressing these boundaries to aesthetic agency, we need to consider how the cosmopolitan ideologies and aesthetic inclinations of cultural actors in Malay film and music played a central role in the project of nation-making. Postcolonial nation states have always created national identities out of cosmopolitan formations, cultural practices and ideologies.[40] The people who contribute to the process of nation-making are often 'cosmopolitans themselves' and alongside 'the mass media' and 'nationalist cultural programs ... provide the most concrete conduits between indigenous arts, cosmopolitan aesthetics, and transnational markets—much as colonial programs did formerly'.[41] Hence, the project of nation-making itself is cosmopolitan, in which the values

---

van der Heide, *Malaysian Cinema, Asian Film: Border Crossings and National Cultures*. Amsterdam: Amsterdam University Press, 2002, pp. 105–60 for accounts of Indian film culture in Malaysia and the use of Indian directors in Malay films. Though by no means a critical or academic book on Malay films, Harding and Ahmad, *P. Ramlee*, pp. 43–82 devotes an entire chapter to the lasting impact of Indian directors who made Malay films in the 1950s.

38 Turino, *Nationalists, Cosmopolitans, and Popular Music*, p. 8.
39 Ibid., p. 9.
40 Joel S. Kahn, *Other Malays: Nationalism and Cosmopolitanism in the Modern Malay World*. Singapore: Singapore University Press, 2006; Cheah Pheng, 'Cosmopolitanism', *Theory, Culture & Society* 23, 2/3 (2006): 486–96.
41 Turino, *Nationalists, Cosmopolitans, and Popular Music*, p. 13.

and characteristics of the local or indigenous are adapted to fit the rigid 'universal' framework of nation states. Turino suggests that this poses a 'twin paradox'. First, specific 'emblems and discourses' derived from 'traditional' local customs and symbols must be accommodated into the 'modern' configuration and ideology of the nation; second, while uniqueness in indigenous culture is favoured, a diversity of local cultures within national boundaries potentially undermines the monocultural notion of statehood.[42] In order to overcome these disjunctures, nation states balance such 'needs and threats ... through the process of *modernist reformism*', in which 'distinctive local arts and lifeways are reformed, or "developed", in light of cosmopolitan ethics, aesthetics, and worldview' due to 'the cultural positions of the reformers'.[43] Turino elaborates that such reformism results in processes of using, diffusing and recontextualising indigenous practices. These processes are particularly relevant in listening to Malay film music.

The notion of reformism and its somewhat aggressive connotation is salient to Malaysian and Singaporean cultural policy from the late 1960s onwards.[44] Cultural reformism in national music was also prevalent throughout Asia during this period, evident in notable studies on the formalisation or classicisation of music in Southeast Asia and South Asia.[45] Prior to the 1960s, a less radical approach to nation-making was taking place, through which cosmopolitan Malay film music composers

---

[42]   Ibid., pp. 15–16.

[43]   Ibid., p. 16.

[44]   Tan Sooi Beng, 'The performing arts in Malaysia: state and society', *Asian Music* 21, 1 (1989): 137–71; Tan Sooi Beng, 'Counterpoints in the performing arts of Malaysia', in *Fragmented Vision: Culture and Politics in Contemporary Malaysia*, ed. Joel S. Kahn and Francis Kok Wah Loh. Honolulu: University of Hawai'i Press, 1992, pp. 282–305; Tan Sooi Beng, *Bangsawan: A Social and Stylistic History of Popular Malay Opera*. Singapore: Oxford University Press, 1993; Sarkissian, *D'Albuquerque's Children*; Margaret Sarkissian, 'Playing Portuguese: Constructing identity in Malaysia's Portuguese community', *Diaspora: A Journal of Transnational Studies* 11, 2 (2002): 215–32.

[45]   Pamela Moro, 'Constructions of nation and the classicisation of music: Comparative perspectives from Southeast and South Asia', *Journal of Southeast Asian Studies* 35, 2 (2004): 187–211; Weidman, *Singing the Classical*; Lakshmi Subramanian, 'Culture and consumption: Classical music in contemporary India and the diaspora', *Transforming Cultures* 3, 1 (2008): 75–92; Bakhle, *Two Men and Music*.

had already internalised non-indigenous conventions of music-making. It was the rise of post-war Malay national and ethnic consciousness that inspired these composers to incorporate local musical practices to evoke a sense of indigeneity in their music. Such notions of indigeneity contributed to a larger narrative of Malay ethnicity and nationhood that had been championed by young activists in the Malay Peninsula and Indonesia since the late 1930s.[46]

Joel S. Kahn provides an insightful account of the 'nationalist narratives' that were being articulated by the Malay cultural intelligentsia in Singapore in the 1950s.[47] By then notions of a Malay '*bangsa*' (race-nation) and '*kebangsaan*' (nationality), and a consequent 'exclusionary nationalist narrative', had matured and were being popularised by emerging radical nationalists.[48] A common nationalist trope in Malay films is based on the notion of *bangsa* as rooted culturally in the *kampung* (village), with its attendant communitarian values forming a potent benchmark for Malayness. This notion of Malayness initially propagated by Malay cultural leaders at the beginning of the twentieth century was also a product of the discursive structural boundaries and conception of 'race' encouraged by British colonial policies and education in Malaya.[49]

Cultural anthropologists who examine the Malay Peninsula have suggested that a 'hegemony of indigenousness'[50] and a discourse of

---

[46] In particular, activists like Burhanuddin al-Helmy and Ibrahim Yaacob, who founded the left-wing, labour-based Kesatuan Melayu Muda (Young Malays Union), were active in writing Malay nationalist literature that was critical of the colonial administration. Barbara Watson Andaya and Leonard Andaya, *A History of Malaysia*. 2nd ed., Honolulu: University of Hawai'i Press, 2001, pp. 246–47. For a study of postcolonial politics of the Malay world, with a focus on the ideas of Burhanuddin al-Helmy, see Syed Muhd Khairudin Aljunied, 'A theory of colonialism in the Malay world', *Postcolonial Studies* 14, 1 (2011): 7–21.

[47] Kahn, *Other Malays*, pp. 114–17.

[48] Ibid., pp. 113–14.

[49] Benedict Anderson, *Imagined Communities: Reflections on the Origins and Spread of Nationalism*. Rev. ed., London: Verso, 2006, pp. 164–70 notes how censuses in the Federated Malay States under the British were used to discursively concretise notions of race and subsequently prescribed national identity in ethnic terms in Malaysia.

[50] Judith Nagata, 'Boundaries of Malayness: "We have made Malaysia: now it is time to (re)make the Malays but who interprets the history?"', in *Melayu: Politics, Poetics and*

'authority-defined' Malayness[51] have permeated the politics and culture of the independent Malaysian nation state well into the twenty-first century. While the hegemony of indigenousness and authority-defined Malayness are applicable to post-1970s Malaysia, these notions do not directly address Malayness across borders, particularly Malay identity in Singapore.[52] As evident in the contemporary contestations of Malayness across the Malay world, the history of Malay nationalism is pluralistic, paradoxical and intensely cosmopolitan.[53] Analysing Malay film and music from the 1950s and 1960s reveals such nuanced articulations of ethnonational nation-making.

Aside from drawing on historical and political examples, in his study of Malay cosmopolitanism Kahn engages a repertoire of Malay films made in the 1950s and 1960s, focusing on those directed by P. Ramlee. He uncovers in these films a recurring narrative of idyllic *kampung* life in contention with urban modernity. The values and customs (*adat*) associated with *kampung* Malays, such as communalism, generosity and humility, are always favoured over the associations of modern city life such as individualism, greed and arrogance. Furthermore, Kahn suggests that P. Ramlee's films underscore ideas of Malay nationalism resonant with the nationalist movements for independence in the 1950s and 1960s.[54] Malay nationalism in P. Ramlee's films was linked to a 'vision of a Kampung Nation' that 'constituted a form of mediation between the nationalist narratives of Malay intellectuals and the

Paradoxes of Malayness, ed. Maznah Mohamad and Syed Muhd Khairudin Aljunied. Singapore: NUS Press, 2011, p. 23.

51 Shamsul A.B., 'A history of an identity, an identity of a history: The idea and practice of "Malayness" in Malaysia reconsidered', in *Contesting Malayness: Malay Identity Across Boundaries*, ed. Timothy P. Barnard. Singapore: Singapore University Press, 2004, pp. 147–48.

52 Lily Zubaidah Rahim, *Singapore in the Malay World: Building and Breaching Regional Bridges*. London: Routledge, 2009.

53 Timothy P. Barnard, ed. *Contesting Malayness: Malay Identity across Boundaries*. Singapore: Singapore University Press, 2004; Anthony Milner, *The Malays*. Chichester: Wiley-Blackwell, 2008; Maznah Mohamad and Syed Muhd Khairudin Aljunied, eds. *Melayu: Politics, Poetics and Paradoxes of Malayness*. Singapore: NUS Press, 2011.

54 Kahn, *Other Malays*, pp. 126–31.

experience of a broader Malay public'.[55] This mediation of modernity
with Malay tradition is particularly pronounced in the social films of
the early 1960s.[56] The social themes expressed in P. Ramlee's films were
concomitant with ideas about emergent postcolonial nation-making
circulating among Malay intellectuals in Singapore.

Along with a 'highly politicised Malay artistic and literary scene',[57]
Singapore was also the birthplace of Angkatan Sasterawan '50 (ASAS
'50, Literary Generation of 1950), a Malay activist literary collective that
comprised 'schoolteachers, journalists and writers dedicated to the cause
of "art for society"'.[58] Initially, this organisation was primarily concerned
with emphasising 'the role that Malay language and literature could
play in developing modernity' among Malays in Singapore.[59] Following
that, their public activities in advancing Malay literature through
book fairs, print media and journalism led to the furthering of their
activism by promoting modernism in 'schools, the newly developing
genre of film, labour activism and ultimately nationalism'. The Malay
film industry, while profit-driven, provided an 'avenue for reaching a
mass audience' with the modernist-nationalist notions of 'young Malay
activists' underscoring 'the stories on the screen'.[60] Timothy Barnard
and Jan van der Putten believe that it was the cosmopolitan intellectual
environment of Singapore in the 1950s that led to significant creative
and political advances in Malay arts and literature throughout the
region. A cosmopolitan conception of Malayness was being formed and

55 Ibid., p. 130.
56 Malay social films differed from Malay *bangsawan* or historical films in that they were
    set in contemporary urban settings. More importantly, such films overtly articulated
    social issues concerning modernity, urbanisation and morality—issues that reflected
    the social concerns of a Malay society facing rapid modernisation and urbanisation.
    Directly influencing Malay social films were their precursors found in India, analysed
    in Ravi Vasudevan, 'Addressing the spectator of a "Third World" national cinema: The
    Bombay "social" film of the 1940s and 1950s', *Screen* 36, 4 (1995): 305–24; and Ravi
    Vasudevan, 'Shifting codes, dissolving identities: The Hindi social film of the 1950s as
    popular culture', *Third Text* 10, 34 (1996): 59–77.
57 Barnard and van der Putten, 'Malay cosmopolitan activism in post-war Singapore', p. 114.
58 Ibid., p. 115.
59 Ibid., p. 140.
60 Ibid., p. 144.

the imperative for the creation of a modern Malaysian state was being articulated with utmost agency 'in the Malay language'.[61]

The creative agency of Malay activists, writers, film-makers and composers during this period would have lasting effects on conceptions of nationhood and artistic identity among future generations of Singaporeans and Malaysians. In line with a conception of cosmopolitanism, agency was not achieved through thoroughly indigenous practices but through modern ideas and mediums that recontextualised indigeneity in the form of nationalism. The music of Malay film songs may have used Western orchestration or samba rhythms, but the newly composed songs were written in the Malay language and sung with a Malay cosmopolitan aesthetic.[62] This aesthetic was expressed in a plurality of ways using a diversity of musical styles and instruments, both local and foreign. For example, modern Western orchestral instruments (violins, cellos, trumpets) were combined with Malay percussion (*rebana* and *gendang* frame drums), saxophones were used to 'sing' Malay-sounding melodies, vibraphones were used to evoke Javanese gamelan, Malay lyrics were sung with Latin American samba, rumba and mambo rhythmic accompaniment. Further evident in all the musical examples analysed in this book is the intertextual articulation of nation-making that reflected the aspirations, contestations and paradoxes of the independence era in the Malay Peninsula.

The Paradoxical Omnipresence of P. Ramlee

Unavoidable in any discussion of nation-making and music in the Malay Peninsula is the aesthetic agency of P. Ramlee, an undeniably cosmopolitan figure whose music and films articulated and continue to reflect the aspirations, contestations and paradoxes of emergent and current Malay nationhood. As should already be obvious, P. Ramlee was and remains a central icon of the Malay world of film and music. Aside

---

[61] Ibid., p. 148. See also T.N. Harper, *The End of Empire and the Making of Malaya*. 2nd ed. Cambridge: Cambridge University Press, 2001, pp. 296–306.

[62] This aesthetic in a singing style present in Malay film song performance has been identified by Tan, *Bangsawan*, p. 98.

from being the first Malay to direct a commercially successful film, *Penarek Becha* (Trishaw Puller, 1955), he was a prolific singer, songwriter and actor.[63] He acted in 62 films, of which he directed 33, all involving him composing and performing his own songs.[64] Moreover, he recorded a total of 359 songs for films and records.[65]

P. Ramlee was born in Penang in 1929 as Teuku Zakaria bin Teuku Nyak Puteh, but had his name changed to 'the more fashionable and enigmatic sounding P. Ramlee at the dawn of his foray into music and show business'.[66] He was born of a Malay-Penangite mother and an Acehnese father with cultural links to the latter evident in his name. The modern self-fashioning of his name obscures his Acehnese lineage.

The source of his success in the entertainment industry was his musical talent. At the age of 19, already composing his own songs and actively playing the violin in *keroncong* bands, he joined an annual singing competition hosted by Radio Malaya in Penang for the third time and won.[67] It was there that the Shaw Brothers' director B.S. Rajhans, who was scouting young Malay talent for his films, spotted him. P. Ramlee then moved to Singapore to begin his singing and acting career.

---

[63] Haji Mahadi was the first Malay to direct a Malay film, *Permata di Perlimbahan* (Jewels in the Valley, 1952), but it was a commercial failure. See Hassan Abdul Muthalib, *Malaysian Cinema in a Bottle: A Century (and a Bit More) of Wayang*. Petaling Jaya: Merpati Jingga, 2013, p. 56.

[64] Ahmad, *P. Ramlee*, p. 63.

[65] Ibid., pp. 133–45.

[66] The exact birth date and year of P. Ramlee is an issue of much contention and mystery. Jan Uhde and Yvonne Ng Uhde, *Latent Images: Film in Singapore*. 2nd ed., Singapore: NUS Press, 2010, p. 30 note his birthday as Wednesday 13 March 1929. This date was likely ascertained from personal interviews in which P. Ramlee claimed he was born on a Wednesday that fell on the first day of Syawal that year (Eid-ul-Fitr). P. Ramlee's official identification documentation lists 22 March 1929, but his birth certificate documents him as being 10 years older, as related by Jamil Sulong, *Kaca Permata: Memoir Seorang Pengarah*. Kuala Lumpur: Dewan Bahasa dan Pustaka, 1990. A news feature suggests that the year on the birth certificate may have been altered by P. Ramlee himself to appear more mature to his new employers when he moved to Singapore in 1948. Nazeri Nong Samah, 'Allahyarham P. Ramlee: Tetap seniman misteri', *Utusan Online*, 29 May 2003. Available at http://ww1.utusan.com.my/utusan/info.asp?y=2003&dt=0529&pub=utusan_malaysia&sec=Hiburan&pg=hi_02.htm [accessed 5 March 2018].

[67] Ahmad, *P. Ramlee*, p. 264.

By 1951 he was recording his film songs for HMV Records in Singapore alongside popular Malay singers.[68] Up to his untimely death in 1973, P. Ramlee had composed a repertoire of songs that would be definitive of modern yet what was considered 'authentic' Malay music.

Most authors who write about P. Ramlee embrace this standard narrative. Ahmad Sarji notes that 'the rhythms [*rentak*, rhythmic stylings] of P. Ramlee's singing and compositions are at one with the heart and soul of Malay peoples', specifically in his use of Malay genres such as *inang, zapin, masri, asli, joget* and *boria*.[69] He also states that 'P. Ramlee was ingenious in arranging and adapting foreign musics with Malay songs', mentioning as examples the waltz, Middle Eastern rhythms, samba, beguine, bolero, rumba, slow beguine, slow rumba, twist and mambo.[70] While P. Ramlee was adept at interpreting a plethora of musical styles for a Malay audience, he eventually encountered obstacles to his creative omnipotence. In 1964 he left Singapore for the soon-to-be separate nation state of Malaysia,[71] continuing his film career at the newly established, underfunded and inexperienced Merdeka Film Productions studio in Kuala Lumpur.[72] Towards the late 1960s he found his popularity waning due to the changing musical tastes of Malaysian youth. To keep up with the Beatlemania craze and the rise of *kugiran* bands,[73] P. Ramlee had to use the new twist style for the song 'Bunyi Gitar' (Sound of the Guitar) in the film *Tiga Abdul* (The Three Abduls, 1964, dir. P. Ramlee) and 'Ai Ai Twist' in the film *Masam-Masam Manis* (Sweet and Sour, 1965, dir. P. Ramlee).[74] Despite being 'closely attuned

---

[68]   Ibid., pp. 265–66.

[69]   Ibid., p. 275: '*Rentak lagu-lagu gubahan dan nyanyian P. Ramlee adalah sejiwa dengan orang-orang Melayu.*'

[70]   Ibid. '*P. Ramlee amat bijak dalam mengadun dan menyesuaikan muzik-muzik asing dengan lagu-lagu Melayu.*'

[71]   Singapore separated from the Federation of Malaysia on 9 August 1965.

[72]   Uhde and Uhde, *Latent Images*, pp. 33–34; Craig A. Lockard, 'From folk to computer songs: The evolution of Malaysian popular music, 1930–1990', *Journal of Popular Culture* 30, 3 (1996): 5.

[73]   An abbreviation of *kumpulan gitar rancak*, meaning 'upbeat guitar group'.

[74]   Ahmad, *P. Ramlee*, p. 277. See Chapter Five for a detailed discussion of 'Bunyi Gitar' and *Masam-Masam Manis*.

to the socio-cultural changes of the time',[75] he was quite reactionary in his attitudes towards the new popular music that was prevalent in the mid-1960s:

> Pop songs and music that are not of quality will give birth to a wild generation in the future. Youths that sing self-indulgently, play music self-indulgently, [and] dress self-indulgently, will be exposed to qualities that are disagreeable and out of that will be born a generation that is without discipline.[76]

In 1971 P. Ramlee also gave a negative speech at a congress on national culture in Kuala Lumpur, where he denounced similar pop music cultures, pointed out a decline of traditional music in Malaysia and proposed solutions for this 'problem'. He lamented the encroachment of Hindustani music from India (of which he was, ironically, an ardent fan), pop music from the West and the influx of youth culture such as long-haired males, miniskirted women and marijuana smoking.[77] He then stated that the government had to take aggressive measures to encourage and sponsor the education, performance and presentation of 'Malaysian traditional' and *asli* music in the media, schools and even 'night-clubs, hotels and restaurants'.[78] P. Ramlee's comments contributed to a homogenising conception of Malaysian national culture that endures until the present day, an issue I examine at length in Chapter Six.

Such reactionary statements suggest that P. Ramlee was experiencing a decline in commercial success as well. His music and films, once considered cosmopolitan and new, were being overshadowed and, in effect, made antiquated by an influx of commoditised trends

---

75 Lockard, 'From folk to computer songs', p. 5.
76 Ahmad, *P. Ramlee*, pp. 276–77, citing an interview with P. Ramlee in *Utusan Zaman*, n.d.
77 P. Ramlee, 'Cara-cara meninggikan mutu dan memperkayakan muzik jenis asli dan tradisional Malaysia demi kepentingan negara' [Ways to elevate and enrich the original and traditional music of Malaysia for the benefit of the nation], in *Asas Kebudayaan Kebangsaan*, 1st ed. Kuala Lumpur: Kementerian Kebudayaan Belia dan Sukan Malaysia, 1973, p. 205.
78 Ibid., pp. 206–7.

disseminated by more rapid technologies of global capitalism. However, due to these changes, his music was also acquiring an 'indisputable' Malay indigeneity that was compatible with Malay cultural nationalist rhetoric. Yusnor Ef, a staunch advocate and disciple of P. Ramlee, considers his impact on Malay music in the following terms:

> Malay songs are an integral part of a Malay person's identity, in which external influences can be accepted while Malayness must be central, just like the music or songs of P. Ramlee; the foundations are Malay, but Western, latin [sic] and Indian elements are absorbed subconsciously [internalised]. Elements from jazz, bossa nova, mambo and cha-cha are found in his songs, but his soul [enduringly] remains a Malay soul.[79]

Regardless of how Malay or cosmopolitan P. Ramlee's songs actually are, his music has provided the basis for an ethnonational discourse of homogeneity or indigeneity, in which Malayness in music is perceived to be rooted in the 'soul' and 'heart', which are therefore the exemplary identifiers of 'Malayness'—something that is actually difficult to discern musically. 'Malay music' thus becomes more of an ideological and political term than it is a descriptive marker in musical form, structure or style. In effect, discourses about Malayness in music mainly act to articulate debates over cultural nationalism.

Andrew Clay McGraw provides some useful observations concerning the impact of P. Ramlee's film music on conceptions of modernity and indigenous identity in Malaysia.

> If, in his early films, Ramlee suggests that modern, Westernized living is corrupt and potentially dangerous to Malay society and culture, then his use of music presents a significantly more complex image, one that suggests that certain aspects of Western culture and modernity fit well with Malaysian aesthetics and values, and indeed can be hybridized and adopted as Malaysian. Furthermore, any attempt to neatly categorize and evaluate instances of Malay (or, in this case Ramlee's) music as

---

[79] Yusnor Ef, *Muzik Melayu Sejak 1940-an*. Kuala Lumpur: YKNA Network, 2011, p. xix.

either Western/modern or Malay/traditional is to grossly oversimplify the case. Musics in Ramlee's films that might otherwise be identified as 'western' (especially jazz, Hawaiian, and Latin music) have a long lineage in Malaysia, having been performed and transformed in the colony within contexts such as bangsawan since before Ramlee's birth. Furthermore, later generations of Malaysian viewers have come to understand Ramlee's rumbas and jazz and rock (& roll) tunes as distinctly Malaysian, sometimes unaware of their global roots.[80]

He further states that the realm of musical taste in P. Ramlee's music goes beyond the polarised dichotomy of degenerate modernity in contrast to pure indigeneity, and instead reflects 'a spirit of aesthetic cosmopolitanism'.[81] While this idealistic aesthetic may have been expressed in earlier film songs by P. Ramlee, McGraw still leaves much to be discussed with regard to the politics of national culture and the changing discourses of nation-making evident in a continuum of nationhood.

While Malay film music from the 1950s and 1960s may have had global roots, it is impossible to deny the nationalist resonance that it has with the contemporary Malaysian public. What about contemporary Singaporeans' reception to such music? Yusnor Ef is a Singaporean citizen but remains a strong advocate of an essentialised Malay culture in music. An aspect of McGraw's study that requires expansion is the impact of P. Ramlee's music beyond the confines of the modern nation state of Malaysia. I address this issue by focusing on Malayness and film music in present-day Malaysia and Singapore, comparing the political remembering of P. Ramlee in the former and Zubir Said in the latter (Chapter Six). On one hand, Zubir Said's iconicity, due to his status as the composer of Singapore's national anthem, is mobilised by present-day Malay Singaporeans to claim cultural relevance in a nation that marginalises their culture. P. Ramlee's iconicity, on the other hand, has been predominantly claimed by the Malaysian state as an unquestionable

---

[80] McGraw, 'Music and meaning', pp. 46–47.
[81] Ibid.

marker of Malay cultural hegemony in the arts. The fact that most of
P. Ramlee's successful films and enduring compositions were actually
produced in Singapore in the mid-1950s to early 1960s is conveniently
forgotten.

Further, how can the complexities of P. Ramlee's music and iconicity
be understood in terms of their potent and enduring articulation in
Malay and, by extension, Malaysian culture? While such aesthetic
cosmopolitanism is undoubtedly heard in P. Ramlee's film music, when
contextualised historically, it is the *cosmopolitan intimacy* or culturally
specific sentiment of Malay nation-making that endows such music with
its enduring potency.[82]

Cultural Intimacies of Malay Film Music

Threads of intimacy are present throughout all the films analysed in
this book. Ultimately, music amplifies a film's emotional content and
culturally intimate expressions, providing clear postcolonial articulations
of a nation-in-the-making. Throughout these analyses of film music
and narratives, cultural intimacy accounts for the sentiments of nation-

---

[82] Precedents to the convergence of cosmopolitanism and intimacy include the call by
Katharyne Mitchell, 'Geographies of identity: The intimate cosmopolitan', *Progress in
Human Geography* 31, 5 (2007): 706–20 for the genealogical analysis of intimacies
in transnational contexts of social change and revolution that considers ethics,
community, education and non-violence rooted in feminist perspectives. Barry King,
'Idol in a small country: *New Zealand Idol* as the commoditization of cosmopolitan
intimacy', in *TV Formats Worldwide: Localizing Global Programs*, ed. Albert
Moran. Bristol: Intellect, 2007, pp. 271–89 problematises cosmopolitan intimacy
in his analysis of the *New Zealand Idol* television singing contest, in which the non-
white, Maori/Pasifika winner of the contest is representative of a national vision of
indigenous inclusivity; however, the marketability of such artists fades after the contest
itself; white artists dominate in terms of the market value of the pop stardom image
in local and global music industry markets. Another angle cosmopolitan intimacy is
approached is in the study of gender and social movements; specifically, the global
transnational flows of sexuality activism, the relationships of power of the North
over the South, and the negotiation of such power relationships through sexually
personal interactions and affinities. See Hakan Seckinelgin, 'Cosmopolitan intimacies
and sexual politics in global civil society', in *Bottom-up Politics: An Agency-Centred
Approach to Globalization*, ed. Denisa Kostovicova and Marlies Glasius. London:
Palgrave Macmillan, 2011, pp. 61–74.

making that are embedded in the films' melodramatic narratives. Film music is the affective 'space' in which the nascent nationalist *sentiments* of Malay film composers materialised and continue to endure.

Stokes's musical study of cultural intimacy and nationhood considers the importance of sentimentalism and love in Turkish national discourses and how musicians, from the 1950s to the present, have been crucial in articulating such national discourses of cultural intimacy.[83] He draws attention 'to a sustained and consequential imagination of public life in affectionate terms, and to popular music as the vehicle to this imagination'.[84] Along these lines, the music of Malay films articulated such intimacies to form affectionate imaginings of Malay society, weaved through the emotional discourses of their narratives. For example, sentiments of decolonisation are expressed in diverging ways in Malay films made in the mid-1950s, the period of Malayan national independence. The music of *Hang Tuah* (1956, dir. Phani Majumdar) amplifies subversive anti-colonial hopes and aspirations through tragic narratives, while the music of *Sergeant Hassan* (1958, dir. Lamberto V. Avellana) uses Western orchestral conventions to support romantic narratives that affectively idealise colonialism (Chapter Two). In the 1960s musical intimacies expressed in Malay films enabled social class-crossings of working-class male musicians with upper-class women (Chapter Four). Retrospectively, when screened and heard in the current period of nationhood, such culturally intimate articulations are weaved into the nostalgic imaginings of a nation's

> paradoxical … longing for an age before that state, for the primordial and self-regulating birthright that the state continually invokes—that citizens can turn against the authority of the state itself, along with all the other similarly vulnerable symbols of official fixity.[85]

---

[83] Martin Stokes, *The Republic of Love: Cultural Intimacy in Turkish Popular Music*. Chicago: University of Chicago Press, 2010, pp. 1–34.

[84] Ibid., p. 193.

[85] Michael Herzfeld, *Cultural Intimacy: Social Poetics and the Real Life of States, Societies, and Institutions*. 3rd ed., London: Routledge, 2016, p. 28.

In the case of P. Ramlee as a national icon, I consider the cultural intimacies expressed in the narrative of his decline. Interestingly, this decline narrative is utilised and embodied by both official and independent actors—from state officials to state-friendly film-makers, from opposition politicians to independent music producers. The overarching sentiment expressed about P. Ramlee is 'kasihan', that is—for lack of a better translation of the uniquely culturally specific Malay word—an immense empathic pity for his tragic circumstances. Wazir Jahan Karim's anthropological study of Malay emotion explains that the word kasihan is semantically linked to the word kasih, which means 'love', forming 'a common lexical item with two sets of semantic references'.[86] She elaborates:

> The word for pity, kasihan, is generally used to indicate or express sympathy or compassion for a particular person suffering from a misfortune. It is sometimes substituted for sayang which may be taken to mean 'what a pity' or 'the pity of it all'. It is significant that in the Malay language, 'love' and 'pity' ... [may express] both the participant's condition [when confronted with this emotion] and the observer's perception of this condition, particularly when such experiences are unsettling, personally traumatic, or require sacrifices, compromises, and resolutions that are difficult to meet.[87]

P. Ramlee's narrative of decline and resultant nationalist iconicity is fuelled by this culturally potent sentiment of pity. This emotionally charged remembrance of P. Ramlee is then deeply embedded as an articulation of 'structural nostalgia'.[88] The peak of his art was achieved in the transitional period of state formation—after the war, the final years of colonial rule and independence. More interestingly, our best, or arguably clearest, memories of him are during his time in Singapore when it was

---

[86] Wazir Jahan Karim, 'Prelude to madness: The language of emotion in courtship and early marriage', in *Emotions of Culture: A Malay Perspective*, ed. Wazir Jahan Karim. Singapore: Oxford University Press, 1990, p. 29.

[87] Ibid., pp. 28–29.

[88] Herzfeld, *Cultural Intimacy*.

still not officially a part of the Federation of Malaysia, but was the centre for producing the most vivid imaginings of a Malayan nation through the silver screen. P. Ramlee's face, voice, music and directorial decisions were the spotlight of this nation-making on celluloid. This is the reason Malaysia and its citizens are unable to escape his memory. This is also why any notion of Malaysian-ness in the arts, especially music and film, recalls nostalgically not the era of independence but the era of P. Ramlee.

However, it is only though the identities rooted in 'external embarrassment ... that nevertheless provide insiders with their assurance of common sociality'.[89] This 'embarrassment' can be discerned from the ability of Malays today to relate the admonishment of musicians to the remark of the condescending mother-in-law in *Ibu Mertua-ku—'ahli muzik?'* Even more so, it is the deeply embedded collective embarrassment of neglecting P. Ramlee while he was alive that paradoxically fuels a sense of nationalist 'pride'. It is the collective sadness felt by those who watch P. Ramlee's tragic narrative unfold in Shuhaimi Baba's biographical documentary (Chapter Six). It is the need for young Malaysian musicians (like myself at an earlier stage) to learn P. Ramlee's music, embarrassed that they may not be considered 'Malaysian enough' if they do not. Thus, it is the collective embarrassment of P. Ramlee's neglect, of his tragic *kasihan* narrative, by both the state and its citizens, that fuels his ubiquity in the embodiment of Malaysian-ness. My analysis of Malay film music considers these intimacies expressed during the period of nation-making and its continued musical reiterations of nationalist sentiment in recent times.

Analysing Film Music

The study of music in film is a well-established field.[90] However, of all the ethnomusicological studies on screened music, McGraw's article is the only one to consider the film music of the Malay Peninsula.[91] Particularly

---

[89] Ibid., p. 7. See also Stokes, *The Republic of Love*, pp. 190–91.
[90] See Kathryn Kalinak, *Film Music: A Very Short Introduction*. Oxford: Oxford University Press, 2010.
[91] McGraw, 'Music and meaning'.

useful to this book has been the extensive field of research on South Asian, particularly Hindi, film music.[92] Malay film music aesthetics of the 1950s and 1960s were closely linked to those of Hindi film music from the same era, as many film directors were imported from India in the early post-war days of the Malay film studio industry. But claiming a dominant influence for Indian films over Malay film music aesthetics is problematic, as Malay film composers adopted musical approaches and aesthetics that were unique to Malay culture and the Straits region. The film scholar William van der Heide, for one, falls into the trap of unduly attributing the aesthetic and narrative qualities of Malayan and Malaysian films to the external border-crossing influences of Indian, American and Japanese films.[93] While this may be true, to an extent, of the visual-cinematic aesthetic of films in the 1950s and 1960s, I argue that Malay film music was uniquely local—which means that it was also inherently cosmopolitan. Indian film music was definitely a major influence, avidly consumed by Malay audiences and musicians of the time, including P. Ramlee. However, Malay film composers were also interested in creating music that could satiate the cosmopolitan tastes of their local audiences while also contributing to the exciting process of nation-making.

Due to the dearth of film music research on the Malay world and the intertwined film history of South Asia and the Malay Peninsula, studies of Hindi film music offer the most salient methodological approaches and comparative springboards for this book. An article published in 2000

---

[92] See, for example, Anna Morcom, 'An understanding between Bollywood and Hollywood? The meaning of Hollywood-style music in Hindi films', *Ethnomusicology Forum* 10, 1 (2001): 63–84; Anna Morcom, *Hindi Film Songs and the Cinema*. Aldershot: Ashgate, 2007; Gregory D. Booth, 'Religion, gossip, narrative conventions and the construction of meaning in Hindi film songs', *Popular Music* 19, 2 (2000): 125–45; Gregory D. Booth, *Behind the Curtain: Making Music in Mumbai's Film Studios*. New York: Oxford University Press, 2008; Alison E. Arnold, 'Popular film music in India: A case of mass-market musical eclecticism', *Popular Music* 7, 2 (1988): 177–88; Alison E. Arnold, 'Hindi Filmigit: On the History of Commercial Indian Popular Music'. PhD thesis, University of Illinois, 1991; Alison E. Arnold, 'Aspects of production and consumption in the popular Hindi film song industry', *Asian Music* 24, 1 (1992): 122–36.

[93] Van der Heide, *Malaysian Cinema, Asian Film*.

by Gregory D. Booth is especially valuable in highlighting the social and musical importance of Hindi film songs that were previously seen as inconsequential to film narratives or a manifestation of crass capitalist musical production. Booth introduces the concept of 'music scenes' in examining the narrative function of film song sequences and analyses how Hindi film songs are 'embedded within a complex of conventional and cultural code systems'.[94] Taking the latter into consideration, I analyse Zubir Said's use of a specific musical aesthetic code to evoke a Malay musical 'tradition' in his film scores (Chapter Three). Additionally, the bulk of musical examples analysed in this book are music scenes that interact in meaningful ways with the films' narratives.

A seminal work on South Asian film music is Anna Morcom's comprehensive study of Hindi film songs, in which she emphasises the need to consider film music, alongside its social milieu, in its narrative context. The context of the 'reel world' is equally important to the context of the 'real world'.[95] She explains that

> [b]ecause film songs are consumed apart from Hindi films and the visual medium to a certain extent, have a very high profile in Indian society and culture, and are clearly interacting with the 'real world' context in fascinating ways, it has possibly led to the 'reel world' (as opposed to the real world) being overlooked as a major context of film music in its own right.[96]

Morcom thus draws attention to the kinds of musical agency that can only be discerned in its filmic context. This is an approach I apply, in which my analyses of film music are always read alongside and against the narrative of the films in which they are expressed. This mode of analysis, emphasising the reel world as much as the real world of film music, leads me to suggest that Malay film music constitutes

---

[94] Booth, 'Religion, gossip, narrative conventions', pp. 127–28. See also Peter Manuel, *Popular Music of the Non-Western World*. Oxford: Oxford University Press, 1988; and Peter Manuel, *Cassette Culture: Popular Music and Technology in North India*. Chicago: University of Chicago Press, 1993.

[95] Morcom, *Hindi Film Songs*, p. 11.

[96] Ibid.

ethnonationalism as much as it challenges it within its narrative and post-narrative articulations. For example, I note how the film *Ibu Mertua-ku*, which is commonly read as a reflection of Malay anxiety towards modern Western immorality, actually embraces an inherently cosmopolitan Malay modernity through its musical themes and content (Chapter Four). This observation is only made possible through an examination of music in its filmic context. In fact, because of the limited number of informants available for this study—all the film composers and musicians from the Malay film industry based in Singapore in the 1950s and 1960s are no longer alive[97]—this study relies significantly on filmic contexts to analyse film music (aside from secondary sources and primary sources such as film magazines and newspaper articles).

Morcom also examines how Hollywood musical conventions merge and interact with Hindi film music, noting the use of large symphony orchestras and Western scoring aesthetics, Western instruments such as the piano and saxophone, and eclectic combinations of Western popular music genres.[98] She points out that despite the general assumption that the West poses a threat to Indian tradition, culture and morality, Western film music practices were in fact very much integrated with Hindi film music to advance the emotional and melodramatic content of the films' narratives.[99] Western music in Malay film, I argue, is even more integrated with the aesthetics of Malay film music. The integration of Western or pluralistic influences had already occurred in Malay music long prior to the advent of films. I thus consider Malay film music as inherently cosmopolitan due to the history of musical practices preceding and surrounding Malay films in the 1950s and 1960s.

---

[97] I was fortunate to interview Kassim Masdor, the last surviving Singaporean Malay film composer, in 2013. He died in January 2014. Another Malay film composer I managed to interview was Ahmad Nawab Khan in 2013, and he is still alive, but he wrote music for Malay films made in Malaysia from the mid-1960s onwards and was not involved in the Singapore film industry. For an extensive biography of Malay Singaporean musicians, most of whom played for the Malay studio film industry in Singapore, see Azlan Mohamed Said, *Musika: Malaya's Early Music Scene (Arena Muzik Silam di Malaya)*, ed. Juffri Supa'at. Singapore: Stamford Printing, 2013.

[98] Morcom, *Hindi Film Songs*, pp. 139–45. See also Arnold, 'Popular film music in India'.

[99] Morcom, *Hindi Film Songs*, pp. 178–79.

As useful as these prominent studies of Hindi film song are to my musical analysis, they do not specifically address film music in the context of nation-making. This is perhaps due to the copious amount of existing research on film and South Asian nationalism and the complexity of nationalism in relation to the Indian film industry. However, in the context of the Singapore-based Malay film industry in the 1950s and 1960s, it is impossible to ignore the pervasive impact of nation-making on film music and vice versa. Moreover, unlike the studies on Indian film music that are based on an extended historical period, the musical approach of studio-produced Malay films of the 1950s and 1960s largely waned from the 1970s onwards, when it became increasingly rare to feature film songs or music scenes in Malaysian-made films.[100] Interestingly, while Malay musical films can now be considered extinct, film songs from independence-era films, particularly those composed and performed by P. Ramlee, are still widely consumed by Singaporeans and Malaysians and are subject to tribute performances and albums as well as new musical interpretations (Chapter Six).

Studies of film music elsewhere in Southeast Asia, such as Indonesia, are scarce. Sumarsam's book chapter on music in Indonesian historical films is, to my knowledge, the only scholarly publication on the topic. His study has been a useful point of comparison for my work, as he highlights how traditional Javanese music—especially gamelan—is scored in historical-political films that narrate Indonesia's postcolonial independence.[101] In line with Hamid Naficy's views, Sumarsam further

---

[100] Notably, the film *Kami* (1982, dir. Patrick Yeoh) features the male Malay-Malaysian superstar singer, Sudirman, in music scenes that are well-suited to his aspiring singer-protagonist. There are also some recent films—perhaps in nostalgic reference to Malay films of the 1950s and 1960s—such as Amir Muhammad's documentary *The Last Communist* (2006) which features song and dance sequences in between its historical narrative of Malaysia's communist insurgency. Yasmin Ahmad's *Talentime* (2009) features many original songs written for the film by the songwriter Pete Teo. The songs' performances fit neatly into the film's narrative that revolves around a secondary school talent competition. The controversial Chinese-Malaysian rapper Wee Meng Chee @ Namewee also directed, starred and performed in two films that feature musical numbers, *Nasi Lemak 2.0* (Coconut Milk Rice 2.0, 2011) and *Hantu Gangster* (Gangster Ghost, 2012).

[101] Sumarsam, 'Music in Indonesian "historical" films: Reading *Nopember 1828*', in *Global*

stresses the importance of reading film music 'intertextually (that is, synchronically and diachronically) and as a crosscultural phenomenon, as fictional, and as documentary and ethnographic'.[102] In adopting this approach, my analysis of music in Malay films is intertextual in its reading of musical expressions in historical and contemporary cultural contexts of Malay nation-making.

Stokes's chapter in the same volume discusses the film music of the Egyptian singer and film star Abd al-Halim Hafiz, noting the enduring impact of his film music on Egyptian national consciousness.[103] P. Ramlee shares many striking resonances, in terms of his national iconicity, with the case of Abd al-Halim, whose

> music is, in a sense, monumental: deeply internalized and naturalized as part of the legitimate cultural order and as materially tangible as a historic mosque or a portrait of a president. In another sense, it is the pedagogical resource: something to be studied, dissected, picked over, discussed, and appreciated by people seeking to gain serious musical knowledge, a knowledge that will produce new things as well as simply reproduce the past.[104]

Similarly, P. Ramlee's musical presence is just as 'monumental' as well as deeply internalised and naturalised as part of the legitimate cultural order in Malaysia.

Applied throughout this study is Mark Slobin's consideration of film music as an ethnography of the culture it represents.[105] He examines

Soundtracks: Worlds of Film Music, ed. Mark Slobin. Middletown, CT: Wesleyan University Press, 2008, p. 232.

[102] Ibid., p. 235. See also Hamid Naficy, 'Phobic spaces and liminal panics: Independent transnational film genre', in *Multiculturalism, Postcoloniality, and Transnational Media*, ed. Ella Shohat and Robert Stam. New Brunswick, NJ: Rutgers University Press, 2003, p. 205.

[103] Martin Stokes, 'Listening to Abd Al-Halim Hafiz', in *Global Soundtracks: Worlds of Film Music*, ed. Mark Slobin. Middletown, CT: Wesleyan University Press, 2008, pp. 309–33.

[104] Ibid., p. 327.

[105] Mark Slobin, 'The Steiner superculture', in *Global Soundtracks: Worlds of Film Music*, ed. Mark Slobin. Middletown, CT: Wesleyan University Press, 2008, pp. 3–4.

the ethnographic representations of non-Western music through the orchestral American film music system he calls the 'Steiner superculture'— music scoring traceable to the composer Max Steiner, which became 'an extremely effective technical and aesthetic practice that spread to the rest of the world as, simply, the way music works' in film.[106] Slobin goes on to problematise this music producer-powered relationship of arbitrarily constituting non-Western musical cultures by suggesting that such music is an 'assumed vernacular' music.[107] However, this is not merely a one-way power dynamic. Despite the authoritative position of American film producers and composers in defining (through the globally adopted conventions of the Steiner superculture) what would constitute the musically familiar and foreign, the self and the other in film music, there are also spaces for resistance and subversion that seep through these musical articulations in film.[108] This conception of a musical superculture is useful in unravelling the constituted homogeneities as well as subversive articulations and paradoxes of Malay film music made during the independence era. The ethnomusicological approach to film music beyond American films is thus useful in understanding how Hollywood film music aesthetics pervade Malay film music as much as it provides a structural format that may be subverted musically with political meaning. While Malay film music may be heard as reproducing the Steiner superculture, it was also unique to the region and rootedly cosmopolitan.[109] Thus, while relevant to the pervasive reach of European colonialism and Western capitalism on a global scale, Slobin's approach does not explicitly account for the agency of non-Western film music makers.

In my view, the music of Malay film in the 1950s and 1960s, instead of an 'assumed' vernacular, actually expressed a *constitutive* vernacular

---

[106] Ibid., p. 3.

[107] Ibid., pp. 25–29.

[108] Ibid., p. 29.

[109] Tan Sooi Beng, 'Negotiating "His Master's Voice": Gramophone music and cosmopolitan modernity in British Malaya in the 1930s and early 1940s', *Bijdragen tot de Taal-, Land- en Volkenkunde* 169, 4 (2013): 457–94; Benedict Anderson, 'Colonial cosmopolitanism', in *Social Science and Knowledge in a Globalising World*, ed. Zawawi Ibrahim. Kajang: Malaysian Social Science Association and Petaling Jaya: Strategic Information and Research Development Centre, 2012, pp. 371–88.

aesthetic. Malay film composers were actively creating their own vernacular film music aesthetic that was inherently cosmopolitan. As Tan Sooi Beng suggests, preceding and influencing the music of the post-war film industry was the rootedly cosmopolitan and widely popular music of Malay-language recording artists in the Malay Peninsula in the 1930s, who

> did not travel outside the Malay world but were exposed to and absorbed universal ideas about change which circulated in the region. They used Malay, the local lingua franca, which had no fixed form, and mixed it with other languages to spread their messages. They interacted with Indian, Chinese, Arab and other diasporic people at the port cities where they performed and mixed Anglo-American music with their own to speak to and attract audiences that were not limited to any one community or nation.[110]

Tan views the rooted cosmopolitanism of these musicians and their music as counter-cultural to more essentialised conceptions of Malay nationalism that were circulating during the independence era. This rooted cosmopolitan musical aesthetic and social outlook pervade Malay film music after the 1940s, despite the more homogeneous Malay nationalist rhetoric that was prevalent at the time.[111] Taking into account the rooted cosmopolitanism of Malay music and film, the notion of a 'superculture' in analysing Malay film music, while useful, does not provide a complete picture of how nationalism was constituted through vernacular identities that had already embraced a culturally pluralistic conception of the foreign and the local.

Methods and Sources

This book is as much an ethnomusicological study of music in film as it is a historical and political ethnography of Malay nationalism

---

[110] Tan, 'Negotiating "His Master's Voice"', p. 460.
[111] Anthony C. Milner, *The Invention of Politics in Colonial Malaya: Contesting Nationalism and the Expansion of the Public Sphere*. Cambridge: Cambridge University Press, 1995, cited in ibid.

in the 1950s and 1960s. I draw upon a variety of research methods in my collection and use of data. The primary sources include the textual materials of films, the songs and music contained in these films, newspaper articles and film magazines. The face-to-face interviews, listed in the bibliography, were conducted with Malay film music composers, historians, authors, museum officials, music journalists and event organisers. I have also used oral history materials consisting of pre-recorded interviews of actors and music producers collected under the Singapore Oral History Project of the National Archives of Singapore. The mixed method research has been extremely useful, allowing me to conduct this study within an appropriate intertextual framework.

The book seeks to understand musical cosmopolitanism, nation-making and cultural intimacy by analysing the musical articulations and discourses about music contained in Malay films. Far from being an auxiliary element, music plays a crucial role in constituting film narratives.[112] Conversely, music often has the ability to subvert a film's narrative and reveal emotional and ideological antipathies that are not overtly present. Music interacts with a film's story, dialogue and visual context not only to enhance or subvert meanings 'already present' but it also functions as 'an active parameter in the creation and emergence of narrative and meaning'.[113]

The musical constitution of meaning in film is a complex process. I therefore employ the ethnomusicological notion of 'screened music' to observe how processes of national or 'self-representation' can be decontextualised and recontextualised in myriad ways while highlighting 'issues of agency, ... process, active or contrived representation or re-representation, ... mediation and media-isation'.[114] In sum, this book seeks to understand Malay film music by paying attention to the mutually constitutive and interactive texts of a film's narrative and its

---

[112] Kathryn Kalinak, *Settling the Score: Music and the Classical Hollywood Film*. Madison, WI: University of Wisconsin Press, 1992, pp. 30–31.

[113] Morcom, *Hindi Film Songs*, p. 16.

[114] Miguel Mera and Anna Morcom, 'Introduction: Screened music, trans-contextualisation and ethnomusicological approaches', *Ethnomusicology Forum* 18, 1 (2009): 5.

music, reading them against the social and cultural context in which they were historically produced and are currently remembered in the public sphere. I find that such an intertextual analysis of music in Malay film from the 1950s and 1960s unravels the seemingly homogenising yet contested and paradoxical tropes of Malay culture and nationalism that are equally relevant to nation-making in the past as they are to the present.

Organisation of the Book

The book is organised in seven chapters. Chapters Two to Six examine the issues set down in this introduction through in-depth case studies of music in selected films released from the mid-1950s to the late 1960s. I do not attempt to provide an exhaustive study of Malay films and music. But the selection of films analysed contains, in my view, musical narratives that clearly represent the era of nation-making on the silver screen. Each chapter is organised by specific themes concerned with the cosmopolitan intimacies of nation-making: the sentiments of musical decolonisation; postcoloniality, tradition and the musical constitution of nation; technologically mediated modernity and inter-class intimacies; ethnonationalism in music and the moral policing of youth culture; and national culturalism and nostalgia. Each chapter introduces the sociological framework for the nation-making themes highlighted above and proceeds with a detailed intertextual analysis of music, narrative and history in relation to that theme in one or two films.

Chapter Two uncovers sentiments of decolonisation by analysing the music of two films made in the mid-1950s—*Hang Tuah* and *Sergeant Hassan*—with reference to the political history of nascent anti-colonial social movements leading up to Malayan independence (*merdeka*) in 1957 and a communist insurgency that saw a proliferation of pro-British propaganda and censorship in local cinemas. These films are chosen specifically because the former was made a year before independence and the latter a year after. *Hang Tuah* and *Sergeant Hassan* also contrast significantly in their narrative themes, genre and setting. The latter is a 'modern' Second World War film while the former is a 'traditional' epic set in precolonial times. These contrasting projections of nation-making—the modern and traditional—are precedents to the next chapter's discussion of the modern construction of musical tradition in Malay film music.

Chapter Three focuses on the film composer Zubir Said, analysing his increasingly 'traditionalised' music in films in the early 1960s that had a precolonial theme. The film *Dang Anom* (1962, dir. Hussein Haniff), which features Zubir Said's music, incorporates a *traditionalised* aesthetic representation of Malay music as a way of articulating an aspiring ethnonationalist and anti-colonial sentiment. In this chapter, only one film is chosen as it highlights the synergy between the radical Malay director Hussein Haniff and the Malay-nationalist music icon Zubir Said. In my view, *Dang Anom* is a pertinent film because it features Zubir Said's traditionalist and Malay nationalist music aesthetic interacting with Hussein Haniff's anti-feudalist interpretation of precolonial Malay society.

Chapter Four continues to analyse films of the early 1960s, but considers how modernity, modern musical technologies and cosmopolitan ideals are featured in social films set within contemporary urban contexts. It also highlights how intimate expressions through film music allow protagonists to transcend class differences. The films analysed in this chapter, *Antara Dua Darjat* (Between Two Classes, 1960) and *Ibu Mertua-ku* (My Mother-in-law, 1962), are P. Ramlee's most prominent social films from the pinnacle of his directing and musical career in Singapore. Additionally, the songs featured in these films are arguably his best known, in particular 'Getaran Jiwa' (Vibrations of the Soul) from *Antara Dua Darjat* and 'Di Mana Kan Ku Cari Ganti' (Where Will I Find a Replacement) from *Ibu Mertua-ku*. I argue that the musical content conveyed through intimate contexts, as well as the discourses about music and musicians in these films, mediate the social fissures between modernity and tradition, urban and rural, working class and elites, and autocracy and self-determination.

Chapter Five examines the slow but musically spirited unravelling of the Malay film studio industry from the mid-1960s to the early 1970s. This was a period that saw the increased inclusion of rock 'n' roll music and youth culture in Malay films, marking a substantial aesthetic shift in film music away from the cosmopolitan and traditional sounds of the previous period. I analyse how a nationalist musical discourse was articulated in Zubir Said's and P. Ramlee's commentaries on developing and preserving national musical culture—how their ideas, despite earlier cosmopolitan leanings, had essentially become ethnonationalist and reactionary to cultural change. I contrast their views to the introduction of the Malay *pop yeh yeh* youth music style in P. Ramlee's last film made in Singapore, *Tiga Abdul* (The Three Abduls, 1964, dir. P. Ramlee). I then analyse two films that highlight the youth culture of this period, *Muda Mudi* (The Youths, 1965, dir. M. Amin) and *A Go Go '67* (1967, dir. Omar Rojik). I choose to examine *Muda Mudi* as it features the prominent Malay actress and singer of the 1940s and 1950s, Siput Sarawak, who portrays an ageing film star in the film. The film's self-referentiality parallels the actual dilemmas of a Malay film industry that was uncertain of but also cautiously appropriating the new youth culture emerging in the mid-1960s. *A Go Go '67* is selected because it features *pop yeh yeh* bands, singers and dancers, and was one of the last films to be made at Shaw Brothers' Malay Film Productions' studios in Singapore, truly marking the twilight of Malay films in the Peninsula. Despite the studio's closure, the music director of the film, Kassim Masdor, went on to shape the Malay popular music industry in the late 1960s to late 1970s as a prominent composer, producer and artists and repertoire (A&R) representative for EMI's Malay music division.

A state-defined national culture that appropriates Malay film music aesthetics and its icons, P. Ramlee and Zubir Said, as emblematic of a refined and fixed national music culture grounds my discussion of nostalgia in Chapter Six. This provides an ethnography of how Malay film music and its icons from the 1950s and 1960s are remembered, historicised and canonised through emotional narratives in present-day Malaysia and Singapore. Analysing the music of the nation-making past in the present, I depict how P. Ramlee's film music is interpreted by contemporary Malaysian musicians, paradoxically articulating the subversion of a homogeneous national music culture while perpetuating a commodified nostalgia towards the past.

Chapter 2

Decolonising Motifs

Berkorban apa saja
Harta ataupun nyawa
Itulah kasih mesra
Sejati dan mulia
(To sacrifice anything at all
Material possessions or your life
That is a joyous love
Genuine and noble)
'Berkorban Apa Saja', music by P. Ramlee, lyrics by Jamil Sulong

Tunggu sekejap
Dalam pelukan asmaraku
(Just wait for a while
In my passionate embrace)
'Tunggu Sekejap', music by P. Ramlee, lyrics by S. Sudarmaji

By the mid-1950s P. Ramlee was a cinematic icon and archetype of the Malay hero. The star's presence on the silver screen was pervasive, cast in leading roles for comedies, historical epics and modern melodramas alike. His musical input was even more influential than his acting. His compositions were at the forefront of developing a recognisable Malay vernacular aesthetic of film music that was intensely cosmopolitan. As cosmopolitan as they were, P. Ramlee's compositions for film have become canonical markers of Malaysian and, more explicitly, Malay national identity in music. Since his death in 1973, numerous reproductions and adaptations of his film songs have been heard on the radio, television, (new) films, stage productions and the internet. In understanding the omnipresence of P. Ramlee's music, it is useful to trace the rise of Malay film and his music against the backdrop of an emergent nationhood in the Malay world. The post-war Malay film industry was instrumental in providing a musical representation of a nation-in-the-making for its growing audience.

In this chapter, I examine how Malay film music articulated, within the frames of a cosmopolitan, commercial, vernacular industry, the sentiments of emergent postcolonial nation-making during the transition between post-war colonial rule and Malayan independence. Music in Malay-language films in the mid-1950s is analysed in the context of decolonisation. These films were produced within a commodified enterprise that sought revenue streams from a vernacular audience. As such, Malay films from this period were not overtly political due to colonial censorship, but still contained covert postcolonial nationalist ideas of resistance and self-determination. At the very least, such films articulated in their narratives the tension, anxieties, aspirations and disjunctures of postcolonial nationhood. I analyse how such ideas of emergent cosmopolitan nationalism were expressed musically in such film narratives through the use of linked musical motifs and culturally referential songs. In particular, I focus on the music in two films produced by Shaw Brothers' Malay Film Productions that reflected the growing consciousness of nationhood among the Malay community. Significantly, these films also articulate two phases of nation-making in the Malay Peninsula: one was made a year prior to the declaration of Malayan independence (1957) and the other a year after. *Hang Tuah* (1956, dir. Phani Majumdar) reflects Malay nationalism expressed through a popular historical narrative, while *Sergeant Hassan* (1958, dir. Lamberto V. Avellana) is a military story set during the Japanese occupation of Malaya during the Second World War that actually articulates the anti-communist sentiment of the government during the period in which it was produced. Both films starred and featured music composed by P. Ramlee.

Set during a precolonial and premodern period, *Hang Tuah* articulates a Malay nationalist narrative in a historical manner. It is not without ideological contradictions. A British scholar administrator Mubin Sheppard, who was an enthusiastic documenter of Malay history and cultural practices, wrote the screenplay. The story depicts the popular Malay hero Hang Tuah (played by P. Ramlee) of the precolonial sultanate of Melaka (c.1400–1511). The narrative nonetheless paints the hero in a *modern* light—his actions and virtues of unquestioning loyalty to the king are put through critical questioning. When read musically, the film displays simultaneous instances of cultural displacement, omission and resistance. What is clear is that traditional Malay musical cultures are misrepresented in the historical setting of the film, reflecting instead the commercial and cosmopolitan approaches to musical production that were part of a Western 'superculture' of film music practices.[1] However, the film's music also incorporates a vernacular approach that suggests the ethnonationalist agenda of the composer. Nevertheless, a modern construction of national identity is relayed in the film in its depiction of internal others who are relegated outside the boundaries of the constructed, 'authentic' Malay nation. This is complicated by instances of musical *othering* that marginalise certain groups and individuals in the narrative and concurrently provide an alternative to autocratic feudal patriarchy and, by extension, articulate a musical resistance to colonial rule. I unravel these ideas through an analysis of numerous songs and dances featured in the film and emphasise a reading of colonial resistance through an analysis of a recurring motif representative of the hero's love interest, Melur (Saadiah).

In the second film, *Sergeant Hassan*, a leitmotif of decolonisation is derived from the melody of the film's featured song, 'Tunggu Sekejap' (Wait for a While), composed by P. Ramlee, with lyrics by S. Sudarmaji. The musical and lyrical content of the song in relation to the film's narrative reflects the ambivalence of an emergent ethnonational identity in the wake of Malayan independence. The film, in its depiction of the Malay and British resistance movement against the Japanese occupation during the Second World War, also mirrors the state of emergency that involved extensive guerrilla warfare by communist insurgents against local and Commonwealth troops. *Sergeant Hassan* exhibits a very colonial-friendly

---

[1]   Mark Slobin, 'The Steiner superculture', in *Global Soundtracks: Worlds of Film Music*, ed. Mark Slobin. Middletown, CT: Wesleyan University Press, 2008, pp. 3–35.

stance in its depiction of Malay soldiers who demonstrate military bravery and national pride in defending their homeland. The film's narrative is a prelude to Malay national autonomy albeit within the framework of a British colonial notion of nationhood. This framework is clearly heard in the film's Western-styled monothematic score in its use of 'Tunggu Sekejap' that is developed as a leitmotif throughout the narrative to symbolise an independent nation-in-waiting.

Decolonisation and the Transition to Nationhood

The 1950s was a period of intense social unrest and political change. The years immediately following the end of the Second World War saw a growth in political mobilisation for postcolonial autonomy. These local movements for independence frame the films made in Malaya in the mid-1950s: Malay films had to appeal to a vernacular audience who were becoming increasingly political, if not already cognisant of their potential position as citizens in a future nation state. Commercial films produced by private companies had to walk a fine line between highlighting current political issues and providing entertainment. While non-Malay collaborators owned and mostly produced these Malay films subject to strict British censorship, their musical production was helmed by Malay composer-directors such as P. Ramlee and composers such as Zubir Said and Kassim Masdor.[2] This racialised division of labour in the Malay film industry significantly parallels the ethnicised social and occupational structures of late colonial, post-war Malaya. Marginal voices and ideas were surfacing to exert structural changes and challenge the hegemony of colonial and local elites. In 1950s Malaya, with independence looming, communism and leftist politics were major concerns for the British. A brief history of these political tensions helps to situate the analysis of Malay film music in this period.

Having signed the Atlantic Charter (1941) in cooperation with the United States's international policy of decolonisation, the returning

---

[2]   Mohd Raman Daud, ed. *7 Magnificient [sic] Composers: 7 Tokoh Muzik*. Singapore: Perkamus, 2002.

British colonial administration was compelled to facilitate Malayan independence.[3] However, in doing so, the British remained opposed to radical organisations with affinities to communist or leftist ideologies. These groups had an organised labour and militant base that had been fostered in the resistance movement against the Japanese occupation. The occupation also gave rise to Malay radicalism and a political consciousness that was closely tied to the ideas fuelling Indonesia's anti-colonial and independence movement following the war. In their haste to form a Malayan nation state, the British administration was met with unpredicted resistance from politicised Indian, Chinese and Malay communities. Drawing from Barbara Watson Andaya and Leonard Andaya's insightful historical narrative, four junctures contextualised the political milieu of nation-making in post-war Malaya: the end of the Japanese occupation in the Malay Peninsula; the proposal of and opposition to the Malayan Union; the state of emergency due to the communist insurrection; and the declaration of independence in 1957.[4] These events demonstrate the rise of ethnonationalism in a period of decolonisation that resonated with Malay film narratives produced in the 1950s. A sense of a Malay(an) nation was forming and this was reflected in film narratives and music.

When the majority of British forces fled Malaya during the war, the Malayan People's Anti-Japanese Army (MPAJA), comprising mostly local leftist groups including the Malayan Communist Party (MCP), was prominent in the armed resistance to the Japanese. After Japan's surrender in 1945, the MPAJA was swift to gain control of the Peninsula before the return of the British administration. During the occupation, the Malay community, who were considered indigenous to the region, were given more favourable treatment by the Japanese in comparison to other ethnic groups; many were recruited into administrative and law enforcement positions. By contrast, the Chinese community suffered considerably due to existing enmities from the Sino-Japanese War which started in 1937. When the Japanese conceded defeat, the predominantly

---

[3]   Barbara Watson Andaya and Leonard Andaya, *A History of Malaysia*. 2nd ed., Honolulu: University of Hawai'i Press, 2001, p. 265.

[4]   Ibid.

Chinese MPAJA or MCP elements retaliated by capturing and executing Malay district officials and police officers. Such interethnic violence formed the backdrop to the communal tensions that would infuse the politics of the post-war period.

After recapturing Malaya, the British initiated plans to form a Malayan Union, comprising the Federated Malay States, Unfederated Malay States, and the Straits Settlements of Penang and Melaka. The proposed Malayan Union, under the direct authority of the British Crown, threatened to greatly reduce the power of the sultans of the Malay states. Nevertheless, most sultans were coerced into signing the agreement, and equal citizenship rights were granted to all ethnic communities, whether immigrant or native to the Malay Peninsula. The Malayan Union's official inauguration in 1946 galvanised the Malay community politically in 'united, vehement and unforseen' opposition to it, leading to the formation of the United Malays National Organisation (UMNO).[5] UMNO effectively provided a platform for Malays of all backgrounds—radicals, nobility, religious leaders, educators—to articulate a sense of ethnonational self-determination. Malay women also played a prominent role in rallying support from their community. The mass mobilisation to oppose the Malayan Union resulted in its replacement with the Federation of Malaya in 1948, a product of negotiations between Malay rulers, UMNO leaders and British officials. Still under British colonial authority, the Federation of Malaya had more rigid terms of citizenship for non-Malays and defined in strict terms who constituted members of the *Melayu* (Malay) 'race': those who practised Islam, adopted Malay customs and habitually conversed in Malay. While UMNO advanced Malay rights significantly on the path to independence, the Federation of Malaya also paved the way for a factionalised communal or ethnic-orientated politics. The ethnic dimensions of the state of emergency exacerbated some of that communal tension.

Two years after the end of the war, a rise in strike action by rubber plantation workers and increasing colonial suppression of leftist labour organisations prompted the predominantly Chinese MCP, led by its new

---

[5]   Ibid., p. 267.

secretary-general Chin Peng, to initiate an armed insurrection against the colonial state. In 1948 the British declared a state of emergency resulting in an increased military and police presence throughout the country, the delegalisation of militant groups such as the MCP,[6] the implementation of regulations that allowed for the arrest and detention of suspects without trial, and the mass resettlement of working-class Chinese communities into so-called 'new villages'—by 1952, 400 government-administered villages housed 100,000 Chinese residents.[7] Due to its predominantly Chinese membership and the MCP's ties to China, the Chinese community found themselves marginalised as 'victims in a quarrel that was not of their making'.[8] In addition, while the British established their control over Chinese livelihoods, Malays looked on the Chinese community with increasing suspicion regarding their loyalty to the country. By 1958 violent clashes with communist insurgents had decreased markedly with the surrender of 500 guerillas. In July 1960 the state of emergency officially ended.

The five years leading up to independence in 1957 established a lasting political alliance between UMNO and the Malayan Chinese Association (MCA). They were later joined by the Malayan Indian Congress (MIC) in 1955. During the Emergency, the MCA, led by Tan Cheng Lock, gained support from diverse factions of the Chinese community while cooperating with UMNO and the British authorities 'in the fight against Communism'.[9] The alliance of the two parties—both had racially exclusive membership—resulted in landslide victories in the municipal town council elections of 1952 and 1954. With the MIC

---

6   There were also Malay members active in the MCP and in the insurrection. Other Malay leftist groups (including Malay members of the MCP) such as Kesatuan Melayu Muda (KMM, Young Malays Union) and Kesatuan Rakyat Indonesia Semenanjung (KRIS, Indonesian Peoples of the Peninsula Organisation), who felt affinities with the post-war independence movement in Indonesia, formed Partai Kebangsaan Melayu Malaya (PKMM, Malay Nationalist Party of Malaya), led by Burhanuddin al-Helmy, in late 1945.

7   Andaya and Andaya, *A History of Malaysia*, p. 272; T.N. Harper, *The End of Empire and the Making of Malaya*. 2nd ed. Cambridge: Cambridge University Press, 2001, pp. 149, 182–88.

8   Andaya and Andaya, *A History of Malaysia*, p. 274.

9   Ibid., p. 275.

joining in 1955, the Alliance won 51 of 52 contested seats for the first federal council elections. The political cooperation between members of the Alliance finally led to the ratification of a new constitution that afforded citizenship to all non-Malay residents born in the Peninsula with additional requirements for others. UMNO's acceptance of non-Malay citizenship was given on condition that special privileges be granted to Malays and that such rights would be safeguarded by a paramount ruler (Yang di-Pertuan Agong, elected from a council of sovereign Malay sultans). On 31 August 1957 independence (*merdeka*) was proclaimed for the Federation of Malaya.

This intense and racialised political history of nation-making coincided with the consolidation of the Malay-language film industry, which peaked in productivity and popularity in the mid-1950s to early 1960s, a period of pronounced nationalist sentiment and political ambivalence.

Screening Decolonisation

The Malay film industry of the 1950s reflected the tensions and complications of a plural Malayan nation. The period preceding independence was marked by 'negotiation, tension and deliberation over how the state would function and who would be its members', which resulted in the newly formed nation being led by an alliance 'of ethnically-based parties'.[10] The term '*merdeka*' (independence) was commonly used to denote 'the transfer of political power', but ideologically it signified the need for 'a revolutionary change in the outlook of all the members of the new nation, from the elites to the *rakyat* [citizens], or masses, and this was a process that was fought on a number of battlefields and was not simply a binary equation'.[11] Underneath the spirit of *merdeka*, however, was a growing tension brought about by a racially orientated political landscape that would eventually culminate in racial riots in May 1969.[12] Here I draw

---

[10] Timothy P. Barnard, 'Decolonization and the nation in Malay film, 1955–1965', *South East Asia Research* 17, 1 (2009): 66.

[11] Ibid., pp. 66–67.

[12] Leon Comber, *13 May 1969: The Darkest Day in Malaysian History*. 2nd ed., Singapore: Marshall Cavendish, 2009.

attention to a less violent decolonising battlefield that helped negotiate this new national consciousness: the emerging Malay film industry based in Singapore.

Singapore was a particularly diverse and lucrative centre of entertainment, art and literature and attracted many intellectual and creative Malays from the rest of the peninsula.

> Singapore was part of the Malay world, but it was radically different from any part of the Peninsula as it was a British colony and a strategic military base for the British. The port city was attractive to many Malays who sought employment as well as an environment that was less restrictive than those under the Emergency laws enforced in wider Malaya.[13]

Singapore in the 1950s was a cosmopolitan hub for the creative and intellectual advancement of Malays and for nascent ideas about Malay culture and nationhood. The creative industries such as print, film and music were fertile arenas for the articulation of Malay nationalist ideas. Young Malay men[14] in Singapore, whose ideas permeated film scripts, were part of an activist community that 'promoted the ideal of an iconic Malay nationalist ... who honoured traditions while embracing the possibilities of a rapidly changing nation' while being 'squarely rooted in the Malay community ... rarely' considering 'the larger multi-ethnic nation, or at most' reactionary to such diversity.[15] Malays were a minority in the Chinese-majority population of Singapore. Ironically, it was this position of relative marginality that provided a creative space for voicing the Malay-majority politics of the entire Malay Peninsula. This creative

---

[13]   Hassan Abdul Muthalib, '"Winning hearts and minds": Representations of Malays and their milieu in the films of British Malaya', *South East Asia Research* 17, 1 (2009): 50.

[14]   Nearly all of the main creative agents in the Malay film industry were men with the exception of the popular film star Maria Menado, who did not write for films but would eventually own a film production company, and another popular actress and singer, Siput Sarawak, who wrote the script for *Mata Syaitan* (Devil's Eye, 1962, dir. Hussein Haniff). See Timothy P. Barnard, 'Vampires, heroes and jesters: A history of Cathay Keris', in *The Cathay Story*, ed. Ain-ling Wong. Hong Kong: Hong Kong Film Archives, 2002, pp. 128, 133.

[15]   Barnard, 'Decolonization and the nation', p. 71.

space for the articulation of nascent Malay nationalism was also limited to the commercial context of a film industry not under direct state control but nonetheless subject to strict British censorship.[16]

Despite the communal political orientation of some Malay activists, Singapore was a vibrant space for the convergence and interaction of people, cultures and ideas from all over Asia, Europe and the Americas. Thus, when reading the social narratives of Malay cultural practices and productions, we must consider the plural interactions of these diverse cultural perspectives as a key element of their cosmopolitanism. Ideas of Malay nationhood and decolonisation expressed through music and narratives via the Singapore film industry were undoubtedly shaped by plural and mixed creative practices in a cosmopolitan environment.[17] While there were latent tensions between the Peninsula's ethnic communities there were also economies of integration and cooperation that reflected the ideal of Malayan multiculturalism. The Malay film industry in the 1950s, for example, was financed by Chinese businessmen, operated by a combination of Indian, Chinese and Malay technical staff, helmed largely by Indian directors and showcased Malays as musical performers, composers and actors.[18] This apparently pluralistic version of interethnic collaboration must be tempered by the fact that these films were made for a Malay vernacular audience. Viewed from the audience's perspective, the films presented an exclusive ethnic space for the articulation of Malay nationhood. Their vernacular frames spoke to the hopes and aspirations of its Malay-speaking consumers.[19]

---

[16] For more on Malaysian state-sponsored films and censorship, specifically of the British-initiated Malayan Film Unit, see Hassan, 'Winning hearts and minds'; and Hassan Abdul Muthalib, 'The end of empire: The films of the Malayan Film Unit in 1950s British Malaya', in *Film and the End of Empire*, ed. Lee Grieveson and Colin MacCabe. London: British Film Institute, 2011, pp. 177–96.

[17] See Timothy P. Barnard and Jan van der Putten, 'Malay cosmopolitan activism in post-war Singapore', in *Paths Not Taken: Political Pluralism in Post-War Singapore*, ed. Michael D. Barr and Carl A. Trocki. Singapore: NUS Press, 2008, pp. 132–53; Joel S. Kahn, *Other Malays: Nationalism and Cosmopolitanism in the Modern Malay World*. Singapore: Singapore University Press, 2006.

[18] Barnard, 'Vampires, heroes and jesters', p. 128.

[19] Beyond this monocultural appeal there were Malay films of the period that successfully attracted a multiethnic audience; particularly popular across communities was the

However, this articulation of Malay nationalism was still mediated by the presence of multiethnic and transnational agents.

The Malay films of the 1950s reflected the disjunctures of postcolonial nationalist ideals that were toned down or subtly expressed within the commercial confines of a profit-orientated industry and stringent British censorship.[20] Barnard observes that a great number of Malay film-makers in Singapore were activists 'who promoted a modern, individualistic outlook'.[21] But this also coincided with the reality that they worked for profit-orientated businesses, which constrained their creativity to market-driven goals.[22] These limitations, I suggest, contributed to many of the ideological disjunctures inherent in the political narratives of such films. Such disjunctures are also observed as an 'ambivalence' in the social messages expressed by film directors and writers with regards to the 'feelings that Malays were experiencing during the 1950s' in the wake of increasing urban migration and changing lifestyles that departed from Malay rural practices and values.[23] This is further complicated by the observation that the Japanese occupation had made an impact on local film-making, particularly in comedy genres, 'narrative style and cinematography'.[24] P. Ramlee famously received his musical education as a cadet at a Japanese naval school in Penang during the war.[25]

These socio-historical ambivalences and disjunctures in the Malay film industry paradoxically contributed to the conditions that allowed for instances of creative agency in the films and music. Considering the

---

horror genre, notably *Pontianak* (Vampire, 1957) and *Sumpah Pontianak* (Curse of the Vampire, 1958). Ibid., pp. 129–30.

[20] Hassan, 'Winning hearts and minds', p. 53.

[21] Barnard, 'Decolonization and the nation', p. 66.

[22] Ibid., p. 68.

[23] Rohayati Paseng Barnard and Timothy P. Barnard, 'The ambivalence of P. Ramlee: *Penarek Beca* and *Bujang Lapok* in perspective', *Asian Cinema* 13, 2 (2002): 21; Hassan, '"Winning hearts and minds"', p. 51.

[24] Timothy White, 'Historical poetics, Malaysian cinema and the Japanese occupation', *Kinema* 6 (1996): 5–27.

[25] Mohd Raman Daud, ed. *7 Magnificient* [*sic*] *Composers*, p. 119. This is particularly ironic, given that in the film *Sergeant Hassan* P. Ramlee portrays a soldier who fights against the Japanese army in Malaya.

disjunctures between Malay ethnonationalism and a commercial film industry, a cosmopolitan milieu of production and creative agency was still able to emerge from structural limitations, thus providing a context for a nuanced interpretation of music and nation-making in Malay films.

While an ethnonationalist ideal was embedded in Malay film narratives, the music contained in these films, by contrast, was modern, hybrid, and in many instances aesthetically Western. This musical aesthetic resonated with the modern nationalist content of the films' narratives. However, such music was also reflective of a period of decolonisation represented by the commercial production of vernacular films for a mass entertainment market. Thus films like *Hang Tuah* set in precolonial times could contain covert anti-colonial ideas in the guise of criticising Malay feudalism. By contrast, a film like *Sergeant Hassan* that negatively depicts the period of the Japanese occupation expresses British political ideology and, more covertly, anti-communist propaganda.

Reinventing the Past: *Hang Tuah* (1956)

The historical epic *Hang Tuah* provided Malay audiences with a complex script for postcolonial nationhood. Set in an idealised precolonial past, the film anticipated the approaching formation of the Federation of Malaysia. The semi-mythical legend of Hang Tuah is a classical Malay epic that depicts an admiral (*laksamana*) of the Melaka sultanate in the fifteenth century. Early accounts of the admiral's exploits are found in the precolonial chronicles *Hikayat Hang Tuah* (*Romance of Hang Tuah*) and *Sejarah Melayu* (*The Malay Annals*).[26] These court-produced texts were 'highly respected receptacles if not sacred objects' that were instrumental in validating the authority of the Malay monarchy.[27] In their development of vernacular education syllabi for Malays, the British

---

[26] Its original title was *Sulalatus Salatin*, edited and compiled by Tun Sri Lanang in 1612, and was initially translated to English in 1821 as John Leyden, trans. *Sejarah Melayu: The Malay Annals*. Kuala Lumpur: Silverfish Books, 2012 (Orig. publ. 1821).

[27] Jan van der Putten and Timothy P. Barnard, 'Old Malay heroes never die: The story of Hang Tuah in films and comics', in *Film and Comic Books*, ed. Ian Gordon, Mark Jancovich and Matthew P. McAllister. Jackson: University Press of Mississippi, 2007, p. 257.

favoured using these texts because they underscore Hang Tuah's fealty to his king, and values such as unquestioning loyalty to one's ruler were easily transferred to the project of instilling Malay support of the colonial administration.[28] As such, these texts were two of the first British publications in the Malay language, valued for their 'clear and simple' use of Malay unencumbered by 'Arabic loan-words, and therefore in line with nineteenth-century western ideals of a "pure" original language which was important for western understandings of a Malay "nation".[29] The Hang Tuah story blossomed in popularity among the Malay-speaking population during the post-war period with a proliferation of *bangsawan* plays,[30] fiction, comic books, dramatic stage acts and film.[31] I am particularly interested here in how music was used in Shaw Brothers' large-budget cinematic production of the story.[32]

Musically Reinventing Melaka

During the opening credits of the film, a percussive Malay rhythm on *rebana* drums is heard followed by an unaccompanied solo voice singing in a *syair* style. Malay film audiences of the 1950s would have recognised the unmistakable voice of P. Ramlee, the star of the film and by then a prominent singing and acting icon of the entertainment industry. More

---

[28] Ibid. See also Ian Proudfoot, *Early Malay Printed Books: A Provisional Account of Materials Published in the Singapore-Malaysia Area up to 1920, Noting Holdings in Major Public Collections*. Kuala Lumpur: Academy of Malay Studies and the Library, University of Malaya, 1993.

[29] Van der Putten and Barnard, 'Old Malay heroes never die', p. 258.

[30] Ibid., p. 246. The period prior to the Second World War also saw adaptations of the Hang Tuah narrative in *bangsawan* plays. See Tan Sooi Beng, *Bangsawan: A Social and Stylistic History of Popular Malay Opera*. Singapore: Oxford University Press, 1993; and Rahmah Bujang, *Sejarah Perkembangan Drama Bangsawan di Tanah Melayu dan Singapura* [The History of the Development of *Bangsawan* Drama in Malaya and Singapore]. Kuala Lumpur: Dewan Bahasa dan Pustaka, 1975.

[31] Two of the notable films about Hang Tuah are Majumdar's *Hang Tuah* (1956) produced by Shaw Brothers' Malay Film Productions and the more daring adaptation, *Hang Jebat* (1961).

[32] Far exceeding the standard cost of a typical Malay film production (below $30,000), the total cost of the production was $300,000—at the time one Malayan dollar was equal to 14 British pence. See van der Putten and Barnard, 'Old Malay heroes never die'.

importantly, this musical presentation immediately signals for a Malay audience a precolonial setting for the narrative. *Syair* is a poetic form of storytelling structured in four-line verses and is sung in a melodic pattern using Arabic *maqam* or modes that are used in Qur'anic recitation.[33] *Syair* singing and verse structures are present in Malay music styles like *ghazal* and incorporated aesthetically and textually to represent 'Malay elements' in *bangsawan* music.[34] Mulaika Hijjas notes the pervasiveness of *syair* in the nineteenth-century Malay world as a poetic and narrative structure 'used not only for religious but romantic allegories ... reportage ... and romantic narratives of all kinds', while the connection between *syair* and music may be discerned from the 'teasing songs performed by *biduan*, or female court singers ... in *Hikayat Hang Tuah*' and descriptions in *Sejarah Melayu* of *syair* in musical contexts.[35] Thus, the use of *syair* at the beginning of the film evokes an aesthetic of Malayness that audibly signifies a premodern Malay past to set the tone for the film's historical narrative. This musical device is simultaneously a narrative, historical and ethnic marker. Despite the complex history of *syair*, notably its popularity as an oral and written form during the period of Western colonial contact with the Malay world in the nineteenth century and its adaptation to modern forms of entertainment in the twentieth, its use here sonically frames the film as a distinctly precolonial Malay story. In addition to this musical-historical placement a Malay nationalist tenor is articulated in the glorification of the Melaka sultanate (see Appendix A.1).

The opening song that details the 'greatness' of Melaka connects the sentiments of 1950s Malay nationalism to a precolonial past in which a traceable and discrete Malay—or, more specifically, *Melayu*—ethnicity centred on specific histories of kingship. Such a sentiment is clearly articulated in the third verse that espouses Melaka as the 'well-known'

---

[33]   Patricia Matusky and Tan Sooi Beng, *The Music of Malaysia: The Classical, Folk and Syncretic Traditions*. Aldershot: Ashgate, 2004, pp. 77, 265.

[34]   Ibid., pp. 353, 77.

[35]   Mulaika Hijjas, *Victorious Wives: The Disguised Heroine in 19th-Century Malay Syair*. Singapore: NUS Press, 2011, pp. 4–5; Matusky and Tan, *The Music of Malaysia*, pp. 276–77.

Malay 'state of origin'. In tracing the origins of the ethnic concept of *Melayu*, Anthony Reid highlights the significance of royal lineages traced historically to ambiguous associations with the Srivijaya Empire in the seventh century up to the clearer identifications of *Melayu* culture with sixteenth-century Melaka.[36] Indeed, it is the conception of Melaka as a 'polity of substance' that acts as the source for a cohesive Malay identity from the sixteenth century to the present in the form of literary and filmic adaptations of history as an 'inspiration for modern state builders'.[37] While Melaka was a Malay polity of note, there were also many other sultanates associated with the Malay world that were similar 'in their mode of living, their language and literature, their state rituals and titular systems, and the particular logic of their political and cultural systems'.[38] Anthony Milner asserts that a unifying factor in the concept of Malayness lies in the 'civilisational logic' of the '*kerajaan* system', in which the sultan or the raja was the highest authority in a hierarchy of ranked subjects to which the monarch had a reciprocal relationship: the more *rakyat* (subjects) in his polity, the more power and prestige he was bestowed.[39] What makes this unitary system more complex is that many discrete cultural polities existed in a networked and feudal space of *kerajaan* (kingdoms). While these were fluidly linked identities, the shared cultural characteristics that encompassed an affiliation with a Malay monarch would form the basis of greater ethnic homogenisation through colonial European as well as local understandings of 'race'. Thus the song 'Melaka', on textual, conceptual and historical levels, relates a

---

[36] Anthony Reid, 'Understanding *Melayu* (Malay) as a source of diverse modern identities', in *Contesting Malayness: Malay Identity Across Boundaries*, ed. Timothy P. Barnard. Singapore: Singapore University Press, 2004, pp. 3–8.

[37] Anthony Milner, *The Malays*. Chichester: Wiley-Blackwell, 2008, p. 47. Malay films drew from a genre of *bangsawan* plays that were historical stories based on precolonial Malay texts. See Tan, *Bangsawan*, for more information. Some prominent Malay films aside from *Hang Tuah* that were of this historical genre include *Semerah Padi* (1956, dir. P. Ramlee), *Hang Jebat* (1961, dir. Hussein Haniff) and *Raja Bersiong* (Vampire King, 1968, dir. Jamil Sulong).

[38] Milner, *The Malays*, pp. 47, 49. These other sultanates include 'Brunei in north Borneo, Patani in present-day southern Thailand, Aru and Siak in eastern Sumatra and Melaka's successor polity, Johor'.

[39] Ibid., p. 66.

message of emerging nationalism that could galvanise a conception of a unified Malay race in a period of decolonisation.

The unaccompanied solo vocal theme is then transformed into a *dikir barat* in the second verse with the added accompaniment of a percussive ensemble and a chorus of men and women that sing in response to P. Ramlee's solo verses. *Dikir barat*, popular in the northern states of peninsular Malaysia (including Penang, where P. Ramlee was born and raised), involves solo lines sung by a lead singer (*tok juara*) that is responded to by a chorus of 10 to 15 singers (*awok-awok*) accompanied by a percussive ensemble consisting of a mixed assortment of *rebana* frame drums, a *gedumbak* drum, maracas and a *tetawak* or *canang* gong.[40] Here we see the influences of two normally separate Malay music styles converging in a manner that could be construed as 'inauthentic' or 'cosmopolitan' depending upon one's viewpoint. I observe this with no intention of questioning musical 'authenticity', but rather to note how different styles may be merged creatively in the commercial context of film music to intensify 'Malay' aesthetic signifiers. It is the commercial context of Malay film music production that facilitates this musical intermingling of styles. The purpose of the music was not to be historically accurate but to refer to a precolonial Malayness while simultaneously providing lively musical entertainment for its cosmopolitan audience. This convergence of styles for a film theme indicates at once the commercial context of film music as well as the ethnonationalist message that underscores the film.

Taking into account the diverse range of individuals involved, the history of the film's production reveals a more complex account of cosmopolitan interaction and commercial production goals than a simplistic reading of it as ethnonationalist. Much criticism was levelled at the film by activists from the Malay community. Mahmud Ahmad, one of the cultural advisers to the film, unhappy with his limited input and meagre remuneration, was critical of the 'vibrant' and thus inauthentic colours of the film's costumes. He further found the 'inordinate amount of input' by the British author of the script, Mubin Sheppard, troubling

---

[40] Matusky and Tan, *The Music of Malaysia*, pp. 355–64.

and was further exasperated by the use of English at the meetings he attended, interpreting this 'as a tool of colonial oppression'.[41] Other critics were wary of an Indian director helming the production, dissatisfied with the 'simplification' of a complex narrative, and opposed to the portrayal of a 'singing Hang Tuah' in that it made the film 'too Indian'.[42] Despite the film's commercial success, it did not appeal to all those invested in a postcolonial conception of Malay nationalism.

These critical opinions reveal the anti-colonial political discourse that concerned Malay activists at the time. Ironically, the narrative of the film actually aligns with such anti-colonial critique in its departure from the classic Malay theme of being loyal to one's monarch, thereby suggesting ideas of self-determination and resistance to autocratic rule. Despite the criticisms levelled at the film after its release, it can be read as an appeal to modern Malay nationalist sentiments that articulates a critique of feudal and colonial rule. The contradictory responses and readings solicited from the film could be explained as reflecting the social ambivalence and anxieties that the Malay community felt in the midst of political uncertainty and rapid urban migration and modernisation.[43] The music contained in the film, however, depicts less ambivalence than is revealed in the film's social and narrative contexts. Beneath this textual ambivalence, from the outset the film possesses an overtly masculine and Malay ethnonationalist agenda in the music.[44] Further analysis also reveals how subversive ideas are expressed through the film's female characters.

In *Hang Tuah*'s historical commercial narrative of a precolonial Malay past, musical meaning is linked to the complex conditions of

---

[41] Van der Putten and Barnard, 'Old Malay heroes never die', pp. 262–63.

[42] Ibid., p. 263; James Harding and Ahmad Sarji, *P. Ramlee: The Bright Star*. 2nd ed., Petaling Jaya: MPH, 2011, p. 72. Adding to the film's questionable authenticity to Malay culture are a Western storybook-style opening credit sequence and the use of the end title 'The End'.

[43] Barnard and Barnard, 'The ambivalence of P. Ramlee'.

[44] For a detailed analysis of the politics of masculinity and subtextual homoeroticism in the Hang Tuah narrative across different filmic and literary contexts, see Khoo Gaik Cheng, *Reclaiming Adat: Contemporary Malaysian Film and Literature*. Singapore: NUS Press, 2006, pp. 22–55.

authorship and production. While the musical content of *Hang Tuah* reflects the commercial cosmopolitan constraints of production, it also reveals a vernacular authorship—a fashioning of national identity in a 'rooted cosmopolitan' framework.[45] In the authorship and production of the film, music was the only domain that was led by Malays—the songs were composed and performed by P. Ramlee. In considering the authorship of the film's narrative, further complexities arise. The scriptwriter Mubin Sheppard, a British colonial administrator who had immersed himself in Malay culture and converted to Islam, authored an adaptation and translation of *Hikayat Hang Tuah* (*Romance of Hang Tuah*) that formed the basis of the film's script.[46] The directorship of the film was awarded to an Indian national, Phani Majumdar, who had a track record of directing films with postcolonial nationalist themes in his home country.[47] Hence the production context of *Hang Tuah* was representative of the cosmopolitan interactions of locals with foreigners,

[45] Tan Sooi Beng, 'Negotiating "His Master's Voice": Gramophone music and cosmopolitan modernity in British Malaya in the 1930s and early 1940s', *Bijdragen tot de Taal-, Land- en Volkenkunde* 169, 4 (2013): 457–94.

[46] Mubin Sheppard's involvement with documenting and eventually adopting Malay culture is especially interesting. Having arrived in Malaya in the late 1920s, he stayed on through the Japanese occupation and after Malayan independence to eventually become a Malaysian citizen and converting to Islam. See Mubin Sheppard, *Taman Budiman: Memoirs of an Unorthodox Civil Servant*. Kuala Lumpur: Heinemann Educational Books, 1979. His documentation of Malay culture culminated in a series of publications on customs and cultural practices, including music and the arts. See Mubin Sheppard, *Malay Courtesy: A Narrative Account of Malay Manners and Customs in Everyday Use*. Singapore: Eastern Universities Press, 1959; Mubin Sheppard, *Taman Indera: A Royal Pleasure Ground: Malay Decorative Arts and Pastimes*. Kuala Lumpur: Oxford University Press, 1972; Mubin Sheppard, *Living Crafts of Malaysia*. Singapore: Times Books International, 1978; and Mubin Sheppard, *Taman Saujana: Dance, Drama, Music and Magic in Malaya, Long and Not-so-Long Ago*. Petaling Jaya: International Book Service, 1983. A complete bibliography of his publications on Malaysia is listed in H.S. Barlow, 'Bibliography of Tan Sri Dato Dr Haji Mubin Sheppard', *Journal of the Malaysian Branch of the Royal Asiatic Society* 68, 2 (1995): 59–66.

[47] Van der Putten and Barnard, 'Old Malay heroes never die', p. 261. Phani Majumdar was brought from India to reorganise Shaw Brothers' Malay Film Productions' studio to maximise its output efficiency. He proved this in his rapid shooting of *Hang Tuah* in 28 days. See Tamaki Matsuoka Kanda, 'Indian film directors in Malaya', in *Frames of Mind: Reflections on Indian Cinema*, ed. Aruna Vasudev. New Delhi: Indian Council for Public Relations, 1995, p. 48.

but more than this, foreigners who were sympathetic to the cultures and political concerns of locals during a period of rapid decolonisation. All these complex interactions and relationships between individuals of different ethnicities, nationalities and motivations reflect the cosmopolitan idealism and nascent ethnonationalist contestations that fuelled the film's production.

In examining music in films during this period of decolonisation, Malay agency is most evident in the music, and in musical moments that signal a modern sense of Malay citizenship. The musical moments in *Hang Tuah* that best represent such agential musical articulations relate the ambivalences of citizenship in Malaya in the mid-1950s. Two key examples are the song 'Berkorban Apa Saja' (To Sacrifice Anything at All) and a recurring melody or leitmotif sung by Hang Tuah and Melur (Saadiah), an indigenous woman and love interest. The traces of modernity that contrast with the film's premodern setting are also found in the dance sequence of the 'Joget Pahang' song.

Dance of Deception, Song of Sacrifice

Musical performances wedded to the film's narrative occur in the second act of the film. All of the film songs performed by P. Ramlee on screen occur during Hang Tuah's excursion in Pahang, where he is given the task of courting the daughter of Pahang's *bendahara*, Tun Tijah (Zaiton), for the Sultan of Melaka.[48] This section of the film contains the song and dance sequence of 'Joget Pahang' and two performances of the ballad 'Berkorban Apa Saja'. The narrative context of the latter portrays Hang Tuah in his first moment of self-doubt, the first instance in which he questions his actions—though not his loyalty—in service to the desires of his monarch.

This section of the film is initiated when the Sultan of Melaka declares his interest in marrying Tijah, the princess of Pahang. Unfortunately for the sultan, she is already betrothed to a prince from another kingdom. Without receiving direct orders, Hang Tuah decides to take matters into his own hands by 'claiming' Tijah for his sultan. He

---

[48] A *bendahara* was a viceroy or representative of a sultan who oversaw many provinces.

embarks for Pahang and on arrival gains the trust of the *bendahara* by declaring that he has defected from the Melaka court. The *bendahara*, who has a strained relationship with Melaka, is thrilled to have the famous warrior in his court and welcomes him with open arms. Immediately, Hang Tuah is seen adapting himself to the Pahang court, immersed in the singing and dancing of 'Joget Pahang'. It is an upbeat performance that sees Hang Tuah dancing and singing jovially with Tijah's brother and other men of the court. Outside the room where the merriment is taking place the princess and her female entourage watch with curiosity and interest. Tijah is immediately attracted to the famous Hang Tuah.

This musical interlude embedded in the narrative represents an interesting case of an appropriation of a postcolonial *joget* song style for a precolonial setting in Malay film. The modern *joget* used in the film is a style that developed in *ronggeng* ensembles and *bangsawan* theatre after colonial contact in the Malay Peninsula.[49] This was possibly a reference to the courtly *joget gamelan* that has its origins in the Pahang court of the early twentieth century, but which is markedly different in musical and dance style from the form presented in the film.[50] The earliest documentation of *joget gamelan* situates its performance in the Riau-Lingga royal courts of the eighteenth century.[51] Then, through a royal marriage between Riau-Lingga and Pahang, court dancers and the accompanying Javanese gamelan ensemble and instruments were transported to the court at Pahang, where it developed further during the mid-nineteenth century and was known as *gamelan Pahang* or *joget Pahang*. The divergence from the Javanese-style gamelan accompaniment only occurred after *joget gamelan*'s development in the Terengganu courts—brought there through another royal marriage—in the early twentieth century.[52] While the title of the film's song, 'Joget Pahang', appropriately reflects the function and context of such courtly music—

---

[49] Tan Sooi Beng, 'From folk to national popular music: Recreating *ronggeng* in Malaysia', *Journal of Musicological Research* 24, 3 (2005): 287–307.

[50] Matusky and Tan, *The Music of Malaysia*, pp. 108–9; Sheppard, *Taman Saujana*, pp. 1–16.

[51] Matusky and Tan, *The Music of Malaysia*, p. 108.

[52] Ibid., pp. 108–9.

used for celebrations that ranged from the crowning of a new sultan to welcoming and honouring official state visitors—*Hang Tuah*'s music and dance sequence in no way approximates the real practice of Javanese-style gamelan accompaniment and female court dancers.[53] Neither does the chronology correlate with the fifteenth-century setting of the film; the *joget gamelan* dance is displaced by about five centuries! This musical-historical displacement and conflation of *joget gamelan* or *joget Pahang* with modern *joget* betray the Malay film industry's commercial goals and the attendant limitations of historical verisimilitude.[54] The Malay past was creatively being reinvented through the unintended misrepresentation of Malay music and dance on the silver screen.

'Joget Pahang', written and performed by P. Ramlee with lyrics by Jamil Sulong, served an explicit commercial purpose to provide entertainment for the film's audience, showcasing P. Ramlee as a 'singing Hang Tuah', while linking the popular song to the precolonial Pahang sultanate in the narrative.[55] The performance may be read as a *dance of deception* on two levels: first, in the film's narrative context, Hang Tuah is deceiving the Pahang court; and second, in the film's musical misrepresentation of a precolonial setting a postcolonial *joget* style is used.

The historical-musical 'error' is mainly interesting for what such a musical conflation reveals about the active fashioning of a 'timeless' conception of Malay nationhood through strategically employed music.

---

[53] Ibid., p. 109, citing Marion F. D'Cruz, 'Joget Gamelan: A Study of Its Contemporary Practice'. MA thesis, Universiti Sains Malaysia, 1979.

[54] The choreographic and musical displacement of the 'Joget Pahang' scene could be due to a number of factors. The choreographer Devdatta Jetley may not have been familiar with traditional Malay dance as is clear from the exoticised or stylised choreography throughout the film. The music of modern *joget* was also more suited to showcase P. Ramlee's composition and singing. Moreover, considering the speed with which the film was shot (28 days) and limited involvement of Malay cultural advisers (see Mahmud Ahmad's complaints) it is no surprise that the musical and choreographic content was produced with efficiency and popular appeal in mind. What is curious is the lack of input from Mubin Sheppard, who was quite attuned to traditional Malay music and dance. See his chapter on *joget Pahang* in *Taman Saujana*, pp. 1–16. Perhaps Sheppard had not refined his knowledge of traditional Malay dance in 1956.

[55] Van der Putten and Barnard, 'Old Malay heroes never die', p. 263; Harding and Ahmad, *P. Ramlee*, p. 72. Harding and Ahmad point out how critics of the film lamented the overt Indian influences that permeated *Hang Tuah*, resulting in a singing and dancing hero.

P. Ramlee and Jamil Sulong penned a 'precolonial' musical theme for Pahang that resonated with the popular music taste of a mid-1950s Malay audience. What is evident in this song is its appeal to the audience via a commercial cosmopolitan and ethnonationalist narrative—at once presenting a grand narrative of a Malay national hero in a timeless Malay cultural space while appealing to the contemporary tastes of popular music consumers. The Malay Film Productions' employee and film song composer Kassim Masdor stresses that it was the 'commercial appeal' and singability (*mudah dinyanyikan*) of the company's film music that contributed to its success.[56] This commercial appeal of P. Ramlee's music can be seen as a form of cosmopolitan 'deception' as well. Henk Maier's analysis of the inherent heterogeneity of Hang Tuah as evidenced in a detailed reading of historical texts reveals that the hero's cultural identity was extremely fluid, if not 'hybrid' and mixed (*kacukan*). Maier notes how 'tradition' is in itself 'deceptive', whereby 'every recitation' and 'every reading' of a traditional text results in 'a difference within a repetition'.[57] P. Ramlee's music, dancing and singing Hang Tuah embodies this plurality and mutability of Malay culture. And his musical articulations in the film, while not concerned with historical accuracy, certainly capture the spirit of the character being represented. Despite the appropriation of Hang Tuah as a Malay nationalist icon before and after independence, any reading or rereading of the figure ultimately reveal the cosmopolitan plurality and paradoxes of Malayness.

The historical disjunctures in Hang Tuah's personality are further revealed in the modern representation of his conflicted sense of loyalty to his ruler, something that is unquestioned in pre-filmic representations of him.[58] This questioning of loyalty is articulated strongly in the song 'Berkorban Apa Saja'—a song that presents the *double entendre* of sacrifice *for* love and Hang Tuah's sacrifice *of* love. After the night of

---

[56] Kassim Masdor, Oral History Interviews, Reel/Disc 6, Accession Number 002141, National Archives of Singapore, 1 May 1999; Interview with Kassim Masdor, Experience in the Malay Film and Popular Music Industry, 2013.

[57] Henk Maier, '"We are playing relatives": Riau, the cradle of reality and hybridity', *Bijdragen Tot de Taal-, Land- En Volkenkunde* 153, 4 (1997): 696.

[58] For instance, Mubin Sheppard's English version of the story, on which the film is based, depicts an unquestioningly loyal figure of Hang Tuah.

merriment and display of Hang Tuah's musical prowess, he befriends Tijah's personal maid or *mak inang* (nursemaid) to devise a way to meet with the princess in person. At a prearranged secret meeting at the maid's home, Tijah is smitten by Hang Tuah's charm and intelligence as they exchange romantic *pantun* verses.[59] In classic Malay texts, this was considered a form of flirtation or expression of intimacy that would not cross physical boundaries. At the end of their *pantun* exchanges, Tijah asks Hang Tuah: 'What is the meaning of love? Can you explain [its meaning]?'[60] To which he replies: 'I can, but not with ordinary words.'[61] Hang Tuah then proceeds to sing the first performance of 'Berkorban Apa Saja' (Appendix A.2).

Hang Tuah thus wins Tijah's heart by explaining 'love' as one's ability to 'sacrifice' anything for their beloved. After Tijah leaves satisfied with his musical answer, Hang Tuah experiences his first moment of self-doubt over his loyalty to the Sultan of Melaka. He echoes the song's title as he asks himself, 'sacrifice anything at all? Could I [really] do that?'[62] He then catches himself in doubt and reasserts his unquestioning loyalty: 'Perhaps I may never get to love. My love is only for my king and country. But Melur. I can't stop thinking about you, Melur.'[63] His proto-nationalist declaration of loyalty is tempered by thoughts of his 'true' love interest as depicted in the film, the Jakun or Orang Asli (indigenous) maiden Melur (Saadiah). He then sings the Melur motif (discussed below).

This moment of self-doubt is further amplified in the second performance of the song. When Hang Tuah finally convinces (or

---

[59] A *pantun* is a poetic form consisting of a rhyming quatrain, usually extemporised in different social contexts. In romantic encounters, couples will extemporise *pantun* to solicit or gauge each other's mutual feelings or attraction in an indirect manner; essentially, as a courteous form of flirtation. See Wazir Jahan Karim, 'Prelude to madness: The language of emotion in courtship and early marriage', in *Emotions of Culture: A Malay Perspective*, ed. Wazir Jahan Karim. Singapore: Oxford University Press, 1990, p. 30; William van der Heide, *Malaysian Cinema, Asian Film: Border Crossings and National Cultures*. Amsterdam: Amsterdam University Press, 2002, p. 182.

[60] 'Apakah erti kasih sayang? Bolehkah Tuah terangkan?'

[61] 'Boleh, tetapi tidak dengan kata biasa.'

[62] 'Berkorban apa saja. Bolehkah aku berbuat begitu?'

[63] 'Barang kali aku tidak boleh bercinta. Cintaku hanya kepada rajaku dan tanah airku sahaja. Tetapi Melur. Aku tak dapat melupakan kau Melur.'

deceives) Tijah to elope with him, he reveals his true intentions on their boat journey to Melaka. Upon revealing the devastating truth to Tijah, he tells her to eat a magical betel quid (*sirih jampi*) to forever forget her feelings for him. Following this, Tijah, devastated and crying in her cabin, sings 'Berkorban Apa Saja', now imbued with an alternative meaning from its initial rendition. She is now sacrificing her love for Hang Tuah, to allow him to serve his sultan's wishes. As Tijah and Hang Tuah leave behind their 'false' romance in Pahang, the song's second performance diverges from its original romantic meaning to symbolise Tijah's sacrifice while questioning the morality of Hang Tuah's actions. The song foregrounds Hang Tuah's personal doubts over his unquestioning loyalty to his king at the cost of Tijah's and his own happiness. Moreover, it places Tijah, as a woman of the court, in sacrificial servitude to the desires of men in power—a victim of the autocratic patriarchal state. She is unable to escape an arranged marriage and her brief romance with Hang Tuah was merely a deception. In *Hang Tuah* women and feminine inclinations such as romantic love ultimately fall victim to an autocratic patriarchal nationalism. However, the musical portrayal of melodramatic tragedy in Tijah's despair and Hang Tuah's ambivalence can also be read as a critique of that determining patriarchy. In line with these intertextual disjunctures, the song is a motif of anti-feudal and anti-colonial critique, one that may be heard in light of a period of nascent nationhood in Malaya.[64] It is through the musically expressed intimacies of the film's poetic narrative that such notions of postcolonial agency emerge.

The Melur Motif

Such intimacies are further expressed through a recurring musical motif in the film that centres on the hero's love interest, Melur. Melur is

---

[64] Of the *bangsawan* adaptations of the Hang Tuah story from 1914 to 1956 that preceded the film, the motif of love was only present in one adaptation, 'Cinta di Negara Hang Tuah' (Love in the Land of Hang Tuah) as listed by Rahmah, *Sejarah Perkembangan Drama Bangsawan*. Van der Putten and Barnard, 'Old Malay heroes never die', p. 259 postulate that this play may have depicted the story of Tun Tijah similarly as portrayed in Majumdar's film.

presented in very musical ways and her character and relationship to the main protagonist loudly express the anti-feudal and anti-colonial critique embedded in the film's narrative. Unfortunately, Melur also embodies the role of the ill-fated and eroticised 'celluloid maiden'. This is not dissimilar to the fate of the Native American heroine in Hollywood cinema, who 'enables, helps, loves, or aligns herself with a white European American colonizer and dies as a result of that choice'.[65] Indeed, Melur mirrors this neocolonial American archetype of the sacrificial internal other translated to a masculine Malay nationalist discourse. In the film, Melur is a Melakan girl who is kidnapped by an indigenous tribe. She becomes Hang Tuah's enduring love interest throughout the film but dies when she kills a corrupt Melaka court official in her attempt to exact revenge for Hang Tuah's presumed execution. While her character represents the feminine and affectionate side of Hang Tuah's sensibilities—in contrast to his masculine and martial patriotism—she sacrifices herself violently in parallel to Hang Tuah's sacrifice of love for nationalistic duty. Melur's death has been viewed as secondary if not inconsequential to the death of Hang Jebat who dies at the hands of Hang Tuah for violently revolting against the Sultan of Melaka.[66] However, the relevance of her death to Hang Tuah's ambivalence is far from inconsequential. Melur's character anchors the narrative and Hang Tuah's sense of morality as

---

[65] M. Elise Marubbio, *Killing the Indian Maiden: Images of Native American Women in Film.* Lexington: University Press of Kentucky, 2006, p. ix. Much has been written about the ill-fated and exoticised heroine in European opera. The orientalist and sacrificial representation of female opera characters from Bizet's *Carmen* and Delibes's *Lakmé* are discussed at length in these studies: Ralph P. Locke, 'Constructing the oriental "other": Saint-Saëns's "Samson et Dalila"', *Cambridge Opera Journal* 3, 3 (1991): 261–302; Ralph P. Locke, 'Cutthroats and casbah dancers, muezzins and timeless sands: Musical images of the Middle East', *19th-Century Music* 22, 1 (1998): 20–53; Ralph P. Locke, *Musical Exoticism: Images and Reflections.* Cambridge: Cambridge University Press, 2009; Susan McClary, *George Bizet: Carmen.* Cambridge: Cambridge University Press, 1992; James Parakilas, 'The soldier and the exotic: Operatic variations on a theme of racial encounter', *Opera Quarterly* 10, 3 (1994): 43–69; Derek B. Scott, 'Orientalism and musical style', *Musical Quarterly* 82, 2 (1998): 309–35; Elizabeth Kertesz and Michael Christofordis, 'Confronting *Carmen* beyond the Pyrenees: Bizet's opera in Madrid, 1887–1888', *Cambridge Opera Journal* 20, 1 (2008): 79–110.

[66] Van der Heide, *Malaysian Cinema, Asian Film*, p. 180.

the film's 'throbbing emotional heart'.[67] Beyond all the violence, death and sacrifice, however, a rejection of blind patriotism is offered in the musical text of the film and Melur's character and musical articulations in the film's narrative resonate with postcolonial conceptions of ethnonationalism and resistance (however futile) to repressive feudal or colonial regimes.

Melur is first seen standing beside the mysterious martial arts master, Adi Putra of Gunung Ledang (Ledang Mountain), as he watches through his magical fire Hang Tuah and his companions scaling the mountain to seek his instruction in advanced *silat* fighting techniques.[68] Melur is then seen again and introduced more prominently as a lead dancer in an exoticised dance of a Jakun or indigenous tribe. It is learned later that Melur was actually a child of Melaka who was kidnapped and raised by the tribe. Hang Tuah stumbles upon this dance in his search for food and is saved from being shot with a poisonous blowpipe by Melur who vouches for him to her tribe members, thereby initiating the ill-fated relationship between Hang Tuah and Melur. While Hang Tuah is an outsider to the musical practices of the tribe, Melur, despite being born of the kingdom, is forever an outsider to Melaka and Hang Tuah's sense of duty to his sultan.

The Jakun song and dance sequence is a sensationalised representation of indigenous people similar to primitivist portrayals in Western films of 'tribal' or exotic communities.[69] McGraw observes the dance in this scene as 'suspiciously Hawaiian', indicating the inclination of Malay film production companies to reproduce representations of 'the generic Pacific/Eastern savage' perpetuated in post-war Hollywood cinema.[70] He also rightly notes that the term 'Jakun'—indicating a specific indigenous group (Orang Asli) in Peninsular Malaysia—is a reductive term used

---

[67] Amir Muhammad, *120 Malay Movies*. Petaling Jaya: Matahari Books, 2010, p. 102.

[68] A useful anthropological study of *silat* martial arts practices in Malay culture is Razha Rashid, 'Martial arts and the Malay superman', in *Emotions of Culture: A Malay Perspective*, ed. Wazir Jahan Karim. Singapore: Oxford University Press, 1990, pp. 64–95.

[69] Van der Heide, *Malaysian Cinema, Asian Film*, p. 179.

[70] Andrew Clay McGraw, 'Music and meaning in the independence-era Malaysian films of P. Ramlee', *Asian Cinema* 20, 1 (2009): 50.

by Malays to denote all the various Orang Asli communities in the country.[71] Slobin considers the notion of an 'assumed vernacular' in American film music practices since the 1930s that assigned generic music for 'tribal' or 'savage' people depicted on screen.[72] Applied to denote any exotic or savage group ranging from Hawaiian islanders to African tribes to Native Americans, such generic 'assumed vernacular' music was characterised by a mixture of monotonous or complex drumming and pentatonicism, in contrast to the use of symphonic arrangements and chromatic melodies for (white) protagonists and familiar or non-threatening locations or cultures.[73] Slobin's notion of the 'Steiner superculture' of film music practices in portrayals of cultural alterity is useful for analysing the Jakun music scene in *Hang Tuah*.[74] Although the Malay film industry was obviously not located in the West and used music composed by Malays, the cosmopolitan and commercial practices of film music in the industry possessed considerable potential to reproduce through similar sonic means Western colonial notions of the national–ethnic–self as mutually constitutive of the nationless–exotic–other. Moreover, in American films, Africans and Native Americans occupy the representational space of 'internal Others that could be generalized and ... "profiled".[75] In the Malay ethnonational film context, Melur and the Jakun tribe are likewise portrayed as *internal others* in relation to the historical Malay nationalist hero archetype embodied in Hang Tuah.[76]

---

[71] Ibid., p. 49.
[72] Slobin, 'The Steiner superculture', p. 6; see also McGraw, 'Music and meaning', p. 50.
[73] Ibid., pp. 7, 11–15.
[74] Max Steiner was one of the first Hollywood film composers who was known for incorporating the European symphony orchestra and (post-classical era) romantic aesthetics for film music. His aesthetic approach to film scoring has been consistently reproduced by his successors in Hollywood and around the world to this day. Slobin, ibid., pp. 6–17, analyses the musical 'ethnography' inherent in Steiner's musical representations of non-Western peoples in the films *Birds of Paradise* (1932, dir. King Vidor) and *King Kong* (1932, dir. Merian Cooper).
[75] Ibid., p. 13.
[76] My understanding of musical othering is drawn from views of the same exoticising musical tropes found in Western music discussed extensively in Georgina Born and David Hesmondhalgh, *Western Music and Its Others: Difference, Representation, and Appropriation and Music*. Berkeley: University of California Press, 2000.

Thus, in line with this musical 'profiling' of Orang Asli, the first half of the dance and music in this scene represents the imaginary Jakun tribe as an internal other by not incorporating any noticeable Malay music styles while providing a visceral and exotic spectacle for the film's audience. Melur is seen as a lead or featured dancer in front of a group of dancing girls. The dance is overtly exotic in its choreography with movements that include coordinated spinning, raising and waving of hands, and seductive swaying of hips. At one point in the more upbeat second half of the dance, the 'chorus girls' stand side-by-side in a line reminiscent of the cancan of nineteenth-century Parisian music halls that was then popularised in American cabaret dance halls in the early 1900s. The music for the dance is characterised by vigorous hand-drumming, melismatic unison singing by a chorus of female and male voices using the syllables 'ah' and 'oh', and punctuated by unmelodic vocal exclamations of 'ha!' by a responding chorus. In the second half of the song, violins and (what sounds like) an electric guitar accompany the chorus melody, sometimes in unison with the chorus and at times in response to the chorus. The music has an overall diatonic tonality with the exception of a few minor-second intervals. The most telling moment of this diatonicism occurs when a repeated ascending major pentatonic scale sung by the female and male chorus in unison ends the song.

While the presentation of exoticised or primitivising musical tropes is pronounced, traces of actual Orang Asli culture are visually present in this dance scene, as if to underpin the 'reality' of what is being shown. Throughout the dance, there is a woman sitting on a ledge playing an instrument that appears to be a *kereb*—a bamboo, plucked, two-stringed heterochordic tube zither usually played by women of the Temiar community in Kelantan (Figure 2.1).[77] Barely visible in the scene, sitting on the ground behind the dancers, is a man hitting a bamboo block with a stick. Prominent in Orang Asli music, long bamboo poles, *ding galung* and *goh*, are used in a stamping fashion, but these are not visible in the scene.[78] What the man in the scene appears to be hitting may be closer

---

[77] Matusky and Tan, *The Music of Malaysia*, p. 299.
[78] Ibid., p. 213.

to *togunggak* or *togunggu* found among the Murut and Kadazan-Dusun communities of Sabah in East Malaysia.[79]

Figure 2.1 Woman playing a *kereb* (third from left)

Thus, on a more prominent level, the music uses Western signifiers of exoticism in its representation of otherness. I further suggest that it is also exoticised from the perspective of a Malay cosmopolitan aesthetic. Urban-based Malay music producers were exoticising an 'internal' but unfamiliar local musical culture. The dances were choreographed by the Indian dancer Devdatta Jetley, who was perhaps more concerned with choreographing exoticism by drawing from familiar Hollywood tropes of assumed vernacular musical representations of non-Western cultures.[80] There is limited understanding or reference to Orang Asli musical practices and, at most, such elements are used in visual

---

[79]   Ibid., p. 216.
[80]   Slobin, 'The Steiner superculture', p. 6.

representations. The instrumentation remains thoroughly modern and globalised—the hand drums are Latin American bongos and congas. The Jakun dance scene presents Melur and the tribe as internalised others. This is quite literally internal, as the Orang Asli communities occupied the hinterlands away from the coastal locations of the Malay kingdoms, and were thus excluded from the ethnonational space of sovereign and 'civilised' Malays such as Hang Tuah. The Jakun dance scene is an internally exoticised representation. The Orang Asli are internal to the Malay national space but on the margins of Malayness. It is very interesting that Western representational means are used to exoticise the Orang Asli in this musical moment.

The musical othering of the Jakun is further complicated by Melur's love connection with Hang Tuah. In many ways, she is portrayed as innocent and genuine in her affection for Hang Tuah and sheltered from the nationalistic sense of duty that deters him from engaging in a committed relationship with her. Thus, what I call the 'Melur motif' is sung by both Melur and Hang Tuah throughout the narrative as a signal for the marginality of their relationship. Even more so, the motif is antipathetic to the blind feudal loyalty embodied in Hang Tuah's actions. However, this reading of resistance in the Melur motif has to be tempered by an understanding of the film as a modern, cosmopolitan and commercial production. The use of a leitmotif is indeed a cosmopolitan construct and can be linked to both Indian and Western film music practices.

The first performance of the motif is sung by Melur and Hang Tuah in the forests of Gunung Ledang in a scene that follows a vigorous *silat* training session in Adi Putra's cave. It is apparent at this point that Hang Tuah and his friends have reached the end of their training. Melur begins by singing the melody with lyrics in what is presumably supposed to be an Orang Asli language. Figure 2.2 provides an approximate transcription of the motif sung by Melur in standard Western notation using a ¾ time signature at 60 beats per minute. This is merely an approximation to indicate the F-sharp Dorian mode (with raised seventh) of the melody that is accompanied by an accordion (or harmonium) drone on the same root note, while indicating the general contour of the melody. The sung melody has many embellishments and bent pitches and is performed in a free tempo. Therefore, this melody is not a conventional Western melody by any means. It is more reminiscent of a vaguely Malay traditional folk style of singing in its use of characteristic embellishments that include trills, turns and bent pitches, commonly found in *asli* and *dondang sayang*. However, the Dorian mode mixed with a raised seventh is uncommon to traditional Malay vocal genres. The modality heard in this motif contrasts greatly with the *syair* mode heard in opening credits. From a Western supercultural perspective, the melody has an exotic and haunting quality—overtly marked as foreign or external to the other Malay musical themes that underscore the film.

In the scene, Melur's call is then answered by Hang Tuah singing the same motif a minor third above. It appears that the melody is a personal call and response game that the two lovers have developed to find each other in the mountain forest. After some flirtatious exchanges, the mood of their conversation takes a dramatic turn when Hang Tuah tells Melur that he must leave Gunung Ledang for Melaka the following day. As she cries in dismay, he tells her in a fatalistic tone: 'But what can I do? My responsibility to my homeland [*tanah air*] beckons'.[81] The recurring use of the Malay term '*tanah air*' denotes a sense of obligatory patriotism to a homeland or nation. The nationalistic discourse of homeland and sacrifice is thus present intertextually across time. The next day, Melur secretly watches Hang Tuah and his friends leave Gunung Ledang. As the men descend the mountain, the shot focuses on Melur sadly watching her lover leave and singing the Melur motif. Here the motif, reproduced verbatim from its first performance (including the accompanying accordion drone), takes on a different meaning—one of sadness, yearning and, in line with the overarching theme of the narrative, sacrifice.

---

[81] '*Tetapi apa boleh buat? Kewajipan tanah air telah memanggil.*' The nationalistic tenor of this statement is also present in *Sergeant Hassan*, analysed below. In that film, the P. Ramlee protagonist also leaves his lover—also played by Saadiah—with a sacrificial sense of duty to his nation.

Figure 2.2 Melur motif

We hear Melur's motif again when she enters the city of Melaka in search of Hang Tuah. This happens while a group of court officials who bear animosity towards Hang Tuah are plotting to defame him. One of the officials mentions a rumour that Hang Tuah is 'crazy' for an indigenous girl in Gunung Ledang, using the derogatory term '*perempuan darat*', or woman of the hinterlands, implying a discriminatory hierarchy of coastal peoples over interior peoples.[82] Thus, Hang Tuah's relationship with a low-status woman would be more than enough to place his credentials in disrepute. Just as she is mentioned, Melur's voice is heard singing the motif. She uses it to call for Hang Tuah just as she did in the mountain. Unfortunately, Hang Tuah is away in Pahang, courting Tijah for the Sultan of Melaka. The plotting officials seize an opportunity by interrogating Melur. In her innocence she reveals to them her intention of seeking Hang Tuah. They then ask her to sing for them but she tells them she only sings for 'her Tuah'.[83] Infuriated, one of the officials slaps her across the face demanding her to sing. Amid fearful sobs Melur sings the motif again, now aware of her subjugated position. This time Hang Tuah's friends hear her singing voice from outside the building

---

[82] '*Dia gilakan perempuan darat di sana.*'
[83] '*Oh tak boleh. Aku nyanyi untuk Tuahku sahaja.*'

where Melur is being interrogated. Despite the officials' attempt to hide her presence, Hang Jebat discovers she is in their custody but is unable to save her. Melur is consequently indentured to serve the court as a courtesan, kept close to Hang Tuah's enemies to be used against him.

Meanwhile, in Pahang, Hang Tuah's romantic deception of Tijah has reached its head. Sparked by his false romance with Tijah, Hang Tuah sings the Melur motif in his room to express his longing for Melur. He sings it antagonistically to his proclamation of nationalistic duty, further revealing the tension between such notions of selfless loyalty and his personal desires. Here the motif more clearly provides a musical critique of feudalism in the narrative and, by extension, could be heard as a questioning of colonial rule in this period. This aspirational sense of autonomy is then heard again in Tijah's appropriation of the Melur motif. She hears Hang Tuah singing the motif from a distance and echoes, in Tuah's key, the last two phrases (bars 5–9 in Figure 2.2). Tijah's performance of the motif, unlike Hang Tuah's, is hopeful—in anticipation of absconding to Melaka and avoiding her dreaded arranged marriage with a Terengganu prince. Thus, the motif is now reflective of an aspiring freedom for Tijah, a hopeful sense of self-determination that she places in her love for Hang Tuah. Intertextually, this hope for an autonomous future also echoes nationalist aspirations leading up to Malayan independence. However, Tijah's articulation of the Melur motif is its last appearance in the film as the hope for freedom is violently quelled in the ensuing sacrificial deaths of the film's key characters.

Resistance in Death

While the hope for Tijah's freedom is crushed, more tragedy ensues for Melur. Upon Hang Tuah's triumphant return from Pahang, he is distraught to learn of Melur being made a courtesan, deeming any personal contact between them illegal and an affront to the sultan's authority—an offence punishable by death. Hang Tuah's enemies devise a way to frame him in front of the sultan and he is charged accordingly. The sympathetic prime minister saves Hang Tuah from execution by secretly hiding him in an undisclosed village. Melur, believing that Hang Tuah has been executed, exacts revenge upon of one of Hang

Tuah's enemies, the Javanese representative from the Majapahit Empire, Karma Vijaya. She performs a semi-seductive dance for him and a group of court officials incorporating a small curved dagger (*kerambit*) into her dance.[84] At the climax of the dance, she slices Karma Vijaya's throat, killing him, but is immediately impaled by a palace guard's spear, uttering Hang Tuah's name in her dying breath.

Melur's dance of death articulates multiple representations of otherness or marginalised identities. Given that it has similar choreography to the Jakun dance described earlier, McGraw suggests that Melur's final dance is adapted from styles performed in Burmese courts. He further argues that music and dances in 1950s Malay film that portray external cultures exhibit a supercultural 'tendency towards musical displacements and erasures and the musical leveling of distinct ethnic groups into stereotyped cues'.[85] McGraw observes in *Hang Tuah* musical 'displacements' such as the substitution of Johor gamelan for Javanese court music and, as I demonstrated earlier, musical 'erasures' in the exoticised indigenous dance.[86] The process of othering is also evident in the deaths of individuals who fall outside the bounds of acceptable Malayness. The outsider Javanese official, Karma Vijaya, is the only court official to die for Hang Tuah's wrongful punishment. Melur, as an exoticised and eroticised internal other, also dies violently.

The sacrifice of Melur contributes to Hang Tuah's disenchantment with his role of servitude to the kingdom. The final scene involves the death of Hang Jebat (Ahmad Mahmud), Hang Tuah's best friend. Hang Jebat dies at the hands of Hang Tuah for revolting against the Sultan of Melaka, a grave and treasonous act. The overarching irony is that Hang Jebat did so in retaliation for Hang Tuah's unjust (and presumed) execution. With no one able to subdue him, the prime minister reveals his deception to the sultan and suggests that Hang Tuah be pardoned and summoned to end Hang Jebat's rebellion. Thus, Hang Tuah proves his loyalty to the sultan, despite his wrongful conviction, and commits the ultimate act of sacrifice by killing his closest and most loyal friend.

---

84   Amir, *120 Malay Movies*, p. 102.
85   McGraw, 'Music and meaning', p. 50.
86   Ibid., pp. 49–50.

Hang Tuah is awarded handsomely for his actions, but at the end of the film he is demonstrably remorseful of his actions. As his mother consoles him in his sadness he says:

> If I release all my tears for but once, it would not be able to wash away the flow of blood from the bodies of Melur and Jebat. They have sacrificed their lives because of my death. In truth, I still live.

As he says this, the villagers surrounding his house chant, 'Long live Hang Tuah!' and 'Long live the admiral!'[87] He then walks to his window and pensively asks, 'Who was right? Was Jebat right or was I right?'[88]

All these statements in which Hang Tuah questions his absolute sense of duty provide an antithesis to the original historical narrative, making it a revisionist account of Hang Tuah, who is commonly depicted as being unfaltering in his loyalty to the sultan.[89] Further, *Hang Tuah* becomes a 'thoughtful modern critique' of feudal values that 'continually throws a challenge to its audience' with its open-ended final quandary. Thus, while characters such as Hang Jebat and Melur who pose a challenge to the status quo are ultimately sacrificed, Hang Tuah in the end embodies the position of an anti-hero, bearing the burden of injustice in his loneliness. The background music in the final scene is sombre, providing ironic counterpoint to the triumphant and patriotic chanting of the village in the background. In line with the moralistic challenge posed in the narrative, the music amplifies for the audience a sense of resistance to blind patriotism and autocracy. If the narrative of *Hang Tuah* can be read as an allegory of resistance, the music embedded throughout it further mobilises the questioning of absolute power during a period of nation-making. It reflects, through a reinvented feudal myth, a process of decolonisation characterised by 'the slow, fractious, blood-soaked decomposition of the British Empire'.[90]

---

[87] *'Hidup Hang Tuah!', 'Hidup Laksamana!'*

[88] *'Siapakah benar? Jebatkah benar atau akukah benar?'*

[89] Van der Heide, *Malaysian Cinema, Asian Film*, p. 183.

[90] Paul Gilroy, 'Great games: Film, history and working-through Britain's colonial legacy', in *Film and the End of Empire*, ed. Lee Grieveson and Colin MacCabe. London: British Film Institute, 2011, p. 14.

Projecting the Future: *Sergeant Hassan* (1958)

In contrast to *Hang Tuah*, *Sergeant Hassan*, starring P. Ramlee and directed by Lamberto V. Avellana from the Philippines, articulates a narrative of nascent independence from a perspective that supports British colonial rule. The film, released on 28 August 1958, a year after Malaya gained independence, is set during the Second World War.[91] It was also a period when war films were emerging as a popular genre and Malay Film Productions sought to capitalise on the commercial success of this global trend.[92] Its fictional story chronicles the exploits of Hassan, a young man who joins the Malay Regiment just prior to the onset of the war, and sees himself in a heroic position to liberate Malaya from the occupation of Japanese forces. The narrative also revolves around the romance of Hassan and his childhood friend Salmah, who patiently waits for him during the occupation. The theme of their patient and enduring love underscores the patriotic and militaristic narrative. The first half of the film features the tribulations of Hassan growing up as an orphan, falling in love with Salmah and eventually becoming a sergeant in the Malay Regiment. The second half is set during the Japanese invasion and occupation and involves Hassan fighting in the jungle until the end of the war as part of a guerrilla resistance force against the Japanese.

This fictional narrative of a Malay war hero parallels and was most likely inspired by the more gruesome and widely known exploits of Lieutenant Adnan Saidi, a real-life war hero who died in his fearless and

---

[91] Ahmad Sarji, *P. Ramlee: Erti Yang Sakti* [P. Ramlee: The Sacred Reality]. 2nd ed., Petaling Jaya: MPH, 2011, p. 353.

[92] Mustafar Abdul Rahim and Aziz Sattar, *Filem-Filem P. Ramlee* [The Films of P. Ramlee]. Senawang: MZA Terbit Enterprise, 2008, p. 175. The popularity of Second World War films, evident around the world in this period, was due (but not limited) to the popular acclaim of David Lean's *A Bridge Over River Kwai* released in 1957. The following year also saw the release of another Malay film set during the war, *Matahari*, by the Filipino director Ramon A. Estella, starring Maria Menado and produced by Malay Film Productions. Some notable British films released in 1958 that are set in the Second World War include *Ice Cold in Alex* (dir. J. Lee Thompson), *Dunkirk* (dir. Leslie Norman), *Sea of Sand* (dir. Guy Green) and *The Silent Enemy* (dir. William Fairchild). Another notable US war film from that year is *The Young Lions* (dir. Edward Dmytryk), starring Marlon Brando, Montgomery Clift and Dean Martin.

stubborn defence of Singapore during the Japanese invasion.[93] Adnan commanded the C Company of the Malay Regiment's 1st Battalion, stubbornly defending Pasir Panjang Ridge and Bukit Chandu (Opium Hill). After two days of intense fighting, Adnan's forces gave way to the Japanese and he was executed. His exploits are dramatised in a Malaysian film, *Leftenan Adnan* (2000), directed by Aziz M. Osman and starring Hairie Othman.

Here I draw attention to the use of the film's theme song 'Tunggu Sekejap' (Wait for a While) as a leitmotif of decolonisation that projects a future aspiration and ambivalence for a Malay nation-in-the-making. Unlike most Malay films of the 1950s and 1960s, there is only one song in this film. The song and its melody, composed by P. Ramlee with lyrics by S. Sudarmaji, are utilised and expanded upon creatively at different junctures in the narrative. An intertextual reading of the film's music, narrative and historical context reveals that articulations of colonialism, postcolonial independence and nationalism are expressed through a cosmopolitan aesthetic of nation-making.

Narrative Utilisation of the Leitmotif

The 'Tunggu Sekejap' leitmotif in *Sergeant Hassan* articulates sentiments of nation-making during the period of decolonisation in Singapore and Malaysia in the mid-1950s (see Figure 2.3). Unlike *Hang Tuah*, the narrative of *Sergeant Hassan* evokes a jingoistic patriotic fervour that is overwhelmingly favourable towards the British colonial administration. The overt use of a single theme song throughout the film—uncommon in Malay films that usually contained at least three varying musical numbers—indicates an unusual Western aesthetic that aptly resonates with its pro-colonial message. The leitmotif of decolonisation thus underpins a conservative vision of Malay nationhood, one that was very favourable towards the capitalist and British-facilitated postcolonial regime and its aversion to radical and leftist politics.

---

93 Nureza Ahmad and Nor-Afidah A. Rahman, 'Lieutenant Adnan Saidi', Singapore Infopedia, Singapore Library Board, 2005. Available at http://eresources.nlb.gov.sg/ infopedia/articles/SIP_456_2005-01-18.html [accessed 18 December 2017].

Figure 2.3 The 'Tunggu Sekejap' motif

A leitmotif is a melody, 'theme, or other coherent musical idea, clearly defined so as to retain its identity if modified on subsequent appearances', which is used 'to represent or symbolise a person, object, place, idea, state of mind, supernatural force or any other ingredient in a dramatic work'.[94] *Sergeant Hassan* utilises a monothematic or theme score, in which 'Tunggu Sekejap' is used as a leitmotif, 'arranged as an integral piece of music that is extractable from the score'; however, the theme or song is also 'varied and repeated in response to the dramatic and emotional needs of the film'.[95] In their classic account of the nature of film music aesthetics, Theodor Adorno and Hanns Eisler were pessimistic about the use of the leitmotif in cinema. They view its use in film as a far cry from the deeper symbolisms and meanings that could be associated with Wagnerian musical dramas, for example, and attributed the leitmotif's use in film as merely an efficient but unimaginative compositional tool for scorers under pressure from high volumes of work in a film industry of capitalist mass production.[96] It is possible that the use of the theme score in *Sergeant Hassan* may be a reflection of the commercial pressures of the

---

[94] Arnold Whittall, 'Leitmotif', *Grove Music Online*, Oxford Music Online, 2012. Available at https://doi.org/10.1093/gmo/9781561592630.article.16360 [accessed 18 December 2017].

[95] Kathryn Kalinak, *Settling the Score: Music and the Classical Hollywood Film*. Madison, WI: University of Wisconsin Press, 1992, pp. 185–86.

[96] Theodor Adorno and Hanns Eisler, *Composing for the Films*. New York: Oxford University Press, 1947, pp. 4–6.

Singapore film industry. Films had to be made quickly and on a limited budget. Kathryn Kalinak, however, believes that the use of classically influenced film scores that included leitmotifs did not degrade the classical tradition, but rather revealed the 'force of that structural foundation and the flexibility of its idiom'.[97] She observes complex uses of the theme score, in which musical themes vary in tempo, style and instrumentation to 'clarify and comment' or even reinterpret or 'undercut' the 'visual content' and narrative of a film.[98] The discussion here considers such possibilities for reading social meaning in leitmotifs in the interactive relationships between music, narrative and history in *Sergeant Hassan*.

The 'Tunggu Sekejap' title theme is introduced in the opening credits.[99] As is typical of most theme scores, the opening credits are underpinned by an orchestral arrangement of the theme song that operates to present 'the musical ideas which unify the score', so that the theme will eventually be varied in relation to the visual narrative.[100] The first image is a close-up of a *songkok*, a traditional Malay headpiece, pinned with a metal badge denoting the formal attire of the Malay Regiment. The opening credits are then superimposed over the *songkok* (Figure 2.4). The music that accompanies the credits opens with an energetic snare drum roll and trumpet fanfare, followed by an upbeat march version of the theme song, effectively evoking a militaristic style and clearly denoting the war film genre. In this instance, the style of the theme song in conjunction with the image of formal military headgear also articulates symbols of Malay national pride and military might. The *songkok* is a definitive marker of Malay ethnicity, an image that signals a forthcoming narrative of triumphant nationhood. This ethnic nationalism is expressed with supercultural Western musical conventions; no trace of vernacular Malay music is heard. However, the juxtaposition of Western music over the image of a *songkok* suggests a colonial, cosmopolitan

---

[97] Kalinak, *Settling the Score*, p. 159.
[98] Ibid., pp. 170–71.
[99] In the film, the Malay Film Productions studio orchestra is given screen credits for 'musical scoring', with P. Ramlee getting a credit for 'original composition [of] theme: "Tunggu Sekejap". No particular credit is given for orchestration.
[100] Kalinak, *Settling the Score*, p. 186.

version of Malayness. After this opening sequence, the *songkok* is picked up and worn by P. Ramlee and a shot of him from the waist up shows him in formal, non-combat Malay military attire. The protagonist introduces himself as Hassan and begins to tell his story. The moment that Hassan speaks there is no musical score, signalling a brief shift to the present-day reality of the film to break with the non-diegetic music of the opening credits and to segue into Hassan's ensuing story.[101]

The 'Tunggu Sekejap' leitmotif is reintroduced as soon as Hassan begins his story, this time in a slower and more melancholic style. As he starts, the camera pans upwards and dissolves to the next scene. Now Hassan is shown as a child at the grave of his recently deceased father. In this scene, the musical theme continues in the slower melancholic arrangement. Prominent in the instrumentation is a string section playing the lead melody with a brass accompaniment. The use of the theme score effectively functions to smooth the transition of the story from the present to the past. Here, the theme has already established its relationship to the protagonist Hassan. The two stark variations of the musical theme suggest that Hassan will emerge victorious, but not without some form of hardship, struggle or conflict. All this is conveyed intertextually, through the interaction of music with images, in less than three minutes.

Another aspect of this leitmotif is its association with place. In the first scene, the score is heard at the same time that Hassan's village and home are introduced. As I noted in the introductory chapter, the concept of the *kampung* (village) as the source of Malayness was an important aspect of the nationalist narrative among Malays in post-war Malaya and Singapore. The musical theme, from the outset, underscores Hassan's rootedness to the land and village. The theme plays during the image of him planting a tree at his father's grave until being introduced to his new adoptive father's home. A sense of self, place and belonging has already been associated with the theme song within a few minutes, albeit with a

---

[101] Diegetic music is music that can be located 'with a source visible on screen' in the film and can be heard by the film's characters, while non-diegetic music is usually not located on screen, 'heard by the audience but inaudible to the film's characters'. See Kathryn Kalinak, *How the West Was Sung: Music in the Westerns of John Ford.* Berkeley: University of California Press, 2007.

Figure 2.4 Film credits superimposed on a Malay Regiment *songkok*

Western classical or supercultural musical approach. The audience does not hear *zapin* music or *rebana* drums to symbolise the Malay village and identity, but lush orchestral arrangements inspired by the European musical tradition.

Clearly articulated in the thematic score to the film's introductory scenes, then, is a utilisation of Western or supercultural film music conventions to support the narrative. Was the use of a Western score intended to give the film more emotional weight? Or was its use merely a 'universal' convention that most non-Western films utilised? Was the choice of a lush orchestral score intended to signify the sophistication of a newly independent and modern Malaysian nation? As I will argue, what is evident is that *Sergeant Hassan* musically articulates a notion of nation-making that is much less subversive than *Hang Tuah*. This more passive and conservative approach to nation-making is expressed in the theme of longing and waiting that encapsulates the film and its monothematic score. The 'Tunggu Sekejap' motif projects an ambivalent future of postcolonial Malay nationhood that parallels the uncertain and contentious historical period of decolonisation in which it was made.

Musical Projections

A prominent theme articulated by *Sergeant Hassan* and 'Tunggu Sekejap' is that of longing and sacrifice. This is the main theme of the song, in which Hassan leaves Salmah to join the Malay Regiment in Port Dickson. Salmah is forced to wait for him, a sacrifice she must bear while her lover defends his nation, which is ironically a British colony. A narrative of nationhood is being formed here, in which intimate sentiments of affection, longing, loyalty and sacrifice feature prominently. The song articulates this theme of nation-making in a less overt manner, serving the dual purpose of love song and patriotic anthem. Intimacy is intertwined with national identity—very much a cosmopolitan notion that may have roots in the Malay culture of loyalty to a sultanate as in *Hang Tuah*. However, unlike *Hang Tuah*'s embedded message of anti-colonial resistance, *Sergeant Hassan*'s narrative and music articulate a passive idealism towards national identity and intimacy, as the main protagonists wait patiently to be united. This sense of waiting and longing for independence, clearly expressed in the film's theme song, parallels the protracted and tumultuous nation-making process in post-war Malaya.

The narrative of nation-making is implicit in the development of the two main protagonists, Salmah and Hassan, who transition visually from childhood to adulthood within the time frame of a single performance of 'Tunggu Sekejap'. The scene where the song is introduced in its entirety shows Salmah as a young girl (Habibah Harun) singing the first verse of the song while hanging laundry outside her house. She sings the first three lines of the verse but melodically replaces the 'adult' lyrics with 'las' (replaced lyrics in parentheses).

Tunggu sekejap wahai kawan (/kasih) — Wait for a while my friend (/love)
Kerana hujan masih renyai — Because the rain is still pouring
Tunggu sekejap dalam pelukan — Wait for a while in an embrace that's
la la la la ... — la la la la ...
(Tunggu sekejap dalam pelukan asmaraku) — (Wait for a while in my passionate embrace)

The lyrics here are modified from the adult version to accommodate Salmah's innocence as a child. When Salmah sings the 'las' in place of the adult lyrics, two young boys are shown looking at her cheekily and throw a stone in the water vase that she leans over. A shot of the stone dropping into the rippling water of the vase is shown while a dramatic orchestral interlude is heard that eventually introduces an adult female voice singing a much more mature melodic interlude of 'las' (see Appendix C.1, bars 11–14). The camera pans upwards from the vase to reveal an adult Salmah played by Saadiah continuing the song.[102]

... Malam ini	... Tonight
Belum puas ku bercumbu dengan kanda	I am not satisfied flirting with you
Sayang ...	My love ...

She continues to sing the second verse of the song:

Tunggu sekejap wahai kasih	Wait for a while my love
Tunggulah sampai hujan teduh	Wait for the rain to subside
Mari ku dendang	Let me serenade you
Jangan mengenang orang jauh	Don't long for those who are far away
Jangan pulang	When you return
Jangan tinggalkan daku seorang	Don't leave me all alone
Tunggu sekejap kasih	Wait for a while my love
Tunggu	Wait

While Salmah sings she is hanging laundry, replacing the scene of her as a child. This time a shot of Aziz (Jins Shamsuddin), Hassan's stepbrother and rival, is shown smiling at her, but she is taken aback and retreats into her house. She closes a window to avert Aziz's stares and turns to another window that frames the now adult Hassan, standing in a masculine pose with his arms crossed and smiling at her charmingly. All this occurs while Salmah sings the second verse of the song.

---

[102] The playback vocal for Saadiah's character was sung by the popular singer Saloma whose real name is, coincidentally, Salmah Ismail. Mustafar and Aziz, *Filem-Filem P. Ramlee*, p. 176.

It is evident at this point that Salmah's childhood friendship with Hassan has transformed into an adult romance. The melodic theme of the song that was initially introduced in the background score has now matured along with the film's protagonists to the foreground of the narrative. Symbolic associations with the theme not only encompass a sense of Hassan's self and place but also Salmah's and, more importantly, the couple's romance. The musical theme in a very overt way has grown up and grown on the audience, its development signalling positive associations with the leitmotif as the film's narrative progresses. Following this juncture, the 'Tunggu Sekejap' leitmotif is repeated in the score with a string arrangement to accompany Salmah and Hassan's flirtatious and humorous exchanges. Salmah longs for Hassan to admit his love for her but he awkwardly avoids telling her directly. This signifies that Hassan is still in a liminal stage in his life, as he has yet to find his calling as a soldier. Regardless, he has already affirmed a sense of where his home and heart reside, and the repeated use of the leitmotif indicates this clearly.

This musical metamorphosis is symbolic of a slow process of a young nation achieving maturity or independence. A conservative and gradualist approach to independence is implied, unlike the radical questioning of authority in *Hang Tuah*. Ideologically embedded in the music is an established sense of self and place and now evoked in the subtext is a sense of love and affection for that place. This articulates a narrative of nation-making, in which conceptions of an autochthonous identity are coupled with a patriotic and unquestioning love for one's country. Thus, through the conventions of supercultural film music, the transformational presentation of the theme song articulates a Western musical aesthetic that subdues the possibility of radical or subversive (that is, communist, Marxist or socialist) notions of nation-making. The local self and sense of belonging are naturalised within the Western musical aesthetic of the 'Tunggu Sekejap' leitmotif.

The final and most complete performance of 'Tunggu Sekejap' occurs towards the middle of the film, marking the end of the pre-war period leading up to the Japanese occupation. The song is performed by Hassan after he completes his basic training at the Malay Regiment camp in Port Dickson. The final performance also signals the complete realisation of Hassan's identity as a man, soldier and dutiful citizen of the (colonial)

Malay nation that he is entrusted to defend. Here the musical expression of Hassan's military identity suggests the realisation of a postcolonial nation—albeit a passive one subjected to British rule—in the process of being conceived.

After receiving the rank of sergeant, Hassan sends a *selendang* (shawl) to Salmah. In the following scene, Salmah is seen in her room with Minah (Annie Jasmin), and is wearing her new *selendang*. An organ is heard playing a monophonic melody. When Minah leaves, a close-up shot from behind Salmah shows her holding a photograph to her chest. She lifts the photograph to reveal to the camera a studio-posed shot of Hassan in army attire. At the same moment, the organ plays the theme song melody. Here the leitmotif is used to recall Hassan's fully realised identity and Salmah's love for him, but the sparseness in instrumentation suggests the melancholic yearning of the two protagonists who are apart from each other. Salmah says longingly: 'Hassan, when will you return to me?'[103]

This is followed by a jump cut to a shot of Hassan in a T-shirt and sarong sitting on a bed and strumming an acoustic guitar as he begins to sing 'Tunggu Sekejap'.[104] He sings the first verse of the song with a sparse rubato guitar accompaniment (Appendix C.2, bars 1–6). He is singing casually in the army barracks in the company of fellow soldiers. The performance transitions from a diegetic to non-diegetic context towards the second verse, when an orchestral accompaniment is heard, overshadowing his sparse guitar playing (Appendix C.2, bar 7 onwards). The accompaniment includes a flute, string section, brass section and piano, arranged in a grandiose style. Together with the musical accompaniment that grows in texture, so does the crowd of soldiers surrounding Hassan to watch him perform. The transition from diegetic to non-diegetic music is particularly significant here in the intensification of the song's emotional content. The song's lyrics and form are also heard in their entirety (Appendix A.3; see Appendix C.2 for musical transcription).

This is the last sung performance of the song in the film, marking the end of the second act that precedes the war scenes that follow. This

---

[103] '*Hassan, bilakah kau akan kembali padaku.*'

[104] Malay men use sarongs as casual wear or nightwear. In this scene, it depicts a leisurely moment in contrast to the military uniforms worn by Hassan in the military training scenes.

performance signifies the full maturation of Hassan's identity as well as his love for Salmah. The character has now completed the first stage of metamorphosis from passive orphan child to fully fledged soldier-lover. In correspondence with Hassan's identity, the song itself has also been fully realised. Perhaps the climactic performance also marks the last days of innocent love as the ensuing narrative involves the beginning of war in Malaya and eventual occupation by the Japanese. The song is only heard in the (background) score from this point onwards.

While the song does not return as a sung performance, there are two more notable uses of the leitmotif in the film. After a third act of substantial fighting scenes, Hassan narrowly escapes a Japanese prisoner of war camp and is washed up against a riverbank. A Malay soldier and Captain Holiday, a member of a British intelligence and resistance outfit, find him. Holiday helps Hassan to his feet and says, 'Don't be afraid. You're among friends. Let me help you.' As Hassan is being helped, the leitmotif is heard as a lush string arrangement reminiscent of the first string leitmotif heard when introducing Hassan's village. Hassan reveals that he is a local to the area and he offers his knowledge of the environs to help Holiday's resistance force.[105] One of the last times the theme is heard is toward the end of the film. Hassan recaptures his village and kills the film's primary villain, Buang (Salleh Kamil), who is a member of the Japanese military police (Kempetai). The leitmotif is heard immediately after he kills Buang and makes an overtly nationalist speech proclaiming: 'Our nation is still young and weak. That does not bother me. My only hope is that we unite as a nation.'[106] The leitmotif is then reiterated when Salmah comes to embrace him.[107]

---

[105] Amir, *120 Malay Movies*, p. 144 notes that Holiday's group is a reference to the British Force 136 which operated in Japanese-occupied Malaya. For more on Force 136, see Tan Chong Tee, *Force 136: Story of a WWII Resistance Fighter*. Singapore: Asiapac, 1994; Ian Trenowden, *Malayan Operations Most Secret: Force 136*. Singapore: Heinemann Asia, 1983; C.G. Taylor, *The Forgotten Ones of 'South East Asia Command' and 'Force 136'*. Ilfracombe: Stockwell, 1989; and Margaret Shennan, *Our Man in Malaya: John Davis, CBE, DSO, Force 136 SOE and Post-War Counter-Insurgency*. Singapore: Monsoon Books, 2014.

[106] Translation in Barnard, 'Decolonization and the nation', p. 65.

[107] '*Memang bangsa kita masih muda dan masih lemah. Aku tak peduli itu semua. Harapanku hanyalah kita sama bangsa bersatu-padulah hendaknya.*'

In these uses of the theme, strong positive associations are made with Hassan's sense of home or homeland. The leitmotif signals his freedom and renewed determination to fight the Japanese. It also marks the end of his patriotic speech, his conclusive union with Salmah and the return to his *kampung*. More importantly, this final iteration of the leitmotif also marks the end of the Japanese occupation and the war, projecting a hopeful future for a Malay–British post-war alliance.

Awaiting Independence

The final performance of 'Tunggu Sekejap' and its culminating melodic development as a leitmotif symbolises the establishment of a firm notion of national identity. The completion of Hassan's identity as a man parallels the national narrative of Malay consciousness, specifically the ethnic consciousness of a Malay 'race-nation', the first step to creating or projecting a tangible nation state. There is also an overarching theme of longing and delay in the film, in which the local population has to wait for the Japanese occupation to end for their British colonial 'partners' to return. While this may be a problematic association, the ideological affinities felt by Malays with the British in the context of the war and decolonisation are particularly relevant. For example, middle- and upper-class Malays (including P. Ramlee) in the 1950s were criticised for their Western affectations including 'big houses, big cars … appreciating Beethoven and Picasso, doing their cocktail rounds, and wearing coats and ties in equatorial heat', in addition to their conservative political stance towards obtaining national autonomy from the British.[108] Malay culture was quite intertwined with Western cultural practices, evidenced further in the vernacular cosmopolitan musical practices that had existed since the turn of the century.[109]

Towards the end of the film, nationalist associations with the leitmotif become clearer. But a sense of national autonomy apparent

---

[108] Harper, *The End of Empire*, p. 226, citing Nordin Selat, *Renungan*. Kuala Lumpur: Utusan, 1978, p. 56.

[109] Tan, 'Negotiating "His Master's Voice"'; Peter Keppy, 'Southeast Asia in the age of jazz: Locating popular culture in the colonial Philippines and Indonesia', *Journal of Southeast Asian Studies* 44, 3 (2013): 444–64.

in the patriotic tenor of the film is unsettled by its rosy portrayal of colonialism. The British forces and colonial administration are never critiqued. In fact, the British soldiers in the film are revered as kind and friendly superiors, so that a narrative of paternalistic colonialism also emerges from the conventions of orchestration. This is symbolically poignant as the music of the film, while evoking a sentiment of autonomous Malay nationalism, is thoroughly Western in style and instrumentation, save for its use of the Malay language and Malay protagonists. The paradox of Malay nationalism in Singapore and Malaya is that agency is expressed in modern Western terms and mediums. Cosmopolitan aesthetic conceptions reflect the paradoxical relationship between local/internal agency and foreign/external modes of aesthetic production. As such, the themes of nation-making and decolonisation apparent in the music of *Sergeant Hassan* evoke the transitory nature of early independence in the Malay Peninsula. As Barnard notes:

> Traditions were to be honoured, but Malays living in an independent Malaya were to be open to a future of debate, complexity and modernity. By the late 1950s, the world of Malay film was promoting a modern outlook, engendering a community open to change. Yet the nation-state remained largely absent from comment on the screen. It was the modern individual, clearly rooted in his or her own ethnic community, which mattered.[110]

The transition between colonialism and independence represented a contestation between modernity and tradition. Central to this transition was the subject of the Malay individual in facing these changes while upholding an ethnic rootedness. However, change was the constant that was inevitable, and individual agency was at the centre of such change.

The use of the 'Tunggu Sekejap' leitmotif in *Sergeant Hassan* as a narrative device is an example of a cosmopolitan aesthetic in which conceptions of a local identity embrace a friendly foreign power, resulting in a passive decolonisation. The film's narrative and use of musical devices

---

[110] Barnard, 'Decolonization and the nation', p. 80.

are relevant to a postcolonial reading in which independence from colonial rule is subject to a British-sanctioned freedom—specifically, an autonomy that is restrained by the boundaries of Western parameters and conditions of nationhood. In *Sergeant Hassan*, independence from Japanese occupation is achieved with the leadership of British commanders. In its music, Hassan and Salmah's patient romance is intimated by a thoroughly Western approach to film scoring in the form of a monothematic leitmotif. The production of the film itself was helmed by a Filipino director, Lamberto V. Avellana, who gave the film a more American-inspired aesthetic and pace, along with a lush orchestral score atypical of most Malay movies from the period.[111] As such, a universalist cosmopolitanism is present in the construction here of Malay national identity. In fact, I would argue that the conception of Malayan and Singaporean nationhood in this film is thoroughly cosmopolitan. Such a conception of statehood is achieved by the film's projection of the universal aspiration to be liberated from the evil and inhumane Axis forces. In this case, the defeat of Japan is the rallying point that ideologically merges subservient local Malay soldiers and villagers with compassionate and determined British forces. A utopian myth of collaboration and goodwill is created to ease past the British censors based in Singapore while inspiring a sense of patriotism among the cinema-going public.[112]

Even more striking in this intertextual reading is the ambivalence of national belonging. For what allegiance are Salmah and Hassan sacrificing their love? Malaya prior to the war was still a colony of the British Empire. Yet in the film there is constant mention of loyalty to the *bangsa* (race) and *negara* (nation) with no reference to the (many) sultanates of the Malay Peninsula—unlike the overt reference to Malay

---

[111] Amir, *120 Malay Movies*, notes how *Sergeant Hassan*'s 'full orchestration for the music makes it seem more expensive' than other Malay films of the time, particularly in comparison to another Malay film set during the Japanese occupation, *Matahari* (Sunshine, 1958, dir. Ramon A. Estella).

[112] Barnard, 'Decolonization and the nation', p. 83 observes that there was a 'continuing presence of former British civil servants in positions of authority in Singapore and Malaysia … and [this] had been an important issue in the negotiations leading up to political independence'.

royalty in *Hang Tuah*. Thus *Sergeant Hassan* expresses the ambivalence of decolonisation and a nation-in-the-making in both musical and narrative ways. 'Tunggu Sekejap' comes to represent the leitmotif and soundtrack to this historical process. In the same way that it expresses the intimacy between Salmah and Hassan, the song articulates the values of love and sacrifice that are part and parcel of patriotism, albeit for an ambiguous nation whose parameters of citizenship or, more specifically, ethnonational belonging had not yet been clearly defined. For an emerging nation to truly gain an emotional and ideological independence, the people of Malaya and Singapore, like Hassan and Salmah, had to wait for a while.

Conclusion

For the increasingly politicised Malay community of the mid-1950s, independence was looming but not firmly at hand—the shadow cast by the British Empire was pervasive in matters of forming a new nation. In considering the nationalist-masculinist narrative of *Hang Tuah*, the women who are sacrificed are objectified reflections of the anxieties and struggles of emerging nationhood. Both Tijah and Melur become victims of the patriarchal order and their embodiment of the anxieties of decolonisation are heard in the film's music. However, beyond their deaths, the songs and musical motifs in *Hang Tuah* greatly amplify a sentiment of resistance that is embedded in the film's narrative. This is unlike the more conventional use of the monothematic leitmotif found in *Sergeant Hassan*, in which the nation is required to submissively wait for a while for its fully realised autonomy. The passivity of *Sergeant Hassan*'s message is an indication of British anxieties towards decolonisation as a result of mounting resistance in the form of a communist insurgency. The film reflects the need for a strong and positive depiction of the British Empire, something that is evident in the distinctly overt musical structure of the film. As Paul Gilroy observes, commercial films produced during the twilight of British colonialism had 'the dual significance as a governmental tool for simultaneously "engineering" the consent of domestic forces while maintaining the colonial order and perhaps re-enchanting it for its primary victims overseas.'[113]

However, just as much as an overarching agenda of re-enchantment was overtly present in British-sanctioned Malay films, narratives of resistance were embedded within the frames of vernacular films and resonated through the musical intimations of the restless colonies. My analysis of music in Malay film in the mid-1950s has attempted to tune in to the intertextually subversive voices of an aspiring anti-colonial national consciousness that permeated the social spaces of film studios and cinema halls. As *Hang Tuah* and *Sergeant Hassan* demonstrate, there were divergent ways of reinventing the past and projecting the future. *Sergeant Hassan* achieved it with a positive portrayal of colonial rule in defending the new nation against its enemy—the communists—while *Hang Tuah* used precolonial Malay feudal excess as the justification for resisting European colonialism.

Music in Malay films, despite their commercial frames of production, expresses ideas of agency in their musical articulations, especially when read intertextually against the films' narratives and historical context. While marginal in the means of cultural production, Malays were able to embed sentiments of self-determination in covert and possibly subconscious ways. This social agency or resistance in film music therefore echoed the Malay activist sentiments and political tensions that were circulating in the 1940s and 1950s. This period saw the mass mobilisation of the Malay community against the British-imposed Malayan Union, a burgeoning Malayan independence that would, in principle, be authored by locals on ethnonational terms, a rise of class consciousness and labour movements of the left and, most fractiously, the communist insurgency that resulted in an outpouring of colonial government propaganda and increased autocratic control. While the Malay films of the mid-1950s reflect the cosmopolitan and commercial frames of production of the studio film industry, an intertextual musical analysis of these films draws out the politics of decolonisation and resistance that could not be articulated on the visual surface of the silver screen.

---

[113] Gilroy, 'Great games', p. 24.

The radical critique of feudal regimes in the Malay world in adaptations of the Hang Tuah narrative was propagated more overtly in modern Malay stage plays and films such as *Hang Jebat* (1960, dir. Hussein Haniff). I do not discuss the music of this film here.[114] Rather, I develop my exploration of postcolonial nationalist critique and ideology in the next chapter by presenting a biography of the film composer Zubir Said, alongside an analysis of his music in Hussein Haniff's historical epic *Dang Anom* (1962). While musical narratives of covert resistance were articulated in Malay films, the late 1950s and early 1960s saw more overtly anti-colonial narratives due to the increasing presence of Malay directors. This dovetailed with the musical nationalist ideologies of composers like Zubir Said who were inspired by the possibilities of an emerging Malay nation beyond colonial rule. While films like *Hang Tuah* employ a commercial approach to the representation of precolonial Malay history, films by Hussein Haniff, set in a similar era, express a more auteurist approach to postcolonial and modernist discourse. Zubir's music corroborated Hussein Haniff's progressive inclinations by emphasising a distinct aesthetic conception of a nationalised Malay tradition in his film scores.

---

[114] For a detailed analysis of the Hang Tuah–Hang Jebat narrative in Malaysian film and literature, see Khoo, *Reclaiming Adat*.

Chapter 3

Nationalising Tradition or Traditionalising Nation?[1]

Aku menabuh hati nan rindu
Saat sangat genting luas terbentang
Debaran hati bertambah kencang
Cemat[2] gelisah semakin bergoncang
Semakin bergoncang
Mudah-mudahan dikau selamat pulang
(I possess a heart in longing
A second so perilous and spread open widely
My heart beats with increasing turbulence
My anxieties increasingly shaken
Increasingly shaken
With hopes that you may return safely)
'Saat demi Saat' (Second after Second), music and lyrics by Zubir Said

In 1953 the release of the first Malay film to include original background music by a local composer marked a watershed in the musical history of the Malay Peninsula.[3] Zubir Said was already a prolific *bangsawan*

---

[1] This chapter is an expanded version of a paper presented at the 8th Asian Graduate Forum on Southeast Asian Studies, Singapore (22–26 July 2013), organised by the Asia Research Institute, National University of Singapore. Portions of the chapter have been published in Adil Johan, 'Scoring tradition, making nation: Zubir Said's traditionalised film music for *Dang Anom*', *Malaysian Music Journal* 6, 1 (2017): 50–72.
[2] 'Cemat' refers to the rope that ties a boat to a dock.
[3] *Buloh Perindu* (1953, dir. B.S. Rajhans) was also the first film produced by the newly established Cathay-Keris Film Productions. See Hamzah Hussin, 'Zubir Said: Man of music', in *Majulah! The Film Music of Zubir Said*. Singapore: National Museum of Singapore, 2012, p. 63.

musician, record producer and film song composer. Until then, films of the Singapore-based Malay film industry used prerecorded European orchestral music to save on production costs.[4] Following his foray into scoring film music, Zubir Said won two Asian Film Festival awards, at the sixth edition in the Best Film Portraying Traditions and Folk Music category for the film *Jula Juli Bintang Tiga* (The Magical Tale of the Three Stars, 1959, dir. B.N. Rao), and then at the ninth edition in the Best Folk Songs and Dances category for the film *Dang Anom* (1962, dir. Hussein Haniff). Aside from film music, Zubir Said is best known as the composer of independent Singapore's national anthem 'Majulah Singapura' (Onwards Singapore), which had previously been made the island's anthem in 1959 when it attained self-government.

Zubir Said was a paragon of the fluid Malay cosmopolitan of the post-war years. Born of Minangkabau descent in Bukit Tinggi, Sumatra, he embarked on a professional music career in Singapore in 1928 and eventually became a citizen in 1967, two years after Singapore's separation from Malaysia and its independence. Before composing for film, he worked as a photographer for the Indonesian embassy and managed the Indonesian Club in Singapore.[5] He was invited in 1957 to write a national anthem for the Federation of Malaya, but all three of his submissions were rejected.[6] Riding on the wave of emerging nationalism leading to independence, Zubir Said was a passionate advocate of Malay nationalism in music by composing numerous patriotic songs and writing nationalist articles.[7]

---

4   Rohana Zubir, *Zubir Said, the Composer of Majulah Singapura*. Singapore: ISEAS Publishing, 2012, pp. 82, 84, citing Zubir bin Said, Oral History Interviews, Reel 13, Accession Number 000293, National Archives of Singapore, 13 September 1984.

5   Rohana, *Zubir Said*, p. 74.

6   Ibid., pp. 106–7; Saidah Rastam, *Rosalie and Other Love Songs*. 2nd ed., Petaling Jaya: Strategic Information and Research Development Centre, 2017, pp. 265–70.

7   Rohana, *Zubir Said*, pp. 102–20; Zubir Said, 'Bahasa Melayu dalam nyanyian' [The Malay language in song], Paper presented at the Third Congress on Malay Language and Literature, Singapore and Johor Bahru, 1956/1957; Zubir Said, 'Menuju tahun 1967' [Towards 1967], *Filem Malaysia*, June 1967; Zubir Said, 'Music in the age of Merdeka', in *Majulah! The Film Music of Zubir Said*. Singapore: National Museum of Singapore, 2012, pp. 94–97; Zubir Said, 'The development of Malay music', in *Majulah! The Film Music of Zubir Said*. Singapore: National Museum of Singapore, 2012, pp. 98–103.

Zubir Said's prolific background in music and his involvement in emerging Malay nationalism frame this chapter on how aesthetic practices and political ideas intersect in the medium of film through the construction and promotion of a traditionalised conception of nation. I observe how tradition and nation were imagined and created in film music of the 1950s and 1960s through a vernacular film industry that indirectly expressed the ideologies and aspirations of post-war cosmopolitan Malay nationalism. A Malay musical aesthetic was established systematically through the musical compositions of Zubir Said in historically themed Malay films such as *Dang Anom* (1962, dir. Hussein Haniff). During this period, an essentialised 'pure' Malay tradition was sought as part of a postcolonial nation-making discourse, but it was expressed in complex and contradictory ways. In the previous chapter, I examined how Malay film music in the mid-1950s articulated the politics of decolonisation. Yet the music of these earlier films did not express an explicitly Malay nation-making aesthetic. The discussion in this chapter is concerned with how the aesthetically cosmopolitan Malay film songs of the early 1960s—particularly the works of Zubir Said—articulated the notion of a national Malay tradition in music. Films such as *Dang Anom* are examples of the historical shift to complete Malay authorial control in the film industry: the film's narrative, aesthetic and musical directions were driven by Malay individuals with an explicit nationalist agenda. *Dang Anom*'s director Hussein Haniff was widely known for his modernist approach to precolonial narratives that indirectly critiqued colonial rule and autocratic leadership. The film's composer Zubir Said was a passionate Malay cultural nationalist, profoundly inspired by the period of nascent independence in the Malay Peninsula. An intertextual reading of *Dang Anom* shows that the creation of a Malay tradition in film music was a paradoxical articulation of the nation-making process that involved the creative agency of individuals operating within the restraints of a commercial film industry and the discursive boundaries of postcolonial modernity.

Nationalising Tradition

A Traditional Aesthetic?

The Malay aesthetic of films combined evocations of customs and practices from the premodern past, previously repressed or challenged, with the ideas of the modern colonial and then postcolonial present.[8] Such cultural referentiality was indicative of the modernist ideologies of emergent nation-making articulated by Malay screenwriters and directors.[9] As Anthony R. Gunaratne observes of Hussein Haniff, the seminal director of *Hang Jebat* (1961) and *Dang Anom* (1962) for Cathay-Keris:

> Haniff's films appear to have been a vehicle for his world-view rather than views of the world he lived in: his epics, set in a feudal past of warring states … appear to have been set in stylized worlds that were allegories of contemporary society and its various ills rather than representative portrayals of them.[10]

In much the same way that Hussein Haniff's worldview was inclusive of a modern, cosmopolitan social critique of his times, Zubir Said's musical compositions for film, despite being intended to represent a traditional Malay sound or mood, were more indicative of the musical conventions

---

[8]   Joel S. Kahn, *Other Malays: Nationalism and Cosmopolitanism in the Modern Malay World*. Singapore: Singapore University Press, 2006 uncovers a consistent narrative in politics, arts and literature that places the *kampung* as the locus of Malay identity. As such, the *kampung* becomes a discursive site for the source of Malay customs and morality, which are either challenged or defended through nationalist ideologies.

[9]   The issue of modern nation-making and traditional referentiality is explored in Sanjay Srivastava's article on the iconic and gendered meanings derived from Lata Mangeshkar's voice in Hindi film music. Mangeshkar's omnipresent voice is regarded as a stable marker and embodiment of Indian national identity on film, while also representing 'the ideal of Indian performative femininity'. Sanjay Srivastava, 'Voice, gender and space in time of five-year plans: The idea of Lata Mangeshkar', *Economic and Political Weekly* 39, 20 (2004): 2019.

[10] Anthony R. Guneratne, 'The urban and the urbane: Modernization, modernism and the rebirth of Singaporean cinema', in *Theorizing the Southeast Asian City as Text: Urban Landscapes, Cultural Documents, and Interpretive Experiences*, ed. Robbie B.H. Goh and Brenda S.A. Goh. Singapore: World Scientific, 2003, p. 163.

and aesthetic preferences of the 1950s and 1960s than the aesthetics of a 'traditional' Malay music.[11] Moreover, his aesthetic concerns were intertwined with his Malay nationalist aspiration to create music that was at once suitably unique in its Malayness while adaptable to the conventions and technologies of modern nationhood such as films and national anthems.

The film music of Zubir Said relied on aesthetic references to Malay culture such as melodies and accompanying percussive rhythms drawn from regional folk song genres.[12] In addition to the use of existing musical styles there was also a marked creative agency in the work of composers like Zubir Said for whom institutional and social limitations determined the boundaries of their assumed aesthetic parameters. Zubir Said's musical innovations were born out of budgetary constraints imposed by the film production studios in Singapore. He could only employ about eight musicians per film, but the resulting sparseness in orchestration (in comparison to Western and Indian film scores) inadvertently contributed to the uniqueness of his sound. An aesthetic subjectivity and creative agency are ever-present in his music, bound to the structural limitations of a profit-orientated film industry in the immediate postcolonial era.

In relation to the musical aesthetics of nation-making and the process of traditionalising nation through Malay film music, the discussion considers two specific ideological and structural aspects: the use of the Malay language and literary forms; and the inequities of postcolonial power relationships in the conception of an ethnicised, national self. Beyond these limitations, I propose that Zubir Said and the cultural product (the film and its music) simultaneously challenged these structural limitations through articulations of self-actualising political

---

[11] It is fitting to mention Richard Taruskin's study of musical authenticity that disputes claims of authenticity in baroque performance practices of the nineteenth century. He argues that performances of the premodern era in fact applied modernist aesthetics, thereby falsely claiming 'authenticity' of the performed material. The same can be applied to modern artistic interpretations of 'traditional' practices in the postcolonial era of national narrative constructions in film and music. See Richard Taruskin, *Text and Act: Essays on Music and Performance*. New York: Oxford University Press, 1995.

[12] A useful reference for Malay folk song genres with musical transcriptions, stylistic and instrumental descriptions is Patricia Matusky and Tan Sooi Beng, *The Music of Malaysia: The Classical, Folk and Syncretic Traditions*. Aldershot: Ashgate, 2004.

awareness and artistic agency. While confined to the use of the Malay language, vernacular musical styles and the budgetary constraints, Zubir Said seized the opportunity to realise a musical soundscape of Malay aesthetic autonomy that was set apart from other hegemonic cultural film music canons (for example, American, Chinese and Indian). This resulted in unique and original compositions that were far from conventional or traditional. His compositions were in fact very modern and conveyed a more cosmopolitan than a supposedly purely Malay aesthetic.

Linguistic Agency

While musical creation was part of a process of nation-making, the creative productions of Malay individuals in the film and literary community were dominated ideologically by ethnolinguistic nationalism. As Eric Hobsbawm notes,

> *any* body of people considering themselves a 'nation' claimed the right to self-determination which ... meant the right to a separate sovereign independent state for their territory.... and in consequence of this multiplication of potential 'unhistorical' nations, ethnicity and language became the central, increasingly the decisive or even the only criteria of potential nationhood.[13]

The independent Malay nation was constituted of diverse Malay and non-Malay linguistic and ethnic communities, but was bound by the ethnolinguistic unifier of the Malay language.[14] In the cosmopolitan

---

[13] Eric J. Hobsbawm, *Nations and Nationalism Since 1780: Programme, Myth, Reality.* 2nd ed., Cambridge: Cambridge University Press, 1992, p. 102.

[14] Timothy P. Barnard, ed. *Contesting Malayness: Malay Identity across Boundaries.* Singapore: Singapore University Press, 2004; Kahn, *Other Malays*; Anthony Milner, *The Malays.* Chichester: Wiley-Blackwell, 2008. For demographic data on ethnicity and linguistic groups in the late colonial Malay Peninsula, see Benedict Anderson, *Imagined Communities: Reflections on the Origins and Spread of Nationalism.* Rev. ed., London: Verso, 2006; and for specific data on ethnic demographics in Malaya/ Malaysia from 1911 to 2005, see Khoo Boo Teik, 'Ethnic structure, inequality and governance in the public sector: Malaysian experiences', Democracy, Governance and Human Rights Programme Paper Number 20, 2005, pp. 1–45.

environment of Singapore, where the seeds of such nationalism were planted and coming into fruition, the industries and technologies of print media, film and music played a vital role in defining this ethnolinguistic conception of a 'Malay' nation.

The influence of the Malay literary group Angkatan Sasterawan '50 (ASAS '50, Literary Generation of 1950) in creating this unified sense of being was pervasive. Very much a product of the creative cosmopolitan and politically charged environment of Singapore, the members of ASAS '50 championed the use of the Malay language to promote Malay nationalism. Nationalism was promoted overtly and covertly in Malay films and print media. A convergence of the two forms of media occurred in film magazines such as *Bintang*, edited by P. Ramlee, that was known for nationalist content that encouraged 'readers to question their colonial mentality' while 'promoting a vision of an independent Malaya'.[15] Film magazines articulated this vision of Malay independence explicitly through the promotion of the national language. The first issue of *Majallah Filem* contained an editorial by P. Ramlee that echoes this linguistic nationalist sentiment:

> '*MAJALLAH FILEM*' will expand widely in [our] society as a 'benchmark to guide its readers in their foray into the world of films; also as an important instrument to raise the standard of the National Language.
>
> As this magazine is published in the National Language and its [official] spelling, it is not wrong for me to say '*MAJALLAH FILEM*' is a courageous magazine. Courageous to strive in the midst of an arena that is in the process of being built.
>
> The courageousness of '*MAJALLAH FILEM*' that is needed in initiating this process will endure and be ever fertile until its goal—[to be the] Magazine of Our National Language—is achieved.[16]

---

15 Timothy P. Barnard, '*Gelanggang Film*', *Cinemas of Asia* 1 (2012). The magazine *Bintang*, established in 1953, operated as a fan magazine for the ever-prominent P. Ramlee. This magazine was replaced by *Bulanan Gelanggang Film* in 1958, also under the editorship of P. Ramlee and even more popular than its predecessor.

16 P. Ramlee, 'Kata sambutan dari P. Ramlee' [The speeches of P. Ramlee], *Majallah Filem*, April 1960, p. 4.

The pride displayed in promoting the use of the national language in a monthly publication for a popular market signals a shift towards an explicit sentiment of rising nation-making. This period also saw an increased interest in modernising the Malay language—the reference to national spelling denotes the replacement of Jawi, the Arabic script that was used in most film magazines prior to the 1960s, with Rumi or romanised Malay. It was in this modern nationalist literary milieu, then, that a unified Malay 'tradition' was being created through the imagination and authorial agency of individuals who suddenly found themselves in positions of national influence.

Zubir Said himself was no stranger to the vibrant political exchanges of the Malay community in Singapore. During the post-war period, he had weekly informal group meetings with his peers of Minangkabau descent who included important figures such as Singapore's first president Yusof Ishak, the prominent journalist Abdul Rahim Kajai, and the author Zainal Abidin Ahmad @ Za'aba.[17] It is highly likely that Malay nationalist concepts about language and culture were exchanged in these meetings, with ideas from Zubir Said's more politicised peers having a direct impact on him and his subsequent work.

While drawing on this activist literary environment, Zubir Said contributed to the nation-making project of Singapore and Malaya through a selection of patriotic songs written for a concert in celebration of the Federation of Malaya's independence, most notably of course 'Majulah Singapura'. However, his own identity was complicated with fluid attachments to multiple spaces and identities: he had been a citizen of the Dutch East Indies who migrated to Singapore to earn a living. While he subscribed to a general patriotic attachment to 'Malay' (linguistic and cosmopolitan) nationalism, Zubir Said wrote the national anthem of a country that stood apart from its neighbours as a non-Malay state surrounded by the Malay world.[18] Despite this apparent contradiction, it is undeniable that he was influential in the process of Malay nation-making through music.

---

[17] Zubir bin Said, Oral History Interviews, Reel 12, Accession Number 000293, National Archives of Singapore, 7 September 1984.

[18] Lily Zubaidah Rahim, *Singapore in the Malay World: Building and Breaching Regional Bridges*. London: Routledge, 2009.

Parallel with Zubir Said's musical articulations of self-determination, however, there was a disjuncture between the new radical ideas of Malay film-makers and the rigid colonial structures of knowledge and power that remained largely in place. The Malay film studio industry in the 1950s had a social structure that loosely reflected the British colonial ideology of organising racial groups into specific occupational roles: Chinese entrepreneurs owned the studios and occupied technical positions (camera operators, sound recordists, studio managers); Indians were the creatives who directed, wrote scripts and occupied technical roles as well; and Malays were the performers—the stars, musicians and composers.[19] By the early 1960s Malays began taking on more authoritative roles in the studios as directors and writers, replacing imported directors from India.[20] This period of transition from non-Malay to Malay authorship is my focus in the reading of *Dang Anom* here. Specifically, I am interested in the articulation of postcolonial nationalist ideas that were expressed subversively in Zubir Said's film music.

Postcolonial Considerations

Zubir Said's film music was composed with the intention of articulating a 'natural' cultural style that embodied a Malay musical aesthetic. But

---

[19]   The British authorities categorised the economic activities of colonised people by 'race': Chinese were small business owners and traders; Indians were estate workers and labourers (although some South Asian castes occupied professional positions and operated businesses); Malays were mostly farmers and fishermen. See Syed Hussein Alatas, *The Myth of the Lazy Native: A Study of the Image of the Malays, Filipinos and Javanese from the 16th to the 20th Century and Its Function in the Ideology of Colonial Capitalism*. London: Frank Cass, 1977; and Lim Teck Ghee, 'British colonial administration and the "ethnic division of labour" in Malaya', *Kajian Malaysia* 2, 2 (1984): 28–66. Malays formed a sizable proportion of the entertainment class both before and after the Second World War.

[20]   While these directors were actually imported from India and were Indian nationals, it is worthwhile noting that South Asian communities existed in the Malay world centuries prior to European colonialism. The Indian director of Malay films, L. Krishnan, would stay on and eventually become a Malaysian citizen and successful producer of Malay films after the demise of Singaporean Malay studio film industry. See Prem K. Pasha, *The Krishnan Odyssey: A Pictorial Biography of Dato' L. Krishnan*. Kuala Lumpur: NASARRE, 2003.

he did this in a postcolonial environment that, to an extent, insisted on conceptual goals of fixing a 'pure' musical tradition. While drawing from local folk music practices, though, he also had to adapt his music to the formal methods and structures of Western orchestration for film.[21] His authorial agency could largely be imposed on what could or would not be included to represent a Malay 'mood' or sound in his selection of instrumentation, melodies and textures.[22]

In order to unravel the complexities of the postcolonial structures of knowledge that governed Zubir Said's creativity I apply intertextual musical analysis to consider the relationship of authorial agency to larger structures of power. The application of postcolonial analysis in studying music requires

> meticulous attention to textual detail, but always sees such analysis as subsidiary to the larger project of thinking through the implications of cultural expression for understanding asymmetrical power relations and concomitant processes of marginalization and denigration.[23]

This sets the tone for my use of intertextual analysis to unravel the power relationships present in processes of authoring a national identity through film music. This provides a catalyst for the following question: to what extent are internal process of marginalisation and denigration present in Zubir Said's music? Instances of exclusion are more appropriately observed in the traditionalising of Malay identity in Zubir Said's compositions. His film composition and arrangement methods involved a working process that ultimately left out certain local musical practices and traditional instruments in favour of modern instrumentation as this was what he deemed aesthetically acceptable for the medium of film.

---

[21] See Mark Slobin, 'The Steiner superculture', in *Global Soundtracks: Worlds of Film Music*, ed. Mark Slobin. Middletown, CT: Wesleyan University Press, 2008, pp. 3–35.

[22] Rohana, *Zubir Said*, p. 82.

[23] Georgina Born and David Hesmondhalgh, *Western Music and Its Others: Difference, Representation, and Appropriation and Music*. Berkeley: University of California Press, 2000, p. 5.

It could be argued that Zubir Said was also exoticising, to an extent, the musical cultures of the Malay Peninsula and subsuming them under his aesthetic boundaries of what would be considered 'traditional' Malay music. This is perhaps not as explicitly problematic as the music of the non-West portrayed in films made in the West—'assumed vernacular' film music.[24] The apparent auto-exoticism that can be heard in Zubir Said's film music could, instead, be considered a *constitutive vernacular*, as the postcolonial power relations that are present in Western films musically representing the non-West were not an issue in Malay films. Rather, Zubir Said's film music articulates the desire of Malay nationalists in the mid-1950s to early 1960s to actively create a modern national culture that was independent of colonial rule, but, ironically, not free of Western criteria of nationhood. Thus, while he was retrospectively reproducing a (Western) superculture of film music, this system of musical production was 'neither monolithic nor omnipotent' and consistently gave way to 'systematic cracks' that allowed 'for variation and even subversion'. This was especially true in the hands of aspiring composers such as Zubir Said and P. Ramlee, who saw themselves as important agents of postcolonial nationalism.[25]

This discussion is therefore not limited to postcolonial observations and analysis, as such an approach can easily ignore 'questions of agency'.[26] Zubir Said and his compositions for film—despite the colonial and modernist limits within which they were created—had an agential role in creating the sound palette of Malay national identity. His personal motivations appear in his own writings on Malay music, which are enthusiastic about the future prospects of Malay national autonomy. The following is an excerpt from an article he wrote in 1958, shortly after Malayan independence:

During the age of *merdeka* music should as far as possible exert a positive influence on society. The music must be original, not imitations. Music should be the pride of the nation and convey the beliefs and values of the nation.

---

[24] Slobin, 'The Steiner superculture', pp. 25–29.

[25] Mark Slobin, 'The superculture beyond Steiner', in *Global Soundtracks: Worlds of Film Music*, ed. Mark Slobin. Middletown, CT: Wesleyan University Press, 2008, p. 60.

[26] Born and Hesmondhalgh, *Western Music and Its Others*, p. 7.

> During the age of *merdeka* music should arise from a creativity that is free to explore new forms and ideas, but at the same time rational, while staying true to what is indigenous to the nation, even for modern compositions.
>
> During the age of *merdeka* there should be an understanding that a nation's creativity should not be an exercise in imitation, rather it should be an effort to discover new forms of national music, grounded on the artistic expressions of the nation.[27]

Zubir Said's manifesto on the importance of music in the construction of Malay nationalism reveals how he intended to create original music in his films that were also 'rational' in their references to a traditional Malay sound. More than that, he believed his compositions were 'staying true to what ... [was] indigenous to the nation, even for modern compositions'. Further, the manifesto indicates the unquestionable importance that Zubir Said accorded his musical compositions in shaping the culture and character of the newly independent Malay nation.

His statement indicates that he considered his compositions 'modern' musical works that were integral to the making of an independent nation. He emphasises the promotion of a national aesthetic that should be 'original', that is not imitative, while containing references to indigenous forms and styles. Indeed, Zubir Said's film music evokes all of these seemingly 'national' qualities through his stylistic adherence to (the already inherently cosmopolitan) Malay folk music genres such as *joget* and *dondang sayang* while using iconic Malay instrumentation such as the *rebana* frame drum. The modern aspect of his music includes subtle textural additions from non-indigenous musical sources such as Western tonal harmony and orchestration and non-Malay instruments such as vibraphones and saxophones. This musical Malay–Western hybridity is

---

[27] Zubir, 'Music in the age of Merdeka', p. 95. It is worth noting the striking similarities between Zubir Said's views and those of the English composer and staunch music nationalist, Ralph Vaughan Williams, expressed at length in *National Music and Other Essays*. 2nd ed., Oxford: Oxford University Press, 1987. Vaughan Williams's essay 'National music' was published in 1934, so it is possible that Zubir was inspired by his ideas, although this cannot be confirmed in any existing sources.

thus a product of Zubir Said's position as a 'rooted cosmopolitan' and, as such, reveals the interplay between inclusion and exclusion in seeking an imagined cultural 'purity' or 'naturalness'—an aspiration concomitant with postcolonial ideologies of modern nation-making. Evident in Zubir Said's film music, these contradictions highlight the contested narrative of postcolonial nation-making in the Malay Peninsula.

Traditionalising Nation

Nation-making Narratives in Film Music

As we have seen, music-making operated as a practice of nation-making in the postcolonial era of Singapore's emerging Malay-language film industry. Music in Malay films was a means of making history through implying definitions of a 'tradition' demarcated by ethnonational boundaries. Concomitantly, Zubir Said's music articulated emergent nationhood through the genre of historically themed films.[28] This expressive space required him to imagine and create a sonically Malay aesthetic by drawing from his experience in local popular performing arts such as *bangsawan* musical theatre.[29] Music in Malay film thus provides an insightful example of how national narratives are shaped through the authorial and creative agency of individuals in spite of the limits imposed by postcolonial conditions, assumptions and ideologies.

Zubir Said's film music can be analysed, in the terms provided by Christopher A. Waterman, 'as a means of making history: not only as a form of social action directed at realising a future, but also as a

---

[28] 'Historical' Malay films were also termed '*bangsawan*' films in reference to the repertoire of narrative themes derived from *bangsawan* plays set in the feudal precolonial past. These stories derived from classic Malay texts such as *Sejarah Melayu* (*The Malay Annals*), *Hikayat Hang Tuah* (*The Romance of Hang Tuah*), *Hikayat Merong Mahawangsa* (*The Romance of Merong Mahawangsa*) and so on. Interestingly, Malay film magazines such as *Majallah Filem* (1960–1965) refer to such historically themed films as *bangsawan* films in contrast to *masharakat* (social) films set in modern, urban contexts.

[29] Rohana, *Zubir Said*, p. 44; Hamzah 'Zubir Said: Man of music', pp. 67–69.

medium for the retrospective definition of tradition'.[30] His film music is a historical text that uncovers the vibrant nationalist sentiment of the Malay Peninsula in the 1950s and 1960s. The musical biography of Zubir Said and his creative process in composing for films reveals how Malay nationalists of the era conceived postcolonial sovereignty by evoking forms of cultural expression out of a precolonial past. This cultural construction of nationhood, articulated in Benedict Anderson's well-known formulation, is 'an imagined political community—and imagined as both inherently limited and sovereign'.[31] The conception of nation is defined by delimiting boundaries such as geography, cultural communities or linguistic affinities while sovereignty relates to the nation imagined as being autonomous from 'divinely ordained' or 'hierarchical' dynastic spaces.[32] What appeals greatly to music scholars is Anderson's example of how cultural groups are recognised 'not by their falsity/genuineness, but by the style in which they are imagined'.[33] Studies of 'expressive culture' and nationalism thus provide an integral point of departure for observing how nation-making is articulated as creative processes in cultural practices.[34] Music as an expressive practice can be heard as a form of discourse on nation that seeks organic boundaries amid natural conditions of plurality. Music thus operates, in the words of Wimal Dissanayake, as an expression of 'national discourse' understood in its

> relation to boundedness, continuities and discontinuities, unity in plurality, the authority of the past, and the imperatives of the present. It moves along two interesting axes: space and time. In terms of the space axis, the dominant question is territorial sovereignty; in terms of the time axis, the central question is the velocity of history, the continuity with the past. The way these two axes interact produces results that bear

---

[30] Christopher A. Waterman, "'Our tradition is a very modern tradition": Popular music and the construction of a pan-Yoruba identity', *Ethnomusicology* 34, 3 (1990): 369.
[31] Anderson, *Imagined Communities*, p. 6.
[32] Ibid., p. 7.
[33] Ibid., p. 6; see also Waterman, "'Our tradition is a very modern tradition"', p. 376.
[34] Waterman, "'Our tradition is a very modern tradition"', pp. 377–78.

directly and challengingly on the problematic of nationhood. What is important to bear in mind is that the manifold issues related to these axes are man-made and not natural givens. *They are human constructs seeking the status of the natural.* The privileged narrative of nationhood tends to submerge the local narratives of resistance that attempt to bring into play the historically determined discourses of memory and the challenges to the hegemony of the nationhood.[35]

It is in this way that the musical aesthetics found in the film music of Zubir Said refer to a discourse about emergent nationhood by actively creating an imaginary 'traditional' style that nonetheless assumes a 'natural' status of Malayness. The notion that this 'narrative of nationhood' was created or imagined musically is evident in Rohana Zubir's observations about her father when composing music for Malay films:

> Having composed contemporary, modern music and now legendary music … [Zubir Said] … found composing the legendary [historical epic or mythical themed film] music more challenging. For modern music he could listen to other recordings, but not so for legendary music, where he had to depend much on his own imagination.[36]

For Zubir Said, composing music for films on premodern themes was most challenging because, unlike films set in the modern era, he had no examples of Malay music to reference. Thus, in his own words, he had 'to imagine it' or conjure a suitably Malay musical aesthetic based on his own creativity.[37] In effect, he invented Malay musical 'tradition' in his film music. This creation of tradition was far from arbitrary as he had his own personal *preferences*—as opposed to references—as to what constituted Malay music. Moreover, in the absence of a specific Malay film music tradition, there were nonetheless Western art music

---

[35] Wimal Dissanayake, 'Nationhood, history, and cinema: reflections on the Asian scene', in *Colonialism and Nationalism in Asian Cinema*, ed. Wimal Dissanayake. Bloomington: Indiana University Press, 1994, p. xi (my emphasis).

[36] Rohana, *Zubir Said*, p. 83.

[37] Zubir bin Said, Oral History Interviews, Reel 13.

conventions that Zubir Said drew upon for his original film scores. He was not making traditional or folk music. Rather, he was re-presenting the Malay tradition musically.

To complicate matters further, Zubir Said was originally trained in the practices of *bangsawan* theatre.[38] This music-theatre form was already immensely diverse in cultural influences and was a hugely popular form of entertainment in the Malay Peninsula for a predominantly Malay-speaking audience.[39] As well as coming from a *bangsawan* background, Zubir Said also wrote music for films adapted from famous *bangsawan* plays including *Jula Juli Bintang Tiga, Yatim Mustapha* (Orphan Mustapha) and *Gul Bakawali*.[40] However, a major difference between performing music for *bangsawan* and scoring music for Malay film was Zubir Said's authorial agency as a composer in creating a 'traditional' Malay musical aesthetic. As we have already seen, the historical Malay film was a potent means for the promotion of a Malay nation through narratives of a precolonial past that offered visual and aural representations of Malayness. Malay audiences could actualise their cultural selves on the silver screen as part of a cohesive national imaginary framed by the Malay language, and articulated through culturally resonant tropes and narratives such as mythical stories, prose and *pantun*. These elements were used in the films' dialogue and songs, but they were also underpinned in the film score by sonic markers of Malayness in the form of Malay-sounding melodies, rhythms and instrumentation. Taking into account Zubir Said's vibrant cosmopolitan experience of music-making in Singapore in his *bangsawan* days, as well as his clearly defined yet complicated Malay nationalist stance on the

---

[38] Rohana, *Zubir Said*, pp. 43–53. Rohana Zubir relates her father's musical career in prewar Singapore that started in 1928 (p. 43). He started his professional musical career at the *bangsawan* Happy Valley opera company playing the violin, where he also learned to read Western staff notation (prior to this he was only adept with Sumatran numerical notation), Western music theory, taught himself how to play the piano, and would eventually go on to arrange music for and lead the company's orchestra (pp. 44–49). Following this, until the war, he became a talent scout and record producer of Malay-language music for HMV, based primarily in Jakarta (pp. 49–53).

[39] Tan Sooi Beng, *Bangsawan: A Social and Stylistic History of Popular Malay Opera*. Singapore: Oxford University Press, 1993.

[40] Rohana, *Zubir Said*, p. 44; Hamzah 'Zubir Said: Man of music', p. 69.

arts, the discussion below unpacks how his experiences and ideologies are present in the traditionalised Malay music aesthetic of his film compositions.

Before engaging an analysis of music and narrative in *Dang Anom*, two concepts are crucial to framing my intertextual analysis: first, the process of 'traditionalising' music in Malay film; and second, the observance of melodramatic cinematic form. The concept of nationhood in Zubir Said's film music was actualised through traditionalising processes that were in fact a hallmark of modern consciousness or, more than that, reflected a global aesthetic and commercial trends in film music in the 1950s and 1960s. *Dang Anom* demands to be read as a melodrama—a common cinematic genre in Hollywood films of the same period.[41] Interpreting films as melodrama provides a critical approach for discerning social and gendered power relations in film narratives beyond the surface of cinematic (and musical) style or aesthetics. *Dang Anom* is in fact a modern take on a historical narrative and reading this narrative alongside and against Zubir Said's aesthetic expressions of a Malay musical tradition in the film reveals disjunctive and conjunctive relationships to the film's ideological undertones. It is therefore important to consider the melodramatic articulations of *Dang Anom*'s narrative in order to understand the musical tradition or traditionalising representations that occur in the film's music.

Music Traditionalised

In what way, then, is Zubir Said's film music 'traditional' to the Malay Peninsula? A comprehensive analysis of his film music by Joe Peters appears in the booklet of a 10-day film festival titled 'Majulah! The Film Music of Zubir Said', hosted by the National Museum of Singapore Cinémathèque.[42] These screenings were held to commemorate his

---

41 Christine Gledhill, 'The melodramatic field: An investigation', in *Home Is Where the Heart Is: Studies in Melodrama and the Woman's Film*, ed. Christine Gledhill. London: BFI Publishing, 1987, pp. 5–6.

42 Joe Peters, 'Zubir Said and his music for film', in *Majulah! The Film Music of Zubir Said*. Singapore: National Museum of Singapore, 2012, pp. 74–90. In an interview with

contributions to music in Singapore, most notably the national anthem. Peters's essay attempts to systematically analyse Zubir Said's music from a collection of 48 films, in which he notes a 'neo-traditional' style of composition that reflected an attempt to stitch together the disjunctures between the commercial film industry and creative expression. Peters observes the synthesis between popular Western styles and traditional folk music through processes of 'on-loading' and 'in-loading'.[43] The on-loading process involves the addition of local elements 'on top' of foreign (read: Western) structures, or conversely adding foreign elements to local forms.[44] For example, additional Malay lyrics and singing on top of a Latin American rhythmic and harmonic accompaniment are commonly found in Malay film music. In-loading involves a more self-contained representation of an external musical style and form with little or no addition or integration from foreign elements. Peters argues that Zubir Said's increased use of in-loading resulted in the production of 'original forms' that 'are now invaluable historical documents of local culture and customs'.[45] Peters's approach here is quite slippery, as it is difficult to discern what practices or forms were internal or external. If Zubir Said wrote a Malay-sounding melody to be performed by a Western orchestral arrangement, could that not also be considered on-loading?

This mechanistic and ambiguous view of musical creation is quite problematic as it does not account for the longer history of interaction between diverse musical genres and styles in the Malay region. Peters assumes a 'pure' or absolute aesthetic of Malay musical practices without problematising their diverse and pluralistic origins. As I noted in Chapter Two, many musical practices in the region were already hybrid and cosmopolitan prior to European colonialism. This was certainly true of many of the popular folk music styles familiar to Zubir Said, with his early career in *bangsawan* music ensembles. Unfortunately, Peters does not describe in detail specific musical examples that differentiate on-loading and in-

---

Peters, he informed me that the essay published in the booklet is considerably shorter than his original contribution, which included more ethnomusicological analysis.

[43]   Ibid., pp. 76–77.

[44]   Ibid., p. 77.

[45]   Ibid.

loading approaches in Zubir Said's film music. What is more convincing in Peters's analysis is evidence of the individuality of his style of film scoring, discerned from his use of repeated and recognisable melodic motifs.

Peters presents the idea of a 'freedom motif' evident in Zubir Said's traditional-sounding compositions, one that contains 'ascending and almost bugle-like movement of notes on the harmonic series and also a falling melisma that is usually heard in *dondang* [*sayang*] and *asli*'.[46] Aside from observing multiple instances of this musical motif in films such as *Dang Anom, Bawang Puteh Bawang Merah* (Garlic and Onions, 1959, dir. S. Roomai Noor) and *Sri Mersing* (1961, dir. Salleh Ghani), he points out that the freedom motif was part of an eight-bar section that was removed from the original draft of the City Council anthem that became the national anthem of Singapore.[47] In short, Peters's systematic analysis is insightful in its observation of a traditionalised nationalist narrative in the musical themes that are reproduced across films. A national-traditional aesthetic is clearly evident in Zubir Said's Malay film compositions.

While Peters notes in passing issues such as cultural synthesis and capitalist production, there is greater need to consider the postcolonial process of conceiving a 'tradition' and 'nation' through musical signifying in film. His empirical analysis is limited to the musical motifs of Zubir Said's film scores and unfortunately overlooks the interactive relationship between his music and specific film narratives. The unequal power relations between agents of independence and colonial structures of knowledge are intertextually articulated in Zubir Said's film music, and this requires a detailed and qualitative analysis of film music operating within a specific film narrative.

Melodramatic Modernities

Dang Anom is, on the surface, a historical Malay epic. It is in fact a modern

---

46   Ibid., p. 87. For a detailed description of the *dondang sayang* genre, see Matusky and Tan, *The Music of Malaysia*, pp. 333–42. The falling melismas noted by Peters can be seen in Matusky and Tan's transcript of a *dondang sayang* melody (pp. 335–37). *Asli* suggests both a rhythmic pattern and a repertoire of Malay folk songs.

47   Peters, 'Zubir Said and his music for film', p. 88.

melodrama, in which its female lead (the eponymous protagonist) is the primary subject of a narrative that questions feudal or precolonial Malay values. Christine Gledhill observes that melodramatic films in the 1960s, despite their pejorative and commercial associations, offered critical cinematic possibilities for 'apparently ideologically complicit films to be read "against the grain" for their covert critique of the represented status quo'.[48] Elsewhere, she posits how melodramatic forms are concerned with

> what cannot be said in the available codes of social discourse; … [operating] in the field of the known and familiar, but also … [attempting] to short-circuit language to allow the 'beneath' or 'behind'—the unthinkable and repressed—to achieve material presence. This dual recognition—how things are and how they are not—gives popular culture much of its strength, suggesting the way it may be drawn to occupy gaps in political, ideological, and cultural systems, and how the subordinated may find a negotiable space in which certain contradictions and repressed desires are rehearsed.[49]

Here I discuss how the narrative structure and music of *Dang Anom*, while seemingly traditional in style and context, actually criticise and reimagine tradition in subversive and modern ways. Beyond the internal critique of feudalism in the film's narrative there is also an underlying anti-colonial sentiment that resonates with the 'repressed desire' for a fully realised ethnonational autonomy. What I aim to highlight are the convergences and disjunctures of film narrative, postcolonial power relationships, expressions of modernity, emergent nationhood and creative agency.

Dang Anom (1962)

Historical Setting, Modernist Narrative

The narrative of *Dang Anom* is steeped in tragedy. It is framed as a Malay

---

48   Gledhill, 'The melodramatic field', p. 6.
49   Christine Gledhill, 'Dialogue: Christine Gledhill on "Stella Dallas" and feminist theory', *Cinema Journal* 25, 4 (1986): 45.

historical epic centred on the invasion of the Temasek kingdom by the Javanese Majapahit Empire. The film is actually a modern melodrama that places idealistic agency in its female protagonist, Dang Anom (Fatimah Ahmad), while overtly critiquing the precolonial Malay feudal system as immoral and unjust. The film is set in precolonial Temasek, today's Singapore. Dang Anom is the daughter of Sang Rajuna Tapa (Ahmad Nisfu), a high-ranking minister in the court of the Malay Sultan of Temasek (M. Amin). She is forced to become the concubine of the lustful sultan when her lover, the warrior Malang (Noordin Ahmad), is sent to lead a war against the Majapahit Empire. When Malang returns from his successful campaign he is distraught to learn of Dang Anom's situation. Eventually, the lovers are framed for treason by Malang's jealous enemy, Dato' Bijasura (Mahmud June), and are sentenced to death. Desperate to save his daughter, Dang Anom's father reluctantly conspires with Majapahit spies to open the fortified gates to Temasek to facilitate an invasion of the sultan's palace. The film ends tragically with the deaths of Malang, Dang Anom and her parents. Dato' Bijasura kills Dang Anom's mother (Siti Tanjung Perak) who pleads to the sultan for her daughter's life. And while the sultan escapes Temasek with his consort, Dang Anom is brutally raped and murdered at the hands of Dato' Bijasura while her father dies trying to save her. The film, then, is a Malay historical epic that paradoxically challenges the concept of feudal power. This is achieved through a narrative of tragedy and injustice experienced by the lead character that also reveals her ethical aspirations for self-determination and freedom.

Central to the film's narrative is Dang Anom's position as a woman subjugated by patriarchal forms of control. Her body is contested between the sultan and her lover Malang, while her father mediates the exchange of her ownership. In this gendered power relationship the sultan is symbolic of the antiquated and anti-modern practices of precolonial Malay society, while Malang is the archetype of a blindly loyal and powerless subject of feudal oppression. Intertextually, this character, whose name means 'unfortunate' in Malay, represents an antithesis to the meaning of Hang Tuah's name—'Tuah' derived from 'bertuah' means 'fortunate'. Dang Anom's quest for self-determination and freedom positions her as a mediator of postcolonial modernist ideals.

This portrayal is in sharp contrast to the historical source of inspiration for the film, *Sejarah Melayu* (*The Malay Annals*).[50] C.C. Brown's translation of *Sejarah Melayu* contains the story of an unnamed daughter of the Temasek sultan's treasurer, Sang Rajuna Tapa, who was the 'mistress' of Sri Sultan Iskandar Shah. She is slanderously accused of 'misconduct' by other women in the sultan's court and is 'publicly exposed' in the local market.[51] In R.O. Winstedt's earlier version of the text, she is similarly accused of disloyalty to the sultan and without investigation 'impaled in the market square'.[52] The main focus of this story in the text is the humiliation of Sang Rajuna Tapa and his consequent treasonous role in assisting the Majapahit Empire's conquest of Temasek. Unlike the film *Dang Anom*, the female concubine is not even named and merely a minor character in the narrative. The story of Sang Rajuna Tapa's betrayal is linked to a generational curse due to the ruthless actions of the sultan's father. In the moralistic vein of *Sejarah Melayu*, the sultan, in repeating an unjust act, is then punished with the loss of his kingdom to Majapahit. Cheah Boon Kheng reads the women in this story as 'capable of great guile, manipulation and ruthlessness which could produce deadly results', and further observes in *Sejarah*

---

[50] This text was promoted extensively and operated to discursively construct a homogeneous identity based on the selective codification and canonisation of linguistic and literary sources that were deemed Malay by the colonial British administration. See Adrian Vickers, '"Malay identity": Modernity, invented tradition and forms of knowledge', in *Contesting Malayness: Malay Identity Across Boundaries*, ed. Timothy P. Barnard. Singapore: Singapore University Press, 2004, pp. 33–35.

[51] C.C. Brown, trans. *Sejarah Melayu, or, The Malay Annals*. Kuala Lumpur: Oxford University Press, 1970 (Orig. publ. 1953), pp. 50–51.

[52] R.O. Winstedt, *The Malay Annals, or, Sejarah Melayu: The Earliest Recension from Ms. No. 18 of the Raffles Collection in the Library of the Royal Asiatic Society*, London, Singapore: Malayan Branch of the Royal Asiatic Society, 1938, cited in Cheah Boon Kheng, 'Power behind the throne: The role of queens and court ladies in Malay history', *Journal of the Malaysian Branch of the Royal Asiatic Society* 66, 1 (1993): 2. Again, parallels can be drawn to South Asian musical and film culture. The tragic history of subjugation of a northern Indian female courtesan that ties this story with a typecast tragic narrative trajectory in Hindi film representations is elaborated in Katherine Butler Schofield (née Brown), 'The courtesan tale: Female musicians and dancers in Mughal historical chronicles, c.1556–1748', *Gender & History* 24, 1 (2012): 165, citing Gregory D. Booth, 'Making a woman from a *Tawaif*: Courtesans as heroes in Hindi cinema', *New Zealand Journal of Asian Studies* 9, 2 (2007): 7.

Melayu instances of courtly women assassinating sultans and acting as major forces of resistance to oppressive monarchs.[53] Hussein Haniff's *Dang Anom* propels this precolonial proto-feminist role of women found in classical Malay narratives into a modern vision of women's resistance to feudal regimes.

What role, then, does music play in Malay feudal history? Contrary to the screened music of *Dang Anom* in which music challenges feudal authority, rulers in precolonial Malay society used music to assert their divine sovereignty. Barbara Andaya discusses the extension of Malay monarchical power through the use of loud sounds, particularly the *nobat* drum and wind ensemble.[54] She argues that the use of sound-producing instruments in premodern society sonically and symbolically reminded Malay villagers 'of their subordination to the temporal power of the ruler' while reassuring them of their protection 'by the supernatural powers such sounds evoked'. More importantly, sounds 'were part of an interactive acoustical space, conveying messages that helped to define a community's cultural parameters and affirm the place of the ruler at its emotional core'.[55] Andaya's observation resonates with Zubir Said's music that attempted to portray a Malay tradition in *Dang Anom*'s film music. The traditionalised music and dance in the film were used to symbolise feudalistic control over the film's protagonists. Considering Andaya's concept of 'sounded authority' in the commercial and cosmopolitan context of Malay film music production highlights a paradoxical, musical critique of the inherent acoustic–kingship–kinship association. As I demonstrate below, traditional-sounding music is not only used to denote and impose monarchical power, it is also applied in a disjunctive aesthetic articulation for depicting that power in a negative light. The interaction of these musical discourses, congruent and disjunctive with the film's melodramatic narrative, exposes a concealed

---

53   Cheah, 'Power behind the throne', p. 2.
54   Barbara Watson Andaya, 'Distant drums and thunderous cannon: Sounding authority in traditional Malay society', *International Journal of Asia Pacific Studies* 7, 2 (2011): 19–35. See also Raja Iskandar bin Raja Halid, 'Malay Nobat: A History of Encounters, Accommodation and Development'. PhD thesis, King's College London, 2015.
55   Andaya, 'Distant drums and thunderous cannon', p. 32.

critique of sounded authority and, by extension, questions the structural inequities of a postcolonial condition.

Traditionalising Music

Music is evidently used and represented in discourses about tradition in Malay film of the 1950s and 1960s. Here, musical motifs present in the opening title theme of *Dang Anom* are analysed to uncover other musical moments throughout the film. In order to contextualise traditionalising discourses about music in this film, I show how music in films produced by Cathay-Keris studios were known for their overt Malayness and inaccessibility to audiences in comparison with the more contemporary and commercial songs of the rival Malay Film Productions. The evocation of tradition in Zubir Said's film music was not a straightforward process. Despite *Dang Anom*'s feudal Malay setting and tragic narrative, the ethnonationalist and cosmopolitan ideals of both the composer and director are articulated covertly in a subtextual critique of Western imperialism that signals postcolonial aspirations for agency and self-determination.

The music of Zubir Said interacts with the melodramatic narrative of *Dang Anom* in unique ways by drawing on Malay melodies and styles combined with dark or sombre-sounding, non-traditional textures to underscore the tragic narrative and modern subtext of the film. The orchestration sounds rich and full—despite using only eight studio musicians—but is coded culturally and affectively through varying use of instrumentation. The instrumental music for the opening credits (title theme) starts with a distinct resonating gong strike followed by a gamelan-sounding descending melody played on a vibraphone (Figure 3.1; see Appendix C.3 for transcription). This acts as an indexical code for Javanese music, relating to the involvement of the Majapahit Empire in the narrative. This 'Javanese' melody reappears in bar 9 and is hinted at with an ascending vibraphone melody at bar 23 towards the end of the piece (Figure 3.2, bar 23). In addition, the use of a descending chromatic passage (Figure 3.3, bars 15–17) uncommon in Malay traditional and folk music provides melodic contrast to the culturally coded Malay-sounding theme that recurs frequently throughout the title theme, background music and songs in the film. All these musical devices converge with and complement the film's overarching allegory of self-determination in the face of unjust authoritarian rule.

Figure 3.1 Gong hit and descending 'gamelan' melody (bars 1–2)

Figure 3.2 Ascending vibraphone (bar 23)

Figure 3.3 Chromatic descent (bars 15–17)

The instrumental music of the opening credits reiterate the 'freedom motif' as described by Peters in various configurations.[56] I call this melody and related variations the 'Dang Anom motif' due

---

56   Peters, 'Zubir Said and his music for film', p. 87.

to its frequency in the film and the centrality of the main character. Following the Javanese melody, the Dang Anom motif is announced by the violins (Figure 3.4, bars 2–7), rearticulated by a two-part saxophone section (Figure 3.5, bars 17–20), and finally a solo electric guitar melody (Figure 3.6, bars 25–28). This motif is repeated in various orchestrations throughout the film, especially in the love duet between Dang Anom and Malang, Dang Anom's lament,[57] and the final scene of the film where Dang Anom's father discovers his dead daughter.[58] For example, the Dang Anom motif is articulated by flute and saxophone in this excerpt from the instrumental introduction to the love duet (Figure 3.7, bars 1–5).

Figure 3.4 Violin motif (bars 1–5)

Figure 3.5 Saxophone motif (bars 17–20)

Figure 3.6 Guitar motif (bars 25–28)

---

57 I cannot confirm the title for the lament as it is not stated in the film or any other sources. For the purposes of this analysis the song is titled 'Saat demi Saat' (Second by Second). The love duet from this film, 'Paduan Budi' (United in Obligations), can be found in the companion CD to Rohana, *Zubir Said.*

58 Peters, 'Zubir Said and his music for film', pp. 87–88.

Figure 3.7 Instrumental introduction to 'Paduan Budi'

The sequence of musical codes in the title theme sonically encapsulate the major narrative themes of the film. The musical themes are framed by the Javanese gamelan melody indicating the major role played by the Majapahit Empire in the story, despite its limited direct appearance. The Dang Anom theme played by the violin section refers to the cautiously optimistic idealism and love between the two main protagonists. In this, the violin signifies a purportedly 'pure' Malay tradition as it has for centuries been used in folk ensembles.[59] The tension between 'tradition' and 'modernity' or, in the context of the story, between individual aspirations and feudal restrictions, can be heard in the use of saxophones and electric guitar to play the Dang Anom motif. Moreover, the saxophones are harmonised in sixths in an expression of Western (or modern) tonality. While saxophones and other Western

---

[59] The combined use of *rebana* and violin is one example of premodern cosmopolitan Malay instrumentation. Margaret Kartomi, 'Kapri: A synthesis of Malay and Portuguese music on the west coast of North Sumatra', in *Cultures and Societies of North Sumatra*, ed. Rainer Carle. Berlin: Dietrich Reimer, 1987, pp. 351–93 suggests its connection to Moorish culture imported by Portuguese colonists to the Malay Archipelago. See also Tan, *Bangsawan*, p. 77; and Tan Sooi Beng, 'From folk to national popular music: Recreating *ronggeng* in Malaysia', *Journal of Musicological Research* 24, 3 (2005): 287–307.

instruments were common in the *orkes Melayu* (Malay music ensembles) used in *bangsawan* theatre, it is uncommon and therefore striking to hear such instrumentation in a 'traditional' Malay film epic.[60]

Zubir Said's creative musical authorship can be heard in relation to the aspiring agency of the film's female protagonist, as an aesthetic disjuncture between modernity and tradition. When made a concubine, Dang Anom is resolutely unhappy. Unlike the other concubines who eventually warm to the lustful but charming sultan, she expresses her displeasure openly to the point of her execution, rejecting the sultan's plea to her to ask for his forgiveness in exchange for her life. The musical references in conjunction with the actions of Dang Anom are allegorical to the struggle for independence from colonial rule. The music therefore expresses a nation-making aesthetic inspired by modern cosmopolitan ideas of emergent national autonomy.

Further oppositions are observed in the composer's use of musical moods. When composing for films, Zubir Said understood 'Malay' music to be rooted in vocal melody limited to two moods: 'happy singing …and sad singing.'[61] This contrasting use of musical moods can be heard clearly in the two songs featuring Dang Anom: initially, an aspirational love duet between Dang Anom and Malang; and later, a tragic lament sung by Dang Anom. Zubir Said's writing process involved extensive experimentation on the piano to create instrumental (background) music that he considered aesthetically suitable to a Malay film. Moreover, he worked with a restricted budget of $3,000 per film and a meagre ensemble of only eight musicians, which limited his ambition to create lush and grand textures easily achieved with a larger orchestra.[62] Because of this, he devised ingenious techniques to achieve his intended sounds by using more percussive instruments such as gongs and frame drums.[63]

---

[60] Andrew N. Weintraub, *Dangdut Stories: A Social and Musical History of Indonesia's Most Popular Music.* New York: Oxford University Press, 2010, pp. 38–41; Tan, *Bangsawan*, pp. 76–78.

[61] Zubir bin Said, Oral History Interviews, Reel 13.

[62] The currency stated is in Malaysian ringgit ($) which was at the time valued at £0.14 to $1.00. Most Malay films would have an overall budget of $30,000. Hence, the budget for music was only one-tenth of the whole.

[63] Zubir bin Said, Oral History Interviews, Reel 13.

In place of large or atmospheric orchestral textures, the vibraphone is heard extensively, providing a lush, dark, dreamy and perhaps ominous presence throughout the film. The vibraphone is not an instrument common to Malay folk music, but it was immensely popular in Malay films of the 1950s and 1960s. Zubir Said's use of the vibraphone can be heard in most of his film scores, notably for films set in mythical or historical settings such as *Bawang Puteh Bawang Merah* and *Jula Juli Bintang Tujoh*. While restricting his music to self-imposed cultural boundaries, Zubir Said nonetheless composed with a modernist aesthetic using Western instruments. His approach to composing and arranging film music in fact challenged a rigid conception of tradition in music. However, in line with a postcolonial conception of nationhood, a Malay musical tradition, no matter how contested, had to be made visible even if it was not heard. A photograph of musicians recording at Cathay-Keris in the presence of Hussein Haniff (Figure 3.8) presents a purely Southeast Asian spectacle: two *angklung* players, a *gambus* player, a flautist with a wooden and metal flute, a *kompang* or *rebana tar* (tambourine frame drum) player, a man standing by an Indonesian gong set and Zubir Said holding a *kompang* and what appears to be three wooden flutes, a crash cymbal on a stand beside him, a harmonium and clarinet in front of him.[64] It appears this photo was taken as a publicity shot in the recording studio, so additional instruments were placed for display such as more *angklung*, a floor tom drum, a *gendang* and a *rebana*. Absent from this photo are the modern instruments actually heard in Zubir Said's film scores like the vibraphone, piano, guitar and saxophones. The most modern 'instrument' is the large microphone in front of Hussein Haniff.[65] I can only speculate whether this was a traditional instrument recording session or a conscious effort to promote the Cathay-Keris brand as being distinctly Malay.

---

[64] Peters, 'Zubir Said and his music for film', p. 76; Rohana, *Zubir Said*, p. 29. The man standing by the Indonesian gong set is Wahid Satay, a popular actor at Cathay-Keris known for comedy and singing.

[65] I discuss the role of the microphone in shaping Malay film music aesthetics in Chapter Four.

Figure 3.8 Zubir Said (seated, front row, right)
and Hussein Haniff (standing, far right)[66]

    In fact, Cathay-Keris distinguished its productions from Malay Film
Productions by focusing on the Malay epic genre. Cathay-Keris was the
only Malay film production company that allowed its composers to write
original background music, whereas Malay Film Productions' composers
focused more on writing commercially viable songs. Cathay-Keris was
thus known for its more traditional aesthetic offerings. Kassim Masdor,
a composer and musician who worked for Malay Film Productions
as a continuity clerk, suggests that the more aesthetically modern
commercially inclined film songs had greater mass appeal compared with
Cathay-Keris film songs that were 'more ... traditional, which are harder
to sing'.[67] He elaborates:

---

[66] Peters, 'Zubir Said and his music for film', p. 76; Rohana, *Zubir Said*, p. 26.

[67] Kassim Masdor, Oral History Interviews, Reel/Disc 6, Accession Number 002141,
     National Archives of Singapore, 1 May 1999. '*Kita punya [lagu]* more to modern.
     Cathay-Keris punya more to *traditional yang payah dinyanyikan.*'

A lot of the film songs from Cathay-Keris were too excessively Malay. So, they were not accepted by society possibly because, sorry to say, they weren't that exciting but despite the Shaw Brothers' films not having any, what people call very typical Malay songs ... [Shaw Brothers' film songs] have a *commercial touch*.[68]

This statement does not necessarily disparage the musical productions of Cathay-Keris but rather indicates the reality of the Malay film audience's musical taste in that period. The 'commercial touch' of prominent Malay Film Productions' songwriters like P. Ramlee and Kassim Masdor constituted a cosmopolitan popular music aesthetic that included non-Malay styles of music such as jazz, samba and later rock 'n' roll, though sung in the Malay language. The commercial musical approach of Shaw Brothers' studio culminated in the final transition out of Malay folk and traditional music in *A Go Go '67* (1967, dir. Omar Rojik) which featured *pop yeh yeh* bands—rock guitar groups with singers in the style of the Beatles and the Rolling Stones.[69] This film was one of the last Malay films produced by the studio in Singapore, marking the beginning of the end of a vibrant era of music in Malay films.[70]

Challenging Tradition

The traditionalising discourse that positions the music of Cathay-Keris films as 'excessively Malay' and 'very typical Malay' is ironic in retrospect, considering the modern approach and critique of tradition contained in those films. This modern approach is evident in the ample

---

[68] Kassim Masdor, Oral History Interviews, Reel/Disc 7, Accession Number 002141, National Archives of Singapore, 13 May 1999 (my emphasis).

[69] Ironically, Cathay-Keris was the first to produce a rock 'n' roll-themed Malay film. *Muda Mudi* (Youths, dir. M. Amin) starring Siput Sarawak and Roseyatimah was released in 1965, two years prior to *A Go Go '67*.

[70] Adil Johan, 'Disquieting degeneracy: Policing Malaysian and Singaporean popular music culture from the mid-1960s to early-1970s', in *Sonic Modernities in the Malay World: A History of Popular Music, Social Distinction and Novel Lifestyles (1930s–2000s)*, ed. Bart Barendregt. Leiden: Brill, 2014, pp. 135–61. I discuss the musical currents that coincided with the end of the Malay film studio system in Chapter Six.

use of diegetic and non-diegetic disjunctures that articulate a discourse of cultural and emotional conflict among the protagonists. The characters Malang and Dang Anom are trapped within the boundaries of their culture and customs (*adat*), in which unquestioning loyalty to the sultan is paramount. However, their cultural loyalties are challenged when they affect their personal relationship. Music is used as a contrast to their emotions at crucial points of conflict in the narrative. Furthermore, the use of a traditional-sounding music disjunct to the narrative amplifies the anti-authoritarian themes of the film's story. These music narrative disjuncts are observed in two crucial scenes. Hussein Haniff's modern melodramatic narrative interacts with the multilayered representations of tradition contained in Zubir Said's music, articulating poetically and musically the contestations of power tied to postcolonial Malay nation-making.

First, I consider the lament sung by Dang Anom when she discovers her fate of becoming the sultan's concubine. It is performed in a *dondang sayang* style replete with traditional-sounding melodies and instrumentation.[71] The song occurs as a dream that Dang Anom experiences the night before she is bound for the sultan's palace to become a concubine. As such, it fittingly portrays the protagonist's despair (Appendix A.4). The song initially articulates Dang Anom's sadness in the form of her desperate longing for her lover, Malang. It expresses her many anxieties regarding the safety of Malang confronting the Majapahit Empire and her own impending subjugation as part of the sultan's harem. It also conveys her anxiety for the anguish that Malang will feel if he returns safely, only to discover that she is a concubine. When Malang enters the song sequence to advise her not to 'idolise shadows', she is elated to see him and just as he embraces her from behind he drops a stone into the pond below them. The shot of the stone dropping into the pond synchronises with a loud and punctuated F minor chord played on the vibraphone. The chord seems out of place

---

[71] Matusky and Tan, *The Music of Malaysia*, pp. 333–34. Matusky and Tan indicate that *dondang sayang*, translated as 'love song', has two possible origins. The first locates it in Penyengat in the Riau archipelago and the second locates it 'in Malacca at the height of the Malay kingdom in the 15th century' (p. 334). Evidence of this performance style can be dated to the seventeenth and eighteenth centuries in the Malay world in the classical Malay texts, *Tuhfat al-Nafis* and *Hikayat Hang Tuah*.

with the accompanying music and is used as a sound effect. They are both shown singing the final line of the song together in their distorted reflection in the pond. The next shot clearly reveals the sultan singing next to Dang Anom in place of Malang. During the final line, Dang Anom turns around to face who she thinks is Malang but is horrified to see the sultan instead. She then pushes herself away from him, and the song transitions into an energetic and harrowing instrumental and visual sequence that amplifies her horror. The song ends with Dang Anom's terrified screams as she wakes up sobbing from her nightmare. The lyrics towards the end of the song imply that Dang Anom's longing for a 'pure' and unimpeded union with Malang ('We, who are pure cannot be restrained') is merely a false hope ('Don't always idolise shadows'). The idolisation of shadows is also in reference to the false idolisation of the sultan; the lyrics suggest the sultan is a false idol. He is clearly portrayed as an obstruction to Malang and Dang Anom's 'pure' love. As the final song sequence, this scene anticipates the tragic fate of Dang Anom at the end of the film. Ultimately, the melodramatic, foreboding lyrics and interpretative context of the song articulate an overt critique of the injustices of blind loyalty to feudal power.

This 'excessively' Malay song is juxtaposed to an impressionistic *mise-en-scène* of Dang Anom's dream that includes shots of her face and the sultan in multiple exposures and long-angle shots of her silhouette next to a barren tree on a hill. The most famous and iconic still from this film—the multiple exposure shot of Dang Anom's face—is also from this song sequence. A prominent film-maker, U-Wei Haji Saari, notes the modern aesthetics of this particular song sequence and image:

> The scene that particularly strikes me, and I've watched it recently, is Fatimah Ahmad's [Dang Anom's] daydream scene. The way it was edited makes it look like the earliest MTV-style Malay music clip ever produced.... It's a good song to edit around ... and indeed director Hussein Haniff started as an editor.[72]

---

[72] U-Wei Haji Saari, 'Zubir Said, semoga bahagia' [Zubir Said, may you achieve happiness], in *Majulah! The Film Music of Zubir Said*. Singapore: National Museum of Singapore, 2012, pp. 59–60.

In other words, this scene and Hussein Haniff's editing techniques were at the time considered comparatively modern and experimental in comparison with other Malay films. At the end of the song sequence, the sultan's image is multiplied as double exposures to amplify the horror felt by Dang Anom. The duplication of his image suggests the inescapable reach of his incessant lustful desires due to his unquestionable position of power. These modern visuals juxtaposed with the tragic melodramatic narrative and the traditional-sounding music of Zubir Said act to separate the protagonist from traditional notions of Malay loyalty to feudal order.

Another important aspect of this song is the intricate orchestration and arrangement. While the song is sung in a *dondang sayang* style, especially in the vocals, the instrumentation is more rigidly structured and melodically repetitive. The instrumental introduction refers back to the Dang Anom motif present in the opening theme and love duet. This melodic motif is deployed as a responding phrase to Dang Anom's sung verses. Each sung line is answered by the Dang Anom motif, indicating a rigid but organised compositional structure. This is an explicit reference to the *dondang sayang* genre, in which a call and response between singers and instrumentalists (usually a solo violinist) is typically heard. However, the instrumental responses are usually performed in a more fluid and extemporised manner. Zubir Said's arrangement, by contrast, formalises the *dondang sayang*. In this way, this song begins to articulate a musical aesthetic of a traditionalised nationhood by mixing Malay folk music practices with Western compositional practices—practices from the past are effectively modernised. The film's narrative can be viewed as paralleling the musical structure. The past is referenced in its historical setting but the modern desire for post-feudal and postcolonial autonomy is the dominant structuring theme. The film's music and narrative analysed together reveal some of the antipathies and aspirations that constituted the paradoxes of a Malay nation-in-the-making.

The next scene for analysis is set in the court of the sultan, in which a group of female dancers is performing to celebrate Malang's triumphant return to Temasek.[73] The sultan summons his concubines to be present

---

[73] The dance here features Lela Sani who is mentioned in the title credits.

for the festivities and Dang Anom enters the room to a slow and melancholic melody that is diegetically heard as the introduction of a new dance. Suddenly, just as Malang notices her, the music is punctuated by a loud accent that becomes a fast and lively percussive *joget* rhythm.[74] This sped-up tempo is in stark contrast to Malang's unsettling realisation that his lover is now a concubine. Infuriated, he leaves the court in haste during the festive dance performance. The interplay of diegetic music in contrast with the repressed emotions of Malang and Dang Anom highlights the overarching anti-feudal theme in the film. The traditional dance music heard above everything else represents the subsuming limitations of a feudal culture in which individual desires and actions (except the sultan's) need to be repressed. Additionally, the dance performances represent an embodied expression of loyalty to culture and tradition as well as a sexualised objectification of female subjects in service to the king's lustful desires. At this crucial point of the film, Malang leaves the court abruptly as he is unable to stomach the reality of his predicament: he fought for his sultan and country only to have his heart broken by the cultural order that he served without question.

This scene resonates with the notion of sounded authority already noted.[75] The portrayal of traditional Malay music and dance as a representation of the sultan's authority in a disjunctive relationship to the narrative amplifies the critique of Malay feudal power. While the sultan's authority and even his magnanimity are reflected in the festive occasion, they contrast with the anger felt by Malang and the despair of Dang Anom when they see each other across the room. After Malang's abrupt exit, he immediately goes to confront Dang Anom's father. The exchange between Malang and Dang Anom's father, Rajuna Tapa, clearly indicates the radical critique of tradition or customs (*adat*) that fuels the film's narrative. Malang learns that Rajuna Tapa had no choice in giving up his daughter to the sultan. This infuriates Malang even more. When Rajuna Tapa asks him to be patient, here is their exchange:

---

[74] Matusky and Tan, *The Music of Malaysia*, p. 108.
[75] Andaya, 'Distant drums and thunderous cannon'.

Malang:	Sir, everything in this world has its limits. The same goes with patience.... If the sultan is free to appease his lustful desires then I too as a free human being should be free to express the words from my heart that are true.
Rajuna Tapa:	Your words are true but the citizens cannot be treasonous to the sultan. Moreover, it is wrong on the side of our customs.
Malang:	Ah! Customs! Are not customs a manifestation of desire to spread cruelty? Meanwhile, the sultan is free to abduct people's children and wives to fulfil his lustful desires, but the citizens, the citizens are bound to ruthless customs. Where is the justice, sir?
Rajuna Tapa:	Malang, do not give in to your the feelings of your young blood. It will destroy your body.
Malang:	Never, never. For the safety of Anom and the truth I am willing to sacrifice anything at all to demolish these ruthless customs.[76]

Here, Malang's overtly anti-feudal opinions criticise *adat* or traditions that allow for a monarch's unjust abuse of power. The exchange between Malang and Rajuna Tapa also reflects the tensions between the younger and older generations. Indeed, the Malay community in the 1960s was divided across a spectrum of beliefs: liberals, conservatives, monarchists, Islamists, socialists and Marxists. The exchange not only articulates the tensions between Malay nationalists and the colonial order but also the antipathies within a diverse community in a period of decolonisation and nascent independence. Some sought a more conservative approach to independence that upheld the integrity of the monarchy, while others wanted a more radical change and a dissolution of the monarchy altogether. Another subtext is a critique of colonial rule—the uncontrollable lust of the sultan can be likened to unbridled capitalism and political domination of the colonial administration. The women and

---

[76] This is an apt intertextual reference by Hussein Haniff to P. Ramlee's song 'Berkorban Apa Saja' (To Sacrifice Anything at All) in *Hang Tuah*, analysed in Chapter Two.

children of the citizens of Temasek are ruthlessly abducted just as the natural resources of the Malay Peninsula had been violently appropriated by the erstwhile colonial rulers.

The social critique derived from the film's narrative and dialogue is even more complex when considering the film's music. What can be heard in the music is a representation of tradition that contrasts with the radical, anti-tradition message of the film. *Traditionalising* music is used to signify the sounded authority of the Malay feudal order but a closer, intertextual reading of this music reveals a more nuanced relationship. In Chapter Two, I demonstrated how the use of the leitmotif indicates a cosmopolitan musical approach rooted in Western art music. Such a leitmotif in the context of a film's narrative can also signal an aesthetic of emergent nation-making. The Dang Anom motif functions similarly in its articulation of two opposing notions. On the one hand, the motif may be heard as a rigid structural imposition of formal Western compositional practices. It assumes the baggage of colonial modes of structuring, simplifying and othering the culture of the colonised. On the other hand, the musical convergence of Western conventions with local music is congruent with the postcolonial process of nation-making. Zubir Said and Hussein Haniff were actively creating their own nuanced discourse about Malay nationhood in *Dang Anom*. It was a discourse about the paradoxes and contestations of an emerging Malay nation that was potentially bound by conservative notions of tradition and a colonial mentality of dependence. The tragic narrative of *Dang Anom*, however, loudly implores its audience to challenge corrupt leaders who derive their power from tradition, customs or archaic belief systems. In this allegory for ethical nation-making, the musical tradition that Zubir Said created actually represented his own desire for a modern Malay nation that could free itself from colonial dependency by adapting the local musical practices of the past to the aspirations of the present.

I have analysed intertextually how musical modernism clashed with notions of Malay tradition. Evident in Zubir Said's film music is an interplay between a traditionalised national music aesthetic with classical narrative themes about a premodern feudal society. Issues of feudalism and class inequities are highlighted in films such as *Dang Anom*, while the aesthetically modern approaches used in Zubir Said's compositions underscore a critique of antiquated notions of Malayness. However, such film music simultaneously challenged precolonial Malay feudal culture while reinforcing Western conceptions of modern nationalism through the supercultural aesthetic conventions of film music and the economic demands and limitations of a commercial film industry. Beyond this unequal relationship of power between a postcolonial economy and aspirant nationalists, there are instances of agency that emerge between the lines of discourse about tradition and modernity. For instance, there is the integral role of the film's female protagonist, Dang Anom, whose tragic predicament and resolute and moralistic stand for autonomy parallel the composer's and director's personal aspirations for postcolonial self-determination. As Zubir Said's own views on music and nationalism demonstrate, the notion of national or traditional authenticity was ambiguous at best. My interpretations of modernity and agency do not describe Zubir Said's true intentions; they reflect his unique musical, cultural and political experience in Singapore during a period of burgeoning nation-making and imagining.

Conclusion

Listening to Zubir Said's film music uncovers how a postcolonial nation is imagined through the evocation of tradition. Traditions are not authentic practices that a nation draws from. Rather, the process of creating or reimagining traditions is constitutive of nationhood. In drawing from Christopher Waterman's insights, tradition-making is indeed very much a process bound up with postcolonial modernity.[77] A musical and historical analysis of *Dang Anom* reveals how the notion of tradition and nation was imagined and discursively formed through a commercial film market that intersected with the ideologies and aspirations of post-war cosmopolitan Malay nationalism. Zubir Said deployed the 'traditional' aesthetically in his music to express an ethnonational Malay discourse. As part of the cosmopolitan discourses on nation-making during the period, an essentialised 'pure' Malay

---

[77] Waterman, "'Our tradition is a very modern tradition'".

tradition was seemingly evoked. But closer attention to musical content reveals a modernising musical approach that used Western instrumentation and compositional practices. Beyond that, despite budgetary constraints, he found solutions that further contributed to the uniqueness of his music and that led to the development of a distinctive Malay musical aesthetic of nation-making in historically themed Malay films. While music from Cathay-Keris films may be heard as canonical symbols of a national Malay culture in Malaysia and Singapore, it articulated a more nuanced and contested notion of Malay statehood grounded in modern ideals of freedom and resistance to the feudal/colonial order.

Nationalising a tradition is strongly predicated upon the existence of a supposedly unchanging repository of culture. This is negated by a case study of Zubir Said and his musical compositions. His film music actually demonstrates the reverse in that he was instrumental in the process of creating an aesthetic of Malay musical tradition for the nascent postcolonial nation.[78] As already highlighted, Malay

---

[78] Inspiring the argument here are studies that deal with modernist reformism and the construction of musical traditions in Malaysia. See Tan, *Bangsawan*; Tan, 'From folk to national popular music'; Margaret Sarkissian, *D'Albuquerque's Children: Performing Tradition in Malaysia's Portuguese Settlement*. London: University of Chicago Press, 2000; Margaret Sarkissian, 'Playing Portuguese: Constructing identity in Malaysia's Portuguese community', *Diaspora: A Journal of Transnational Studies* 11, 2 (2002): 215–32. A comparative study of how Southeast Asian and South Asian music is formalised as an elite national cultural practice or 'classicised' is found in Pamela Moro, 'Constructions of nation and the classicisation of music: Comparative perspectives from Southeast and South Asia', *Journal of Southeast Asian Studies* 35, 2 (2004): 187–211. Additionally, substantial scholarly discussion exists on modernist reformism in the classicisation of South Asian music with regard to nationalism and postcoloniality. See Lakshmi Subramanian, 'The reinvention of tradition: Nationalism, Carnatic music and the Madras Music Academy, 1900–1947', *Indian Economic and Social History Review* 36, 2 (1999): 131–63; Lakshmi Subramanian, *From the Tanjore Court to the Madras Music Academy: A Social History of Music in South India*. 2nd ed., Oxford: Oxford University Press, 2011; Janaki Bakhle, *Two Men and Music: Nationalism in the Making of an Indian Classical Tradition*. Oxford: Oxford University Press, 2005; Amanda J. Weidman, *Singing the Classical, Voicing the Modern: The Postcolonial Politics of Music in South India*. London: Duke University Press, 2006; Katherine Butler Schofield (née Brown), 'Reviving the golden age again: "Classicization", Hindustani music, and the Mughals', *Ethnomusicology* 54, 3 (2010): 484–517.

musical practices prior to colonial rule were intensely pluralistic and cosmopolitan. Therefore, the process of creating a musical tradition for an emergent Malay nation was a selective process facilitated by creative individuals in positions of nation-making. Zubir Said was a composer who was given the opportunity to compose a 'modern' musical 'tradition' for an emerging Malay nation, using ambiguous cultural boundaries of Malayness that were and remain highly contested. As such, Zubir Said had to construct a Malay musical tradition for the silver screen, drawing on, at his own discretion, selected musical genres, instrumentation and folk melodies to portray a sense of musical authenticity rooted in an imagined organic past. While Malay films drew on feudal history as a source of their vernacular cultural past, the traditional-sounding music and melodramatic narratives of such films actually challenged archaic notions of tradition to articulate a subversive message of ethical modernity, freedom and self-determination. From the disjunctural narrative juxtaposition of Malay folk music and dances like *dondang sayang* and *joget* to harmonising a Malay melody in sixths on saxophones, Zubir Said's film music—in tandem with the radical ideology of Malay nationalists active in the literary, print, film and music community—sounded a subversive postcolonial critique of unequal power relations between despotic rulers and innocent subjects, British rule and Malay activism, colonial oppression and self-determination. Malay literary activists, film-makers and composers championed new postcolonial ideals by challenging antiquated notions of feudalism. As one of the first film composers in the post-war Malay film industry, Zubir Said was instrumental in initiating a musical aesthetic discourse of Malay nation-making that resonated throughout films of the early 1960s.

This chapter has examined how the precolonial past was represented in Malay films in the early 1960s, a period that saw a rise of Malay authorship in films and music. These emerging directors, writers and composers also saw a need to portray the social issues and problems that were facing a rapidly modernising Malay society. The early 1960s saw more social films (*filem masharakat*) made by Malay directors. These films, especially those directed by P. Ramlee, also featured musician protagonists in prominent roles. As we shall see in the next chapter, musician protagonists effectively mediated the concerns and anxieties of the changing Malay community that faced increased urbanisation and the social inequities of class in a modern capitalist economy. Moreover, the cosmopolitan music and musical technologies of such films also played a role in mediating an acceptable and embodied modernity in a period of emergent national consciousness in Malaysia and Singapore.

Chapter 4

Technologies of Classiness and Narratives of Class[1]

Tak mungkin hilang irama dan lagu
Bagaikan kumbang sentiasa bermadu
Andai dipisah lagu dan irama
Lemah tiada berjiwa
Hampa
(The rhythm and melody cannot be lost
Like a bee always making honey [making love]
If the melody and rhythm are separated
My soul will be weakened
Disappointed)
'Getaran Jiwa' (Vibrations of the Soul), music by P. Ramlee, lyrics by S. Sudarmaji

A man in shirt and tie is seen sitting behind a large broadcast microphone announcing in Malay, 'This is Radio Singapore!'[2] This scene cuts to an image of a pair of hands striking a bongo. Then, in sequence with the developing musical arrangement, there are images of hands on musical instruments playing a double bass ostinato, an accordion striking a minor chord, a piano doubling the bass pattern, a drum kit

---

[1] Portions of this chapter were presented at the University of North Carolina—King's College London Joint Graduate Student Conference, Technology in Music: Production, Preservation, and Dissemination, University of North Carolina, 22–24 May 2014; and at the Jazz Beyond Borders Conference, Conservatorium van Amsterdam, 4–7 September 2014.

[2] *'Inilah Radio Singapura!'*

playing a fill, a pair of maracas outlining the beat and finally, to mark a break in the groove, P. Ramlee is playing a melody on a tenor saxophone that brings the whole band together.[3] He makes a gesture with his hands to signal the last phrase of the song, ending the band's performance in unison. The radio announcer goes on to say, 'That was the opening song by the Kassim Selamat Orchestra, led by Kassim Selamat.'[4] The scene then cuts to a young woman dusting a table beside a large radio cabinet. On hearing Kassim Selamat's name, she rushes downstairs to alert her employer's daughter of around the same age about the bandleader's radio appearance.

This is the opening scene of *Ibu Mertua-ku* (My Mother-in-law, 1962), arguably the most loved, influential and critically acclaimed film directed by P. Ramlee. Critics and scholars observe in this film a fluid portrayal of the complications of class and the anxieties of modernity in the Malay-speaking world of the 1960s.[5] Beyond this view, I highlight in this chapter how 'social' films such as these used music, musical instruments, musical technologies, musicians and music listeners as integral subjects in the articulation of modernity. While these representations of modernity may have been regarded with ambivalence in Malay film narratives, the musical discourses and practices presented in these films reveal a greater consonance with Western modernity and the ideologies and expressions that are presumed to be exogenous to Malay culture. The films of the 1960s were inclusive of an indigenous cosmopolitan aesthetic that reflected the increasingly urbanised and nation-conscious inclinations of their producers and consumers. These complex articulations of modernity and nascent nationhood are evident

---

[3] All the tenor saxophone parts were performed by Yusof B., a prominent film song composer who worked for Shaw Brothers' Malay Film Productions. He is shown in the film playing a jazz song (reminiscent of Lester Young's saxophone style) in the blind date scene set at the Capitol Blue Room cabaret nightclub.

[4] '*Itulah lagu pembukaan Orkestra Kassim Selamat, yang di bawah pimpinan Kassim Selamat.*'

[5] Amir Muhammad, *120 Malay Movies*. Petaling Jaya: Matahari Books, 2010; Timothy P. Barnard, '*Sedih sampai buta*: Blindness, modernity and tradition in Malay films of the 1950s and 1960s', *Bijdragen Tot de Taal-, Land- en Volkenkunde* 161, 4 (2005): 433–53; William van der Heide, *Malaysian Cinema, Asian Film: Border Crossings and National Cultures*. Amsterdam: Amsterdam University Press, 2002.

in the films' class-based narratives that negotiate traditional rural Malay values with musical expressions that convey a modern cosmopolitan aesthetic.

The films I examine also include culturally poignant statements about the placement of musicianship as an occupation representing a liminal position in a class-based modern society.[6] The infamous lines remembered by most fans of P. Ramlee's films are proclaimed by the rich and domineering mother-in-law of *Ibu Mertua-ku* when she inquires about the occupation of her daughter's new love interest. The daughter Sabariah (Sarimah) replies that he is a musician (*ahli muzik*) to which her mother angrily responds: 'A musician? My ancestors curse this! A musician. You ungrateful child.'[7] These lines are delivered by Mak Dara, who plays Nyonya Mansur, the eponymous mother-in-law. Prior to her film career, Mak Dara was herself a famous singer and actor of *bangsawan* operas.[8] This admonishment and its attendant ironies

6   My understanding of the liminality of musicians considers them as being in an adaptable social position that affords access to both the upper-class and lower-class spaces of cultural production and social interaction. This draws on Katherine Butler Brown's view of how 'musicians ... possess social liminality—unusual cultural sanction to cross ordinarily strict boundaries that are of particular significance to a particular society'. Katherine Butler Brown, 'The social liminality of musicians: Case studies from Mughal India and beyond', *Twentieth-century Music* 3, 1 (2007): 6. Brown expands on Alan Merriam's observation of the high cultural value accorded to musicians despite their 'low social status'. Further, musicians are integral in 'representing the voice of the masses to the powerful' and hence are 'institutionally liminal' and 'continually moving between fixed categories'. Alan Merriam, *The Anthropology of Music*. Evanston, IL: Northwestern University Press, 1964, pp. 137–38. See also Victor Turner, 'Liminality and communitas', in *The Ritual Process: Structure and Anti-Structure*. New Jersey: Transaction Publishers, 1969, pp. 94–130.

7   '*Ahli muzik? Memang pantang datuk nenek aku! Ahli muzik. Anak yang tak mengenang jasa!*' See Amir, *120 Malay Movies*, pp. 225–36; Alfian Bin Sa'at, 'Hinterland, heartland, home: Affective topography in Singapore films', in *Southeast Asian Independent Cinema: Essays, Documents, Interviews*, ed. Tilman Baumgärtel. Singapore: NUS Press, 2012, pp. 33–50.

8   A notable performance by Mak Dara singing and dancing an improvisatory *dondang sayang* style song can be viewed in the film *Sri Mersing* (1961, dir. Salleh Ghani). This performance is a useful reference to sung performance styles found in *bangsawan* theatre. For a brief overview of *bangsawan* music styles see Tan Sooi Beng, 'From folk to national popular music: Recreating *ronggeng* in Malaysia', *Journal of Musicological Research* 24, 3 (2005): 294–98.

also echo in the cultural memory of contemporary Malaysians and Singaporeans.[9] P. Ramlee's musician-themed films such as *Ibu Mertua-ku* poetically articulated a performative discourse about music, musicians, class and modernity that would resonate throughout Malay culture until the present.[10]

This chapter analyses music as articulating and mediating modernity in the films *Ibu Mertua-ku* and *Antara Dua Darjat* (Between Two Classes, 1960, dir. P. Ramlee). These are significant examples of social films (*filem masharakat*) that address issues of class inequality in an increasingly urbanised and modernising Malay Peninsula from the mid-1950s to early 1960s.[11] These films and their musical content provide insights into the social issues that concerned scriptwriters and the diverse musical styles that were popular among the urban population of Malaysia, Singapore and Indonesia. The early 1960s was a transitional period of nationhood. The Federation of Malaya was officially independent, but Singapore—the centre of Malay film production—was in an ambiguous, sometimes fraught, relationship with the federation. In time, Malaysia was formed in 1963 from nine Malay states, the Straits Settlements of Penang and Melaka, and the Crown colonies of Singapore, North Borneo (Sabah) and Sarawak. Within two years, Singapore was expelled from Malaysia and gained its independence as the Republic of Singapore in 1965. Thus films from this era reflect and document daily life issues, directly or indirectly commenting on the concerns and

---

9   When I was an aspiring music undergraduate, my mother and older Malay relatives would jokingly quote Mak Dara's statement—'*Ahli muzik?*'—when I mentioned pursuing a career in music.

10   Prior to this, P. Ramlee directed, starred in and wrote music for the class-themed social film *Antara Dua Darjat* (1960), in which he plays a pianist. Another notable film, *Ibu* (1953, dir. S. Ramanathan), features him as a trumpet player but does not deal with class issues as explicitly as his films from the 1960s.

11   The monthly magazine *Majallah Filem* devoted three issues in 1960 to fan letters debating the value of *filem masharakat* over *filem bangsawan* (premodern themed films). The term 'social film' is also employed in Ravi Vasudevan's studies of films of a similar genre in Hindi cinema of the 1950s. Ravi Vasudevan, 'Addressing the spectator of a "Third World" national cinema: The Bombay "social" film of the 1940s and 1950s', *Screen* 36, 4 (1995): 305–24; Ravi Vasudevan, 'Shifting codes, dissolving identities: The Hindi social film of the 1950s as popular culture', *Third Text* 10, 34 (1996): 59–77.

anxieties of Malays living in the postcolonial social environment of a modern multicultural society. However, the confines of a vernacular film industry and its expressions of ethnonational ideologies presented a more homogeneous vision of nation in such social narratives. My reading of nation-making narratives in the films should therefore be understood within the context of an era in which the shaping of a modern Malay citizen—adaptable to changing times, but also true to traditional values—was essential to the emerging nation.

The discussion analyses the discourses of modernity through and about music in P. Ramlee's social films. Music from his films indicates a history of pluralistic practices in the region that ultimately articulate a conciliation with modernity. The music of social films expressed the complexities of modernity and emerging nationhood with *narratives of class* and what I call *technologies of classiness*. Activist film-makers used class-orientated narratives in an attempt to instil a sense of social consciousness in their audiences. However, since the Malay film industry was profit-driven and subjected to censorship, overtly radical ideas were tempered with ambiguous narratives and mediating characters. Historical and critical analyses of P. Ramlee's social films draw attention to the tensions between traditional Malay morality conflicting with the social ills brought about by modernity and wealth. While such films present melodramatic narrative themes of poor against rich, rural against urban, tradition against modernity, a closer intertextual analysis reveals multilayered interactions and negotiations of these themes.

Musical technologies in the form of modern, Western and cosmopolitan instruments and genres further mediate such class and cultural tensions aesthetically. The term 'classiness', then, is a reference to the cosmopolitan practices mediated by such technologies and further embodied by the films' characters. Musician protagonists, who represent the working class, dress in Western clothes, play modern musical instruments and perform cosmopolitan music in cabaret dance halls and radio studios. The visual and sonic portrayals of such elements are representations of classiness in the sense of style, as opposed to economic status. Moreover, the medium of film itself is a modern technology that frames these class-conscious narratives of nation-making. A further social interplay is present in the commercial aesthetic shaped and facilitated by technologies of music and film—the musical styles and instruments affected by on-screen protagonists are representative of a cosmopolitan and global capitalist sphere of entertainment production and consumption.[12]

Female characters were especially important in negotiating the tensions between commoners and nobility, lower and upper classes, tradition and modernity.[13] These negotiations were facilitated through contexts of intimacy. Women protagonists in class-based narratives generally belonged to the upper class but forged intimate relationships with the lower-class male musician heroes (portrayed by P. Ramlee). As such, the gendered constructions of modern Malay women characters in social films were, to an extent, liberating. Women were portrayed as possessing considerable agency in their roles of bridging the gap between traditional ignorance and modern excess. Of course, the extent of women's agency in these films is limited, as traditional roles highlighting female submission are also perpetuated throughout the films' male-authored scripts. For instance, the two contrasting female heroines in *Ibu Mertua-ku* are objectified as a dichotomous allegorical representation of urban superficiality against small-town compassion.

---

[12] The history of capitalist production for the consumption of a discrete Malay demographic dates to the Great Depression of the 1930s. The construction of a Malay consumer market in that period is examined in Jan van der Putten, 'Negotiating the Great Depression: The rise of popular culture and consumerism in early-1930s Malaya', *Journal of Southeast Asian Studies* 41, 1 (2010): 21–45. The capitalist production and consumption of Malay-language music via the European-based gramophone industry in the 1930s is discussed in Tan Sooi Beng, 'The 78 RPM record industry in Malaya prior to World War II', *Asian Music* 28, 1 (1996/97): 1–41; and Tan Sooi Beng, 'Negotiating "His Master's Voice": Gramophone music and cosmopolitan modernity in British Malaya in the 1930s and early 1940s', *Bijdragen tot de Taal-, Land- en Volkenkunde* 169, 4 (2013): 457–94. The pre-war history of the consumption of films through film magazines is discussed in Timothy P. Barnard, 'Film Melayu: Nationalism, modernity and film in a pre-World War Two Malay magazine', *Journal of Southeast Asian Studies* 41, 1 (2010): 47–70.

[13] For further analyses on the role of women in Malay-language films, see Khoo Gaik Cheng, *Reclaiming Adat: Contemporary Malaysian Film and Literature*. Singapore: NUS Press, 2006, pp. 125–57; Fuziah Kartini Hassan Basri, 'Representations of gender in Malaysian Malay cinema: Implications for human security', *Asian Cinema* 19, 2 (2008): 135–49; and Alicia Izharuddin, 'Pain and pleasures of the look: The female gaze in Malaysian horror film', *Asian Cinema* 26, 2 (2015): 135–52.

Exceptionally, the earlier film, *Antara Dua Darjat*, presents for the first time—at least in Malay films—a female protagonist learning and playing a musical instrument (piano) to accompany the male protagonist's singing. Malay films until then featured the reverse (female singer, male instrumentalist). In fact, it is generally overlooked that the film's female character is featured as a skilful musician who does *not* sing in duet with P. Ramlee.

Considering the history of cosmopolitan musical practices in the Malay world, the discussion focuses on the narratives of modernity and the technologies of musical expression that articulated the nation-making aesthetic particular to Malay films from the 1950s and 1960s. Before an analysis of music in *Antara Dua Darjat* and *Ibu Mertua-ku*, I discuss the role of musical technologies in the Malay film industry that effectively shaped a modern and cosmopolitan aesthetic. This is followed by a social history of class-conscious narratives expressed by independence-era Malay activists and film-writers to provide a frame of reference for analysing the two films.

Technologies of Classiness

The Malay recording and film industry introduced a plethora of post-war musical styles that extended the pluralistic aesthetics of *bangsawan* theatre music. These aesthetic developments were a result of new musical technologies that mediated a sense of postcolonial modernity and emerging nationhood. The industry portrayed modern urban and cosmopolitan themes, characters, narratives and music, especially in social films. The music and representations of musicians in their spaces of performance, such as nightclubs, hotels and private parties hosted by wealthy patrons, presented the film-going audience with a sonic and visual display of *classiness*. This classiness was depicted through iconic musical styles such as jazz, rumba and samba, and specific instruments— pianos, saxophones, accordions, violins, congas and bongos. These musical technologies of classiness mediated the disjunctures of social class structures articulated in social films. As mediators of modernity, working-class Malay musicians occupied a social position of liminality— with a unique 'cultural sanction to cross ordinarily strict boundaries that are of significance to a particular society'.[14] I discuss the social position of musicians later. The focus of this section is to consider the history and prevalence of technologically shaped aesthetic practices in Malay film music that expose an inherent cultural acceptance and embodiment of modernity in Malay society of the 1960s. The technologically shaped musical aesthetics of the post-war Malay music and film industries reconciled a modern and cosmopolitan lifestyle with a traditional and rural Malay identity, a theme that is reflected clearly in social films of the period.

My analysis of musical mediation relates to the way music articulates the space between structural expression and social meaning. Antoine Hennion suggests art and mediation as 'the reciprocal, local, heterogeneous relations between art and public through precise devices, places, institutions, objects and human abilities, constructing identities, bodies, and subjectivities'.[15] Moving beyond a strictly sociological paradigm of music research, Hennion argues for a reacknowledgement of the autonomous 'work' of music to be considered alongside the sociological factors that determine the distribution and reception of music. Music is thus mediated on multiple levels: transforming society while adapting, autonomously and creatively throughout history and social contexts. It is this approach to musical mediation that I discuss with regard to the shaping of post-independence Malay society by musical technologies and the representation of such technologies on the silver screen. In this way, film narratives and the social-historical context in which they are produced, consumed and reconsumed provide a further space for musical mediations.

Specifically, I am interested in the iconic portrayal of modern musical technologies and cosmopolitan musical aesthetics in Malay films that sonically and visually articulated the aspirations of an era of nascent independence. Such technologically shaped music and its attendant visual representations mediated an aesthetic of cosmopolitan modernity

---

[14] Brown, 'The social liminality of musicians', p. 6.
[15] Antoine Hennion, 'Music and mediation: Toward a new sociology of music', in *The Cultural Study of Music: A Critical Introduction*, ed. Martin Clayton, Trevor Herbert and Richard Middleton. London: Routledge, 2003, p. 81.

in Malay films. Film music was also mediated by the technological, economic and social context of the film studio system. Observing the musical mediation of modernity through specific musical technologies of production, such as playback recording methods, musical instruments and the medium of film itself, exposes an inherent cultural acceptance and embodiment of modernity during this epoch.

Technologically Shaped Aesthetics of Intimacy

Paul Théberge considers how technologies of popular music such as the microphone and electric amplification are crucial—and yet largely ignored—to the formation of popular music since the beginning of the twentieth century. The post-war technologies of musical reproduction contributed significantly to a shift in the vocal aesthetics of Malay music during the era of film and recorded music. According to Théberge, the extensive use of the microphone gave rise to 'a new, intimate style of singing, known as "crooning".[16] This vocal style was popularised by American singers such as Bing Crosby who developed an approach to singing that

> exploited the intimacy offered by the microphone to great effect: his more 'masculine', 'husky' sounding baritone voice not only differed from the style of singing adopted by many of the other early crooners but its low register was also particularly enhanced through the microphone through the physical phenomenon known as the 'proximity effect'.[17]

---

[16] Paul Théberge, "'Plugged in": Technology and popular music', in *The Cambridge Companion to Pop and Rock*, ed. Simon Frith, Will Straw and John Street. Cambridge: Cambridge University Press, p. 5.

[17] Ibid. My discussion of the role of the microphone in shaping national musical cultures is inspired by similar studies of its use in other non-Western musical cultures. Martin Stokes, "Abd al-Halim's microphone', in *Music and the Play of Power in the Middle East, North Africa and Central Asia*, ed. Laudan Nooshin. Aldershot: Ashgate, 2009, pp. 55–73 examines the social, gendered and nostalgic implications of the prominent and iconic use of the microphone by the 1950s Egyptian crooner and film star, 'Abd al-Halim Hafiz. See also Martin Stokes, 'Listening to Abd Al-Halim Hafiz', in *Global Soundtracks: Worlds of Film Music*, ed. Mark Slobin. Middletown, CT: Wesleyan University Press, 2008, pp. 309–33. Amanda J. Weidman, *Singing the Classical, Voicing*

This microphone aesthetic can be heard in the vocal style of the Indonesian comedian and baritone crooner Ahmad Syech Albar who assumed the explicitly referential stage name Bing Selamat. He was well known in the recorded and live music scene of the 1950s and 1960s in both Indonesia and the Malay Peninsula.[18] In the Singapore-based Malay film industry, P. Ramlee's baritone crooner style, as well as the smooth, 'husky' alto voices of Normadiah and Saloma, were suited to the vocal amplification provided by microphones; these vocal qualities could not have been projected adequately in an unamplified context.

There was a gradual aesthetic transition from live *bangsawan* or Malay theatre performances and gramophone recordings prior to the Second World War to the improved recording technologies of the post-war record and film industries. Female *bangsawan* singers such as Mak Dara—still heard in 1960s Malay films—continued to employ the higher registers and nasal timbres that were developed for unamplified projection in large *bangsawan* theatres.[19] Miss Rubiah, in her performance of the *keroncong* song 'Sayang di Sayang' (Sweetheart Is Loved, comp. Zubir Said) in the film *Rachun Dunia* (Poison of the World, 1950, dir. B.S. Rajhans), embodies a transitional style, at times slightly nasal in higher registers but also smooth in lower registers. Prior to being a film playback singer and popular recording artist in the late 1940s, Miss Rubiah was an active *bangsawan* performer.[20] Like most

---

the Modern: *The Postcolonial Politics of Music in South India*. London: Duke University Press, 2006, pp. 59–60, 86–97 discusses the paradoxical and contested politics regarding the use of the microphone in shaping a new aesthetic of classical Indian music since the 1930s.

[18] H. Asby, 'Kalau dia menyanyi menyuroh orang teringat kapada Bing Crosby' [When he sings he asks people to remember Bing Crosby], *Bulanan Gelanggang Film*, April 1961, pp. 6–8; Azlan Mohamed Said, *Musika: Malaya's Early Music Scene (Arena Muzik Silam Di Malaya)*, ed. Juffri Supa'at. Singapore: Stamford Printing, 2013, pp. 240–41.

[19] A notable performance by Mak Dara singing and dancing an improvised *dondang sayang*-style song takes place in the film *Sri Mersing* (1961, dir. Salleh Ghani). This performance is a useful reference to sung performance styles found in *bangsawan*. See Tan, 'From folk to national popular music', pp. 294–98.

[20] Her most famous recording is 'Bunga Tanjung' recorded in 1947 on HMV. See Ahmad Sarji, *P. Ramlee: Erti Yang Sakti* [P. Ramlee: The Sacred Reality]. 2nd ed., Petaling Jaya: MPH, 2011, p. 330; and Azlan, *Musika*, pp. 108–9.

popular singers around the world in the 1950s and 1960s, the successful careers of Rubiah, Normadiah, Saloma, Bing Selamat and P. Ramlee can be attributed in part to the technological mediation of an increasingly electrified film and popular music aesthetic.

This technological and aesthetic shift in Malay films can also be heard in the use of instruments corresponding to specific musical styles. Jazz or jazz-like music was commonly used as a marker of musical modernity and classiness. As such, modern jazz instruments were fetishised in musician-themed film narratives as important markers of character identity. P. Ramlee's unique position as a film star and musician afforded him leading roles that articulated this affectation of modern musical technologies. He took on leading roles as a musician protagonist in the following films: *Ibu* (Mother, 1953, dir. S. Ramanathan) features him as a jazz trumpeter that performs in cabaret halls (Figure 4.1); *Anak-ku Sazali* (My Son Sazali, 1956, dir. Phani Majumdar) showcases him as a commercially successful violinist and composer who gets his songs pressed on records (Figure 4.2); *Antara Dua Darjat* portrays him as jazz pianist, piano tuner and piano teacher (Figure 4.3); in *Ibu Mertua-ku* he is a radio broadcast tenor saxophonist and band leader (Figure 4.4); and *Tiga Abdul* (The Three Abduls, 1964. dir. P. Ramlee) features him wielding an electric guitar as a musical instrument shop owner (Figure 4.5). In all these films, Western instruments and technologies (trumpets, gramophones, pianos, electric guitars, saxophones, radios) and musical styles such as jazz mediate a cosmopolitan modernity for musician protagonists. Furthermore, such music mediated the experience of modernity and capitalism to the films' audience, who were consumers of the mass-produced technology of the cinema and popular music. In considering these heroic musician archetypes, with their iconic instruments, musical technologies presented in screened narratives mediated Malay identities that were modern and cosmopolitan. They were, at the same time, indicative of the social-economic life of urban artists in the entertainment industries of the Malay Peninsula in the mid-twentieth century. While these images or personae signal a cosmopolitan modernity both visually and sonically, what might we discern from the technological processes or practices used to create the portrayals of musical characters in film?

Figure 4.1 P. Ramlee plays the trumpet in a jazz cabaret nightclub in *Ibu*

Figure 4.2 P. Ramlee listens to his composition on the gramophone in *Anak-ku Sazali*

Before you start to play, you should learn to identify musical notes first.

Figure 4.3 P. Ramlee teaches piano in *Antara Dua Darjat*

Figure 4.4 P. Ramlee, the studio recording musician, wields both a saxophone and microphone in *Ibu Mertua-ku*

Figure 4.5 P. Ramlee plays the electric guitar in *Tiga Abdul*

Recording Playback Film Songs

A glimpse of how music was recorded in a film studio environment is presented in the pages of the Malay Film Productions' magazine *Majallah Filem*. In an article titled 'Merekam Lagu Filem' (Recording Film Songs) in May 1960, the process of recording a traditional Malay folk song 'Ikan Kekek' (Kekek Fish) for the film *Sumpah Wanita* (A Woman's Oath, 1960, dir. Omar Rojik) prior to shooting a film is explained.[21] In addition to a list of the musicians, there are photographs

---

[21] This is a process of playback recording, a practice for recording film songs prior to the films being shot in order for the actors to lip-sync to the pre-recorded song while the film is being shot. This production process and its history in Indian cinema are documented and explained in detail in Anna Morcom, *Hindi Film Songs and the Cinema*. Aldershot: Ashgate, 2007, and Gregory D. Booth, *Behind the Curtain: Making Music in Mumbai's Film Studios*. New York: Oxford University Press, 2008.

of them in the recording studio.[22] The photographs include an image of P. Ramlee on the vibraphone and acting as the conductor for the recording. In addition, the vocal parts of the song involved a chorus of male actors and one director (H.M. Rohaizad) who worked for the film studio.[23] The interaction of the film's director with recording technology is aptly noted:

> While the musicians and singers adhere to their individual musical responsibilities, the director, Omar Rojik is not left out [of this process] as he intently watches the meters of the recording console.[24]

The article concludes by stating that the new arrangement and recording will bring 'new life' and 'increased popularity' to the already famous song.[25]

This example from the promotional magazine indicates how technological processes were presented positively to film audiences by depicting the modern aspects of film and music production. Linked to this promotion of modernity was a sense of valuing local tradition in the reproduction of Malay folk songs like 'Ikan Kekek'.[26] Modern musical methods were seen as a way of renewing the practices of the past. At the same time, the involvement of various studio personnel portrays a communal environment resonant of the Malay *kampung* in tandem with these modern technologies. In other words, a *kampung* ideal is enmeshed

---

[22] The musicians listed are Yusoff Osman (bass); Subrinyo, Nordin, Osman Ahmad, Chee Sai, Boon Liew, Wandi, Kam Leng (violins); Yusof B. (tenor saxophone); Ahmad Kassim (piano); A. Rahim (bongos); and Kassim Masdur (Masdor) (guitar). 'Merekam lagu filem' [Recording film song], *Majallah Filem*, May 1960, p. 33.

[23] The male singers listed are H.M. Rohaizad (an emerging film-writer and director), Salleh Kamil, Ali Fiji, Omar Suwita, Muhammad Hamid, Aziz Jaafar, M. Rafie and Omar Harun. Ibid.

[24] Ibid. '*Sementara pemain2 musik dan penyanyi2-nya patoh dengan kewajipan masing2, pengarah Omar Rojik tidak ketinggalan mengamat-amati meter perkakas recording.*'

[25] '*Lagu Melayu yang terkenal ini, di-perchayai akan menjadi lebeh popular dengan susunan musik baru, lagi hidup.*'

[26] For a transcription of this song for a *caklempong* (gong chime) ensemble see Patricia Matusky and Tan Sooi Beng, *The Music of Malaysia: The Classical, Folk and Syncretic Traditions*. Aldershot: Ashgate, 2004, p. 170, citing Mohd Anis Md Nor, *Zapin: Folk Dance of the Malay World*. Singapore: Oxford University Press, 1993.

with the modern urban space of a recording studio.[27] Interestingly, the personnel involved—while exclusively male in this recording—were of different ethnicities, notably the instrumental musicians and staff in the recording booth.[28] The article effectively fetishises a technologically mediated space of film music recording in its idealistic portrayal of the film studio's communal atmosphere and multiethnic personnel. The film music studio was portrayed as a microcosm of the modern Malay nation—a nation constructed from the visionary leadership of a prime minister/director, aided by the technical expertise of its government administration/sound engineers with the collective support of its citizens/musicians and singers.

Such mediations of modernity through musical technologies signal the cosmopolitan aesthetic and active adaptation and embodiment of the modern technologies that permeated Malay films in the period of emergent national autonomy. While much has been said about the expression of postcolonial autonomy in the Malay world through outlets such as newspapers and other print media, less has been said about the political and social impact of musical practices.[29] Musical practices reproduced and disseminated through emerging technologies were important in shaping the narrative culture of nation-making. As indicated by the intersecting music recording and film production economies, the technological mediation of Malay voices and music was a cosmopolitan process that extended the pluralistic interaction of musical

---

[27] Post-war Malay texts and films depicted the idealistic notion of the *kampung* as the source of positive moral and communal values in opposition to the ills of modernity. See Joel S. Kahn, *Other Malays: Nationalism and Cosmopolitanism in the Modern Malay World*. Singapore: Singapore University Press, 2006.

[28] In the recording booth, aside from Omar Rojik, the assistant director Kemat Hassan and recording engineer Kam Sim Boon are mentioned.

[29] The most important studies on the social and political impact of musical practices in Malaysia during this period can be found in Tan Sooi Beng, *Bangsawan: A Social and Stylistic History of Popular Malay Opera*. Singapore: Oxford University Press, 1993 and Mohd Anis Md Nor, *Zapin*. More recently, Tan 'Negotiating "His Master's Voice"' and Peter Keppy, 'Southeast Asia in the age of jazz: Locating popular culture in the colonial Philippines and Indonesia', *Journal of Southeast Asian Studies* 44, 3 (2013): 444–64 have examined cosmopolitan recording musicians who challenged colonial rule in the Malay Archipelago from the 1900s to 1940s.

practices that had existed prior to the local film industry's emergence. Ironically, the mediation of cultural plurality by new technologies was expressed within the homogenised frames of a vernacular Malay film and music industry that was and continues to be imagined as embodying a narrow ethnonational aesthetic.

Ethnonationalist narratives also intersected with concerns about rapid modernisation and a growing class consciousness. The nascent nationalistic and social ideologies of the urban-centred Malay intelligentsia permeated the narratives of film from the mid-1950s to early 1960s. I am particularly interested in social films because until the 1960s they were quite rare due to the fact that *bangsawan* or tradition-themed films were more popular with the mass Malay audience. Thus social films were a new means of relaying contemporary issues amid a modernising environment. In these films, local concerns and traditional values are musically mediated with visual and sonic representations of Western modernity and urban immorality in the postcolonial context. Social films of the 1960s can be said to represent musical 'Westernisms' as a mark of cosmopolitan modernity or progress—qualities deemed to be required of emergent postcolonial nations in need of a definitive national culture. Musical technologies and the representation of those technologies were integral to this portrayal of postcolonial modernity and national autonomy.

As discussed below, Malay society's interaction with and adoption of Western modernity in the 1960s were often contradictory. On the one hand, Western urban traits were regarded with suspicion or anxiety in social films. On the other, Western cosmopolitan music was embodied and expressed as local and natural. *Ibu Mertua-ku* even goes so far as to defend the position of musicians who perform Westernised music. Or was such music just considered 'local' by the musicians performing it?

Narratives of Class

Antara Dua Darjat and *Ibu Mertua-ku* highlight the issue of class inequality brought about by post-war modernisation, urbanisation and capitalism through a focus on musical personalities. These films were largely set in the multiethnic urban centres of Singapore and

Penang, depicting the social life of musicians as part of a communal Malay working class. The narrative of Malay communal values in the face of rapid urbanisation and modernisation was an effective way to articulate ethnonationalist ideology for a mass audience. The emphasis of nationalist, anti-colonial and socially conscious themes in Malay literature and political writing had a direct impact on film narratives. The Malay writers' collective ASAS '50 promoted political themes through literature, modern theatre and film. Direct interaction between ASAS '50 and film-makers occurred through the contributions of the organisation's writers, including A. Samad Said, Masuri S.N. and Noor S.I., to P. Ramlee's *Gelanggang Filem* (Film Arena) magazine.[30] By the early 1960s issues of colonialism, nationalism and class pervaded Malay literary and film culture. These issues were articulated as central to the experience of being a Malay under modern urban conditions. Such Malay-centred social narratives expressed

> a critique of British rule, not only for its cultural impositions, but for its encouragement of a division within Malay society between a Malay bureaucratic elite and the masses. The Malay experience was represented as an interplay between the forces of feudalism and colonialism and the masses. The survival of the suffering and steadfast poor in an inhospitable social environment was contrasted with the lives of hypocritical and callous rulers, obsessed with sensual gratification.... The city, no longer an evil in itself but colonised by Malays on the move, was a chalice of corruption, dominated by upper classes in a state of moral collapse. 'Malayness' was associated with values embedded in the rural masses; it rejected elitism.[31]

Unlike the 1950s, when directors from India were mainly responsible for Malay films, the 1960s saw a surge of Malay film-writers and directors

---

[30] T.N. Harper, *The End of Empire and the Making of Malaya*. 2nd ed., Cambridge: Cambridge University Press, 2001, p. 285; Timothy P. Barnard, 'Gelanggang Film', *Cinemas of Asia* 1 (2012).

[31] Harper, *The End of Empire*, p. 302.

who articulated more class-conscious and nationalist narratives.[32] The slow but steady increase of social films set in contemporary and urban settings also marked a shift from commercial, vernacular themes to more political, nationalist narratives.

Modern-sounding or Westernised popular music flourished as it suited the contemporary setting of these films. The most famous song from the Malay film music canon, 'Getaran Jiwa', featured in the class-conscious social film *Antara Dua Darjat*. The song stands out for its overtly modern style, employing a Latin American beguine rhythm and a pseudo-classical romantic or jazz-like piano introduction and harmonic arrangement. While the song is commonly perceived as a sentimental love song, it was presented in the context of a very socially conscious if not actively political narrative about the ills of a feudal mindset in modern times. Before I analyse the social and musical discourses of this film, I place the trajectory of social themes in Malay films into historical perspective by briefly discussing the first commercially successful activist social film produced and written by Malays in the Singapore film industry.

The Malay Film Productions' film *Penarek Becha* (Trishaw Puller, 1955) was the directorial debut of P. Ramlee, adding to his existing prominence as a film star, singer and songwriter. The film also marked the beginning of Malay activists raising social and political concerns through the wide reach of film. P. Ramlee wrote the film in collaboration with the literary activists Abdullah Hussain and Jamil Sulong, highlighting issues of poverty and class inequalities to convey a message that championed individual—and by extension national—agency in the face of archaic traditions and anxieties towards modernity.[33] In *Penarek*

---

[32] For a table of Malay film productions in Singapore from 1953 to 1965 that indicates film directors by 'race', see Timothy P. Barnard, 'Decolonization and the nation in Malay film, 1955–1965'. *South East Asia Research* 17, 1 (2009): 77. The year 1955 saw the first and only film directed by a Malay (rather than an Indian or Filipino), but that number steadily rose to 14 films directed by Malays in 1965. See also Harper, *The End of Empire*, p. 283 who indicates that by 1960 four Malay directors were employed by Cathay-Keris.

[33] Barnard, 'Decolonization and the nation in Malay film', p. 75; Timothy P. Barnard and Jan van der Putten, 'Malay cosmopolitan activism in post-war Singapore', in *Paths*

Becha, the positive values of modernity are highlighted in strong female characters that mediate moral relations between the impoverished and the wealthy, the traditional and the modern.[34] The film's heroine (and de facto 'hero') Azizah (Saadiah) is a modern and confident young Malay woman from a rich family. She is a student in an all-women's vocational school that teaches young women modern domestic skills such as using sewing machines and baking Western cakes. A similar school in Singapore close to the offices of the film's writers was the inspiration for the Azizah character. Timothy Barnard suggests that the film's poor trishaw pedaller protagonist, Amran (P. Ramlee), is primarily motivated by Azizah 'to look beyond his traditions'—an ideal that captures the modern nationalist aspirations of young Malay activists at the time.[35] William van der Heide views Azizah's self-determination in the face of patriarchal barriers as more blatantly defiant than 'her counterparts in Indian films'.[36] It is useful to draw comparisons across these film cultures—especially considering the avid consumption of Hindi films by Malay-speaking audiences—as van der Heide's observation indicates an agential depiction of female characters particular to a Malay modernist narrative.

The notion of individual agency operates within a class-based narrative that emphasises communal values over selfishness and greed. Joel S. Kahn suggests that the emphasis on communalism in P. Ramlee's films mediates 'between the nationalist narratives of Malay intellectuals and the experience of the broader Malay public'.[37] As such, what is observed by Rohayati Paseng Barnard and Timothy Barnard as 'binary oppositions' in the film—an arrogant and greedy villain versus a humble and poor hero—are used allegorically to facilitate the eventual realisation

---

Not Taken: Political Pluralism in Post-War Singapore, ed. Michael D. Barr and Carl A. Trocki. Singapore: NUS Press, 2008, p. 145.

[34] Rohayati Paseng Barnard and Timothy P. Barnard, 'The ambivalence of P. Ramlee: *Penarek Beca* and *Bujang Lapok* in perspective', *Asian Cinema* 13, 2 (2002): 20.

[35] Barnard, 'Decolonization and the nation in Malay film', p. 75.

[36] Van der Heide, *Malaysian Cinema, Asian Film*, p. 174. Van der Heide cites the films *Awara* (1951, dir. Raj Kapoor) and *Andaz* (1971, dir. Ramesh Sippy) for comparison.

[37] Kahn, *Other Malays*, p. 130.

of positive Malay communal values.[38] Amran's kindness and humility originate in his modest rural community as he works tirelessly on his trishaw to earn a meagre living to support his ailing mother. Conversely, the film's villain, Ghazali (Salleh Kamil), owns a car and obnoxiously requests samba music in preference to traditional Malay *inang* music at a nightclub.[39] Azizah's rich but miserly father (Udo Umar) eventually sees the error of his ways and welcomes Amran into his family. However, it is argued that an ambivalence is present in the mediating role of Azizah—the saintly, upper-class protagonist who sympathises with the poor and lifts Amran from his lack of self-confidence to overcome his dire situation.[40] The character of Azizah can be seen as reflecting the unique position of the activists who wrote the film. P. Ramlee and his collaborators were successful Malay urbanites in bustling Singapore. They were, like Azizah, mediating their modern cosmopolitan aspirations for national autonomy with the concern of the working-class, rural Malay community for upholding traditional values in the face of rapid and uncertain social changes.

Antara Dua Darjat (1960)

Between Class and Music

Antara Dua Darjat, also directed by P. Ramlee, continues the trajectory of class-based narratives in Malay film, but presents discourses shaped by music about Malay modernity, culture and society in the 1960s. The non-linear narrative of this social film focuses on the tragic relationship between Tengku Zaleha (Saadiah), a young woman of royal lineage, and Ghazali (Ramlee), a pianist of humble means.[41] Zaleha meets Ghazali while on holiday with her family at their country mansion Anggrek

---

[38] Barnard and Barnard, 'The ambivalence of P. Ramlee', pp. 12–13.
[39] Through a discussion of Ghazali's character in the film, Kahn, *Other Malays*, p. 163 unravels the complications and paradoxes of hybridity in Malay culture.
[40] Barnard and Barnard, 'The ambivalence of P. Ramlee', pp. 20–21.
[41] For the sake of clarity, I present the plot in a linear fashion. The honorific 'Tengku' is accorded to Malays born of royal lineage.

(Orchid) Villa. Zaleha and her family are residents of Singapore and the country home is situated somewhere across the Causeway in Johor—a quiet rural retreat from the city. Zaleha's father (Ahmad Nisfu) is resolved to ensure that Zaleha does 'not mingle with youngsters who are not of the same royal blood lineage'.[42] Replacing an indisposed band from Singapore, Ghazali and his band, who reside in a nearby village, are hired to perform for Zaleha's birthday party. The band performs in a range of Western and Latin styles, portrayed as a musical montage, slipping from a cha-cha to jazz ballad to samba to waltz for a dancing crowd. On hearing Ghazali mesmerise the party crowd with his original song 'Selamat Panjang Umur' (Best Wishes for a Long Life),[43] Zaleha is smitten and finds a way to spend more time with him by convincing her father to employ him as her piano teacher. Over an undetermined period of time—weeks or months perhaps—screened as a piano-centred musical montage, Zaleha's piano skills progress exceptionally. After Zaleha's remarkable musical progress, Ghazali decides to test her with his own composition, 'Getaran Jiwa'. Aside from marking Zaleha's competence on the piano, the song's performance also confirms the blossoming love between the two. When Zaleha's father learns of their relationship, the lovers are dramatically separated. Ghazali is beaten unconscious and Zaleha is forcefully sedated and immediately taken to Singapore. There, when Zaleha awakens, a confrontation breaks out between her mother (Rahimah Alias) and her stepbrother (Kuswadinata). Zaleha's stepbrother reveals disparagingly that her mother was a 'cabaret woman' and does not have the right to stand up for her daughter. After calling the police to circumvent his potentially violent actions, he kills the mother by hitting her on the head with a heavy object. Zaleha manages to protect herself with a handgun until the police arrive. Her stepbrother is arrested and

---

[42] *'Tidak layak kamu bercampur-gaul dengan pemuda-pemuda yang bukan keturunan darah diRaja.'*

[43] The lyrics for this song were written by S. Sudarmaji. He is also portrayed in the film as a saxophonist for the band performing this song. Before he performs it, Ghazali informs his band to play 'Selamat Hari Jadi' (Happy Birthday). However, the official name for the song is 'Selamat Panjang Umur', as documented in the P. Ramlee songbook. See Arkib Negara Malaysia, *Senandung Warisan* [Song Legacy]. 2nd ed., Kuala Lumpur: Arkib Negara Malaysia, 2008 (Orig. publ. 2004), p. 55.

her father, traumatised, becomes mentally ill, leaving Zaleha with all the family's wealth. She then marries a man of noble blood, Tengku Mukhri (S. Kadarisman), who is intent on appropriating her inheritance. He is revealed to have a love affair with a woman (Rahmah Rahmat) already pregnant with his child. Zaleha, Mukhri and his friend Tengku Aziz (Yusof Latiff) return to a neglected Anggrek Villa for the newly-wed couple's honeymoon. Eventually Zaleha reunites with a dishevelled and broken Ghazali and explains her side of the story. Until then Ghazali had believed her to be dead. Aziz deduces the entire situation but compassionately pleads with his friend to let the lovers be. Mukhri, who does not accept any of this, attempts to kill his friend and Ghazali. In the end, Mukhri, on the verge of shooting Ghazali, is shot dead by Aziz who survives Mukhri's earlier attempt on his life.

While the film highlights status or class as an impediment to morality, the responsibility to be moral lies in the hands of the upper-class protagonists. The moralistic and dramatic conclusion of the film makes Aziz, a man of royal lineage, the accidental hero of the film. On the other hand, Zaleha may be seen as a mediating character similar to Azizah in *Penarek Becha*. But Zaleha is presented as more of a liminal character—she is only partially of royal blood as revealed via her mother's origins as a cabaret artist and commoner. Musically, she also transcends the depiction of the working class as entertainers or producers of music who perform for the enjoyment of the upper classes. Aside from using piano lessons as a foil for her father's restrictions, she excels remarkably on the piano as a producer of music—performing what is arguably the most famous piano introduction to P. Ramlee's best-known film song, 'Getaran Jiwa'.[44] As a woman, like the class-mediating female protagonists of previous films, Zaleha is bound by a restrictive patriarchy but she is simultaneously empowered by her upper-class position. Moreover, this is the first Malay film featuring a woman as an

---

[44] Kassim Masdor informed me that the pianist who performed this film version of 'Getaran Jiwa' was Ahmad Kassim; he was an exception to the emphasis of musical literacy in the film, as he was unable to read musical notation, playing and learning the most challenging classical and jazz repertoire entirely by ear. Interview with Kassim Masdor, Experience in the Malay Film and Popular Music Industry, 2013.

instrumental musician. Prior to this, women were portrayed as singers but never as instrumentalists. In fact the female voice is absent from all of the film's songs, except for the chorus singing the birthday song 'Selamat Panjang Umur'. In representation at least we see the mutually reinforcing roles of music and the upper-class female protagonist as mediators of the tensions between class and modernity in Malay society.[45]

In *Antara Dua Darjat*'s narrative, class differences are mediated through musical production, consumption and expressions of intimacy. Working-class musicians perform music for upper-class consumption. The doomed lovers are separated by social standing but are brought together by musical exchanges. In some instances, music is used as a means of resistance against antiquated restrictions. Music even connects the poor and the rich in brief moments of pleasure; the upper-class birthday party crowd gathers around the piano and sings along to a working-class musician's composition. The village-based musicians use Western instruments and perform modern jazz and Latin music (Figure 4.6). The musician characters are also metaphors for village communalism. In a telling scene, Ghazali's cousin Sudin (S. Shamsuddin) storms off with the band's double bass to serenade his love interest. As he walks off, Ghazali reminds him that they have a practice session later in the evening, to which Sudin retorts, 'I already paid my fees!'[46] One of his bandmates then replies, 'Have we not paid our fees too?'[47] This indicates the communal economy of the village band in which the bandmates pool their resources to rent instruments. The village featured in the film is a very musical one. Scenes set in the village always have the *keroncong* music of the band practising in the background—the scene that introduces the village features Ghazali, Sudin and the band playing the P. Ramlee *keroncong* song 'Alunan Biola' (Sound of the Violin). At

---

[45] The earliest documentation of a Malay woman in a musical role but either singing or dancing is in an article on Salamah Basiron, a young female songwriter. 'Salamah Basiron: Penggubah muda yang berjiwa gelora' [Salamah Basiron: The young composer who is so turbulent], *Bintang dan Lagu*, November 1966, pp. 14–15.

[46] '*Aku pun bayar yuran dah!*'

[47] '*Kita pun tak bayar yuran, ke?*'

the end of their performance, Zaleha's chauffeur approaches them in the pouring rain. The chauffeur's uniform makes Sudin mistake him for being a 'general' and he gets the band to stand to attention in the middle of their song. After correcting this misunderstanding, the chauffeur asks them to help push his car out of the mud and the band obliges without question. The band's helpfulness in this scene also reflects the idealised spirit of village society. Thus, musical practice and musicians are associated directly with the *kampung* and communal living. Music, while presented as the foundation for communal interaction, is also capable of leaving the space of the village and penetrating the modern home and social activities of the urban nobility, acting as a bridge between two classes. Music is the medium that penetrates these class divisions through intimacy.

Figure 4.6 The party band in formal Western attire

Overall, music binds the narrative and moral direction of the film in a recurring poetic metaphor of the film's script. The film starts with interior shots of the abandoned Anggerik Villa amid a turbulent thunderstorm. This metaphor is then introduced during this scene by a ghost-like narration voiced by P. Ramlee. Zaleha is struggling to sleep in Anggerik Villa in the middle of the storm when she hears the disembodied voice of Ghazali utter the following words: 'Zaleha, rhythm and melody cannot be separated. If separated, the melody will be disordered and art will be ruined.'[48] This phrase also emerges as a prominent theme in the lyrics of 'Getaran Jiwa' sung by P. Ramlee (Appendix A.5).[49]

The metaphor of rhythm and melody is repeated again in the middle of the film's narrative by Ghazali and Zaleha as they assure each other of their mutual commitment and inseparability:

Zaleha: Ghazali, why can't rhythm and melody be separated?
Ghazali: If they are separated, song will be disordered and art will be ruined.
Zaleha: What if you and I are separated?
Ghazali: Our romance will be disordered and our lives will be ruined.

Here, the relationship between rhythm and melody obviously speaks to the romantic inseparability of the two protagonists. While *irama* as 'rhythm' and *lagu* as 'melody' are the most logical translations of the terms in relation to the film's narrative, this metaphor is relatively open to multiple interpretations. *Irama* could be used to describe an entire musical style, rhythm, groove and/or melody of a song (*lagu*).[50] For example, *irama Malaysia* is a genre of music that emerged in the 1990s, while the term *irama* is used to denote tempo in Javanese gamelan

---

[48] '*Zaleha, irama dan lagu tidak dapat dipisahkan. Kalau dipisahkan, pincanglah lagu dan rosaklah seni.*'

[49] Mustafar Abdul Rahim and Aziz Sattar, *Filem-Filem P. Ramlee* [The Films of P. Ramlee]. Senawang: MZA Terbit Enterprise, 2008, pp. 196–97 suggest that 'Getaran Jiwa' shares some melodic similarities with 'Wang Bu Liao' (Unforgettable), sung by Lin Dai in the film *Bu Liao Qing* (Love without End, 1961, dir. Doe Chin). The piano introduction to 'Wang Bu Liao' is also similar to the one performed by Ahmad Kassim in 'Getaran Jiwa'.

[50] Based on definitions in *Kamus Dewan*. 4th ed., Kuala Lumpur: Dewan Bahasa dan Pustaka, 2007.

music.[51] *Lagu* is used as the more general term denoting individual songs of different genres or repertoire (for example, *lagu rock* or *lagu* 'Getaran Jiwa'), while in some instances it is synonymous with the term *irama*.[52] Aside from the poetic and ambiguous usage of the terms, *irama* and *lagu* are apt metaphors for the distinctions of class perceived in modern Malay society. As the moralistic narrative tries to demonstrate through this musical metaphor, the rich are connected to common people and both classes are mutually dependent on each other. Working-class servants and entertainers service the lives of the upper class and the latter are responsible for the welfare of the poor.

The mediating role of music is particular to a specific period of modernity and nascent nation-making. In the previous chapter, I highlighted the notion of 'sounded authority' in feudal communities, where Malay rulers used loud sounds as markers of territorial control.[53] By contrast, in narratives about Malay society in the films of the 1950s and 1960s music negotiated authority through intimacy. Morally grounded leaders were still responsible for the dispensation of justice—as seen in Aziz's intervention—but the feudal class divide was no impediment to the inseparable intimacy of two lovers just as melody is intrinsically bound to rhythm. When Ghazali presents the sheet music for 'Getaran Jiwa', Zaleha teasingly says, 'Oh no! Five flats.'[54] This indicates both the difficulty of the song—five flats indicating the challenging piano fingering of D-flat major—and Zaleha's musical proficiency. Moreover, she makes the comment in a flirtatious and affectionate manner—a sentiment that is encapsulated by the Malay term '*manja*'—expressing a veiled confidence in her musical skills. This comment also indicates a naturalisation of Western musical practices into Malay musicality, whereby modern musical knowledge mediates the cultural obstructions that underscore the intimate relationship

---

[51] For a discussion on the *irama Malaysia* genre, see Tan, 'From folk to national popular music', pp. 303–5; and Matusky and Tan, *The Music of Malaysia*, pp. 410–12.

[52] *Kamus Dewan*.

[53] Barbara Watson Andaya, 'Distant drums and thunderous cannon: Sounding authority in traditional Malay society', *International Journal of Asia Pacific Studies* 7, 2 (2011): 19–35.

[54] '*Alamak! Lima flat.*'

between Zaleha and Ghazali. Ghazali, a commoner, is also in a position of authority as Zaleha's teacher. But Zaleha, as a woman, provides instrumental accompaniment for Ghazali's singing in a reversal of the usual Malay musical practices. As a result, multiple layers of authority, class and gender are reversed and rendered ambiguous in the intimate musical interactions between Zaleha and Ghazali.

Antara Dua Darjat provides layers of discourses concerning class, modernity, music and gender in the Malay narrative of emergent nationhood. Despite the nuanced mediations of gender and class through musical intimations, people in predetermined positions of power such as the urbanised nobility ultimately decide the fate of the rural masses. I now turn to a more detailed reading of *Ibu Mertua-ku*, released two years after *Antara Dua Darjat*. Made during the peak of his career in Singapore, *Ibu Mertua-ku* is considered the most critically successful of P. Ramlee's social films. My analysis does not situate *Ibu Mertua-ku* as a canonical film. Rather it is seen as a significant culmination of the themes of music, modernity, class, gender and emergent cosmopolitan nationhood articulated by independence-era Malay films.

Ibu Mertua-ku (1962)

In *Ibu Mertua-ku* musicians and their social environments become symbolic of working-class marginalisation in modern urban portrayals of a postcolonial Malay nation. Aside from the social position of musicians, the tensions between tradition and modernity are expressed in various narrative themes throughout the film. Examining this film intertextually, music mediates modernity and nation-making via three prominent themes: social anxieties towards modernity embodied in the protagonist's physical blindness; constructions of the modern self through musical identity; and an embrace of modernity in the film's musical articulations. While modernity is contested and regarded with suspicion in *Ibu Mertua-ku*, it is also embodied in its musical themes and expressions. The cosmopolitan music of social films mediated the tensions of traditional Malay values coming to terms with the rapid changes in ideology and lifestyle brought about by independence.

Visual Anxieties, Sonic Conciliation

Ibu Mertua-ku deals with the trope of blindness. The musician protagonist Kassim Selamat (P. Ramlee) loses his vision as a result of weeks of crying and two years of isolation after his wife's apparent death in childbirth. It is later revealed that his mother-in-law lied about his wife's death as part of an elaborate scheme to expunge him from her upper-class family. Barnard reads this against other traditional Malay historical and film narratives in which the motif of blindness is present. The loss of sight in P. Ramlee's film is part of a modern narrative that emphasises 'the melancholy (*sedih*) of a character' coming to terms with 'the emptiness of the modern world'.[55] In the context of Singapore in 1962, the theme of blindness functioned metaphorically to represent the alienation of Malays from traditional or rural practices and values in the face of increased urban migration and contested national boundaries.[56] This articulation of moral anxiety towards modernity is expressed through the blindness motif in three Malay films made in the late 1950s and early 1960s in which 'characters denigrate their servants, manipulate their relatives, place a monetary value on all interaction and even kill their mothers'.[57] Thus, a reading of these films reveals how local film-makers were engaging their target audiences' ambivalence towards postcolonial modernity and the attendant social and political changes.

How, then, might blindness and moral anxiety towards modernity be linked to music in Malay film? On the one hand, Kassim's blind musicality and hearing are linked to a moral purity in opposition to the excesses of modern life that are encountered through seeing. On the other, musical practices in the film can be seen as modern or cosmopolitan, but are ultimately naturalised as local or culturally neutral expressions. In fact, modern musical practices are actually defended against the selfish and materialistic goals of the film's modern upper-class

---

[55] Barnard, '*Sedih sampai buta*', p. 439.

[56] Ibid., p. 447.

[57] Ibid., p. 451. Besides *Ibu Mertua-ku*, the films considered in Barnard's study are *Korban Fitnah* (Slanderous Sacrifice, 1959, dir. P.L. Kapur@Usmar Ismail) and *Sayang Si-Buta* (Pity the Blind One, 1965, dir. Omar Rojik).

protagonists. The narrative sympathetically decries the admonishment of musicians as belonging to an inferior working class. After getting married, it is the irrational obstruction of Kassim's musical career by his wife Sabariah (Sarimah) that indicates a conflict in their relationship and a loss of Kassim's identity. Conversely, it is the rediscovery of Kassim's musical self that heals his grief. Beyond the trope of blindness, the discourse of music in the film articulates a desire for modernity through intimacy. Musical discourse also reconnects the protagonist to a morally grounded self that eschews the ills of modernity. In addition, the cosmopolitan musical styles and instruments used in the film further signal an acceptance of modernity through aesthetic practices. While the theme of class reveals antagonisms towards emergent modernities, aesthetic references to classiness provide a more conciliatory approach to modernity in the film's musical expressions of cosmopolitanism.

Musically Shaped Identity

Kassim's musicality is desired, dissolved and renewed at integral points in the film's narrative. In fact, it is his musicality that becomes synonymous with his self, whether through his occupation as a professional entertainer or through the material extension of his musicality in the form of his saxophone. Initially, at the start of the film, Kassim's voice is heard over the radio inducing a display of desire by Sabariah, a young Malay woman from a rich family. This scene portrays the most overtly sexual moment in the film. It is a moment of craving for Kassim's voice and musicality without actually seeing him. Sabariah is so infatuated with his musical persona that she calls the radio station in the hope of setting up a date with him. A flirtatious exchange on the telephone between the two leads to a comic blind date scenario. Kassim and Sabariah only see each other after a series of false set-ups involving their respective friends. Van der Heide reads Sabariah's desire for Kassim as a 'superficial infatuation' implying that merely hearing a voice is not a valid reason for true emotional attachment.[58] This surface desire is also applied

---

[58]   Van der Heide, *Malaysian Cinema, Asian Film*, p. 201.

to Kassim's character who 'is metaphorically blinded by Sabariah's beauty to not notice how fundamentally shallow she is'.[59] While compatible with the thematic emphasis on blindness, these readings are deaf to the profound sensual and emotional impact music and the voice have on the characters. Sound minus vision is reduced to the surface element of romantic desire and connection. Both readings fail to hear the centrality of the film's musical text in charting the narrative trajectory of Kassim's construction, dissolution and renewal of self.

In two crucial moments of his blindness, Kassim symbolically loses his music and later regains it. At the peak of his mourning, Kassim is forced to leave his dark and modest dwelling beneath a house. To show appreciation for his landlord's kindness—allowing him to stay rent-free for two years—he leaves his saxophone as a form of payment. This marks an abandonment of his self. He says to his landlord Ali (Mat Zain): 'This is my life. Take this saxophone and do what you like.'[60] This submission of his life to Ali in the form of his saxophone marks a dissolution of self. Later, when he is housed by the kind-hearted Mami (Zainon Fiji), he hears a tenor saxophone being played by a neighbour. He then asks Mami's daughter Chombi (Zaiton) to bring the neighbour and his saxophone to his room. The young man named Bayen (Ali Fiji) bears a striking resemblance to P. Ramlee in his younger days.[61] In an iconic moment of 'rebirth' he plays Bayen's saxophone and performs an instrumental version of 'Jeritan Batin' (Wailing Soul). He gestures in a stylised portrayal of fluid, natural and masterful musicality that he is Kassim Selamat, the renowned Singaporean bandleader. In contrast to Bayen's unaccompanied playing, the non-diegetic sounds of orchestrated violins and a jazz band—similar to the one heard at the radio station—accompany Kassim's performance. As Kassim plays, Bayen whispers to Chombi that he sounds like Kassim Selamat. This is confirmed by

---

[59] Amir, *120 Malay Movies*, p. 226.

[60] '*Ini nyawa saya. Ambillah saxophone ini dan buatlah apa yang Abang Ali suka.*'

[61] I draw this observation from Amir, *120 Malay Movies*, p. 228: 'I don't think it's an accident that the teenage boy, Chombi's neighbour, who's trying to play the sax looks uncannily like the scrawny youth P. Ramlee was.'

a friend of Mami's, Mahyudin Jelani (Ahmad Nisfu),[62] who overhears the music when entering the house. This musical revelation marks a recovery of self for Kassim, with the conduit for his self symbolised by the saxophone.

It is important to note that when hearing Bayen practising, Kassim says to Chombi, 'I hear the voice [*suara*] of a tenor saxophone.'[63] The choice of the word '*suara*' meaning 'voice' over the expected '*bunyi*' or 'sound' indicates the personification of the instrument. In contrast to this, P. Ramlee does something amusing in his stylised emphasis on the phrase 'tenor saxophone'. The Englishness of the phrase is emphasised in a subtle moment of mockery indicating both a postcolonial sense of irony as well as an attachment to the 'classy' culture of Western popular music. An extended portrayal of this accented poking fun at Englishness is found in the film *Labu dan Labi* (Labu and Labi, 1962, dir. P. Ramlee), in which P. Ramlee and Mat Zain parody 'the pretensions of Britons' by speaking 'a mixture of Malay and English'.[64] Such parodic slippage indicates the complications of decolonisation in that era, in which the affectations of the West were mocked but also deeply entrenched within local cultural practices. That single line in the film indicates several layers of postcolonial identity that are revealed in the character of Kassim as well as the personal position of P. Ramlee as a cosmopolitan musician, composer and film-maker.

It turns out that Mahyudin, the owner of a Malay magazine,[65] is an entrepreneur and offers to bring Kassim on tour 'all around the Malay Peninsula and on radio', guaranteeing his success.[66] Kassim then embarks on a tour as a blind saxophonist-singer, using the pseudonym

---

[62] Ahmad Nisfu is also credited as the scriptwriter of the film. Ahmad's character refers to himself as 'Mamak'. For a Malay-speaking (or contemporary Malaysian) audience, this immediately identifies him as part of the Jawi Peranakan or Indian Muslim community in Penang.

[63] '*Abang Osman dengar suara tenor saxophone.*'

[64] Barnard, 'Decolonization and the nation in Malay film', pp. 85–86.

[65] Mahyudin mentions that he is the owner of a magazine named *Cenderamata Review*. Penang had been a centre for radical Malay-language publications since the 1930s. Barnard and van der Putten, 'Malay cosmopolitan activism in post-war Singapore', p. 133.

[66] '*Kassim Selamat. Mamak ada satu cadangan. Mau tak bersama Mamak kita pusing seluruh Tanah Melayu dengan radio? Mamak dah guarantee tentu baguih (bagus).*'

Osman Jailani. His rising popularity is attributed to the novelty of his blindness paired with his astonishing musical talent. The narrative circle is almost complete as Kassim's self is reborn in a new musical persona. Throughout the narrative, Kassim's identity is discarded, recovered and renewed through musical signifiers. Aside from his voice and musicality, Kassim's saxophone features as a prominent marker of his identity. The saxophone can also be understood as symbolic of embracing modernity against the overarching anxiety towards modern morality commonly read into this film.

Beyond the theme of blindness as a mode of expressing the anxieties and tensions inherent in a modernising Malay society, how do musical styles and instruments operate as signifiers of modernity? While the saxophone signifies Kassim's identification with modernity, unlike the critique of modern morality found in the tragic blindness-by-grief and consequent blindness-by-self-mutilation, the instrument in *Ibu Mertua-ku* comes to represent a modernity that is morally neutral or even compatible with Malay values. It is indeed a Western instrument not found in traditional Malay folk music, and as indicated by the film's music underpins a more jazzy or modern cosmopolitan soundscape. The saxophone, in its associations with modernity, is naturalised as part of a musically cosmopolitan Malay culture. This is indicated in the opening credits that are framed by a tenor saxophone (Figure 4.7). In short, the instrument has become synonymous with the film's fictional character, Kassim Selamat.[67] Ironically, the film gave rise to the common misconception that P. Ramlee was adept at playing the saxophone. The prominent Malay Film Productions' composer Yusof B. actually performed the saxophone parts. In the opening credits, his role as 'solo tenor saxophone' is prominently displayed alongside P. Ramlee's and Saloma's credits as playback singers. Thus, the display and use of the instrument were important markers of the film's character. Alongside the film's pianist, Ahmad Wan Yet, Yusof B. is featured as a stage musician in a jazz cabaret dance hall called the Capitol Blue Room, setting the scene

---

[67]   I recall security personnel at Malaysian airports teasingly making references to me as 'Kassim Selamat' when passing my saxophone through baggage security screenings.

for Kassim and Sabariah's first blind date.[68] Kassim Masdor, who portrays the on-screen pianist in Kassim Selamat's band but actually performs the accordion parts, informed me that Yusof B. was known as a 'sweet … crying tenorist', very much in line with and perhaps the inspiration for the film's narrative theme.[69] When I asked Kassim Masdor if there was a real-life musician who inspired the Kassim Selamat character, he told me that P. Ramlee was inspired by Sadao Watanabe, who in the early 1960s was a fast-rising jazz alto saxophonist from Japan and had just released his first album in 1961. This adds another cosmopolitan twist to the musical articulations of the film. The film's hero was the product of a deeply cosmopolitan understanding of identity, music and modernity in Singapore in the early 1960s.

This film is one of a number that feature P. Ramlee as a musician hero. The construction of the musician hero around P. Ramlee was also a convenient intertextual reference for him, given that he was brought into the Singaporean film industry as a musical talent. Moreover, the use of musician protagonists linked seamlessly to the song sequences of Malay films from the 1950s and 1960s.[70] While all these convenient fictional and real-life connections regarding P. Ramlee's musicality have been noted in existing scholarship on Malay films, there has been a lack of analysis on how the cosmopolitan music of these films intimated a conciliatory expression of postcolonial Malay cultural practices coming to terms with modernity.

---

[68] The scene that momentarily features Yusof B. on the bandstand of Capitol Blue Room is the setting for Kassim and Sabariah's first meeting. The band, featuring Ahmad Wan Yet on the piano and Yusof B. on saxophone, slip into the background from diegetic to 'scource' music (the combined effect of diegetic 'source' and non-diegetic 'score' music) for the ensuing humorous narrative. Kassim and Sabariah are anxious about meeting each other for the first time, not knowing what each other looks like—having only communicated by phone—so both of them send their friends as proxies while they watch on secretly. These false representations play on the theme of not genuinely 'seeing' each other that pervades the film's narrative.

[69] Interview with Kassim Masdor, Experience in the Malay Film and Popular Music Industry, 2013.

[70] Van der Heide, *Malaysian Cinema, Asian Film*, p. 201.

Figure 4.7 Opening credits of *Ibu Mertua-ku* framed by a tenor saxophone

Consonant Modernities

The songs written and sung by P. Ramlee in *Ibu Mertua-ku* indicate in their cosmopolitan musical aesthetic a convergence of modernity with a narrative that seeks to critique modern morality. While an overall anxiety towards the ills of modernity is present in the story, the musical formations accompanying that narrative are paradoxically consonant with modern and pluralistic articulations of musical styles and culture. The narrative direction of *Ibu Mertua-ku* is diegetically complemented by three featured songs performed by P. Ramlee. The lyrical and musical content of these songs is relevant to the dramatic narrative. The songs also express cultural stylistic tropes that diverge and converge with the film's overarching themes of modernity and morality in a cosmopolitan Malay world.

The light-hearted beginning is in stark contrast with the rest of the film which takes on a tragic and melodramatic tone. Parallel to this narrative trajectory, the severity of blindness and the emotional register of featured songs become more sombre towards the end of the film. Musically, the theme of 'blind desire' in the first song 'Jangan Tinggal

Daku' (Don't Leave Me) in relation to the initially comic narrative is contrasted with the more emotionally weighted 'Di Mana Kan Ku Cari Ganti' (Where Would I Find a Replacement)[71] and 'Jeritan Batin' (Wailing Soul). These last two songs are performed at two moments of Kassim Selamat's blindness.

'Di Mana Kan Ku Cari Ganti' is sung in a reflection on his tragic predicament and in sympathy with Chombi (his second love interest) mourning her deceased husband. It marks his realisation of the unfairness of the world and connects him with a kindred spirit who shares his grief. The opening verse is sung in the *syair* style of spoken poetry. P. Ramlee's adaptation, however, approximates the sound and style of a *syair* performance in its use of implied Arabic *maqam* scales—a commonly used tonality in Malay folk singing—and does not match the formal *syair* rhyming verse structure.[72] He sings the following in the opening verse:

Hendak 'ku 'nangis tiada berairmata	I want to cry but there are no more tears
Hendak 'ku senyum tiada siapa nak teman	I want to smile but there is no one with me
Kalaulah nasib sudah tersurat	If fate has been written
Beginilah, apa 'nak buat	It is so, what can I do

Alongside lamentation, the song's introduction signifies indigenous Malay musical and cultural practices and aesthetics. Compared to the film's other songs, this is by far the most 'Malay' musical moment; this indigenous aesthetic is linked to Malay values of humility and honesty. It is thus rhetorically framed in opposition to the excesses of modernity seen and heard in the more cosmopolitan and Western sounds of the city. These sounds can be heard in the contrasting spaces of Singapore and Penang as they are portrayed in the film. Until this moment in the film, the music of the city has been characterised by perceivably modern

---

[71] Lyrics by S. Sudarmaji.

[72] The *syair* rhyming verse structure was adapted to the *bangsawan* and *ghazal* repertoire and in religious Islamic *nasyid* music, in which Arabic *maqam* scales are employed to recite such verse structures. See Matusky and Tan, *The Music of Malaysia*, pp. 77, 265, 353. See also Mulaika Hijjas, *Victorious Wives: The Disguised Heroine in 19th-Century Malay Syair*. Singapore: NUS Press, 2011 for an important study on the agential role of women in *syair* texts from Riau.

styles and contexts: Latin rhythms, jazz cabaret halls and Western instruments. It is significant, then, that at Kassim's moment of grieving a local *syair* style is used to contrast the ills of modernity. Ironically, the *syair*-styled verse is placed over a rubato piano accompaniment, a convergence of modernity with indigeneity via a cosmopolitan aesthetic. This cosmopolitan aesthetic is perpetuated in the rest of the song. Similar instruments to the radio band seen at the beginning of the film—bongos, accordion, piano, double bass with the addition of violins—accompany P. Ramlee's singing in a merged aesthetic of *syair*-inflected modalities in the voice, violin and accordion parts, Malay and Latin percussion, and Western tonal jazz-inflected harmonisation in the piano accompaniment. The song represents a moment of conciliation and healing for Kassim and Chombi. These scenes of Kassim singing the song on his bed and Chombi watching and listening to him intently on the floor are juxtaposed with double exposures of Chombi and her deceased soldier husband, while another double exposure shows Kassim and his presumed-to-be-dead wife, Sabariah. As the visually represented memories of their deceased beloveds are magnified by the song, they are also drawn together sonically by their mutual grief.

Musically, it is important to highlight Chombi's position as a listener in this song in contrast to Sabariah's act of listening in the film's opening song. Chombi's listening is portrayed as deeper and more emotionally sincere compared to Sabariah's 'surface' and sensual response to Kassim's voice over the radio. To elaborate on what was briefly noted earlier, the scene of the radio broadcast of 'Jangan Tinggal Daku' shows Sabariah stroking her radio while listening to Kassim Selamat's saxophone solo (Figure 4.8). She then leans on her bed in uncontrollable ecstasy while listening to the song. This depiction of Sabariah's untamed sexual desire being tied to her 'insincerity' reflects the male authorship of the film and also speaks to conservative Malay values. Acceptable morality and sincerity are more clearly portrayed in Chombi's reaction. Her response to Kassim's music is portrayed as sincere and empathetic. Her emotional listening to 'Di Mana Kan Ku Cari Ganti' becomes a cathartic and therapeutic experience for mourning her lover (Figure 4.9). Sharing Kassim's sense of loss, she watches him praying—without his knowledge—for her well-being.

Figure 4.8 Sabariah stroking her radio during Kassim Selamat's saxophone solo

Figure 4.9 Chombi and Mami listen to Kassim singing 'Di Mana Kan Ku Cari Ganti'

The problematic association of female sexual desire with superficiality arises from these contrasting characterisations. This is of course another moral metaphor articulating the overall thematic anxiety towards modernity. The extroverted, immoral and modern personality of Sabariah presented as a pleasure-seeking and sexualised listener is contrasted to the passive, morally grounded and non-urban personality of Chombi as a melancholic and sympathetic listener. Chombi facilitates and encourages Kassim's career as a blind musician; earlier in the film, Sabariah obstructs him from working as an entertainer. Sabariah becomes the embodiment of the shallow-minded, self-absorbed and extravagant upper-class Singaporean, while Chombi represents the open-minded, self-sacrificing and humble persona of a middle-class Penangite. Thus the women of the film—as consumers, receivers and interpreters of music—are allegories of archetypal opposites: working class and bourgeois, city and village, modernity and morality.

However, there is a convergence or conciliation of those opposing themes, as the perceived dichotomies in *Ibu Mertua-ku*'s narrative are actually more nuanced. Chombi and her mother are in fact from an upper-class family; they live in a large, traditional-looking Malay house, own a car and employ a chauffeur. The idea of Penang as oppositional to Singapore is ambiguous. After all Penang had also been part of the British Straits Settlements and was similarly urban and cosmopolitan. Indeed, when Kassim and Sabariah move to Penang they spend their honeymoon at a luxurious hotel and are entertained over a Western-style dinner with a jazzy cabaret song performed by the popular Malay singer Saloma.[73] In a later scene in Penang, forbidden by his wife from working as a musician, Kassim's humble job as a construction site labourer is punctuated by the loud and modern sounds of a large pile-driving machine. Penang was far from antithetical to the modernity represented

---

[73] Saloma, who was also P. Ramlee's third wife, originally performed the song 'Jelingan Mata' (Flirting Eyes) in the film *Azimat* (1958, dir. Rolf Beyer), but a portion of the film's song scene was included in the hotel honeymoon scenes of *Ibu Mertua-ku*. It cannot be ascertained who composed the music as the title credits portion displaying this information seems to be damaged and was edited out of the existing digital copy. In the scene featuring the Capitol Blue Room nightclub, there is also a brief shot of Saloma's show poster.

in Singapore. The sonic and musical content of seemingly oppositional urban spaces thus indicates a conciliation of modernities.

This conciliation of modernities is further heard in the third P. Ramlee song, 'Jeritan Batin'. The song is performed three times: as an instrumental featuring the song's melody on the tenor saxophone; sung by P. Ramlee with musical accompaniment; and the instrumental version is repeated in the background score in the final scene. In all three versions, the saxophone is present. The first is played in a private space—Mami and Chombi's home in Penang—resulting in the exposure of Kassim's true identity. The sung version includes an instrumental introduction on the tenor saxophone and is performed in a concert hall. Stylistically, all versions of 'Jeritan Batin' are musically cosmopolitan in line with the other songs heard throughout the film. In all its manifestations it is arranged with strings, piano, accordion, Latin percussion (particularly the conga) and double bass as accompaniment for the saxophone and vocal melody. Musically, the song is presented and arranged in a very cosmopolitan if not Western aesthetic. This modern musical aesthetic lends a modern Western style to the film in line with its urban setting and theme.

The song plays an integral role in the narrative development of the film as well. The first performance reveals Kassim's identity and marks a rebirth of his self. The second performance is set in a concert hall in Singapore at the end of Kassim's new musical tour as Osman Jailani (Appendix C.4 for musical transcription). It is during this performance that Sabariah and her new husband, Dr Ismadi (Ahmad Mahmud), are uncomfortably made aware of Kassim's existence and blindness. The melancholic content of the song emphasises the guilt felt by Sabariah and Ismadi over abandoning him for their better lives (Appendix A.6). Sabariah's guilt is then shown in her abruptly leaving the concert in the middle of the song. As the sung verse ends, Kassim plays a saxophone solo. The solo is then slipped into the background of the next scene of Sabariah and Ismadi lying on their bed. Over the echoing and muted saxophone solo, Sabariah asks Ismadi to operate on Kassim's eyes. This sparks the last portion of the tragic narrative, which leads to Kassim's sight-enabled realisation of the world's ills and unjust deceptions. After regaining his sight, Kassim grasps that his presumed deceased wife

Sabariah is alive and married to the doctor who returned his vision. The son he fathered with Sabariah is now four years old and displays musical inclinations. After his mother-in-law's admission of this protracted deception he mutilates his eyes with two forks. The final dramatic scene is set in the foyer of Sabariah and Ismadi's upper-class home. Kassim, with blood dripping from his eyes, leaves the house and is met by Chombi and her family. Following this, the saxophone melody of 'Jeritan Batin' begins to play synchronously with a shot of Sabariah at the entrance of her home crying in remorse. Ismadi walks into the house in shock. As the song is heard, the final image is of Kassim, Chombi, Mami and Mahyudin walking away into darkness.

Metaphorically, they are walking away from the modern ills of Singapore back home to the more morally grounded Penang. As concluding music, the saxophone melody of 'Jeritan Batin' encapsulates the emotional themes of the narrative: melancholy, loss, longing, blindness and alienation. Aside from these negative aspects there are also positive interpretations—a conciliation or negotiation of different kinds of modernity. As Amir Muhammad notes:

> I read a recent critique of this film as being 'defeatist' because the hero chooses to become handicapped at the end. It was obviously written by someone who looked at the film without really seeing it, as *Ibu Mertua-ku* affirms the vital importance of being able to see without prejudice or pretence.[74]

Along the lines of Amir's favourable assessment of the film's nuances, I add that such a reading can also be applied to the musical meanings expressed in the film. Listening to the music in *Ibu Mertua-ku* reveals the conciliatory mediation of modernity through musical style and instrumentation. Music mediates this modernity as a cosmopolitan aesthetic representative of actual cultural practices that were taking place in the Malay Peninsula in the 1960s. While the lifespan of social films may have been fleeting, a plurality of modern musical practices

---

74 Amir, *120 Malay Movies*, p. 228.

had already been present in the region prior to the production of Malay-language films. Thus the themes of modern anxiety and moral decay in the film's narrative were particular to a discourse of ethnonationalism that sought clear binaries in the process of forming a homogenised notion of nationhood. A sense of *kampung* values was set against the moral ills of the city. A working-class male musician was a victim of an upper-class matriarch. The kind and generous inclusivity of Penang was preferred to the cold and superficial exclusivity of Singapore. Beyond these narrative dichotomies, it is more difficult to find such oppositions in the film's music. Even the *syair*-like opening verse of 'Di Mana Kan Ku Cari Ganti' is arranged in a Westernised style. While the use of a Western-derived musical aesthetic can be attributed to the modern urban setting, such musical practices indicate the ambiguities and paradoxes of a modern period of nation-making that was articulated by Malay artists and film-makers in the 1960s. Moreover, the cosmopolitan aesthetics, technologies and narratives about music in Malay films mediated the cultural tensions and social dissonances of a modernising society with an ethical and conciliatory vision of a nation in the process of forging an identity.

Conclusion

P. Ramlee's social films of the 1960s that featured musically orientated narratives were consistent with a modern vision of a Malay nation. Such conciliatory expressions of modernity were mediated through an aesthetic of *classiness* shaped by a history of modern musical technologies, instruments and styles that reflected a vibrant cosmopolitan environment. The urban milieu of Singapore was also conducive for Malay literary activists to spread class-conscious ethnonationalist narratives through the wide-reaching medium of film. In these social narratives, female characters were integral in negotiating modern notions of progress and self-determination with traditional values of Malay communalism. Moreover, the musical intimations and practices of these films provided a conciliatory space for the mediation of binary relationships: poor men serenade rich women; a rich woman learns music from a poor man; a young woman uses music to usurp her controlling father; rich patrons consume the musical performances of poor musicians; a poor musician makes rich people realise their immorality. These narratives were articulated as variegated relationships of power and gender.

The analysis of *Antara Dua Darjat* reveals that while rural communal values and traditional hierarchical notions of leadership are emphasised, multiple layers of authority, class and gender are reversed and made ambiguous in the intimate musical interactions of the film's protagonists. There is a rare portrayal of a woman in a non-singing role, playing an instrument to accompany a male singer. Despite being a student of a male teacher, she displays agency in her confident musicality and cunning deception in using musical lessons to spend time with her love interest, defying the imposed limitations of her class-conscious father. Thus the metaphor of the 'inseparability of rhythm (*irama*) and melody (*lagu*)' employed throughout the film resonates with the mutually dependent gendered and powered relationship between individuals of opposing classes in modern Malay society.

Ibu Mertua-ku depicts a more ambivalent narrative of class but is insightful in its overt music-orientated theme. Beyond a modernist narrative of blindness, the film portrays musicians as representative of a marginalised working class. The protagonist's tenor saxophone is synonymous with the loss, recovery and renewal of his self. Contrary to common interpretations of the narrative as a rejection of modern excesses and immorality, the saxophone is symbolic of a consonant modernity. Western or cosmopolitan musical instruments and styles operate as signifiers of an embraced or assimilated modernity. The featured songs in the films nearly all demonstrate a modern Western aesthetic in instrumentation and arrangement. The exception is the *syair*-like introductory verse of 'Di Mana Kan Ku Cari Ganti', which is at best a reference to musical indigeneity as it is arranged in a hybrid cosmopolitan style. This does not discount the local in this hybridised expression, but indicates the innateness of what are understood as Western, foreign or exogenous musical practices. Indeed, the limited hybridity of the film's music indicates a long history of mediated stylistic differences in the pluralistic musical practices of the Malay Peninsula and Southeast Asia since before the 1900s.[75]

While women feature in few musical performances, they are significant as listeners, interpreters, disruptors and enablers of music. The two female leads of *Ibu Mertua-ku* are allegorically opposed: Sabariah embodies the superficial desires of urban immorality while Chombi personifies the compassionate affection of not-so-urban communal values. Unlike the agential role of Zaleha in *Antara Dua Darjat*, they are objectified as opposing archetypes of the film's Manichaean themes. Nonetheless, there is a more nuanced convergence and conciliation of those themes in the perceived narrative dichotomies. The sonic and musical content of the supposedly oppositional urban spaces of Penang and Singapore indicates a consonant modernity. My own reading of *Ibu Mertua-ku* differs from the common interpretation of the film as a contestation of modern decadence in Malay society. Interpreting musical discourses and practices in social films reveals more positive responses to forms of acceptable modernity.

The fluid pluralities found in Malay film music in the 1960s reveal a trajectory of cosmopolitanism that had long existed in the cultural practices of the region. However, the mediation of such practices through the aesthetic technologies of international mass popular music distribution and consumption is also present in the Western-derived styles, Latin rhythms and jazz instrumentation of the two films' musical aesthetic. While modern social immorality was contested in Malay film narratives, musical discourse and practice were expressions of an innate and local sense of modernity—a 'rooted cosmopolitanism'.[76] Unlike other cultural and political issues of modern nation-making that were regarded with anxiety and ambivalence, music was an aesthetic space where modern Westernisms were negotiated favourably and also naturalised as local cosmopolitan practices.

---

[75] Tan, 'Negotiating "His Master's Voice"'; Keppy, 'Southeast Asia in the age of jazz'.

[76] Tan, 'Negotiating "His Master's Voice"', pp. 460, 490–91; Benedict Anderson, 'Colonial cosmopolitanism', in *Social Science and Knowledge in a Globalising World*, ed. Zawawi Ibrahim. Kajang and Petaling Jaya, Malaysia: Malaysian Social Science Association and Strategic Information and Research Development Centre, 2012, pp. 371–88.

This chapter looked at the period that represented the zenith of the Singapore-based Malay film industry, revealing how the incorporation of supposedly exogenous musical practices into a local and emergent nationalistic artistic expression was favourably mediated. The next chapter discusses a slightly later period of Malay-language films. The adoption of new musical styles and cultures from the West—particularly British and American rock 'n' roll—came to represent a threat to established Malay national conceptions of musical purity. This period from the mid-1960s to the early 1970s marked the era of a self-conscious youth culture: long-haired men, miniskirted women, Beatlemania and a surge of rock guitar bands. These youths challenged the older generation's musical aesthetic sensibilities and presented a cultural and moral threat to the conservative national authorities of Singapore and Malaysia. The rise of *pop yeh yeh* youth culture had an effect on the declining Malay film industry. This is examined in the context of ethnonationalist state policies and ideologies on what constituted 'acceptable' music and youth behaviour, the moral discourse among youth themselves, and the inclusion of youth music culture in Malay film.

Chapter 5

Disquieting Denouement[1]

Oh gitar berbunyi
Menawan hati sedang berahi
Oh rancaknya irama
Dapat mikat sukma
Gadis dan teruna
Mari cari teman gembira
(Oh the guitar sounds
Attracting hearts in passion
Oh how lively this rhythm is
Able to attract youths
Young ladies and bachelors
Let's find a happy partner)
'Bunyi Gitar' (Sound of the Guitar), music by P. Ramlee, lyrics by S.
Sudarmaji

The pleasures and emotional drives of the other (in our midst or just
beyond our borders) so often serves as a focus for the rage of social
groups that feel their core identities are under threat.[2]

---

[1] This is a modified and expanded version of Adil Johan, 'Disquieting degeneracy:
Policing Malaysian and Singaporean popular music culture from the mid-1960s to
early-1970s', in *Sonic Modernities in the Malay World: A History of Popular Music,
Social Distinction and Novel Lifestyles (1930s–2000s)*, ed. Bart Barendregt. Leiden:
Brill, 2014, pp. 135–61.

[2] Martin Stokes, *The Republic of Love: Cultural Intimacy in Turkish Popular Music*.
Chicago: University of Chicago Press, 2010, p. 193.

In October 2012 I visited a modest exhibition on Malay youth music from the mid- to late 1960s at Singapore's Esplanade Library. The minimalist and silent exhibition created by the Malay Heritage Centre of Singapore featured five two-sided panels displaying photographs and historical information about the Malay rock 'n' roll bands of the *pop yeh yeh* era (Figure 5.1). It was part of a series of nostalgic cultural exhibits intended to shed light on a vibrant but often overlooked period of cultural history in the Malay Peninsula. Quite unlike the quiet atmosphere of the exhibition, the Malay youth of the *pop yeh yeh* era expressed a culture that was apparently in need of silencing by the aggressive cultural policies implemented by the governments of Malaysia and Singapore. This chapter examines the renewed interest in *pop yeh yeh* and gives voice to the contested discourses and issues that were articulated by Malay youth that featured prominently in the films of this time.

Figure 5.1 Display on 1960s Malay youth music

The rise of youth culture and music coincided with the demise of the Malay studio film industry. In fact, the incorporation and representation of this musical culture in films of the mid-1960s marked a shift in the production and consumption of Malay music from films to the new youth-orientated record industry. Young film composers such as Kassim Masdor would find new employment in international record companies such as EMI that were interested in cultivating local youth music.[3] This transition also overlapped with the increased promotion of separate Malaysian and Singaporean national cultures. Boundaries of national identity were being enforced and the youth of this burgeoning musical culture found themselves on the margins.

The discussion here seeks to provide some much-needed amplification for the study of Malaysian and Singaporean music by observing the ways in which Malay youth of the mid-1960s to early 1970s were implicated in the cultural policies and conservative regimes of nation-making. These young people negotiated their differences from the older generation in divergent ways: some actively and proudly fashioned themselves according to the subversive styles and sounds of the West, while others voiced conservative concerns about such trends, effectively policing their peers with discourses of morality and tradition. While the analysis is not primarily concerned with government policy in relation to music, I discuss the ideas of two film music icons, Zubir Said and P. Ramlee, whose ideas on Malay music culture inspired the implementation of the Malaysian National Culture Policy that was drafted in 1971. Their reactionary comments about the erosion of Malay culture by youth-related lifestyles and musical dispositions provide an ideological frame of reference for the discourses of cultural nationalism that demonised *pop yeh yeh* youth.

I then discuss youth music culture in Singapore and Malaysia followed by a reading of the 'yellow cultures' or subversive youth trends that caught the negative attention of government authorities.[4] The beat

---

3   Interview with Kassim Masdor, Experience in the Malay Film and Popular Music Industry, 2013.

4   Andrew F. Jones, *Yellow Music: Media Culture and Colonial Modernity in the Chinese Jazz Age*. Durham, NC: Duke University Press, 2001, p. 6 describes how the term 'yellow' was used in China during the Republican era to associate a degenerate and 'pornographic' quality to the popular music of Li Jinhui that blended 'American jazz, Hollywood film music, and Chinese folk music'.

music of English-language bands primarily based in Singapore in the 1960s emulated British rock bands such as the Shadows and the Beatles. In time, English songs were adapted into Malay, and eventually, by the mid-1960s, Malay youth started writing and performing original compositions in the styles of Western rock bands they had previously emulated. A vibrant array of youth fashions went along with this music that included tight-fitting clothing, sunglasses, miniskirts for women and long hair for men. The Singaporean and Malaysian governments were active in policing what were deemed degenerate 'yellow cultures', resulting in youth harassment and the banning of music performances. Some youths themselves were also active in the policing of their peers as fan letters in the Malay music magazine *Bintang dan Lagu* (Stars and Songs) indicate.

Youth music was introduced in Malay films from the mid- to late 1960s. Contrary to suggestions that Malay youth music 'directly corresponded to the decline of the Malay film industry' at the time,[5] youth music featured prominently in Malay films and each influenced the other. Initially, youth music was used parodically or inconsequentially. However, the inclusion of youth music also signalled its immense popularity and the need for Malay film producers to appeal to the new youth audience. This chapter examines how the film *Muda Mudi* (The Youths, 1965, dir. M. Amin), which features the ageing star Siput Sarawak, incorporates youth culture and music into its narrative— but from the perspective of an older generation coming to terms with a culture that was seen as radically different from theirs. In fact, the film does not vilify or demonise Malay youth and their music. Rather, it offers a discourse of conciliation, in which the older generation encourages and advises youths to be cautious in their new-found success. The film is an allegory of the symbiotic relationship that the film industry would have with the emerging youth culture.

In order to provide an insight into contemporary discourses on Malay youth, moral degeneracy and music in the mid-1960s, the

---

5   Craig A. Lockard, *Dance of Life: Popular Music and Politics in Southeast Asia.* Honolulu: University of Hawai'i Press, 1998, p. 226.

discussion turns to the film *A Go Go '67* (1967) directed by Omar Rojik for Shaw Brothers' Malay Film Productions. This film was made during the twilight of Malay film production in Singapore. It exemplifies the effort the film industry made to attract a youth audience whose consumption patterns were straying from Malay cinema and being drawn towards local electric guitar bands and their numerous record releases. The once popular means of disseminating Malay music through film was being usurped by a renewed local record industry and its attendant *pop yeh yeh* culture.[6] The transition from film music to guitar band music contextualises the reactionary comments of film music icons such as P. Ramlee, whose cosmopolitan musical and cinematic practices in the 1950s were being replaced by louder sounds and less conservative fashions.

Malaysian government policy in the 1970s operated within a framework of Malay ethnonationalism that required clear delineations of what constituted 'pure' Malay culture. This led to the removal or avoidance of elements that were regarded as 'foreign', 'un-Malay' and non-Islamic.[7] Catherine Grant suggests that state-enforced ideologies of purity 'can give rise to the opinion that safeguarding—that is, "guarding

---

6   In the 1950s numerous singers for Malay films, including P. Ramlee recorded film songs for labels such as HMV, EMI, Columbia, Parlophone and Pathé. Ahmad Sarji, *P. Ramlee: Erti Yang Sakti* [P. Ramlee: The Sacred Reality]. 2nd ed., Petaling Jaya: MPH, 2011, pp. 290–98. For a detailed account of the record industry in Malaya before the war, see Tan Sooi Beng, 'The 78 RPM record industry in Malaya prior to World War II', *Asian Music* 28, 1 (1996/97): 1–41, and Tan Sooi Beng, 'Negotiating "His Master's Voice": Gramophone music and cosmopolitan modernity in British Malaya in the 1930s and early 1940s', *Bijdragen tot de Taal-, Land- en Volkenkunde* 169, 4 (2013): 457–94. The record industry was renewed through the proliferation of beat music bands in the 1960s. More research is required regarding the record industry centred on Singapore from the 1950s to 1960s, but Joseph C. Pereira says that there were numerous independent record labels emerging in the mid-1960s that capitalised on the proliferation of local youth bands. Interview with Joseph C. Pereira, Beat Music Bands in 1960s Singapore, 2012.

7   Tan Sooi Beng, *Bangsawan: A Social and Stylistic History of Popular Malay Opera*. Singapore: Oxford University Press, 1993, pp. 177–78. See also Tan Sooi Beng, 'From popular to "traditional" theater: The dynamics of change in *bangsawan* of Malaysia', *Ethnomusicology* 33, 2 (1989): 229–74, and Tan Sooi Beng, 'Counterpoints in the performing arts of Malaysia', in *Fragmented Vision: Culture and Politics in Contemporary Malaysia*, ed. Joel S. Kahn and Francis Kok Wah Loh. Honolulu: University of Hawai'i Press, 1992, pp. 282–305.

safe" a tradition—straight-jackets it into a petrified form, forbidding it to be subjected to any processes of innovation and change that would normally feature in living, vital cultural heritage'.[8] This is quite unlike the kinds of created tradition, as examined in Chapter Three, represented by Zubir Said's film music. The mid-1960s was a period in which national traditions were already established and youth cultures featured as a threat to these recently formed 'national' traditions.

In Malaysia and Singapore, there has been a marked disjuncture between development-orientated national agendas based on capitalist ideologies and the 'modern' young population that is 'relentless' in the 'fashioning of ... youthful selves through [the] consumption' of popular culture.[9] These 'self-fashioning' youths spark 'moral panics' and 'social anxieties' in state authorities that respond by retaining and enforcing hegemonic state-sanctioned boundaries of modernity and morality.[10] In line with this youth–state tension, the role of the Malaysian government in controlling the 'threat' of youth cultures has historically run parallel to their initiatives to regulate the performing arts. As Tan Sooi Beng notes:

> By introducing various policies, guidelines and institutions in the 1970s and 1980s, the government has tried to centralize and control the performing arts. Those art forms which are in line with the national culture policy and performances which adhere to the stipulated guidelines have been promoted and encouraged. However, those which are considered 'anti-Islamic', those which are alleged to stimulate 'violence' and those which are generally 'undesirable' have been banned or censored.... Even the popular music industry, dominated by

---

[8]   Catherine Grant, 'Rethinking safeguarding: Objections and responses to protecting and promoting endangered musical heritage', *Ethnomusicology Forum* 21, 1 (2012): 37.

[9]   Maila Stivens, 'The youth, modernity and morality in Malaysia', in *Questioning Modernity in Indonesia and Malaysia*, ed. Wendy Mee and Joel S. Kahn. Singapore: NUS Press, 2012, p. 170.

[10] Ibid., p. 174, citing Jock Young, *The Drugtakers: The Social Meaning of Drug Use*. London: Paladin, 1971, and Stanley Cohen, *Folk Devils and Moral Panic: The Creation of the Mods and Rockers*. London: MacGibbon and Kee, 1972.

transnational companies and show promoters, has been subjected to the same intervening institutions and restrictions.[11]

Tan's observations point to the pervasiveness of Malaysian state intervention in the arts and allude to the role of state policies in constraining youth music cultures. Criteria for inclusion and exclusion are often vague, thus subjecting a range of cultural practices to prosecution, censorship or repression. Hence, the youths who participated in music counter-cultures—transmitted through a commoditised global market of cultural consumption—were at the centre of the government's initiatives to perpetuate a hegemonic national culture. Furthermore, tensions existed (and continue to exist) between the state and the recording and entertainment industries interested in marketing 'subversive' but highly attractive trends to local youths.

In the historical context of the waning Malay film industry in the late 1960s, young Malaysians and Singaporeans actively shaped local music practices based on trends from the West that were at odds with state-defined notions of national culture. It is nevertheless apparent that youth agency was not complete given that the marketing initiatives of the entertainment and print industries mediated the representations of 'degenerate' youth in conflict with the 'repressive' state. The Malay film industry also tried to rejuvenate its appeal to the broader public by featuring youth music. After initially taking a detour away from Malay films, this chapter unravels these issues historically and discursively, with a focus on Malay youths whose bodies and cultural practices were at the centre of contestation between state-sanctioned moral policing and the consumption of globally commoditised musical and cultural trends. Such contestations were articulated loudly in the final films produced by Cathay-Keris and Malay Film Productions. I argue that Malay youth cultural practices initiated such challenges to national cultural ideology in Malaysia and Singapore, providing a template for the discursive and physical repression of youth cultures in the future.

---

[11]   Tan, 'Counterpoints in the performing arts of Malaysia', p. 303.

The Ideas of Zubir Said and P. Ramlee:
Precursors to National Culturalism

Some of the earliest ideas for a Malay national culture can be found in the writings of Zubir Said and P. Ramlee. In the mid-1960s both composers became prominent critics of Westernisation in Malay music practices. Ironically, while both sought to infuse Malayness into their musical creations, they adapted a diverse range of musical styles from the West and other parts of Asia such as Hindustani film songs.[12] Despite their cosmopolitan musical backgrounds, the ideas they later proposed about developing and preserving a national culture would become standardised in the discourse of Malaysian national cultural policies after 1971. Here I look at some of their ideas that set the tone for the National Culture Policy.

There has been renewed interest in Zubir Said resulting in a comprehensive biography by his daughter Rohana Zubir and a series of events to commemorate his cultural contributions to Singapore: a musical tribute concert at the Esplanade concert hall (12 October 2012) and a 10-day series of screenings highlighting his film music at the National Museum of Singapore (10–20 October 2012). These celebrations

---

[12] For an account of the diverse Malay and Western musical styles used by P. Ramlee, see Ahmad, *P. Ramlee*, p. 275, and Clare Chan Suet Ching, 'P. Ramlee's music: An expression of local identity in Malaya during the mid-twentieth century', *Malaysian Music Journal* 1, 1 (2012): 16–32. A more contentious observation is made by Yusnor Ef, who argues that despite the internalisation of foreign musical styles P. Ramlee's music ultimately expresses 'soulfully Malay' qualities. Yusnor Ef, *Muzik Melayu Sejak 1940-An*. Kuala Lumpur: YKNA Network, 2011, p. xix. Andrew Clay McGraw, 'Music and meaning in the independence-era Malaysian films of P. Ramlee', *Asian Cinema* 20, 1 (2009): 53–55, however, argues that P. Ramlee's film music expressed a more heterogeneous but uniquely Malaysian musical aesthetic. As discussed in Chapter Three, Zubir Said, while working with the medium of film music and orchestration, actively used and adapted 'traditional' Malay instruments and styles for his film scores. Joe Peters, 'Zubir Said and his music for film', in *Majulah! The Film Music of Zubir Said*. Singapore: National Museum of Singapore, 2012, pp. 74–90 analyses his film music stylistically as a 'synthesis of musical systems in neo-traditional music', while Rohana Zubir, *Zubir Said, the Composer of Majulah Singapura*. Singapore: ISEAS Publishing, 2012 provides a detailed musical biography of her father emphasising his contribution to Singapore's national music repertoire.

of Zubir Said as a Singaporean national icon are paradoxical given he proposed Malay nationalist initiatives for the development of music and performing arts. Of course, his ideas were proposed during a period when Singapore and Malaysia had a shared national trajectory after colonial rule. In 1957 the Federation of Malaya was declared. Singapore, along with the Borneo states of Sabah and Sarawak, joined the federation to form Malaysia in 1963. In 1965 Singapore separated from Malaysia to form an autonomous republic. This thorny history of national boundaries is further complicated by the politics of ethnicity, in which Malays form an increasingly marginalised minority in Singapore but are a ruling majority in Malaysia. The prominence of Zubir Said's writings of ethnonationalism centred on Malay culture is thus difficult to reconcile with his retrospective invention as a Singaporean icon.

At a presentation given in 1956/1957 on the use of Malay in music, Zubir Said observed a decline in the standards of the language compared to the 'glorious days of the Malay sultanates', stating that under courtly patronage, musicians and artists were highly valued, while 'Malay singing and songs occupied a good position in the field of arts'.[13] In the context of modern Malay society, he further stated:

> The result of changes in the organisation of society leads to changes in the development of Malay sung arts. Singers [artists] and poets do not receive adequate patronage and there are artists born in society that do not take responsibility in the value of their creations. These changes have brought detriment to the songs and language used in songs due to the intrusion of foreign elements.[14]

To overcome this decline of local music culture, he proposed the following actions be taken by the state and the artistic community:

---

[13] '*zaman gemilang Kerajaan2 Melayu ... nyanyian2 dan lagu2 Melayu mendapat kedudokan baik pula dalam bidang kesenian*.' Zubir Said, 'Menuju tahun 1967' [Towards 1967], *Filem Malaysia*, June 1967, p. 20.

[14] Ibid.

1. Foreign elements that are destructive must be eliminated and [those that are] beneficial should be accepted.
2. Songwriters and singers [artists] must possess adequate knowledge of [Malay] language [vocabulary] and language usage [grammar].
3. A [nationalised] system for teaching singing and writing should be implemented in schools.[15]

Zubir Said's suggestions feature the primacy of language in preserving and effectively creating a shared national culture through the arts based on Malay ethnicity. The conscious inclusion of 'national' elements in 'Malay songs' would require an active if not artificial process of shaping a national consciousness through music. While defining a specifically Malay ethnicity is fraught with difficulties,[16] the emphasis on the Malay language as a unifier for a diverse range of peoples that inhabit the Malay Peninsula provides feasible grounds for a national identity. More importantly, this national identity would be forged through literature and music, and solidified by the active preservation and systemisation of knowledge concerning the language.

Another factor that contributed to this national cultural agenda was the selective exclusion of 'external' cultures. This was a process in which cultural boundaries needed to be clearly marked. However, in the post-colonial states of Malaysia and Singapore this was problematic due to their multicultural populations. Zubir Said suggested the need to remove 'foreign elements' that were considered 'destructive' while retaining 'beneficial' ones. The ambiguity here lies in the subjectivity of what was considered 'foreign' and how 'good' and 'bad' influences on Malay cultural practices could be assessed. As further examples below

---

[15] Ibid.
[16] Maznah Mohamad and Syed Muhd Khairudin Aljunied, eds. *Melayu: Politics, Poetics and Paradoxes of Malayness*. Singapore: NUS Press, 2011; Anthony Milner, *The Malays*. Chichester: Wiley-Blackwell, 2008; Timothy P. Barnard, ed. *Contesting Malayness: Malay Identity across Boundaries*. Singapore: Singapore University Press, 2004; Shamsul A.B., 'A history of an identity, an identity of a history: The idea and practice of "Malayness" in Malaysia reconsidered', in *Contesting Malayness: Malay Identity Across Boundaries*, ed. Timothy P. Barnard. Singapore: Singapore University Press, 2004, pp. 125–48.

suggest, the nation state would play a major role in creating criteria of inclusion and exclusion in the arts. Some of these criteria were also drawn from reactionary suggestions by cultural personalities such as P. Ramlee, who was coping with difficulty with the changing musical tastes of Malay youth.

Towards the end of his career in the late 1960s, P. Ramlee experienced a decline in popularity due to the impoverished local film industry and the rapid spread of popular music styles from abroad that rendered his music outdated and unmarketable. In a speech given at a congress on national culture in Kuala Lumpur in 1971, he expressed his frustrations by denouncing youth music cultures and upholding the need to advance traditional Malaysian music. These frustrations were closely tied to his departure from Singapore in 1964 for Malaysia, where he continued his film career at the newly established, underfunded and inexperienced Merdeka Film Productions' studio in Kuala Lumpur. He would make numerous films there until his death in 1973. Critics and historians lament that the quality and reception of his Malaysian productions failed to meet the standards of his Singapore films.[17] Times and tastes were changing. And despite his vibrant and diverse cosmopolitan musical influences, P. Ramlee began to represent a bygone era of antiquated Malay culture that did not speak to the younger, 'groovier', 'long-haired', 'marijuana-smoking' and 'miniskirt-wearing' youth of the 1970s.[18]

In his presentation to the congress, P. Ramlee noted the decline of traditional music and proposed solutions for this so-called problem. He lamented the encroachment of Hindustani music from India and music from the West that had

---

[17] Gordon T. Gray, 'Malaysian Cinema and Negotiations with Modernity: Film and Anthropology'. PhD thesis, Napier University, 2002. Gray identifies the nationwide sentiment that Malaysia's film output at the time was not successful.

[18] As discussed in detail in Chapter Six, the documentary film *P. Ramlee* (2010, dir. Shuhaimi Baba) mentions a concert by the 'Three Ramlees' in the late 1960s when P. Ramlee was 'booed' by the young audience. Conversely, the Malay Heritage Centre exhibition mentioned earlier features a picture of P. Ramlee performing alongside the popular *pop yeh yeh* band the Swallows (photograph: EMI Music).

rapidly influenced the souls of our [Malaysian] youths to the point that these youths are unaware of their long hair (like the Beatles), dress in 'groovy' styles that are unfamiliar, smoke ganja [marijuana] and other things. There are also young women that wear short 'miniskirts' due to the influence of pop musicians.[19]

At the end of his presentation, P. Ramlee proposed eight points to address the decline of traditional music that stressed the importance of government intervention and responsibility:

1. The government must act vigilantly to expand *asli* [indigenous] and traditional music extensively.[20]
2. Radio and television must play an important role in broadcasting as much traditional and *asli* music as possible.
3. A [government-sponsored] programme must be implemented that has two simultaneous outlets for the training of *asli* and traditional Malaysian music.
4. All schools (including vernacular schools) must teach *asli* and traditional music as a subject in the curriculum.
5. Nightclubs, hotels, restaurants and any public places must play and perform *asli* and traditional music.
6. Music that is at odds with Malaysian traditions must be reduced.
7. The government must encourage the producers of *asli* and traditional music by providing commensurate endorsement and sponsorship for their musical works.

---

[19] P. Ramlee, 'Cara-cara meninggikan mutu dan memperkayakan muzik jenis asli dan tradisional Malaysia demi kepentingan negara' [Ways to elevate and enrich the original and traditional music of Malaysia for the benefit of the nation], in *Asas Kebudayaan Kebangsaan*, 1st ed. Kuala Lumpur: Kementerian Kebudayaan Belia dan Sukan Malaysia, 1973, pp. 205–7.

[20] The *asli* genre meaning 'original', 'indigenous' or 'pure' is both a specific Malay rhythm and a repertoire of song types. *Asli* music instrumentation includes regional instruments such as *rebana* frame drum and *gendang* two-headed drum as well as indigenised Western instruments such as the violin and accordion. See Patricia Matusky and Tan Sooi Beng, *The Music of Malaysia: The Classical, Folk and Syncretic Traditions*. Aldershot: Ashgate, 2004, p. 330 for an example of the *asli* rhythmic pattern, and pp. 321, 329–30 for examples of *asli* repertoire.

8. The government must sponsor *asli* and traditional music festivals to [positively] influence Malaysians.[21]

What is evident in these proposed 'solutions' is the constant emphasis and reliance on government assistance and intervention. P. Ramlee portrayed an uphill 'battle' against commercial popular music and sees government sponsorship as the only solution to maintaining a 'declining' indigenous culture. Further, the youth who increasingly overlooked his music for foreign popular music were at the centre of the problem. They were the generation succumbing to 'negative' Western culture, effectively forgetting their local cultures and values. The only solution he saw to this was active state intervention. In this argument, Malaysian national consciousness was being entrusted solely to the machinery of the state. Where Malays once relied on their sovereign rulers to define and symbolise their culture, they now had to turn to the state as an extension or replacement of that sovereignty in the modern world. At the end of the congress where P. Ramlee presented his views about music, the National Culture Policy of 1971 was drafted. This has remained the official government policy concerning culture and the arts until today.[22]

I now explore how youth music cultures in mid-1960s to early 1970s featured as the centre of contention in the debate about national culturalism in Malaysia and Singapore. These youth cultures posed a counter-cultural threat to the two newly emerging countries, and a wealth of reactionary as well as conciliatory discourses were expressed about youth freedom and degeneracy in conflict with conservative and locally rooted morality.

---

[21] P. Ramlee, 'Cara-cara meninggikan mutu', pp. 206–7.

[22] Ministry of Information [Kementerian Penerangan Malaysia], 'Dasar Kebudayaan Kebangsaan', 2018. Available at http://pmr.penerangan.gov.my/index.php/component/content/article/88-dasar-dasar-negara/238-dasar-kebudayaan-kebangsaan.html [accessed 28 January 2018]. The ministry lists the updated policy, but states that three main principles of the policy are based on the initiatives set out by the National Culture Congress of 1971: '*Ketiga-tiga prinsip asas di atas adalah melambangkan penerimaan gagasan Kongres Kebudayaan Kebangsaan 1971.*'

Youth and Popular Music in Singapore and Malaysia in the 1960s

The 1960s in Singapore and Malaysia were a vibrant and creative period for youth music culture.[23] Youth music culture began as emulative practices that would eventually become localised. Rock 'n' roll bands from Britain and the United States were imitated in the form of cover bands. This was followed by the translation of popular English songs into local languages like Malay, and later original songs were written and performed in Malay, English and local Chinese languages. While other languages were present in youth music, I limit my observations to English- and Malay-language bands based in Singapore and Malaysia, with a focus on the musical translatability of youth music and related youth cultural practices that were deemed degenerate by state authorities.

The beat music of British bands such as the Beatles, the Rolling Stones and the Shadows were major influences on the musical styles and band formats embraced by Singaporean and Malaysian youth. Aside from a pervasive culture of emulating Western popular styles among English-language bands, there was also a growing number of Chinese- and Malay-language bands that combined these new beat styles and guitar band formats with lyrics sung in local languages. The Malay-language adaptations of British rock would be termed *pop yeh yeh* in direct reference to the Beatles' 'She Loves You' with its famous 'yeah, yeah, yeah' refrain.[24]

Alongside this loud and rhythmically driven music, fashion statements such as miniskirts for women and long hair for men represented a vivid

---

23 Joseph C. Pereira, *The Story of Singapore Sixties Music*. Vol. 1: *Apache Over Singapore*. Singapore: Select Publishing, 2011; Joseph C. Pereira, *The Story of Singapore Sixties Music*. Vol. 2: *Beyond the Tea Dance*. Singapore: Select Publishing, 2014.

24 Lockard, *Dance of Life*, p. 224; Pereira, *The Story of Singapore Sixties Music*, Vol. 1, p. 1; Matusky and Tan, *The Music of Malaysia*, p. 407; Burhanuddin Bin Buang, 'Pop Yeh Yeh Music in Singapore: 1963–1971'. BA Honours thesis, National University of Singapore, 2000, p. 4. These references to *pop yeh yeh* also constitute the few studies mentioning or dedicated to the genre of music. A comprehensive biography of *pop yeh yeh* bands and singers can be found in Pereira, *The Story of Singapore Sixties Music*. Vol. 2, pp. 10–128.

cosmopolitan counter-culture to the more conservative leaders and lawmakers. Singapore and Malaysia were seeking to assert a distinct national cultural identity that was refined in modernity yet rooted in indigenous traditions. The beat music youth cultures, however, were seen as far from refined and far from local by the older generation of local artists and government officials. In fact, youth music culture of the 1960s represented everything the postcolonial nation-building projects were against. In line with Andrew Jones's reading of the 'doubleness of yellow music' in China in the 1930s, the establishment of Malayan youth music signified a degenerate or 'pornographic' cultural expression that was also modern and translatable across national boundaries.[25] The articulation of *pop yeh yeh* culture represented a threatening sexual freedom along with a borderless cultural practice that could not be bound by the rigid confines of a national culture and traditional morality. Here I examine a few examples of Malayan youth music cultures that posed a counter-cultural threat to Singapore's and Malaysia's national cultural agenda in the late 1960s to early 1970s.

Disquieting Expressions

In the 1960s Singapore was the centre of production for guitar band music for the entire Malay Peninsula. International record labels such as Philips and Columbia-EMI had recording and distribution operations there and were actively promoting and producing local talents. In the early years of that decade a wealth of local bands were recorded performing English songs by American and British artists. A major appeal of this industry was the accessibility of these local bands to local audiences at live shows. Siva Choy, a member of the duo called the Cyclones (Figure 5.2) says:

> In the early '60s, television had not arrived. You heard [foreign] bands on the radio but couldn't see them. Occasionally, a movie might come into Singapore with bands and things. So what do you do? You look

---

[25] Jones, *Yellow Music*, pp. 101–4.

for anything that will substitute. So, suddenly a local band stands up and starts to play Rolling Stones. It was great. No videos, no cassettes. So we became substitutes. Everybody sounded like somebody else. The more you sounded like somebody else, the greater the hero that you became.... As a result, people became extremely imitative.[26]

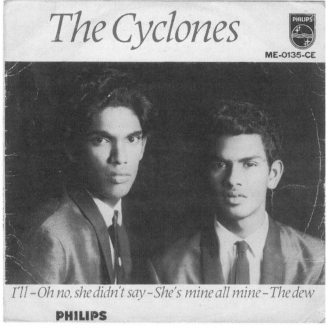

Figure 5.2 Siva and James Choy's debut single, 1965

One of the more successful English-language bands from the era, the Quests, modelled themselves after the Shadows. They initially gained popularity by winning talent competitions in which they would play songs by the Shadows.[27] In fact there were many soundalike band competitions in the early 1960s: local bands such as the Stompers won the Cliff Richard and the Shadows contest, the Astronauts claimed the

---

[26] Interview in Joseph C. Pereira, *Legends of the Golden Venus: Bands That Rocked Singapore from the '60s to the '90s.* Singapore: Times Editions, 1999, p. 18.

[27] Henry Chua, *Call It Shanty: The Story of the Quests.* Singapore: BigO Books, 2001, pp. 33–38.

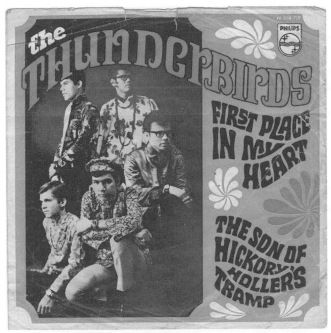

Figure 5.3 The Thunderbirds' single, 1968

Figure 5.4 Naomi and the Boys' debut single, 1964

title of the Ventures of Singapore and the Clifters were winners of the Rolling Stones of Singapore competition.[28] There was also a Beatles versus Rolling Stones competition that involved a finalist play-off between the Thunderbirds (who emulated the former) and Les Kafila's (who mimicked the latter)—the Thunderbirds won the competition (Figure 5.3).[29] Other notable groups such as Naomi and the Boys gained popularity in the Malay Peninsula with their cover version of the song 'Happy, Happy Birthday Baby' by Margo Sylvia and Gilbert Lopez (Figure 5.4).

The adaptation of popular chart-topping English songs to Malay initiated a local recording music industry that emulated the West. The industry, which set the aesthetic tone for local music practices, would eventually be articulated in more local expressions. It is likely that the increase in the number of recordings in Malay was due to its widespread use as the official national language in both the Federation of Malaya (then Malaysia) and Singapore from 1959 to 1965.[30] For example, in 1967, under the TK label, Ismail Haron who sang with the Vigilantes recorded 'Green, Green Grass of Home' (Claude Putman Jr) as 'Senyuman Terakhir' (Last Smile), 'La Bamba' (Ritchie Valens) as 'Mari Menari' (Let's Dance), 'Hang On Sloopy' (Bert Berns and Wes Farrell) as 'Mari Sayang' (Come Here, My Dear) and 'You Better Move On' (Arthur Alexander) as 'Pulang Pada-ku' (Return to Me).[31] Ismail Haron based his recording career in the 1960s on performing, adapting and writing Malay versions of popular English songs. His other notable recordings were 'Enam Belas Lilin' based on 'Sixteen Candles' (Luther Dixon and Allyson R. Khent), 'Delailah' from 'Delilah' (Barry Mason and Les Reed) performed by Tom Jones (Figure 5.5) and 'Jangan Marah Lili' (Don't Be Angry, Lili) adapted from 'Mohair Sam' (Dallas Frazier) performed

28 Pereira, *The Story of Singapore Sixties Music*. Vol. 1, pp. 2–3.
29 Ibid., p. 3.
30 Burhanuddin, 'Pop Yeh Yeh Music in Singapore', pp. 24–25.
31 Ismail Haron, Oral History Interviews, Interview with Ismail Haron by Joseph C. Pereira, Accession Number 003001, National Archives of Singapore, 31 December 2005; Pereira, *The Story of Singapore Sixties Music*. Vol. 1, p. 111; Malay Heritage Centre Singapore, *Malam Pesta Muda Mudi Exhibition*, Library@Esplanade, October 2012.

by Charlie Rich.[32] Ismail Haron asserted that despite being labelled the 'Tom Jones of Singapore', he was more inclined to African-American performers such as James Brown, Lou Rawls, Nat King Cole, Aretha Franklin and Ella Fitzgerald. However, he was constrained to covering white artists due to the demands of recording companies.[33]

Figure 5.5 Ismail Harun's (Haron) single, 1968

The mid-1960s also saw the growth of Malay *kugiran* bands in Singapore and Malaysia.[34] Like the cover groups, the *kugiran* bands usually consisted of a core band fronted by a singer. These singers changed depending on the performance or recording project. Popular singers and bands in the mid-1960s from Singapore included Rafeah Buang, Maria Bachok, Sanisah Huri (Figure 5.6), Siti Zaiton, Ahmad

---

[32] Ismail Haron, Oral History Interviews; Pereira, *The Story of Singapore Sixties Music.* Vol. 1, p. 112.

[33] Ismail Haron, Oral History Interviews.

[34] Matusky and Tan, *The Music of Malaysia*, p. 47. An abbreviation of *kumpulan gitar rancak* (upbeat guitar band).

Daud, Jeffridin and the Siglap Five (Figure 5.7), A. Ramlie and the Rhythm Boys, Kassim Slamat and the Swallows (Figure 5.8), the Terwellos (Figure 5.6), the Hooks and Les Kafila's. The bands were characterised by their original compositions and vernacular or *asli* (indigenous) approach to Malay singing complemented by a Westernised musical style and instrumentation.[35] One notable recording is the song 'La Aube' [*sic*] recorded by Kassim Slamat and the Swallows sung in a Bawean dialect. The song was even a popular hit in Germany, arguably making the group 'the most internationally recognised Malay Pop band of their time'.[36]

Figure 5.6 Sanisah Huri and the Terwellos' single from *A Go Go '67*, 1967

---

35   Lockard, *Dance of Life*, p. 226; Ismail Haron, Oral History Interviews.
36   Malay Heritage Centre Singapore, *Malam Pesta Muda Mudi* Exhibition.

Figure 5.7 Jeffridin and the Siglap Five's single, 1966

Figure 5.8 Kassim Slamat and the Swallows' single, 1965

Degenerate Practices

Youth audiences naturally complemented the music-makers. Young people adopted fashions that were considered outrageous or provocative, listened to their favourite Western or Western-derived music on the radio, actively collected music records, increasingly preferred local television programmes (over local films) featuring local bands and singers, and congregated in music spaces and events such as band competitions and concerts. The most accessible of these live events were tea dances that were aimed at young adults. The most prominent fashion statements included miniskirts and form-fitting outfits for women, tight trousers for men and towards the end of the 1960s long hair for men.

Tea dances in Singapore were held on Saturday and Sunday afternoons for young patrons below the legal drinking age as no alcohol was served. Venues included the notable Golden Venus, a club located on Orchard Road, the Celestial Room, the Palace, Springdale, the Prince's at Prince Hotel Garni and New World cabaret.[37] These were events where youth could have 'clean fun', enjoy live music and congregate in their trendy clothes.

Joseph C. Pereira, the author of three books on Singapore band music in the 1960s, is an avid fan, record collector and producer of numerous compilation albums of beat music from the 1960s (Figure 5.9). During my research, I was fortunate to interview him at his home and view his vast record collection. Pereira is a key member of a modest but enthusiastic network of 1960s music fans and record collectors across Singapore and Malaysia. Aside from his personal vinyl collection he showed me a collection of albums from the 1960s that had been converted to CDs by another fan. His insights and personal memories of growing up in the era provide an intimate perspective on *pop yeh yeh* culture. He shares his personal experience of attending a tea dance in 1969 at the age of 15. The tea dance

---

[37] Pereira, *The Story of Singapore Sixties Music.* Vol. 1, p. 6; Chua, *Call It Shanty*, pp. 85–88.

was held in the afternoon from three to six and it was a basement club … I went with two friends. We paid the grand fee of one dollar which entitled us to a Coke…. But the thing was that straight away, I told myself, 'I'm out of my league' … because we were wearing short sleeve shirts and trousers—we looked like tourists! Then we look[ed] at the rest [of the people], and you know, because they were older teens or … [young] adults—these guys and gals, they looked damn cool, man! We looked like a bunch of tourists, wearing short sleeve shirts…. Some were wearing fringe jackets, some were wearing corduroy, some were wearing Levi's corduroy [jeans], and tailored slacks…. A wide range of fashions … [some who wore] sunglasses. All kinds of sunglasses…. There were a lot of [young women wearing] miniskirts. Of course, some of them wore pantsuits.[38]

Figure 5.9 Joseph C. Pereira and his music collection

---

[38] Interview with Joseph C. Pereira, Beat Music Bands in 1960s Singapore, 2012.

Appropriate fashion was a major consideration among youths at these tea dances. Pereira expresses amazement at the attire of the patrons and emphasises how embarrassed he was to be out of place in his clothing ('we looked like tourists!'). Pereira also describes the setup of the club, which included a 'bandstand', 'dancing stage' and 'tables and chairs where people sit and watch' the performances. Most of the dancing was done by male–female couples on dates, while a majority of the audience comprised males who sat and observed the bands.[39]

This was the first and last tea dance that he would attend as they were banned by the Singapore government on 1 January 1970, just a few months after Pereira and his friends patronised the Golden Venus on Orchard Road.[40] According to Pereira, tea dances at the end of the 1960s were notorious for ending up in fights, so the government viewed them as a breeding ground for 'juvenile delinquency'.[41] In fact, state antagonism towards youth culture in the late 1960s and early 1970s was a major factor in the decline of these and similar musical events, as the earlier government campaign that

> had begun in 1959 to create a Malayan culture and reject 'yellow culture' or what were seen as *degenerate* external cultural influences began to have an impact. As local music was regarded as being heavily influenced by the West and associated with a culture of drug use and disorderliness, this led to the banning of, among other things, tea dances and other events featuring live music.[42]

Indeed, in the late 1960s and early 1970s, the *Straits Times* was full of articles on youth degeneracy couched in terms of 'yellow culture', 'flower people' and the general paranoia about the 'hippie' movement and

---

[39] Ibid.

[40] Ibid.; Pereira, *The Story of Singapore Sixties Music*. Vol. 2, p. 273; Joanna Tan, 'Popular music in 1960s Singapore', *Biblio Asia* 7, 1 (2011): 10–14.

[41] Interview with Joseph C. Pereira, Beat Music Bands in 1960s Singapore, 2012; Pereira, *The Story of Singapore Sixties Music*. Vol. 2, p. 273.

[42] Joanna Tan, 'Popular music in the 1960s', *Singapore Infopedia*. Singapore: National Library of Singapore, 2010. Available at http://eresources.nlb.gov.sg/infopedia/articles/ SIP_1658_2010-04-15.html [accessed 29 January 2018] (my emphasis).

associated music cultures.[43] This included the banning of the American film *Woodstock: Three Days of Peace, Music and Love.*[44]

This concern came to a head around another issue of youth 'degeneracy' in the late 1960s and early 1970s: long-haired males. They were considered such a problem that Singapore government offices instituted a policy of serving 'males with long hair ... last'.[45] In Malaysia, Johor state scholarship holders were banned from having long hair alongside restrictions on participating in demonstrations and marrying without the consent of the scholarship committee.[46] What constituted 'long hair' for males? According to an illustrated Singapore government poster titled 'Males with long hair will be attended to last', the criteria included 'hair falling across the forehead and touching eyebrows', 'hair covering the ears' and 'hair reaching below an ordinary shirt collar'.[47] Pereira informs us, from a personal experience he had with his friends, that police officers in Singapore in the 1970s would randomly harass and find fault with any young males who sported long hair.[48] These examples indicate that it was the bodies of youth that the state sought to control. Unfamiliar and unconventional appearances were somehow linked to degeneracy and moral decadence, and ultimately at odds with the state vision of promoting a subservient national culture among young people.

This policing of the body was internalised among youths themselves. In the mid- to late 1960s Malaysian and Singaporean women were liberating their bodies through 'provocative' or revealing styles of dress. The issue of young Malay women in miniskirts was a frequent topic of fan letters in the Malay-language music magazine, *Bintang dan Lagu* (Stars and Songs). A letter from someone who may be a young woman

43 'Lim warns of flower people, yellow culture', *Straits Times*, 13 January 1968; 'Need to play down "hippie trend" on TV', *Straits Times*, 18 May 1970; Lawrence Basapa, 'Hippism does not start or end with pot and long hair', *Straits Times*, 20 September 1970.
44 Arthur Richards, 'Singapore censors ban pop colour film Woodstock', *Straits Times*, 29 December 1970.
45 Malay Heritage Centre Singapore, *Malam Pesta Muda Mudi* Exhibition; Chua, *Call It Shanty*, pp. 56–57.
46 'Long hair ban on grant holders', *Straits Times*, 17 November 1975.
47 Malay Heritage Centre Singapore, *Malam Pesta Muda Mudi* Exhibition, citing Singapore National Library Archives.
48 Interview with Joseph C. Pereira, Beat Music Bands in 1960s Singapore, 2012.

named N. Hanis denounced the wearing of miniskirts as a provocatively revealing Western form of dress with the sole intention of attracting male attention.[49] The writer asks why women should copy the fashions from abroad while ignoring local and more modest fashions:

> Miniskirts are a type of clothing that exposes [a woman's] calves to the public. Is this what is called progress? Progress can be achieved without having to wear miniskirts. And, by wearing *baju kurong* [traditional Malay dress] we are able to attract males; we don't need to wear miniskirts for this.... If we really want to wear short [revealing] clothes, wear underwear, isn't that even shorter [more revealing]?[50]

The writer adds that local society is to blame for encouraging this indecent form of dress by holding 'miniskirt pageants' and falling victim to the disagreeable influences of the West.[51]

This statement is unique in a number of ways. First, the critique of miniskirts is voiced by someone who was probably a Malay woman. She advocates a style of dress among her female peers that embodies both sartorial modesty and a progressive and modern intellectual outlook. Second, the writer raises interesting issues about feminine sexual objectification: why should women expose their legs just to attract men and why should they be paraded in beauty pageants? Third, the issue of cultural hegemony is touched on, since Western fashion is reckoned to threaten the survival of Malay national dress and cultural values:

> Why must we copy the clothes that come from other countries, like Western countries[?] Aren't there enough clothes in our own country?

---

[49] N. Hanis, 'Untok mengembalikan kesedaran' [To restore awareness], *Bintang dan Lagu*, July 1967, p. 51. It is difficult to verify the gender of the letter writer as there is a possibility that the writer may be using an alias, a male writing as a woman, or even one of the magazine editors intending to generate interest in the magazine. For the purpose of this analysis, the writer's identity is taken at face value. What is important is to ascertain how magazine readers in the mid-1960s would have interpreted or reacted to such letters.

[50] Ibid.

[51] '*Ratu mini-skirt.*' Ibid.

> While Western countries have never ever wanted to use our clothes, why then must we favour clothes that come from the West that are not suitable for us.[52]

The question is whether to view this letter as a conservative statement or a postcolonial feminist one. It seems to present both possibilities, but I interpret the writer as an autonomous female voice that is paradoxically bound by the cultural restraints of patriarchal Malay culture. What complicates a reading of the writer's position is that her notion of 'modesty' is a personal internalisation of patriarchal cultural values. With regard to the culture of wearing miniskirts, N. Hanis employs a discourse similar to conservative critiques of youth culture such as those of P. Ramlee, and subsequently implemented government policies that attempted to promote traditional, non-radical values.

In later issues of *Bintang dan Lagu*, conservative views by another woman (again suggested by the name provided) towards the miniskirt trend are expressed. A letter expresses antagonism towards miniskirts in a very satirical manner:

> For me miniskirts are like jackfruit covers. The top is wrapped tightly, while the calves and thighs are shown to the general public. I feel that instead of wearing miniskirts it is better not to wear anything at all; that is even more attractive for men.[53]

Another more neutral letter, this time by a male writer, observes how new male and female fashions are far from different in their tightness and attendant attitudes:

---

[52] Ibid.

[53] A. Anis Sabirin, 'Jangan pakai baju langsong' [Don't wear clothes at all], *Bintang dan Lagu*, September 1967, p. 51. It is highly likely that this is Anis Sabirin, a Malay feminist who actively wrote in the 1960s. See Alicia Izharuddin, 'Anis Sabirin: Suara feminis lantang yang terkubur' [Anis Sabirin: An articulate feminist voice buried], *Malay Mail Online*, 9 March 2015 for a biography of her often overlooked contributions to feminism in Malaysia; and Lisbeth Littrup, 'Development in Malay criticism', in *The Canon in Southeast Asian Literatures: Literatures of Burma, Cambodia, Indonesia, Laos, Malaysia, the Philippines, Thailand and Vietnam*, ed. David Smyth. Richmond: Curzon, 2000, pp. 76–87.

While young women are stylish with their miniskirts that reveal parts of their thighs, young males show off their shirts and trousers that are tight or 'fancy', as these young adults like to say. No matter what clothes they wear, no one can tell them otherwise because they will reply with an answer that is unsettling [rude or inappropriate].[54]

Both letters indicate a general uneasiness among more conservative female and male youth towards new fashions. It is clear that their stance can be considered conservative in relation to the content of the magazine itself. *Bintang dan Lagu* issues from 1966 and 1967 contain numerous pictures of female artists in miniskirts and other form-fitting attire in line with the youth fashions of the day. These letters perhaps only reflect a minority view of youth styles and their assumed morality. It is also possible that the letters were contrived by magazine editors to entice readers. Whatever the truth, there was a debate over the issue in a publication targeted at young people. Beyond the music, bands and singers, the discourse around fashion directly involved the fans of and participants in the music scene.

The debate over miniskirts in *Bintang dan Lagu* ended on a more liberal note with an article titled 'Miniskirt, apa salahnya gadis2 Melayu memakai miniskirt?'[55] The article summarises previous fan letters for and against miniskirts and makes an attempt to investigate the issue. The writer(s) did so by visiting the predominantly Malay Geylang Serai district in Singapore to assess the extent of miniskirt wearing among young Malay females. They ascertained that the situation wasn't as 'bad' as previous fan letters had depicted as the number of women wearing unreasonably short skirts was 'very small'. The article concludes

---

[54] A. Zainy Nawawi, 'Pakaian lelaki perempuan tak berbedza' [Women's clothing is different], *Bintang dan Lagu*, November 1967, p. 48.

[55] 'Miniskirt: Apa salahnya gadis2 Melayu memakai miniskirt?' [Miniskirts: What is the harm in Malay women wearing miniskirts?], *Bintang dan Lagu*, November 1967, pp. 4–5. The last available copies of the *Bintang dan Lagu* magazine at the British Library are issues from 1967, thus 'ending' the miniskirt debate until more research is done to retrieve later copies. There is also a possibility that this magazine ceased publication after 1967. Archived copies of this particular magazine are rare.

by noting that young Malay women are 'still capable of looking after themselves and adapting to the times'.[56]

Despite conservative reactions towards youth fashions that were viewed as detrimental to local culture, values and morals, there was a discourse that sought to reconcile youth culture as reasonable or even progressive and adaptive to modern times. In effect a cosmopolitan agency was present in the debates and discourses among the youth in the 1960s. This contrasted to the aspiring nationalism expressed by the previous generation. The notion of youth culture featured prominently and presented a discursive and embodied space of contestation. This agency was articulated in different ways with divergent opinions about morality and the role of youth in the emerging nations of Malaysia and Singapore. Conservative or reactionary voices proclaimed a moralistic position by using modern tropes of national culturalism to safeguard traditional values. Arguments in favour of youth cultures sought to reposition the moral compass towards ideas of progress, modernity and adaptability to changing times. Thus, agency exists in both views and their arguments were articulated in cosmopolitan mediums that provided a new space for these oppositional ideas to interact. While the recording industry created music for counter-cultural youths to consume, print media provided a discursive space for youths to expose and express the disjuncture between such counter-cultures and traditional values, national identity and modernity.[57]

The Malay film industry, waning in popularity towards the end of the 1960s, provided a further space for the articulation of this counter-cultural youth discourse. In the next section, I discuss how one film tried

---

[56] Ibid., p. 5: '*maseh lagi pandai menjaga diri dan menyesuaikan diri mereka dengan pengedaran zaman.*'

[57] For a thorough discussion on the cosmopolitanism and Malay nationalist activism in print media see Timothy P. Barnard and Jan van der Putten, 'Malay cosmopolitan activism in post-war Singapore', in *Paths Not Taken: Political Pluralism in Post-War Singapore*, ed. Michael D. Barr and Carl A. Trocki. Singapore: NUS Press, 2008, pp. 132–53. They believe it was the cosmopolitan intellectual environment of Singapore in the 1950s that led to significant creative and political advances in the Malay arts and literature. A cosmopolitan conception of Malayness was being formed and the imperative for the creation of a modern Malaysian state was being articulated with utmost agency 'in the Malay language' (p. 148).

to reconcile older values with the trendy youth music and culture of the late 1960s. In its attempt to draw a young audience, the film provided a narrative that tried to challenge conservative stereotypes of Malay youth degeneracy by portraying these young people as morally capable individuals.

Youth Music in Malay Film

The popularity of *pop yeh yeh* bands coincided with the decline of the musically orientated Malay film industry.[58] It is difficult to ascertain whether *pop yeh yeh* directly affected the decline of Malay cinema, but there were many instances of *pop yeh yeh* or rock 'n' roll in films from the mid-1960s. Contrary to Craig Lockard's view, Burhanuddin Bin Buang suggests that the popularity of *pop yeh yeh* music actually waned *alongside* the Malay film studio system's demise.[59] I go further to argue that *pop yeh yeh* and Malay films had more of a symbiotic and intimate relationship than the contested one suggested by the conservative reactions to youth culture voiced by Malay film music icons such as P. Ramlee. By the early 1970s there was, as noted above, increased policing of youth cultures and fewer avenues for performing, especially in Singapore. Also, the craze for local *kugiran* groups had subsided as local youths gravitated towards 'foreign artists who were much more radical' such as Led Zeppelin, Deep Purple, Black Sabbath and Jimi Hendrix. However, many of the singers from *pop yeh yeh* bands would go on to record successful commercial albums beyond the 1970s.[60]

Pop yeh yeh and youth culture, while treated dismissively by the state, permeated Malay films in the mid-1960s, even though they tended to include this music as frivolous, parodic or secondary to the films' main narrative. The inclusion of Malay youth music was a cautious way for film producers to retain the viewership of the older generation while simultaneously appealing to a younger audience whose musical tastes were radically different from earlier styles. For example, the keyboardist

---

[58]   Lockard, *Dance of Life*, p. 226.
[59]   Burhanuddin, 'Pop Yeh Yeh Music in Singapore', pp. 11–12.
[60]   Ibid., p. 12.

Shah Sarip of the Rhythm Boys remarks: 'At that time, people didn't want to hear traditional music anymore. Everybody wanted to hear *pop yeh yeh* songs. Even at wedding functions, *pop yeh yeh* bands dominated.'[61] Whether the cosmopolitan music of films before the mid-1960s was considered 'traditional' is unclear, but the reactionary comments from P. Ramlee are indicative. Ironically, some of the earliest rock 'n' roll music can be found in his films.

One of the earliest musical scenes featuring a rock 'n' roll guitar song happens to be one of P. Ramlee's most famous songs.[62] Aptly titled 'Bunyi Gitar' (Sound of the Guitar), the song featured in the comedy *Tiga Abdul* (The Three Abduls, 1964, dir. P. Ramlee), his last Singapore film before his move to Kuala Lumpur. The film is set in a fictional country that could be Turkey, where men wear fezzes in a style reminiscent of the pre-Atatürk era. As one of the three Abdul brothers who have amassed a wealthy inheritance, P. Ramlee's character, Abdul Wahub, owns a musical instrument shop, which forms a suitable setting for his performance of 'Bunyi Gitar'. The song is presented in a pedagogical manner as if P. Ramlee is introducing the Malay film audience to a 'new' genre of music. A group of musicians—two electric guitarists and a drummer—are trying out musical instruments in his shop. Abdul Wahub walks up to the band and asks if he can assist them. One of the guitarists (Kassim Masdor) invites Abdul Wahub to join their band. Abdul Wahub then asks each of the musicians which parts and instruments they play, and they proceed to demonstrate by taking turns to play three bars of their parts unaccompanied: rhythm guitar followed by bass guitar followed by drums.[63] Abdul Wahub then determines that they need a lead guitar,

---

[61] Interview with Shah Sarip on 28 January 2001, in ibid., p. 22.

[62] In Chapter Six, I discuss the ironic use of this song in a documentary about P. Ramlee. Numerous Malaysian artists have also reinterpreted the song since the 1980s. The song has been performed by the singers Sheila Majid and Siti Nurhaliza and the rock group the Blues Gang among others. More recently, the song was covered by Subculture for the *Indiepretasi* P. Ramlee tribute album and Kyoto Protocol for the Versus 2 band competition broadcast on TV9. Of the Malaysian film music canon, it is arguably the song that best references the *pop yeh yeh* era.

[63] Here, as was popular with many early *pop yeh yeh* bands, the 'bass' guitar part was a running bass line played on an electric six-string guitar.

picks up an electric guitar from a display stand and plays the opening riff of the song. During the instrumental interlude following Abdul Wahub's singing, a group of customers dance a choreographed twist that could have been considered unruly by a conservative audience; this was quite unlike the traditional or cabaret ballroom dancing screened in earlier films. Abdul Wahub's shop becomes a vibrant cosmopolitan space for the introduction of rock 'n' roll to the film audience. In my view, it was possible to present this new style of music because the film was a comedy. Older or more musically conservative audiences were able to accept the song as a parody of the wild youth culture. Another reason P. Ramlee composed a song in this style could have been his need to demonstrate his musical skills in adapting to a new genre. In a magazine article titled 'Nasihat P. Ramlee' (P. Ramlee's Advice), he expressed his concerns about the young guitar bands and pop musicians who were gaining musical success but did not have the formal musical knowledge that his generation had to acquire:

> One matter that is disappointing is that, based on what I know, many pop singers and musicians cannot read musical notes. For me, this is a weakness that needs to be fixed.… Because if it is not [addressed] … I worry that the future of pop singers cannot be brought to the centre or to the side [as in lacking direction], like a ship sailing with a ruined sail.[64]

Despite P. Ramlee's tongue-in-cheek performance, the inclusion of this style of music also reflects the immense popularity of the genre in 1964. 'Bunyi Gitar' had the dual function of being a cynical musical take on youth music while also appealing to the younger and hipper generation.

The lyrics for the song indicate the stereotypically carefree, party-going, love-seeking and laidback attitude of Malay youths in the mid-1960s. As noted by Zam Zam, a popular singer from that period, *pop yeh yeh* lyrics

---

[64] Noor As Ahmad, 'Nasihat P. Ramlee', *Mastika Filem*, August 1967, p. 31.

were mostly about love, love relationships and partying because those were the concerns of the youth at that time. Since [*sic*] *pop yeh yeh* was a music that catered for the young people of that time, of course the lyrics must be something that touch on their liking and activities.[65]

Indeed, these inclinations towards 'love', 'love relationships' and 'partying' are prominent in the song's lyrics (Appendix A.7).

Pop yeh yeh culture and Malay films influenced each other. Film music and narratives played an active role in shaping *pop yeh yeh* artists, and Malay youth culture and music featured prominently in films. Pereira notes how a *pop yeh yeh* band from Singapore, the Swallows, initially backed the singer Ahmad Daud who managed to get them to appear in a Malay Film Productions' movie, *Sayang Si Buta* (Love the Blind One, 1965, dir. Omar Rojik).[66] The same year, they recorded a second song fronted by Ahmad Daud called 'Dendang Pontianak' (Vampire Song) for the film *Pusaka Pontianak* (Legacy of the Vampire, 1965, dir. Ramon A. Estella).[67] The Swallows then collaborated with a singer named Kasim bin Rahmat who took the stage name Kassim Slamat, referencing the Kassim Selamat character of P. Ramlee's *Ibu Mertua-ku*. In other words, aside from providing music for films, the younger musicians also appropriated references from Malay films, exemplifying a mutually influential intertextual discourse between film music and youth culture.

Likewise, films from the mid-1960s also drew considerably from Malay youth music. The opening scene of P. Ramlee's *Anak Bapak* (Father's Son, 1968) features an upbeat *pop yeh yeh* song for its title credits, with Saloma singing and dancing to the song. The film also includes musical scenes in a nightclub featuring an unnamed and uncredited *pop yeh yeh* band. Here, the film does not parody or critique

---

[65] Interview with Zam Zam on 6 December 2000, in Burhanuddin, 'Pop Yeh Yeh Music in Singapore', p. 22.

[66] Pereira, *The Story of Singapore Sixties Music*. Vol. 2, p. 13.

[67] Ibid. See also Alicia Izharuddin, 'Pain and pleasures of the look: The female gaze in Malaysian horror film', *Asian Cinema* 26, 2 (2015): 135–52 for an in-depth analysis of the 'female gaze' in the *pontianak* genre of Malay horror films.

this style of music like P. Ramlee's earlier films. The band and style of music is diegetic to the nightclub environment (and musical aesthetic) of Malaysia in the 1960s.[68]

None of the examples mentioned above represent the integration of *pop yeh yeh* and youth culture themes directly into the narrative of films. One film that attempted to incorporate *pop yeh yeh* music and articulate the issues of Malay youth culture was *Muda Mudi* (The Young Ones, 1965, dir. M. Amin), produced by Cathay-Keris and starring Siput Sarawak. Siput Sarawak was one of the most prominent Malay film stars from the early 1950s. *Muda Mudi* places her in the reflexive role of an ageing film star named Dayang, a single mother who is coming to terms with her age and her waning popularity in the film scene. Dayang's daughter, Rohana (Roseyatimah), is an ambitious singer in a *pop yeh yeh* band.[69] The film presents the theme of youth culture from the perspective of the older generation. Dayang struggles to accept that she is past her prime for leading roles as a young heroine and is aggressive and confrontational with her producers. She is especially spiteful to a young actress who is quickly surpassing her. At the same time, while proud of her daughter, she also wants her daughter to follow in her footsteps and become an actress. For her part, Rohana is adamant about being a singer. The result is conflict.

The film is replete with musical scenes that explicitly promote the *pop yeh yeh* style. The opening title credits feature an upbeat rock 'n' roll song with Siput Sarawak dancing an a-go-go. At the beginning, Rohana is shown singing a *pop yeh yeh* song by the beach with her friends. She is accompanied by electric guitarists who are not actually plugged into any amplification. Regardless, they perform the obligatory guitar-driven dance movements typical of a *pop yeh yeh* band. This scene is a stereotypical portrayal of carefree youths playing music and having fun. At the end of the song, one of the youths, while reading a

---

[68] *Anak Bapak* was one of P. Ramlee's films made in Shaw Brothers' Merdeka Studios in Kuala Lumpur. By this time, the Singapore film studios had shut down.

[69] In retrospect the film is revealing, as Siput Sarawak's real-life daughter, Anita Sarawak, was a hugely popular and successful singer from the early 1970s. See Amir Muhammad, *120 Malay Movies*. Petaling Jaya: Matahari Books, 2010, p. 316.

film magazine, announces with disappointment that Dayang is being cast in a new film and remarks disrespectfully that she is too old to be taking on lead roles. He is unaware that Rohana, who just sang for him, is Dayang's daughter. In another poignant scene, Dayang attends her daughter's performance at a nightclub and is invited to sing. Towards the middle of the song, the youthful audience jeers her off the stage, strongly disapproving of her performance. In another scene, Dayang is dancing the twist enthusiastically at her daughter's nineteenth birthday party, but eventually becomes exhausted and almost faints, unable to keep up with the youngsters. The musical culture of youths serves as a glaring reminder to Dayang of her age and her declining fame. Through its theme of ageing and narrative focus on the ageing star, *Muda Mudi* can be read as an allegory of the Malay film industry at the time—an older generation of entertainers who were trying to make sense of a radically different youth culture.

In reality, the film's portrayal of adults against youth is quite conciliatory. The film features music by the popular British band the Tornados—credited in the opening titles—and includes many *pop yeh yeh* songs. It is unclear whether the Tornados' instrumental music was used as a backing track for newly composed vocal parts sung in Malay or if it was a fake band taking on the name the Tornados. Whatever the case, British instrumental bands were very influential on the beat music scene and a lot of *pop yeh yeh* bands modelled their style on them.[70] The pervasiveness of this music in a Malay film was quite daring for the mid-1960s, but like P. Ramlee's *Tiga Abdul* the film had to appeal to the older generation by narrating the story from their perspective. At the same time, the incorporation of a *pop yeh yeh* or youth theme also reflects the significance of youth culture in the mid-1960s, which implored film producers to find ways to appeal to the new musical taste of the demographic.

The major narrative thrust of the film centres on the plight of the ageing actress and tries to generate a significant amount of sympathy for the older generation. Young people are portrayed as carefree and fickle-

---

[70] Pereira, *The Story of Singapore Sixties Music.* Vol. 1, p. 1.

minded, without much thought for the future. Dayang advises Jaafar (Tony Kassim) regarding his shaky relationship with her daughter: 'Youngsters like you are always short-sighted. Quick to be hurt, while matters of love are not taken seriously. But, Jaafar, if a love is pure, it will not change.'[71] Young people are portrayed as being in need of the wise counsel of the older generation. They are not vilified and do not need to be suppressed. They just require affectionate guidance. Dayang, for example, encourages Rohana's career in music, attending her nightclub performances while giving her advice about not giving in to quickly gained fame. Rohana excitedly shows off her debut single, but Dayang cautions her:

> Ana, you are new to this world. A debut single or record has no meaning. Today, everyone likes your voice. Tomorrow, people won't listen to you anymore. I want you to be successful and I know your singing is widely appreciated. However, I like to give you advice. You can accept it or not…. Ana, I have experienced everything.

The youth here are portrayed as new to the world and lacking experience. Yet Dayang is encouraging in her advice to her daughter. While she initially tries to steer Rohana away from singing towards acting, she eventually realises the error of her ways and accepts Rohana's decision to be a professional singer. *Muda Mudi*, while narrating from the perspective of the older generation of film stars and producers, provides a cautionary but encouraging message to Malay youth. However, its top-down narrative perspective still leaves much to be desired for the agency of youth and their cultural practices. In the next section, I turn to a film about Malay youth culture and music that more openly articulates the tensions and contestations between the older generation and young people from the youths' perspective.

---

[71] *'Pemuda-pemuda seperti engkau selalu mempunyai fikiran yang singkat. Lekas tersinggung. Berkasih-kasihan pun dipermainkan. Tapi Jaafar, kalau cinta suci, tetap tidak berubah.'*

A Go Go '67 (1967)

A Go Go '67, directed by Omar Rojik, contains a loose plot about a young woman and man who are members of a *kugiran* band and, more importantly, features *pop yeh yeh* performances by 12 bands and four dance groups. The opening credit sequence is reminiscent of *Muda Mudi*'s but is portrayed more artistically, presenting go-go dancers as silhouettes behind screen panels. While the musical performances are the main highlights of the film, the narrative that ties them together contains discourses about *pop yeh yeh* youth culture clashing with conservative Malay values, including state ideology in both Malaysia and Singapore. In the final analysis, *A Go Go '67* provides a moral compromise that favours young people, while critiquing stereotypical conservative views that abhor youth culture.

The film's storyline evolves around a young woman named Fauziah (Nor Azizah) who, against her conservative and well-heeled father's wishes, sings in a *pop yeh yeh* band. Her boyfriend Johari (Aziz Jaafar) is the leader of the band who sings and plays the keyboards. Fauziah's father (Ahmad Nisfu) is extremely antagonistic towards Malay youth culture to the point that he abruptly intervenes in one of her band's rehearsals by kicking a drum kit and scolding her and her bandmates: 'If you want to be Satan, go and be Satan. Don't bring my daughter to be Satan with you! What is all this *yeh yeh yeh*?'[72] Despite his disapproval, Fauziah makes long speeches about how youth are not as bad as her father believes. She admonishes her father about his misconceptions:

> Not all youth are immoral and delinquent, father. Also, not all people who are religious are good, father. I am an adult. I know right from wrong. You know father, a lot of them [youths] do not have permanent jobs. So, by directing their interest towards music, they are able to fill the emptiness of their lives and avoid criminal activities.... Father, do you like hearing of our youths stealing, thieving, extorting because of the emptiness in their lives?

---

[72] *'Ingat! Kalau kau nak jadi syaitan, pergi jadi syaitan. Jangan bawa anak aku jadi syaitan bersama! Apa ni, "yeh yeh yeh" ini apa?'*

Her father does not agree as he views such youths as lost beyond 'repair'. He then laments how the West with its civilised ways and innovations has failed to control their 'wild youth movements' (*angkatan liar*). In order to keep her from her social and musical activities, Fauziah's father arranges for her to be married to her cousin.

Later, Fauziah's father makes a comment about the misfortunes of the world, and mentions the need to do charity work. His wife chides him by saying that his plans for charity never materialise. He then says that if he collects substantial donations he will receive a medal for his contributions to society and the government, and follows up by denouncing young people for their aimless ways, noting that they are never concerned about the welfare of the poor. Overhearing these remarks, Fauziah decides to organise a charity concert for orphans. She gives Johari (Aziz Jaafar) $500 to organise the event and recruit bands. Johari asks why she is suddenly planning this event. Fauziah then makes another proclamation:

> My father always claims that youth like us are the trash of society that are absolutely useless. I want you [Johari] to prove to society, especially my father, that we can be used for a good cause as long as people know how to make use of us.

In the next scene, Fauziah's house is prepared for the marriage but Fauziah is nowhere to be found as she is attending the charity concert. More performances from *kugiran* bands follow. She returns from the concert and tells her father that she has accomplished her duties and is ready to be married according to her father's wishes. But her engagement is called off as her potential in-laws are tired of waiting for her return. Fauziah did not even intentionally avoid the wedding as she was not informed when the wedding was going to be held. Her father is ashamed about the whole escapade and angrily tells Fauziah to leave his sight.

Shortly afterwards, a group of reporters comes into the now gloomy house looking for Fauziah. They glowingly inform her parents that Fauziah and Johari just organised a very successful charity event and are to be commended for their contributions to society. As the reporters congratulate her on her success, she mentions that the *true* organiser of the event was her father. In the end Fauziah's parents are seen apologising to Johari and all is well.

A Go Go '67 provides an informative perspective on the discourses about youth and music in contention with national culturalism in Singapore and Malaysia. The film was shot in Singapore during the last years of Shaw Brothers' Malay Film Productions division, marking the end of an era. Fittingly, the film is an attempt by the industry to appeal to the very youth culture that was assumed to be responsible for the film industry's demise. As such, the narrative tries to portray a conciliatory stance by presenting the youthful protagonists as decent human beings, contrary to many of the statements made by established cultural icons. The film depicts an archetype of reactionary conservatism in the figure of Fauziah's father, replete with statements about the immorality of youth, their futility to society and their devious, delinquent and devilish tendencies. Meanwhile, the film's altruistic protagonist, Fauziah, becomes a staunch advocate of youth culture, proving to her father that young people are morally grounded and with a capacity to care for others and use their art for good causes. Fauziah's character is thus a noble and self-sacrificing exemplar, who both participates in youth culture as well as upholds 'traditional' moral values. In fact, she ends up displaying greater moral initiative than her conservative and opportunistic father.

The film's altruistic narrative also asserts moral expectations of young people and in effect patronises their moral inclinations. Despite this attempt at reconciliation, youth music remained predominantly commercial and government initiatives continued to repress youth culture as indicated in the subsequent banning of activities and venues.[73] While being a commercial production that targeted a youth demographic, the film provides an important document of the discourses and disjunctures that circulated around the vibrant musical culture of Malay youth in the late 1960s. Beyond the one-dimensional characters, moralistic condescension and far from subversive narrative, *A Go Go '67* presents viewers with an idea of the music and lifestyles of Malay youth

---

[73] Pereira, *The Story of Singapore Sixties Music.* Vol. 1; Tan Sooi Beng, 'The performing arts in Malaysia: state and society', *Asian Music* 21, 1 (1989): 137–71; Tan, 'Counterpoints in the performing arts of Malaysia'.

of the *pop yeh yeh* era, albeit through the mediating gaze of a declining local commercial film industry desperately seeking a youth audience.

Kassim Masdor's Transition

The production of *A Go Go '67* also mirrored the rise of the Malay popular music record industry that would be more pervasive than films from the late 1960s to late 1970s. The musical director of the film, Kassim Masdor, was a protégé of P. Ramlee who had officially worked at Malay Film Productions as a continuity clerk from the mid-1950s. By the mid-1960s, aside from appearing in numerous films as an on-screen musician and contributing his own musical skills as a guitarist, accordionist, pianist and songwriter, Kassim Masdor was a part-time music producer and talent scout for EMI Singapore's Malay music division. His increasing musical success in the record industry led to some tension between him and the Malay Film Productions' studio manager Kwek Chip Jian, who saw Kassim Masdor's relationship with EMI as a conflict of interest. This was a complicated situation because Kassim Masdor was composing songs for Malay Film Productions' films and also releasing them as promotional records for their respective films on EMI. In an interview, he speaks about the struggle he experienced over the ownership of his film songs for Malay Film Productions:

> When I wrote songs for film, I would use them on the films as well as record them for EMI. So such recorded songs would be promotional for the film. So, one day the manager of Malay Film Productions [Kwek Chip Jian], he stopped me.... He [tried] to stop me from recording [my film songs] for EMI. He called me and said, 'From today onward, your songs cannot be recorded for EMI.' I said, 'Why?' To which he replied, 'Because we pay you, already ... You [should] pay me [for your EMI recordings].' [In reality] you [Malay Film Productions] borrowed my songs for the films.... [Kwek then responded]: 'You [should] pay me, that means the song(s) ... belong to us [Malay Film Productions].' The reason ... [Kwek] said this was because he was jealous as my songs were already making money, as well, right?.... No such thing ... [I replied]: 'You must remember Mr Kwek, I work in Malay Film Productions.

I work with you not as a composer, you must remember that … I am working with you as a continuity clerk.… If the lawyer [from EMI] comes to see you don't blame me.' [Kwek responded]: 'Why [would a] lawyer [come to see me]?' I answered: 'Because whatever song I write belongs to EMI. I signed the [song-writing] contract with EMI.' … As such, the film songs of … Yusof B. and Osman Ahmad … they were actually working in Jalan Ampas [Malay Film Productions] as composers [by contract] and their songs belonged to Malay Film Productions. Myself and P. Ramlee—P. Ramlee was hired as an actor. I was a continuity clerk. Both of our songs were free [to use in whatever way we wanted]. They could be recorded anywhere. They [Malay Film Productions] have no right to stop [the recording and distribution of] my songs.[74]

Kassim Masdor's exchange with Kwek Chip Jian indicates the anxieties expressed by the Malay film industry over the increasing shift of musical ownership and authorship towards individual agents not tied to film companies' exclusive composer contracts. This incident occurred sometime during the mid-1960s, when Kassim Masdor was rising quickly as a songwriter for radio programmes, records and film—a career that he pursued in parallel to his full-time job as a continuity clerk. However, the supposed 'jealousy' or contention over music ownership by Malay film studio executives clearly indicate that there was a contestation between the transmission of Malay popular songs via film as opposed to records. Even though film songs were initially released on records to promote their respective films, it is apparent that songs on records outshone and possibly even outsold the films. As a result, Malay film studios eventually became adamant about adapting to and claiming some form of ownership of the new musical practices that were quickly overshadowing the popularity of films.

---

[74] Interview with Kassim Masdor, Experience in the Malay Film and Popular Music Industry, 2013. In this interview, Kassim Masdor refers to himself as 'Uncle'. It is common in Malaysian and Singaporean culture for older, non-relatives, to refer to themselves as 'Uncle' or 'Auntie' as a form of respect and endearment. His use of the term indicates his seniority over me, but also conveyed a sense of informality, openness and familiarity with me. I was also quite surprised with his openness, as the interview was my first meeting with him.

A Go Go '67 was the culmination of this symbiotic but contested relationship between the recording industry and film industry. After the closure of the Malay Film Productions' Jalan Ampas studio in 1967, Kassim Masdor moved on to a successful career as a full-time manager for EMI's Malay music division. He relates how the film's conception was closely tied to his experience as a popular music producer outside the film industry:

> When I worked [in Malay Film Productions], I was also a part-time producer for EMI ... as a talent scout ... I recorded artists for EMI and made songs for EMI.... In time, they took a liking to me.... So one day Malay Film Productions wanted to make a film, *A Go Go '67*.... So the musical directors for the film were Yusof B. and myself. So we published an advertisement in the newspaper ... to call all the *kugiran* to come to [Malay Film Productions] for an audition.... Whoever was eligible, good, would appear [in the film].... From there I wrote many songs and from there I found many talents. For example, Sanisah Huri was not yet a singer. She was one of the dancers from the Terwellos band.... So, I ... [as] a talent scout ... I saw her ... [she was] cute, pretty.... So I featured her ... she could not sing. I made her sing in the film *A Go Go '67*.... From there, she [started] singing, and I brought her to EMI. Straight to EMI. Pass.

A Go Go '67 also launched the careers of the musicians and bands featured in the film, in particular Sanisah Huri, Zaiton and the Terwellos. It also marked the last attempt of the Malay film studio industry in Singapore to appeal to a changing audience demographic by adapting to the widely successful local music industry that was centred on youth culture. Kassim Masdor said the film received an 'encouraging reception' (*sambutan yang menggalakkan*) and made a considerable profit for Malay Film Productions, but was not as successful as P. Ramlee's films of the mid-1950s to early 1960s.[75] However, while appealing to youth, the agency of young people was somewhat limited if not altogether illusory. Most of the songs in the film were actually written by Kassim

---

[75]   Ibid.

Masdor and Yusof B., while iconic *pop yeh yeh* musical talents such as Sanisah Huri would go on to be successful recording artists beyond this transitory era. Kassim Masdor himself actually signifies the enduring musical legacy of the Malay film studio system. Unlike P. Ramlee, he was able to adapt the musical skills he learned from the film industry to the changing record industry. Instead of becoming a reactionary towards the youth music of the 1960s he actively embraced it and authored many popular songs, further developing Malay popular music into the next decade and beyond. He would continue to collect royalties from his compositions for EMI until his death in 2014 as the longest surviving film composer from Singapore's Malay film industry.[76]

Conclusion

Youth music cultures in Malaysia and Singapore have always been a locus of contention for nation-making policies and their conservative power brokers. While studies of Malay youth and music have provided some pertinent examples of this struggle with the two governments,[77] it was the music cultures of the 1960s that really ignited the history of contestation between the state and youth cultural practices. The 1960s was a decade of political transition for Malaysia and Singapore. State architects from both countries were desperate to create a local cultural imaginary for their emerging nation states. *Pop yeh yeh*, with its cultural

---

[76] There was a poignant moment at the end of my interview with Kassim Masdor. When he gave me a copy of the book edited by Mohd Raman Daud, *7 Magnificient [sic] Composers: 7 Tokoh Muzik*. Singapore: Perkamus, 2002—featuring the great Singapore-based Malay film composers from the 1950s to 1960s: Zubir Said, Osman Ahmad, Yusof B., Ahmad Jaafar, Wandly Yazid, P. Ramlee and Kassim Masdor—he pointed out that he was the only one still alive (at the time).

[77] Stivens, 'The youth, modernity and morality in Malaysia'; Azmyl Md Yusof, 'Facing the music: Music subcultures and "morality" in Malaysia', in *Media, Culture and Society in Malaysia*, ed. Yeoh Seng Guan. London: Routledge, 2010, pp. 179–96; Tan, 'The performing arts in Malaysia'; Tan Sooi Beng, 'From popular to "traditional" theater'; Tan, 'Counterpoints in the performing arts of Malaysia'; Tan, *Bangsawan*; Tan Sooi Beng, 'Dissonant voices: Contesting control through alternative media in Malaysia', 2006. Available at http://geekrawk.wordpress.com/2006/01/21/dissonant-voices-contesting-control-through-alternative-media-in-malaysia/ [accessed 29 January 2018].

rootlessness, was antithetical to the state vision, seen as a hindrance to the nation-making project. *Pop yeh yeh* music was unmistakably Western in influence, and Malaysian and Singaporean youth were aligning themselves to the more radical and subversive subcultures of the West. In doing so, these young people incited 'moral panic' among the conservative ruling elite.[78] This resulted in the formation and implementation of policies and interventions to limit their activities and spaces of expression. Much like the Malaysian black metal crackdowns in the early 2000s, 'the construction of Malay cultural identities as embodied in the body politics of urbanized Malay youths' led to state actions to control and repress what was deemed as deviant cultural practices.[79] Of course, in the case of commercially based music cultures there are ever-present ironies with regard to ethnocratic state hegemony and capitalist logics of global cultural consumption. In her study of Malaysian youth culture, Maila Stivens notes:

> There are … contradictory links between, on the one hand, the social disciplining imposed by the state and religious moral projects, to produce the hoped-for new, responsible, self-fashioning young citizen-subjects required by the new order discourses—male and female—and on the other, the relentless fashioning of selves by young people through their massive engagement in the new consumption ordained by the enthusiastic embrace of capitalist development.[80]

While not as transgressive or subversive as the more recent heavy metal scene,[81] *pop yeh yeh* culture can at least be seen as counter-cultural in its welcoming embrace of the new through processes of self-fashioning that, while initially emulating external trends, became local in its expression of Malaysian and Singaporean youth aspirations. These young people had music that was enjoyed in Europe (Kassim Slamat and the Swallows),

---

78   Stivens, 'The youth, modernity and morality in Malaysia', p. 174.
79   Azmyl, 'Facing the music', p. 180.
80   Stivens, 'The youth, modernity and morality in Malaysia', p. 190.
81   Ibid.; Tan Sooi Beng, 'Negotiating identities: Reconstructing the 'local' in Malaysia through "world beat"', *Perfect Beat* 5, 4 (2002): 3–20.

they adapted foreign songs to Malay and infused new meanings into them (Ismail Haron), they sparked new interest in the declining film industry, and more importantly they danced the a-go-go in stylish abandon and let their hair down freely—much to the misunderstanding, disgruntlement and embarrassment of the state authorities. All these practices of self-fashioning intersected in complex ways: cosmopolitan expressions of agency were articulated, yet the looming presence of larger market forces such as the print, recording and film industries were instrumental in the dissemination of these cultural practices and lifestyles.

As is clear from the films discussed in this chapter, youth counter-culture featured prominently in Malay film music. For some films, youth music was parodied and included as inconsequential to the narrative. In others such as *Muda Mudi*, Malay youth and *pop yeh yeh* music featured prominently in the narrative but more than that were presented as the antithesis to themes such as ageing. Meanwhile, films like *A Go Go '67* portrayed a youth perspective on youth music and the moral policing of young people. However, it simultaneously conveyed an idealistic and patronising message that young people should uphold consensual moral values and use their music to do good. Nonetheless, it still offered a significant critique of conservative sentiments towards youth culture, sentiments that mirrored the stringent cultural policies of the Malaysian and Singaporean states in the late 1960s and early 1970s. What is evident in the inclusion of youth culture and music in Malay film was the sheer popularity of youth music and dance at the time. Malay film producers were desperate to appeal to the younger generation that was turning away from local films and heading out to *pop yeh yeh* concerts and tea dances, and spending more of their money on the latest records instead of cinema tickets. Moreover, younger film music composers such as Kassim Masdor made a natural transition out of the film industry, after the closure of the Singapore film studios, into the more lucrative local popular music industry. This period thus represents a half-decade denouement of the Malay film studio industry, an unravelling of the musical styles and aesthetics and distribution networks that had seen the industry thrive from the mid-1950s to mid-1960s.

The disquieting musical expressions of Malay youth did not necessarily cause the film industry's demise. Rather they reflected a period during which a state vision of national culture was being cemented in the face of uncertain global social, economic and political changes. The state enforced national cultural policies on Malay youth that imposed an ethnic, traditionalist conception of morality with attendant behavioural expectations. It was the disquieting loudness of 'degenerate' youth practices that unsettled the Singaporean and Malaysian nation-making projects of cultivating a culturally refined and obedient citizenry. The looming presence of the postcolonial music and culture industries of the West still exists to challenge the presumed self-fashioning agency of musical cultures around the world.[82] These postcolonial transnational markets and ideological forces continue to complicate the tensions between youth practices and state policies in Malaysia and Singapore albeit in different cultural manifestations.

The prolonged and nuanced end of the Malay studio film industry involved the conciliation of new musical and cultural aesthetics with the older cosmopolitan styles and narrative conventions of Malay film. The music of Malay films from the 1950s and 1960s, particularly that of P. Ramlee, would gain renewed interest from the 1980s onward, resulting in many new performances and recordings of songs from his films. This music would form the basis of nostalgic references to an idealised nation-making past. In fact, Malay film music from the post-war and independence era would be instrumental in promoting an ethnonationalist aesthetic canon of Malaysian (not necessarily Singaporean) music. In the next chapter, I examine how the film music personalities Zubir Said and P. Ramlee are remembered and mobilised as icons of national culture in present-day Singapore and Malaysia. I then analyse how P. Ramlee's music has been interpreted by young Malaysian indie musicians in a compilation album released in 2010. I aim to show that while the music of Malay film in the 1950s and 1960s articulated the nation-making aesthetic of the independence era, the 'sounds of independence' continue to be rearticulated, reinterpreted and refashioned by those who search for agency in a national cultural paradigm that marginalises them.

---

[82] Martin Stokes, 'Music and the global order', *Annual Review of Anthropology* 33 (2004): 47–72.

Chapter 6

Indiepretations of Zubir Said and P. Ramlee

Di mana kan ku cari ganti
Serupa dengan mu
Tak sanggup ku berpisah
Dan perhati patah, hidup gelisah
(Where will I find a replacement
In your likeness
I will not let you go
Seeing us apart is a life of uncertainty)
'Di Mana Kan Ku Cari Ganti', music by P. Ramlee, lyrics by S. Sudarmaji

If there is one song that any Malaysian could attribute to P. Ramlee, it would undoubtedly be 'Getaran Jiwa' (Vibrations of the Soul). Composed by P. Ramlee and with lyrics by S. Sudarmaji, it was first performed in the film *Antara Dua Darjat* (1960). Numerous renditions of the song have emerged since P. Ramlee's death, from lush instrumental orchestrations to upbeat rock renditions to hip-hop remixes. From my experience as a jazz saxophonist performing in Kuala Lumpur from 2006 to 2011, 'Getaran Jiwa' is undoubtedly the standard or even compulsory Malay song for a predominantly English-language (or sometimes Mandarin) set list of popular songs. Most professional musicians playing live would almost always play 'Getaran Jiwa' if requested to perform a Malay or Malaysian song in a largely English repertoire. Beyond this song, P. Ramlee's film music has continued to inspire new arrangements and interpretations more generally, whether for live gigs, national events, television and radio programmes, and commercial albums. For many Malaysian artists, singing or performing versions of P. Ramlee's film songs is a rite of passage that affords them national recognition. Notable cases of such career-shaping tribute performances include Sheila Majid's *Legenda* album (1990), Siti Nurhaliza's numerous renditions and familiarity with his songs, and the winner of the 2004 *Malaysian Idol* contest Jaclyn Victor's grand finale performance of P. Ramlee's 'Tunggu Sekejap' (Wait for a While).[1]

In this chapter, I examine three cases of how Malay film music from the independence era has been adapted to contemporary contexts that simultaneously perpetuate and contest a 'cultural regime' of Malay national identity.[2] In each case, I argue that cultures of remembering film music icons and their music have formed part of perpetuating a Malay regional culture in Malaysia and Singapore. In these cultures of remembering, Malay film music icons are interpreted in different ways depending on the national context (Malaysia or Singapore), the agents involved (state institutions or individuals) as well as the spaces and media used (museums, documentary films, film festivals, concerts and compilation albums). First, I observe how Zubir Said was remembered as a Malay nationalist icon in a tribute concert that was held alongside the 'Majulah! The Film Music of Zubir Said' festival organised by the National Museum of Singapore in 2012. Next, I cross the border to Malaysia, examining discourses of remembering P. Ramlee as a Malay(sian) national icon at the P. Ramlee Memorial Museum and in the documentary by Shuhaimi Baba, *P. Ramlee*, aired on History Channel Asia in 2010. Finally, I analyse the conception and reception of the compilation album *P. Ramlee … Di Mana Kan Ku Cari Ganti*:

---

[1]   Jaclyn Victor was the first winner of the *Malaysian Idol* series that was broadcast nationally on TV3 and 8TV channels. After her performance of 'Tunggu Sekejap', Roslan Aziz, one of the three judges (who also produced Sheila Majid's *Legenda* album), said: 'Jacyln, in all the many songs that you have sung, this is the song that I like the most. I have never heard anyone else sing Tan Sri P. Ramlee's song "Tunggu Sekejap" this way. Ladies and gentlemen, I present to you another star that can be called a "super singer".' (*Dalam banyak-banyak lagu yang Jac(lyn) menyanyi, inilah lagu yang saya paling gemari sekali. Saya tak pernah dengar lagi orang menyanyi lagu Tan Sri P. Ramlee, 'Tunggu Sekejap', begini. Para hadirin, seorang lagi bintang yang bergelar 'super singer'.*) *Malaysian Idol Grand Finale*, 9 October 2004.

[2]   See Jocelyne Guilbault, *Governing Sound: The Cultural Politics of Trinidad's Carnival Music*. Chicago: University of Chicago Press, 2007.

Satu Indiepretasi (P. Ramlee ... Where Will I Find a Replacement: An Indiepretation, 2010).[3] It is the notion of 'indiepretation' that frames the discussion, particularly how the historically contextualised themes of ethnonationalism in Malay film music discussed earlier have been simultaneously reified and contested in contemporary interpretations of such history. The term 'indie' denotes the do-it-yourself aesthetic of rock bands since the 1990s and has its roots in punk music of the 1970s.[4] I appropriate the term here to signify the additional ideas of national independence articulated in film music of the 1950s and 1960s that have been made iconic in the image and music of P. Ramlee and, to a lesser extent, Zubir Said, to denote a unifying national culture. Since P. Ramlee's death, this notion of national independence has been constantly re-enacted and also subverted by the Malaysian and Singaporean states as well as by Malaysian popular music artists. This chapter seeks to unravel how the intertextual meaning of independence—both ideologically and in practice—is remembered and rearticulated in the national discourse. I examine how the cosmopolitan intimacies of nation-making found in the Malay film music of the 1950s and 1960s are recycled, reconsumed and reinterpreted today.

Solving the National Culture 'Problem'

In understanding the mobilisation of P. Ramlee and Zubir Said as national music icons in Malaysia and Singapore,[5] it is helpful to outline

---

[3]   The title of the compilation is a *double entendre* homage to P. Ramlee's famous film song 'Di Mana Kan Ku Cari Ganti' (Where Could I Find a Replacement), performed in the film *Ibu Mertua-ku* (My Mother-in-law, 1962).

[4]   See David Hesmondhalgh, 'Indie: The institutional politics and aesthetics of a popular music genre', *Cultural Studies* 13, 1 (1999): 34–61 for the background to the 'institutional politics and aesthetics' of the 'indie' category; and Ryan Hibbett, 'What is indie rock?' *Popular Music and Society* 28, 1 (2005): 55–77 for a detailed study of the commercial and contested category of 'indie rock' in predominantly Western popular music.

[5]   The notion of the 'bio-icon' as a technology that articulates social concerns is discussed insightfully in Bishnupriya Ghosh, *Global Icons: Apertures to the Popular*. Durham, NC: Duke University Press, 2011. She notes how the images and related representative ideology of iconic individuals such as Phoolan Devi, Mother Theresa

contemporary debates around the national cultural policy for music in both countries. This approach is in response to the dearth of comparative studies on the two states, especially with regard to music. Due to the politically intertwined histories of colonialism, culture and state formation, and the extensive ongoing cultural and commercial interactions between the two, it is imperative to examine the convergences and divergences of national culture in relation to Malay ethnicity. Malay ethnicity is hegemonic in Malaysia and marginal in Singapore. Nonetheless, both states share an autocratic approach to governance and employ homogenising and reductive discourses of national culture.[6] While this discussion excludes an examination of Indonesia's cultural policies with regard to Malay culture, Zubir Said's Indonesian identity and his transnational articulation of Malay culture should also be borne in mind. The purpose here is to draw attention to the homogenising conception of Singaporean and Malaysian national culture concomitant with postcolonial nation-making that effectively erased the pluralistic and cosmopolitan history of musical practices in the Malay Peninsula. In doing so, I hope to provide a detailed background for the case studies of how Zubir Said and P. Ramlee are presented, represented and remembered as authors and icons of Singaporean and Malaysian national culture.[7]

Refining and Defining Tradition

In Malaysia, a discourse of 'refinement' is particularly evident in the canonisation of a national music culture. This discourse indicates the

---

and Arundhati Roy are mobilised by disenfranchised groups to further their own social needs in complex, discursive, representational and material ways.

[6] Lily Zubaidah Rahim, *Singapore in the Malay World: Building and Breaching Regional Bridges*. London: Routledge, 2009.

[7] In line with Michel Foucault's notion of the role of authorship, I view the music and ideas of Zubir Said and P. Ramlee as 'initiators of discursive practices'. However, the cultural policies that were modelled on their conceptions of national music demonstrate how such initial discursive frameworks—of Malayness and Malay nationalism in music—have been subject to systematisation and subversion over time. See Michel Foucault, 'What is an author?' in *The Foucault Reader*, ed. Paul Rabinow. New York: Pantheon, 1984, pp. 101–20.

postcolonial worldview and cosmopolitan articulations of Malaysian proponents of the arts who sought the creation of a 'respectable' national culture on Western terms. It has resulted in the promotion of certain art forms over others. The terms of refinement also encompass an ethnically defined space of inclusion and exclusion. While Malay-Muslim art forms underwent nationalist projects of refinement, other art forms were aggressively omitted from the canon.

What can be said of Malay film music? P. Ramlee and his music, despite his cosmopolitan orientation and the multiple hybridities of his musical style, were absorbed, appropriated and propagated as Malaysian national music culture. It is P. Ramlee's iconicity rather than his music that has afforded him such a prominent status in Malaysia's national culture. His music was rootedly cosmopolitan, incorporating equally local and foreign musical practices.[8]

Two prominent studies, published in the same year, on the impact of the Malaysian National Culture Policy (1971) on local musical practices in the 1990s offer diverging analyses. Mohd Anis Md Nor's monograph on *zapin* dance offers a subdued critique of national arts discourse, while Tan Sooi Beng's book on the *bangsawan* form of Malay opera employs a more overtly critical analysis of state intervention and cultural control.[9] As a point of entry for their analyses, both cite the three concluding points of the National Culture Congress (Kongres Kebudayaan Kebangsaan) held on 16–20 August 1971 at Universiti Malaya, Kuala Lumpur:

1. Malaysian national culture must be based on the indigenous culture(s) of the citizens of this region;

2. Cultural elements of other cultures that are appropriate and reasonable may be accepted as an element of national culture; and

3. Islam is an important element in the shaping of this national culture.[10]

---

8   Tan Sooi Beng, 'Negotiating "His Master's Voice": Gramophone music and cosmopolitan modernity in British Malaya in the 1930s and early 1940s', *Bijdragen tot de Taal-, Land- en Volkenkunde* 169, 4 (2013): 457–94.

9   Mohd Anis Md Nor, *Zapin: Folk Dance of the Malay World*. Singapore: Oxford University Press, 1993; Tan Sooi Beng, *Bangsawan: A Social and Stylistic History of Popular Malay Opera*. Singapore: Oxford University Press, 1993.

10   Ministry of Culture, Youth and Sports [Kementerian Kebudayaan, Belia dan Sukan

With the added stipulation that 'appropriate' (*sesuai*) and 'reasonable' (*wajar*) cultural elements must be understood within the provisions of the first and third points, this contentious policy has been subject to divergent interpretations and outright critique depending on the cultural practices that are being contested or promoted. Tan's and Mohd Anis's studies clearly indicate the differing impacts of the National Culture Policy on different cultural practices local to the Malay Peninsula. Here I compare the two studies in order to situate my own reading of Malay film music and their icons in contemporary Malaysia. I also include for the first time some of the viewpoints of the papers presented for the music seminar of the National Culture Congress to better trace the discourse on music that contributed to the drafting of the policy.[11]

Despite its hybrid cosmopolitan origins, and informal and participatory contexts of performance, *zapin* has been institutionalised with ease in its adaptation to this national culture framework. Mohd Anis notes:

> Not only is contemporary *zapin* construed as a choreographed dance tradition by most Malaysians, it is also considered a *dignified* dance tradition. In contrast to the glittering era of *bangsawan* and cabarets in the 1930s, and the glorious years of the Malay movies in the 1950s and 1960s, *zapin* today, in the early 1990s, is associated with the *fine artistry* of Malay-Arab syncretic culture. *Zapin* is highly regarded as the *last bastion* of an Arab-derived dance tradition that has contributed to the *enrichment* of Malay performance traditions.[12]

Malaysia], *Asas Kebudayaan Kebangsaan* [Basis of National Culture], Kuala Lumpur: KBBS, 1973, p. vii. My translation of this is closer to Tan's in the use of 'elements' for '*unsur-unsur*' and 'reasonable' for '*wajar*', and is based on the same printed source, whereas Mohd Anis cites 'The National Culture Congress (*Kongres Kebudayaan Kebangsaan*: 91, supra note 16)' but does not mention any specific document as a source.

11 In Chapter Five I discussed P. Ramlee's contribution to the seminar, 'Cara-cara meninggikan mutu dan memperkayakan muzik jenis asli dan tradisional Malaysia demi kepentingan negara' [Ways to elevate and enrich the original and traditional music of Malaysia for the benefit of the nation], in *Asas Kebudayaan Kebangsaan*, 1st ed. Kuala Lumpur: Kementerian Kebudayaan Belia dan Sukan Malaysia, 1973, pp. 205–7.

12 Mohd Anis, *Zapin*, pp. 87–88 (my emphasis).

Mohd Anis indicates how the cultural status of *zapin* has been transformed over time by conforming to government policy that accords greater aesthetic value to certain performing arts over others. This is seen in the privileged positioning of '*zapin* today' compared to its use in previous performance contexts such as '*bangsawan* and cabarets' in the 1930s and Malay films from the independence era. While Mohd Anis alludes to nationalist discourses about *zapin* he does not problematise them in any detail. He indicates a discourse of 'high art' that accords a greater value to '*zapin* today' compared to other Malay or local art forms. For example, he notes a conception of *zapin* as synonymous with 'fine artistry' whose corollary is that *bangsawan* and cabaret music fall outside the bounds of such 'fine artistry'. It is evident that the criteria for what constitutes such 'fine artistry' are based on the three pillars of the National Culture Policy. He further notes how the art form is perceived as 'the *last bastion* of an Arab-derived dance tradition that has contributed to the *enrichment* of Malay performance traditions'. Mohd Anis's observations imply that the National Culture Policy projects the notion of a threat to 'Malay performance traditions' onto un-Islamic foreign elements. For its part, *zapin*, in its Islamic-Arabic-Malay hybridity, forms the ideal 'bastion' of Malaysian art that can 'contribute to the enrichment' of national culture as envisioned in the Malay-Islamic criteria of the policy. Despite the 'low' cultural status associated with Malay film and its music and dance noted in Mohd Anis's work, the position of 'high art' has, paradoxically, been accorded to P. Ramlee's film music. Currently, his music, if not his musical iconicity, has an even higher cultural status than *zapin*.

The discursive conception of *zapin* as a high art form mirrors the tone of papers presented at the National Culture Congress that discussed the need to improve local music by adapting Western music 'values'. In his call for increased adaptation of local music to 'serious/heavy' (*berat*) or Western classical music standards, Ariff Ahmad laments the inability of 'Malay society' to appreciate such intellectual forms of music:

> Malay society, especially, finds it quite difficult to accept serious styles of music because there is no understanding of serious styles of music.

> Indigenous types of music that have form and structure in Malay society
> are primitive and only emphasise rhythms. Because of this, it cannot be
> denied that if Malay society is required to appreciate these serious musical
> arts, their own musical concepts need to be added with Western concepts.[13]

Much like the cases above, this sense of refining Malay cultural practices
is something that Mohd Anis's analysis of *zapin* brings to the surface,
explaining its advantageous position with regard to the National Culture
Policy. While it is ironic that such a Western-centric view contributed
to the drafting of a firmly ethnocentric cultural policy, this was not the
only presentation to give Western music a privileged position. In the
same seminar, Saiful Bahari suggested correcting the tuning of traditional
instruments from Kelantan—specifically *seruling* (bamboo flute), *rebab*
(bowed string instrument) and *serunai* (reed wind instrument)—because
he heard them in relation to each other as 'excessively contrasting' in
tuning 'to the point that it disturbed his ears while listening'.[14] He further
argued for the establishment of a national symphony orchestra that 'aside
from playing national music, must be tasked to perform Western classical
repertoire'.[15] Ariff Ahmad's and Saiful Bahari's intention was to promote a
notion of high art in Malay culture and their suggestions were to 'classicise'
or to refine Malay musical practices and tastes with Western concepts.

Attempts to Westernise local music in many parts of the world were
part of a more widespread process of postcolonial nation-making, as the
refinements of the West were also seen as a means to reclaim national
cultures from a colonial past. Amanda Weidman observes how the use
of the violin since the 1800s in South Indian classical music presents

---

[13] Ariff Ahmad, 'Muzik Malaysia jenis barat (seriosa) dan kedudukannya dalam masyarakat Malaysia baru' [Western (seriosa) Malaysian music and its place in new Malaysian society], in *Asas Kebudayaan Kebangsaan*. Kementerian Kebudayaan Belia dan Sukan Malaysia, 1973, p. 210.

[14] Saiful Bahari, 'Perkembangan muzik Malaysia dan matlamatnya' [The growth of Malaysian music and its objectives], in *Asas Kebudayaan Kebangsaan*. Kuala Lumpur: Kementerian Kebudayaan Belia dan Sukan Malaysia, 1973, pp. 215–21. '*Menurut pendengaran saya alat-alat muzik Kelantan di antara satu dengan lainnya sangat contrast hingga agak mengganggu pendengaran telinga.*'

[15] Ibid. '*Selain memainkan muzik-muzik kebangsaannya sendiri ianya harus sanggup pula memainkan lagu-lagu klasik-Barat.*'

a complex set of mimetic relations between instrument and voice, India and West, colonizer and colonized. The mimetic capacity of the violin guarantees the authenticity of the Karnatic voice, as a colonial instrument is used to ward off—and ultimately redeem Indian music from—the effects of colonialism.[16]

In much the same way, national policymakers in Malaysia envisioned the elevation of the status of local music through Western technologies or frameworks of progress. However, alongside this complex postcolonial mimesis was a need to homogenise a national culture within the frames of Malay and Islamic culture. Jocelyne Guilbaut outlines a similar situation in Trinidad and Tobago where the black community occupied the 'privileged space' in the performance and production of calypso music that was 'in the wake of independence ... emblematic of the nation-state'—however, this 'exclusive domain' for black Trinidadians effectively marginalised diasporic minorities such as the large South Asian community.[17]

In analogous ways, the National Culture Policy in Malaysia was instrumental in shaping 'exclusive domains' of musical practices that privileged a homogeneous conception of Malayness—an ethnocentric articulation of national cultural identity. Judith Nagata observes that 'ethnocratic' tropes have 'politically enclosed ... Malay citizens', allowing UMNO to 'manufacture a Malay political majority and dominance to which it jealously guards access'.[18] So even within Malay society, a bounded conception of cultural identity is imposed, something that is disjunctive to both the diverse ethnic communities of Malaysia and

---

16 Amanda J. Weidman, *Singing the Classical, Voicing the Modern: The Postcolonial Politics of Music in South India*. London: Duke University Press, 2006, p. 59.

17 Guilbault, *Governing Sound*, p. 40.

18 Judith Nagata, 'Boundaries of Malayness: "We have made Malaysia: now it is time to (re)make the Malays but who interprets the history?"', in *Melayu: Politics, Poetics and Paradoxes of Malayness*, ed. Maznah Mohamad and Syed Muhd Khairudin Aljunied. Singapore: NUS Press, 2011, p. 27. The notion of 'ethnocracy' rather than 'ethnocentricity' implies an institutionalised form of ethnic group dominance. In the case of Malaysia, the racialisation of politics is very much ingrained into the constitution and electoral system. See Geoff Wade, 'The origins and evolution of ethnocracy in Malaysia', Asia Research Institute Working Paper, no. 112 (2009): 1–39.

the pluralistic history of Malay culture. It is out of this conception of ethnoculturalism that P. Ramlee's musical iconicity grew—despite his cosmopolitan hybrid plurality. It was actually very easily suited to the national culture project. Here was a Malay personality who composed music exclusively in the Malay language for a Malay vernacular film industry.[19]

In understanding the process of governmentality in musical practices, Tan Sooi Beng's study relates how the implementation of the National Culture Policy led to the subsequent institutionalisation, systematisation and control of *bangsawan*. She observes the shift towards homogenisation in government-sanctioned culture in the form of increased attention and promotion of performing arts that are more compatible with the first and third points of the policy—such as *wayang kulit*, gamelan and *nasyid*—that construct 'national culture' as 'based on the cultures of the people indigenous to the region' while emphasising 'Islam' as 'an important element'.[20] Indirectly, the policy suggests that the cultural practices of non-Malay and non-Muslim communities,

---

[19] However, this is further problematised by his patrilineal Acehnese roots. Beyond his father's Acehnese origins, P. Ramlee's affinity with Aceh is scarcely discussed. Moreover, he was born and raised in highly cosmopolitan and ethnically diverse Penang.

[20] Tan, *Bangsawan*, pp. 176–77. A considerable amount of research has been done on the rise of modern *nasyid* (Islamic religious music sung by all-male or all-female vocal groups) and its place in articulating a post-1990s Malay-Muslim modernity through popular music culture. See Tan Sooi Beng, 'Negotiating identities: Reconstructing the 'local' in Malaysia through "world beat"', *Perfect Beat* 5, 4 (2002): 3–20; Margaret Sarkissian, '"Religion never had it so good": Contemporary *nasyid* and the growth of Islamic popular music in Malaysia', in *Yearbook for Traditional Music* 37 (2005): 124–52; Bart Barendregt, 'Cyber-*nasyid*: Transnational soundscapes in Muslim Southeast Asia', in *Medi@sia: Global Media/tion in and out of Context*, ed. Todd Joseph Miles Holden and Timothy Scrase. London: Routledge, 2006, pp. 170–87; Bart Barendregt, 'The art of no-seduction: Muslim boy-band music in Southeast Asia and the fear of the female voice', *IIAS Newsletter* 40 (2006): 10; Bart Barendregt, 'Pop, politics and piety: *Nasyid* boy band music in Muslim Southeast Asia', in *Islam and Popular Culture in Indonesia and Malaysia*, ed. Andrew N. Weintraub. London: Routledge, 2011, pp. 235–56; Bart Barendregt, 'Sonic discourses on Muslim Malay modernity: The Arqam sound', *Contemporary Islam* 6, 3 (2012): 315–40. Not surprisingly, *nasyid* has thrived in the Malay-Muslim market, fitting comfortably into the vision of the nation's cultural policy. But it has also made an impact among Muslim audiences from Indonesia to Britain.

such as the substantial Chinese and Indian minorities, do not count as 'national culture'.[21] To further illustrate this, Tan observes a process of 'Malayisation' in government-sponsored productions of *bangsawan* that downplay or ignore altogether the abundant non-Malay and non-Muslim elements that were formerly a part of its rich and plural cultural practice.[22] Tan concludes that *bangsawan* in its government-sponsored form is 'no longer able to attract non-Malay audiences or performers' or 'Malays of the younger generation [who] find it difficult to identify with this type of *bangsawan* which has distinctly failed to adapt to the times in terms of themes, music, dances, and setting, and which does not emphasize variety'.[23]

Tan's study demonstrates how interventionist initiatives on the part of the government have failed to invigorate a declining art form. It is adherence to strict ethnocratic agendas that have led directly to the art form's declining appeal to the public. In light of the ethics of intervention in preserving endangered musical cultures, Catherine Grant suggests that the needs and welfare of the related artistic community should be the focus instead of 'overarching policy, systemic or governmental demands, or the interests of academics or others in positions of power'.[24] As Tan's research shows, the National Culture Policy has had little effect on the surviving practitioners of *bangsawan* theatre, most of whom are living in poverty.[25] This is not dissimilar to the neglect of P. Ramlee. He struggled financially after moving from Singapore to Malaysia in 1964 until his death in 1973.

Tan's study demonstrates the failings of an ethnocratic agenda in its inability to accept Malay cultural practices as culturally heterogeneous.

---

[21] This is especially contentious in my view, because point three automatically excludes non-Muslims who may be 'indigenous to the region' (point one). Of course, the definition 'indigenous' is ambiguous, but the inclusion of specifically Malay cultural practice as 'indigenous' is reinforced by the 'Islamic culture' provision, in that Islam is the exclusive religion of Malays in Malaysia.

[22] Tan, *Bangsawan*, pp. 178–87.

[23] Ibid., p. 186.

[24] Catherine Grant, 'Rethinking safeguarding: Objections and responses to protecting and promoting endangered musical heritage', *Ethnomusicology Forum* 21, 1 (2012): 42.

[25] Tan, *Bangsawan*, p. 187.

In providing an insight into the cultural 'purification' of Malay culture through the aggressive removal of elements that are regarded as 'foreign' and un-Islamic, Tan sheds light on how pluralistic and cosmopolitan musical practices such as Malay film music of the 1950s and 1960s may be appropriated to promote a homogeneous national culture agenda by state institutions. While *bangsawan* in the 1990s was performed in the institutionalised context of state universities, P. Ramlee's film music was performed and recorded in both state and commercial contexts. In both manifestations, his music and persona were used to symbolise or evoke a national cultural aesthetic.

The authoritarian ethnocracy of cultural policy in suppressing pluralism and creativity also results in counter-hegemonic or alternative conceptions and practices of Malay culture. In this vein, Judith Nagata contends that the emergence of '*Melayu Baru* [New Malays] ... who think outside the ideological box and are engaged in alternative artistic and civil society movements, ensure the constant production of new images of Malayness' and Malaysian-ness 'as a challenge to the state vision'.[26] The *Indiepretasi* album discussed below provides a case of how a canonised conception of national culture in the form of P. Ramlee's musical works can be subverted by a new generation. Despite the renewed imagining of Malayness that the album offers, it nonetheless perpetuates an ethnocratic and commercial agenda—a Malay musical icon forms the foundation of reimagining national culture in the commodified context of indie music.

The case of national culture and music in Singapore is markedly different despite the two countries' shared history of colonialism and independence. Studies on national culture, music and the performing arts there focus more on the hegemonic control of the ruling People's Action Party through state-sponsored arts initiatives. Lily Kong's study of Singaporean popular music in government-endorsed music campaigns is particularly useful in understanding how music was mobilised to propagate a hegemonic state vision of ideal citizenry based on 'core Asian values', such as 'community over self; upholding the family as the

---

26 Nagata, 'Boundaries of Malayness', p. 28.

basic building block of society; resolving major issues through consensus instead of contention; and stressing racial and religious tolerance and harmony'.[27] However, Kong also observes how state-sponsored music initiatives are contested in parodic musical productions. Popular music is therefore also mobilised by non-state actors to challenge autocratic state values.

While Kong's study notes how the state has been 'harnessing music' for Singaporean nation-making since 'the first days of independence',[28] it stops short of providing a history of nationalistic song-making during the independence era. Moreover, a history of nationalist songs in Singapore would also have to problematise issues of ethnicity and Malay ethnic nationalism in particular—an issue she does not discuss.[29] A number of questions suggest themselves. How are notions of race and ethnonationalism intertwined with nationalist music produced in the shared independence era of Singapore and Malaysia? How are Malay composers and their songs from that era remembered in contemporary Singapore? How do the ethnonationalist ideals of composers such as Zubir Said fit with Singapore's multiethnic (though distinctly Asian) vision of citizenship? How is this contested by the minority Malay community?

These questions are addressed through the ways that Zubir Said's music and iconicity are remembered by the Singapore Malay community. While Kong's study provides an insight into how nationalist songs and their sentiments are challenged through musical parody, I consider how a politically marginalised group reappropriates nationalist music. Singaporean nationalism itself is not scrutinised. Rather, it is the authorship of that national (musical) narrative that is contested and reclaimed by the Malay community through the musical works of Zubir Said.

---

[27] Lily Kong, 'Music and cultural politics: Ideology and resistance in Singapore', *Transactions of the Institute of British Geographers* 20, 4 (1995): 450.

[28] Ibid., p. 457.

[29] An edited volume, Jun Zubillaga-Pow and Ho Chee Kong, eds. *Singapore Soundscape: Musical Renaissance of a Global City*. Singapore: National Library Board Singapore, 2014, includes histories and contemporary cases of popular Malay music within the multicultural backdrop of the city state.

Remembering Icons, Interpreting Independence

P. Ramlee and Zubir Said are memorialised as icons of national identity in museums, events and spaces. But their status is made problematic by the precarious position they occupy in relation to the complex and controversial political, economic and racial histories of Singapore and Malaysia. In Malaysia, P. Ramlee died a tragic death, unable to thrive in the uncertain economic and political conditions of the early 1970s. Yet he is acknowledged posthumously as a national icon. Despite being a markedly cosmopolitan individual during his lifetime, P. Ramlee's image, films and music have come to be represented as unquestionable markers of Malay ethnonationalist pride. By contrast, Zubir Said, despite his Malay nationalist inclinations, remained in Singapore as part of an ethnic minority.[30] His penning of the national anthem 'Majulah Singapura' positions him uniquely as a nation-maker and music icon. The Malay-language national anthem is one of the few tangible reminders of Singapore's position in the Malay world—few non-Malay Singaporeans, especially those born after independence, understand the meaning of their own national song. Here I unravel the parallel paths these two Malay film music icons have occupied, at times converging and at others diverging, but ultimately appropriated by state projects to perpetuate a particular vision of national culture.

Remembering Zubir Said beyond the Causeway

In October 2012 I attended a film festival titled 'Majulah! The Film Music of Zubir Said', organised by the Cinémathèque film division of the National Museum of Singapore. It seems this was an especially auspicious year for remembering the famous film composer. That same year Zubir Said's daughter, Rohana Zubir, released a comprehensive and personal biography of her father, *Zubir Said: The Composer of*

---

[30] Zubir Said's daughter mentions how dedicated he was to Singapore, refusing to live with her in Kuala Lumpur and saying he 'wanted to die in Singapore'. Serene Lim, 'Audience turns misty-eyed at tribute to Zubir', *Straits Times*, 10 March 1990.

Majulah Singapura.[31] Rohana Zubir launched the book on 1 October at the Institute of Southeast Asian Studies, with introductory speeches by the historian Wang Gungwu and the film song lyricist and film-maker Yusnor Ef.[32] The book was then launched in Kuala Lumpur on 21 October, an event attended by the Malaysian minister of information, communications and culture Rais Yatim, the Singapore high commissioner to Malaysia Ong Keng Yong, and the former prime minister of Malaysia Abdullah Badawi.[33] I was not able to go to these exclusive events, but I did attend a tribute concert for Zubir Said on 12 October at Singapore's Esplanade titled '*Bintang Hati—Malam Kenangan Zubir Said*' (Star of the Heart—Remembering Zubir Said). All these events in 2012 indicated a deepening mobilisation of Zubir Said as a Singaporean national icon. More than this, his status has moved beyond the Causeway to Malaysia, making him a binational cultural icon.[34] His cultural iconicity is contested, promoted and remembered through different notions of Malay ethnicity, Singaporean nationalism and the divergent political positions adopted in each nation.

Though born and raised in Bukit Tinggi, Sumatra, there were no notable events in Indonesia to memorialise Zubir Said, highlighting by omission his potency as a Malay nationalist icon in Malaysia and Singapore. While the reach of his status is relatively limited in Malaysia (quite unlike that of P. Ramlee), it is important to note that his Singapore-born daughter is a Malaysian citizen and decorated with a national honorific title. Her book though was sponsored and published by a Singapore-based academic institution, while its title explicitly positions Zubir Said as the composer of Singapore's national

---

[31] Rohana Zubir, *Zubir Said, the Composer of Majulah Singapura*. Singapore: ISEAS Publishing, 2012.

[32] Juliana Lim, 'Tribute to national anthem composer Zubir Said on the 25th anniversary of his demise', 2012. Available at http://julianalim.wordpress.com/2012/10/18/tribute-month/ [accessed 18 December 2017].

[33] 'Singapura kongsi arkib warisan sejarah' [Singapore shares historical heritage archives], *Sinar Harian*, 21 October 2012.

[34] Officially the Johor–Singapore Causeway, built in 1923. The phrase 'across the Causeway' is commonly used by Singaporeans and Malaysians to describe each other's relative locations, and contains meanings, such as nationality, ideology, politics and racial hegemony.

anthem, highlighting his role as a cultural icon for his adopted country. These modes of remembering Zubir Said articulate a 'causeway' to a complex and entangled national, cultural and musical history. At the Kuala Lumpur book launch, both the Malaysian minister and the Singaporean high commissioner agreed on the need to actively cooperate in exchanging the historical resources of their shared national history.[35]

Beyond these diplomatic niceties, however, greater tensions are apparent, particularly in Singapore, with regard to the mobilisation of Zubir Said. The tribute concert at the Esplanade, for example, was performed to a packed hall and predominantly Malay audience, thus articulating a very Malaycentric yet Singaporean nationalist atmosphere. At this event, Zubir Said was the galvanising icon for the besieged Malay minority's cultural stake in Singapore, a country where Malay is an official national language but the majority hardly speak or understand it.[36] This appropriation of Zubir Said as an ethnonational icon was clearly expressed by the concert's artistic director:

> Tonight we celebrate one of the heroes of our race, culture and country. Zubir Said was an artist who carved the soul of the nation with his steadfast talent and upholding tradition through his art. Aside from being the composer of patriotic songs and folk songs, he also wrote many for classic Malay films. Tonight we are proud to present his compositions from that time. These songs have been arranged in a way so as to tell the story of the life of Pak Zubir himself, all with the hope that as we all learn more about him, we will love and cherish keenly, Zubir Said, the pioneer Singapore artist.[37]

Quite clear in this introductory message in the concert programme booklet is an ethnic minority voice mobilising Zubir Said's status as a

35 'Singapura kongsi arkib warisan sejarah', *Sinar Harian*, 21 October 2012.
36 Rahim, *Singapore in the Malay World*, pp. 1–2, citing Ong Soh Chin, 'Who are you? Where do you live?', *Straits Times*, 19 August 2006. Singapore's other three official languages are English, Mandarin and Tamil.
37 Zizi Azah Bte Abdul Majid and Amri Amin, '*Bintang Hati—Malam Kenangan Zubir Said*' [Star of the Heart—Remembering Zubir Said], Concert Programme Booklet, 12 October 2012, p. 8.

hero of 'our race, culture and country'. It is telling how the possessive 'our' is used: it assumes the exclusive racial demographic of the concertgoers. Indeed, the concert was definitely more of a Malay ethnonational event than a multiethnic one—simultaneously occupying and being sanctioned by an official national space (the Esplanade), while also presenting a microcosm of a generalised Malay musical culture onstage. As such, the 'our' also indicates a political position—an overt display of Malayness to the rest of Singapore. The concert articulated the complex polarisation of Singapore's multiethnic society while also amplifying the underlying sense of displacement felt by its Malay minority. The musical contributions of Zubir Said were projected as the pride and joy of the Malay community, thus serving as a reminder of Singapore's precarious geographic position in the surrounding 'Malay' region.

Ethnographically, the contested relations of power between the state and the concert's participants were initially subtle, but became more apparent towards the end of the performance. At the end of the concert, all of the concert performers were invited onstage, along with the most honoured guest, Rohana Zubir, to sing 'Majulah Singapura'. Everyone rose dutifully and sang the anthem loudly and clearly, and at the end of the song, amid sustained applause, I heard a young Malay man jokingly say, '*Hidup Melayu! Hidup UMNO!*' (Long live the Malays! Long live UMNO!). During the singing of the anthem, I reflected on the possible precariousness of Rohana Zubir's position as a Malaysian citizen singing Singapore's national anthem that was composed by her erstwhile Indonesian father. In short, an awareness of the cultural fluidity and political tensions of Malayness were intertwined with the fixities of Singaporean, Malaysian and Indonesian citizenship, all of which coalesced in this moment of the national anthem's performance.

These disjunctures gesture towards the paradoxes and intimacies of Malay nation-making found in the ideas and music of Zubir Said. They reverberate from the mid-1950s to the present. A sense of Malay ethnonational identity is explicitly galvanised around musical practices, yet the performance of these practices in different national spaces reveals the complexities and contested nature of ethnicised sentiments about citizenship. Remembering Zubir Said historically—as opposed to nationalistically or aesthetically—through his music in films provides a clearer insight into the source of the national cultural tensions experienced by Malays in Singapore today.

By contrast, the more overtly state-sanctioned event remembering Zubir Said in the 'Majulah!' film festival attempts to subdue the racialised tensions apparent in the tribute concert by perpetuating a less ethnocentric and more 'inclusive' nationalist discourse (see Figure 6.1). In her foreword to the festival programme, Lee Chor Lin says:

> Zubir Said's life epitomises the story of the many thousands of Singaporeans who originated elsewhere but found roots in Singapore and gave this country unreservedly their life-time's work, heart and soul.... Zubir Said ... gave generations of Singaporeans—and our neighbours in the archipelago—his talent for music-making.... Zubir Said's music should help us recall the time in which we were energised by a singular hope and sense of purpose for the nascent country that was being born. That the anthem is written in Malay by a composer from Bukit Tinggi reminds us of Singapore's place in the Malay world, but also of the inclusive multicultural basis on which our society is built. This society asked not where one had come from, but what one had come to give (and what one would bear).[38]

Lee implies a more racially inclusive vision of Zubir Said as a national icon that conveniently ignores (or perhaps is unaware of) his explicit historical role in the propagation of Malay nationalist ideas. Lee acknowledges Zubir Said's Malayness that 'reminds us of Singapore's place in the Malay world', but stresses in a somewhat overcompensatory manner the inclusivity of Singapore's 'multicultural' society. This nationalised, as opposed to ethnicised, promotion of Zubir Said's iconic status effectively washes over any possibility for ethnic sentiment in claiming a stake to Singapore's nation-making. In its very inception, Singapore is envisioned as a diverse cosmopolis in which anyone from any background could contribute to the national project, provided they

---

[38] Lee Chor Lin, 'Foreword', in *Majulah! The Film Music of Zubir Said*. Singapore: National Museum of Singapore, 2012, pp. 12–13.

contributed significantly. Zubir Said's affiliation with the regional Malay nationalist ideas of the 1950s is downplayed in order to promote a vision of a cosmopolitan nation state comprising dedicated citizens from different backgrounds ('a composer from Bukit Tinggi'). The 'Majulah!' festival thus articulated Zubir Said's cosmopolitan history and music, but also neutralised his role in envisioning a Malay nationalism in his music.

Figure 6.1 The 'Majulah!' billboard on the exterior of Singapore's National Museum

I was informed by Low Zu Boon, the assistant manager of Cinémathèque, that the festival was part of a general 'mandate from the top ... in terms of cultural policy' that was seeing an increased emphasis on 'local content' in 2012.[39] He told me of a shift towards more local cultural content in government organisations that occurred 'quite recently ... post [2011] general elections'.[40] However, even prior to the

---

[39] Interview with Low Zu Boon, 'Majulah!' Film music of Zubir Said, 2012.

[40] The 2011 Singapore general election saw a reduced majority of votes for the ruling PAP. Some of the cultural issues that contributed to discontent towards the ruling party included the increase of immigrants and a sense of deteriorating local culture.

elections, Cinémathèque was keen on exploring local content but did not have the support to do so:

> We were looking at ... how to explore ... to do a programme ... of local film heritage and music ... [as] a big part of it and ... a way to sort of anchor in this whole selection of films ... and, yeah I guess many people can sort of associate with ... icons within our history so Zubir Said is ... known, but not really known.... It's almost like ... I don't know if you would call him a nationalistic figure. In a certain way [he is a national icon] because he composed the national anthem so I guess, we are a bit excited to ... go beyond that racial stereotype.... We [Cinémathèque] always felt there was not enough research done [on Zubir Said], so it's our way of contributing.... In a way we are continuing what has been done before.[41]

I also asked Low how the festival might relate to instilling national pride and whether there was any intention to do so on the part of the National Heritage Board (NHB), the government body that manages the National Museum:

> [National pride] could be derived [from the festival content], definitely. Whether it was something we want to convey, I'm not too sure.... But I guess we are [conveying that sentiment as] it's a national culture situation. It's kind of geared that way.... It is their [NHB's] mission to do this but ... that's not the reason why we did this programme.... I guess it's a close fit so it's kind of well received, as well.[42]

For detailed political analyses of this election, see Terence Chong, 'A return to normal politics: Singapore general elections 2011', in *Southeast Asian Affairs 2012*, ed. Daljit Singh and Pushpa Thambipillai. Singapore: ISEAS–Yusof Ishak Institute, 2012, pp. 283–98; and Stephan Ortmann, 'Singapore: Authoritarian but newly competitive', *Journal of Democracy* 22, 4 (2011): 153–64.

[41] Interview with Low Zu Boon, 'Majulah!' Film music of Zubir Said, 2012. Low was making reference to books such as Juliana Chua and Hawazi Daipi, *Zubir Said: His Songs*. Singapore: Singapore Cultural Foundation, 1990.

[42] Ibid.

The festival was indeed a convenient 'fit' to the more artistic and historical intentions of the organisers, considering that the NHB's official mission statement is 'to preserve and celebrate our shared heritage' by 'safeguarding and promoting the heritage of our diverse communities, for the purpose of education, nation-building and cultural understanding'.[43]

The events of remembering Zubir Said in Singapore underscore the paradoxes and disjunctures of his iconicity in a national and ethnonational context. The events articulate his cosmopolitan life and his musical contributions to national culture, especially in Singapore. However, Zubir Said was also a staunch advocate of Malay nationalism in music. His complex position in between the boundaries of Malaysia, Singapore and Indonesia naturally manifested itself in contested discourses or conflicting mobilisations of his iconicity across the Causeway. For Malays in Singapore, his music, and in particular the national anthem, is a pertinent reminder to the majority population of the Malay minority's presence and relevance in a country that has over the years distanced itself from a Malay national identity. Conversely, across the Causeway, Zubir Said is remembered as an important contributor to a shared Malay musical heritage of Malaysia and Singapore. Since the 2011 general election in Singapore, there has been a greater emphasis on 'local' content in the state's cultural institutions. As the 'Majulah!' festival showed, greater attention has been paid to Zubir Said beyond his commonly remembered role as the composer of the national anthem. But in line with state policy, these events actively downplayed his role as a Malay nationalist, instead choosing to represent him as a paragon of Singapore's inclusive and multicultural citizenry—an idealised vision of the island state that ignores its tumultuous political past and precarious relationship to the surrounding Malay world and its own Malay citizens.

---

[43] National Heritage Board, 'About us—National Heritage Board', 2018. Available at https://www.nhb.gov.sg/who-we-are/about-us/mission-and-vision [accessed 2 February 2018].

Irreplaceable: Memorialising P. Ramlee

In the historical national cultural narrative of Malaysia, the death of P. Ramlee in 1973 is remembered as having stirred the national cultural consciousness from a stupor of decadent, long-haired and sexually depraved pop and rock bands and artists who were shunning local musical practices. This grand narrative of P. Ramlee's resurgence after his death is somewhat misconstrued as his pre-eminence as a nationalist icon would only be truly cemented in 1986 with the establishment of Pustaka Peringatan P. Ramlee (P. Ramlee Memorial Museum) by Arkib Negara (National Archives of Malaysia). The memorial functions as a museum for the artist and his third and final wife, Salmah Ismail, better known by her stage and screen name, Saloma. In its exhibition of memorabilia, the museum presents a grand narrative that casts P. Ramlee and Saloma as virtually undisputed in their artistic greatness as national film and music icons. At the same time, beyond the odd diorama displays of film sets alongside Saloma and P. Ramlee attire rentals,[44] there is a sense of homeliness that lends an intimacy to the museum. This is mainly because it is located in and built out of the interior of the actual home the couple rented when they moved from Singapore to Malaysia in 1964 (Figure 6.2). The National Archives bought the house from its original owners in 1986. In the renovated space, there is a small section that approximates the couple's original study replete with, among other items, P. Ramlee's typewriter and piano—two iconic objects that symbolise the convergence of his auteurship and musicality (Figure 6.3). Despite the display of personal effects, P. Ramlee and Saloma are ultimately objectified and idealised by this exhibition of personal possessions that outlived them: her collection of sunglasses, his film trophies and record player. These objects are now material artefacts that form assemblages of a national cultural narrative based on the undeniable artistic pre-eminence of P. Ramlee as a film-maker, musician and patriot. Such memorials indicate how the authority of the

---

[44] I was informed when I visited in July 2013 that the clothes available for guests to wear and take photos on site were the actual possessions of P. Ramlee and Saloma. The clothes rental was no longer available when I visited again in 2015.

state permeates the cultural authority of P. Ramlee's works and words as an unchallenged benchmark for greatness in Malaysian arts. They also articulate how the music and film iconicity of P. Ramlee is mobilised and appropriated by the Malaysian state to perpetuate an ethnonational discourse of Malay artistic greatness through the grand narrative of his tumultuous life that paralleled the history of the Malaysian nation-in-making. The appropriation of P. Ramlee as a national icon was also due to his artistic career that coincided with Malaysia's (and Singapore's) era of independence.

Figure 6.2 P. Ramlee Memorial Museum

It was P. Ramlee's death, or rather the remembrance of his death, that sparked the Malaysian national cultural narrative. While political independence was a long-established fact by the 1970s, there was a sense that its national identity was being eroded by Western cultural influences. This sentiment had parallels with the New Economic Policy (NEP) implemented in 1971, a controversial affirmative action policy to give Malays a larger stake in the nation's wealth, in response to the increasing economic disparity between Malay and Chinese

Figure 6.3 P. Ramlee's piano and typewriter on display

communities.[45] Connected with the NEP was the need to cement a stronger Malay presence in local cultural practices such as music, which led among other things to the National Culture Policy. As such, the discourses and subsequent implementation of policies aimed at raising the presence of Malay culture also resulted in defensive and reactionary views regarding non-Malay cultures. The popular music of the West that was being consumed by local youths came under particular attack. In the previous chapter, I discussed discourses about the musical tastes of youth during the late 1960s and early 1970s as a reflection of the state's wariness of counter-cultural movements. P. Ramlee's statement on traditional

---

[45] Not much research has been done on the impact of the NEP on music and popular culture. Scholars like Tan Sooi Beng and Mohd Anis Md Nor focus on music in light of the National Culture Policy. Edmund Terence Gomez and Johan Saravanamuttu, eds. *The New Economic Policy in Malaysia: Affirmative Action, Ethnic Inequalities and Social Justice*. Singapore: NUS Press, 2012 is a comprehensive, multidisciplinary volume on the impact of the NEP, but it does not contain any studies on popular culture, music or the arts.

music in 1971 in reaction to youth music indicated, in my view, a general decline in interest for his style of music.

P. Ramlee's supposed support for traditional local music against the encroachment of foreign cultures has been fully mobilised in his (re)construction as a Malay nationalist icon. His strong reactionary sentiments made him instrumental in permitting the state to champion a distinctly Malay national culture. It is the public narrative of his life as a Malaysian citizen—and not as a resident of Singapore—that is utilised to relay his national cultural iconicity. This claim can be illustrated via a close reading of the documentary film *P. Ramlee*, directed by Shuhaimi Baba, that aired regionally in 2010 on History Channel Asia. The film is a particularly explicit national cultural text and highlights the potency of the state-centred narrative that has emanated from the period of P. Ramlee's death to the present.

The Kasihan *Narrative: P. Ramlee's Demise*

The effectiveness of this national narrative lies in the film's emotionally intimate framing of P. Ramlee's biography. It conveys the life story melodramatically and it ends in tragedy. It plays on generating an emotional response that is best captured by the word '*kasihan*', meaning to feel an immense sense of pity and empathy with someone. The script depicts P. Ramlee's death as soliciting a sense of 'guilt' that begins to prick the nation's collective conscience resulting in regret; this in turn leads to a clamour for his songs and films, and calls to have him honoured and remembered. The script and narration exploit this emotion to considerable effect, drawing on interviews with P. Ramlee's family, close friends and colleagues, interspersed with historical photographs and scenes from his films, and all to an instrumental score that uses the melodies of his well-known film songs. Most of the emotional weight of the film centres on the years leading up to his death, emphasising how P. Ramlee died broke and broken. The film's trajectory is laid out in the opening lines of narration:

> Conquering every medium of the entertainment spectrum, P. Ramlee had an infinite charm laced with a healthy dose of humour, warmth

and humility that endeared him to many. But his phenomenal rise from stagehand to screen sensation had ill-prepared him for the downward spiral to rejection and obscurity.… But after death, his popularity soared to incredible heights.

These lines capture the general public perception of P. Ramlee in Malaysia and Singapore and then set up the nationalist narrative that follows. The film explores his life from his childhood and schooling in Penang to his rise to film and music stardom in Singapore during the 1950s and 1960s. The film then takes a tragic turn, outlining the struggles and hardships faced by P. Ramlee after his move from Singapore to Kuala Lumpur in 1964. Aside from the complex relationship he had with his only son, Nasir, the narrative highlights how unappreciated he was in Malaysia for the decade he lived in Kuala Lumpur up to his death. The film explicitly attributes his decline in popularity to the onslaught of Western popular music:

It was the era of the 'Swinging Sixties' and the world(wide) invasion of rock, soul, pop, reggae and blues music. The Bee Gees, the Rolling Stones, the Beatles and the Supremes all became household names displacing P. Ramlee's brand of music and singing style. And while local pop singers struggled to compete with the new musical craze, P. Ramlee remained true to his music. The consequences were disastrous.

This narration has the original recording of P. Ramlee's song, 'Bunyi Gitar' from the film *Tiga Abdul* in the background. The intertextual implications of this scene in the documentary are manifold. As noted earlier, 'Bunyi Gitar' was included in one of the last films that P. Ramlee made at Shaw Brothers' studio in Singapore. The song was made as a parody of the rising popularity of guitar band music in the mid-1960s, a style he was apparently opposed to given what he said in his presentation at the National Culture Congress. Further, 'Bunyi Gitar' is used in the documentary to denote the era that led to P. Ramlee's musical demise. Moreover, the use of the song significantly contradicts the statement that he 'remained true to his music', while the film hardly attempts to demonstrate the kind of music that he was actually making in the late

1960s and early 1970s. P. Ramlee's music in all periods of his career was cosmopolitan and diverse, using a plethora of styles, both local and foreign. It is thus difficult to specify what cultural style or aesthetic could be considered 'true to his music'.

This passage in the narration is remarkably similar to the arguments P. Ramlee put forward at the National Culture Congress. This moment in the documentary is explicit in its appropriation of his views on the role of Western pop music culture in eroding local music. His opinions were then easily appropriated to perpetuate a nationalist narrative based on 'racial purity' or 'Malay homogeneity' in Malaysian music. The viewer is made to empathise with him over the rejection of his music by wayward youth who, it was supposed, had no love for their own culture. A desire to deepen this sense of *kasihan* for P. Ramlee is evident in an interview in the film with Ramli Kecik, P. Ramlee's friend and personal assistant. He relates how P. Ramlee was openly rejected by young Malaysian music fans in 1971:

> P. Ramlee has been 'booed' on stage. At the Malaysian Institute of Language and Literature [Kuala Lumpur]. It was the 'Night of Three Ramlees': P. Ramlee, A. Ramlie and L. Ramli. I was the cameraman. So, when P. Ramlee came out to sing, everyone 'booed'. I noticed … [in] pop [concerts] held in stadiums that had singers from Singapore and Malaysia, when Malaysian singers come out, people had to 'boo'. So, at the time, [Malaysian] people did not like local singers.[46]

Ramli Kecik's observations of the general rejection of local artists actually points to a general sentiment among music fans who favoured Singaporean over Malaysian artists. A. Ramlie, a Singaporean, was

---

[46] See also 'Tiga Ramlee di malam amal banjir '71' [Three Ramlees in the night flood '71], *Berita Harian*, 10 March 1971. Ramli Kechik's account of this concert is corroborated by another account of a P. Ramlee performance in Abdullah Hussain, *Kisah Hidup Seniman Agung P. Ramlee* [The Story of the Great Artist P. Ramlee]. Kuala Lumpur: Dewan Bahasa dan Pustaka, 2016. The author attended a concert in which other Malay and Indonesian pop artists were performing. After Titiek Puspa and Ernie Djohan's segment, it was P. Ramlee's turn. However, heckling was heard in the audience, even before he sang his first note (p. 216).

a particularly popular *pop yeh yeh* singer at the time, and L. Ramli, while Malaysian, was also a *pop yeh yeh* singer. P. Ramlee was evidently associated with an older, outmoded era. Ramli Kecik's anecdote, while generating a shocking sense of *kasihan* compared with P. Ramlee's later status in the national narrative, conveniently frames the film's claims for P. Ramlee as an advocate of local traditional music. Despite being local in origin, *pop yeh yeh* is cast as foreign, external and deviant, grouped with the other impure musical 'invaders' from the West. In the documentary's revisionist narrative, P. Ramlee is portrayed as a champion of a national music that was not appreciated by rebellious and wayward Malay youth.

Following the infamous 'booing' incident, the film shows footage of an interview with P. Ramlee in the early 1970s, in which he talks about the importance of preserving traditional music:

> Songs [or musical styles] such as joget, *orkes-orkes combo* [small Malay orchestras] … *asli* songs, *ghazal* and … *dondang sayang* have never been put on competitions or presented. If these songs are not encouraged, hence in less than 10 or 20 years to come these songs will be fully forgotten and music from the West … will be representative of our music.

Here, P. Ramlee is cast as a visionary sage—a prophet without honour in his own country—foretelling the erosion of local musical cultures as a consequence of the onslaught of foreign decadent music. The juxtaposition of his public rejection (youths 'booing') against his wise and ominous statement draws on the viewer's empathy or pity for him, and perhaps even arouses anger towards the rowdy youth who did not appreciate him while he was still alive. The icon's credibility is thus cemented further in this narrative of rejection and struggle. It is a potent reminder of why P. Ramlee's vision needs to be championed, underpinning as it does a set melodramatic narrative for preserving national culture.

The emotional climax of the film is best depicted in the interview with Aziz Sattar, P. Ramlee's acting colleague.[47] Aziz Sattar remained in

---

[47] Aziz Sattar was Ramlee's co-star in the famous quartet of comedies produced at the

Singapore when P. Ramlee left for Kuala Lumpur. He relates P. Ramlee's sad state when he went to visit him in Kuala Lumpur. In this scene, his teary outburst is the most emotional of all the interviews.

> His life was burdensome. [I felt much] pity [for him]. The last time I went to his home [in Kuala Lumpur]. I saw [*tears welling up in his eyes and looking down*], he was eating rice with egg [*holding back sobs*]. His name was big. People [used to] know who P. Ramlee was. But his life was burdensome.

Aziz Sattar's interview encapsulates the tragic final year of his friend as being reduced to the humbling act of eating plain rice with fried egg, implying the lowest level of poverty for a man that was once the wealthiest and most popular Malay entertainer in the region.

The sincerity of Aziz Sattar's monologue was put in question in my interview with Ahmad Nawab, a close friend of P. Ramlee who composed music for his films made in Kuala Lumpur:

> [In the] Shuhaimi Baba [documentary] there are … many things that are not that perfect. She interviewed me, too.… [In] that interview, I was not very satisfied because there are [certain] people … especially Aziz [Sattar]; I don't want to defame him. He said a story that was not right. He [tells] stories. So, when you seek him [for information], he wants to make a name of himself. It is like he wants to occupy a position whereby everything that you want to know about P. Ramlee, 'you must come to me'. Ah, it's like that. People like him. However, there are other people that are knowledgeable about P. Ramlee that they [the film-makers] do not … go to meet [and interview]. And then, [the people] they [do] meet; they create a story. Today [the story is] different. Tomorrow [the story is] different. If [they were] not [fabricating stories] they would say the same story. They only know P. Ramlee at Jalan

Malay Film Productions' studio in Singapore, all of which were directed by P. Ramlee: *Bujang Lapok* (Ne'er Do Well Bachelors, 1957); *Pendekar Bujang Lapok* (Ne'er Do Well Bachelor Warriors, 1959); *Ali Baba Bujang Lapok* (Ali Baba Ne'er Do Well Bachelors, 1961); and *Seniman Bujang Lapok* (Ne'er Do Well Bachelor Actors, 1961).

Ampas. When P. Ramlee came to Kuala Lumpur [after 1964] they were not around anymore.[48]

While Ahmad Nawab was also interviewed for the documentary, he is clearly not satisfied with the way it framed P. Ramlee's life, highlighting the testimonies of certain individuals over others. Though contentious, Ahmad Nawab implies that some of P. Ramlee's colleagues who only worked with him as actors (as opposed to musicians) were not privy to his private life outside the studio. Ahmad Nawab feels that these studio colleagues do not have the authority or credibility to speak of him on such personal terms. Ahmad Nawab, who had known P. Ramlee since his primary schooldays in Penang, also related to me that P. Ramlee was closer to his musician friends compared with his actor friends. What is important to note is Ahmad Nawab's suspicion of Aziz Sattar as an actor, his positioning of himself as an authority on P. Ramlee and also being able to solicit a melodramatic 'performance' on camera. Of course, it is impossible to ascertain the validity of Aziz Sattar's emotions and credibility, but it is significant how conveniently his melodramatic moment fits into the tragic narrative of the documentary. In my initial viewing of the film, I was also deeply moved by Aziz Sattar's tears and the documentary as a whole. These emotional responses are instrumental in rallying a sense of anguish and sadness concerning the tragedy of P. Ramlee's last days while instilling a sense of national pride in the need to champion his views on local music.

Later in the film, footage from the same interview with P. Ramlee cited earlier highlights his views on instilling local music among local youths:

> If we do not cultivate traditional and *asli* music into the chests of our children, our young children … one day other musics will occupy that space because the inside of their chests are empty. There is nothing. The same goes for when we teach our children to learn religion. However far s/he goes, s/he will rarely change religion because the religion that is taught by her/his parents are kept in the chest. It is the same [with] music … so that other musics cannot fill their soul.

---

[48] Interview with Ahmad Nawab Khan, Malay Film Music and P. Ramlee, 2013.

P. Ramlee's statement here indicates his passion for local music, even comparing it to religious identity. The particular presentation of his statement on how local traditional music can be likened to a connection with the soul also serves to evoke a nationalistic sentiment among the documentary's Malaysian viewers. The film solicits empathy with P. Ramlee's passion for local music and covertly relates it to a strong nationalistic sentiment. National culture is discursively and emotively linked to faith and the soul—designating to local traditional music an untouchable and unquestionable position of purity. P. Ramlee is by extension the embodiment of that cultural purity, the irreplaceable national musical image of that cannot be usurped by outside forces. Thus the melodramatic act of remembering P. Ramlee evokes a nationalistic sentiment of wanting to preserve national cultural practices that are at risk of being forgotten. Far from the cautionary warnings expressed in the film, P. Ramlee's actual omnipresent iconic status as a bastion of national culture makes it impossible to forget him.

These melodramatic remembrances signal the mythical status of his personal narrative that parallels the making of the nation.[49] The ease with which P. Ramlee's biography has been appropriated is well articulated by Bishnupriya Ghosh in her study of global icons:

> Myths are comfortable; they reassure. They encourage passive consumption in habitual encounters that cause little discomfort. But when we come across icons that attract a great deal of affective intensity of the sort … [found] in … mass media biographs … we might assume that the message communicated through the iconic sign is highly contested.[50]

As easily as such a potent nationalist icon as P. Ramlee can take on the status of myth and reinforce a nation's identity it can conversely challenge such a rigid conception of nationhood. Ghosh suggests that it is the

---

[49] Mahyuddin Ahmad and Yuen Beng Lee, 'Negotiating class, ethnicity and modernity: The "Malaynisation" of P. Ramlee and his films', *Asian Journal of Communication* 25, 4 (2015): 417.

[50] Ghosh, *Global Icons*, p. 48.

'affective intensity' of such 'bio-icons' that leads to contestations. It is clear that an affective narrative of remembering P. Ramlee has galvanised a sense of national pride in his music. But how has his iconicity been used to do the opposite—to challenge the hegemonic status of national culture? Earlier, I observed how Zubir Said's iconicity is mobilised to articulate minority politics in Singapore. Here, I examine how P. Ramlee's iconicity is mobilised for a non-conformist approach to music-making, demonstrating how the act of remembering an icon can be, to some extent, counter-hegemonic in the context of contemporary Malaysia.

Indiepretation

From the huge amount of recorded and live interpretations of P. Ramlee's film music, I have chosen to highlight one particular compilation: *P. Ramlee … Di Mana Kan Ku Cari Ganti: Satu Indiepretasi* (henceforth *Indiepretasi*). Songs from the *Indiepretasi* project were broadcast on local radio stations and released on the internet as digital downloads for mobile phone ringtones in 2010, a year that also included the screening of a P. Ramlee festival of films on the Malaysian television network Astro.[51] The *Indiepretasi* project, unlike many state-sanctioned events and institutions such as the P. Ramlee Memorial Museum, involved the collective contributions of young, local, indie solo artists and bands playing a diverse range of musical genres.

The contributors to this album and their styles of music resonate with the spirit of *pop yeh yeh*. As much as *Indiepretasi* was counter-cultural in relation to the state's vision of national culture, it also received considerable public interest due to the sensational prospect of reinterpreting the music of a popular national icon. The generational divide between the musical era being interpreted and the interpreters themselves lent the compilation its novelty value. It was also an act of instrumentalising the nationalistic nostalgia for P. Ramlee's film music. This nostalgic appropriation or reclaiming of national culture was used as a platform to promote the music of artists who did not

---

[51] Daryl Goh, 'P. Ramlee goes indie', *The Star*, 22 October 2010.

Figure 6.4 Sleeve of *Indiepretasi* CD album[52]

consider themselves part of the mainstream popular music industry.[53] The *Indiepretasi* compilation involved a diverse mix of young singers and bands performing a variety of styles; half the artists mainly sing their original material in English. The styles in which they interpret P. Ramlee's songs are in stark contrast to the Malay film song styles of the 1950s and 1960s. Much like the indie scene in Indonesia, Malaysia's indie artists mirror 'the approach of some Western pop traditions with a similar rebellious image', in which genres such as 'punk, metal and ska

---

[52] For the release of the compact disc, the compilation's title was shortened to *P. Ramlee: Satu Indiepretasi* (P. Ramlee: An Indiepretation).

[53] Singers mentioned earlier such as Sheila Majid, Siti Nurhaliza and Jaclyn Victor are definitely considered part of the mainstream popular music industry. These are singers who are signed to and distributed by major labels such as Universal and EMI. Indie artists, by comparison, are not linked to major international labels and usually distribute their music through independent labels such as Laguna Records in Malaysia as well as digital means via the internet. The term 'mainstream' is arguable, however, as some artists from the indie scene such as Zee Avi and Yuna are now distributed by major labels on an international scale. On Zee Avi's career after her 2014 album release, see Daryl Goh, 'Dreamtime with Zee Avi's lullaby album', *The Star Online*, 25 February 2014. Available at https://www.thestar.com.my/lifestyle/entertainment/music/news/2014/02/25/dreamtime-with-zee-avis-lullaby-album/ [accessed 2 February 2018]. Yuna's career in the United States is highlighted in the following interview: 'Malaysian singer-songwriter sensation Yuna blazes US trail', ABC Radio Australia, 12 September 2013. Available at http://www.radioaustralia.net.au/international/radio/program/asia-pacific/malaysian-singersongwriter-sensation-yuna-blazes-us-trail/1189557 [accessed 2 February 2018].

music have … enjoyed enormous popularity among the youth' since the 1990s.[54]

The contributors were also about the same age as the youth who commonly rejected P. Ramlee's music in the 1970s. The compilation presents an enigma: P. Ramlee, who officially shunned the 'foreign' youth music of the late 1960s and early 1970s, is now being represented in musical styles that are, on the surface, not indigenous or traditional in any sense. It is of course problematic to consider music that sounds 'foreign' as not being local. Regardless of its exogenous aesthetics, this music is a product of its local social environment. It is more convincing to situate locally produced Western-sounding music as part of a complex web of intercultural, global and neo-liberal market relationships, in which the modes of production and distribution as well as musical aesthetic styles (such as rock and hip-hop) are seemingly being transmitted, hegemonically, 'downwards' from the North or Western 'core' to the South or Eastern 'fringes'.[55]

The concept of indie music and culture is further complicated by its paradoxical promotion of an independent identity that survives and thrives within the constraints of neo-liberal capitalism. Brent Luvaas's study of do-it-yourself (DIY) indie culture in Indonesia is particularly useful for understanding these complexities. Indie culture today has roots in the punk music and fashion of the United States and Britain in the 1970s. At one ideological extreme, it 'advocated seizing the very means of production, enacting the long-dormant promise of Marxist revolution'; in less overtly politicised and aesthetic practice, it 'pushed a sort of militant amateurism, stripping rock of its virtuoso pretenses and replacing it with an anyone-can-do-it simplicity'.[56] Indie is considered a post-punk phenomenon that at its core espouses a DIY philosophy, ethos or else a

---

[54] Bart Barendregt and Wim van Zanten, 'Popular music in Indonesia since 1998, in particular fusion, indie and Islamic music on video compact discs and the internet', *Yearbook for Traditional Music* 34 (2002): 82.

[55] Martin Stokes, 'Music and the global order', *Annual Review of Anthropology*, 33 (2004): 47–72.

[56] Brent Luvaas, *DIY Style: Fashion, Music and Global Digital Cultures*. London: Berg, 2012, p. 11.

shorthand for a variety of cultural production [e.g. films and music] operating outside the reach of the cultural industries. In a sense, indie is a bourgeois takeover of punk, a middle-classification of DIY.... For many, the indie scene provides a supportive community of like-minded creators, a safe place to express, and an infrastructural apparatus of alternative distribution for those outside of the established commercial media companies.[57]

With regard to the indie music produced in *Indiepretasi*, what is interesting is the intimate refashioning of P. Ramlee's national cultural iconicity through musical practices that its interpreters ultimately consider personal to their own musical—and by extension national— identities. Earlier I emphasised the cosmopolitan intimacies of self- determination in Malay film music in the historical context of nation- making in the Malay Peninsula. These autonomous expressions were also part of the capitalist economy of the film studio industry. Here I link such paradoxes of nation-making idealism to new contexts of 'independence' as articulated in this indie-spirited cultural production. The independent nature of the *Indiepretasi* compilation was defined in relation to both the limited capital that was available to produce it and the subsequent need for it to thrive financially through alternative means of musical distribution. The album's producer Adly Syairi Ramly says:

I hope the [*Indiepretasi*] compilation somehow ... beyond the CD or the music ... [will] have a bigger cultural impact on how it was marketed ... [in] that [aspect] ... it ... [is] way better than *Legenda*. Because *Legenda* was distributed, marketed using the standard industry *punya* [own] procedure, whereas ... [*Indiepretasi*] was [done in way in which] we maximised our lack of financial resources ... that made us more proactive and creative in terms of ... promoting the album, which for me is ... nothing new because it has something that I always ... believe in because [of] my ... punk roots.[58]

---

57   Ibid., pp. 16–17.
58   Interview with Adly Syairi Ramly, *Indiepretasi* Album (2010), 2013.

The *Indiepretasi* compilation was initially conceived to be loosely related to Astro's P. Ramlee film festival in 2010. The television network also runs and owns national radio stations, one of which was XFresh FM (XFM), a station that played entirely local musical content. Adly Syairi Ramly, who helmed the compilation, was concurrently XFM's manager at the time.[59] He relates the almost impromptu manner in which the compilation was conceived:

> So, one day we [XFM] had a meeting with the Astro top management and staff … they came to [the] radio [department] and said, 'Okay, so how can radio be part of this whole [P. Ramlee] campaign?' So, jokingly, I told them, 'Why don't we do a compilation? Get all these new [indie] bands to reinterpret all his songs?' It was a joke. Because at that point I didn't actually … [think] that Astro would buy that idea. For me, because I always have this thing where people don't really look up to all these indie bands and stuff. So, [surprisingly] they said 'Yeah'.… So it started off with … if I'm not mistaken … 10 artists. They said, 'Okay, we [will] give you money to record 10 artists'. So, [at the] time … the basis of the project is very simple. I want interpretation. I do not want covers. Solely because, for me, the essence of music back then, you need to truly digest it, you know, and then like, interpret it yourself. Whereas, [in] a cover version you just … take the melody and stuff and do your cover version. Those are two different things. So, that was the brief given to bands via [a] BBM [BlackBerry Messenger] chat group.… So all the communication was via [the] BBM chat group; so, it started from 10 bands and then, it became 12, became 14, 15, and the last call was 18 bands.[60]

While the project seemingly had corporate sponsorship, the actual production of the compilation was a collective effort between all the artists and bands involved, who received no payment except for a

---

[59] XFM originally aired on Astro Radio as Varia. In 2009 it assumed the name XFM as an abbreviation of XFresh FM. In 2012 XFM no longer broadcast on public radio airwaves and was only available for online streaming on http://dengar.xfm.com.my/.
[60] Interview with Adly Syairi Ramly, *Indiepretasi* Album (2010), 2013.

percentage of the digital sales of their songs as ringtones and a minimal budget for recording their songs:

> Astro gave us, I think around 36,000 [ringgit] to record ... because at that time nobody knew it was going to be that big.... So, at that time, bands were doing it for free. So, our deal—what I told the bands, I put it this way, 'I'm going to give you studio time. Studio time with Kamar Seni studio.' ... I think [it was] 12 hours per band.... If they don't want to record with Kamar Seni I'll give them ... 3,000 ringgit to record wherever they want to record because the cost for each band is 3,000 ringgit to record.... So, I think all of the bands recorded at Kamar Seni studio. Some that had their own recording facilities recorded the songs themselves ... and ... the deal with the band is they do it for free and because we don't have money to actually print the CD, we thought, 'Okay, how are we going to do this?' We have the songs, we have the outlet to play it, which is the radio, but we don't have the place where people can actually purchase the music. So ... this problem became like ... [an] opportunity ... we have no money to print CDs, [so] let's release the compilation as the country['s] first-ever ... digital-only compilation.... To be honest it's not really because of innovation, it's more because of budget [constraints] but it worked to our benefit.[61]

In a faint echo of the budgetary constraints that produced Zubir Said's unique sound, a limited recording budget led to what could be considered an innovative product—in fact a historical moment in Malaysia's popular music industry as *Indiepretasi* was the 'first-ever ... digital-only compilation'. In addition, there was a DIY attitude in the enthusiastic and personal means by which the compilation was promoted prior to its release, mainly through the use of internet-based social media networks. Adly Syairi Ramly says that the individual bands and artists

---

[61] Ibid. It is not ascertained whether the total budget for the compilation was RM36,000 (12 bands) or RM54,000 (18 bands). The confusion for Adly Syairi Ramly could have been due to the initial budget for 10 bands, which would have been RM30,000, but the number of bands rose to 18 making it RM54,000. Also, he may not have remembered the exact figure because the project was completed three years before the interview.

would update their fans and their compilation mates on the progress of their recordings via Twitter. Fans were also interacting directly with the artists as the project was being produced,

> asking which band is involved … which band is doing what song. So, the whole curiosity sparked, like it was quite *giler, kan* [crazy, right]? So it was quite, the buzz … the buzz on Twitter was insane … until the compilation was released. And then, okay, a few months after that, Jeremy [Little] from Laguna Records said, 'Eh, why don't we, we produce a CD for you?'…. So that's how … it … [was released as a] CD.[62]

The buzz generated in the digital sphere resulted in a release of the compilation as a CD. After completion, the songs were broadcast on radio and sold as downloadable ringtones for mobile phones. Adly Syairi Ramly also emphasises the popularity of the compilation in the availability of illegal recordings of songs on YouTube, suggesting that the songs were so hotly anticipated that fans recorded the songs off the radio to be circulated immediately (and freely) on the internet.

Luvaas notes that the pervasiveness of indie culture can be attributed to the persona of the ubiquitous indie 'hipster', a representation of '*a digital age recalculation* of what it means to be "outside" of corporate capitalism'.[63] This presence of the so-called outsider is further complicated by 'an era of media interpenetration … where a genuine outside is no longer possible'.[64] It is equally problematic to consider indie production as a wholesale co-optation by corporations (such as Astro), as indie artists balance a need to thrive independently according to DIY practice by maintaining 'a complicated relationship with capitalism, pushing away with one hand, what it pulls to it with another'.[65] In the case of *Indiepretasi*, however, the interplay of capitalist and independent production was also tied to the reclamation of a national identity—a nostalgic sentiment for independence.

---

[62] Ibid.
[63] Luvaas, *DIY Style*, p. 20 (my emphasis).
[64] Ibid.
[65] Ibid., p. 21.

The success of the compilation was due to the combination of the collective support of the bands' and artists' individual fan bases and the prospect of reinterpreting a national icon's music. The music of P. Ramlee is quite distant from the current generation's awareness and tastes. But the active participation of young musicians in reinterpreting his music provided them with the self-determining means to reclaim a rigidly promoted national cultural icon in a DIY manner. P. Ramlee's iconicity was thus mobilised to instil a sense of a homegrown or local identity to the music of these indie musicians and it was done in a way that was not overtly nationalistic. P. Ramlee was conveniently appropriated as a cultural icon—whether consciously or not—by the *Indiepretasi* artists to promote themselves as legitimate and their music as genuinely Malaysian, and so to appeal to a broader local audience. Adly Syairi Ramly mentions the surprisingly broad reception of the compilation that

cross[ed] over … not only to the Malay market because I met quite a number of … my Chinese friends; my bosses who … [are] not Malay who came to me and said, 'Good job with the compilation.… My son who … never listen[s] to Malay music … bought the compilation and [as a result] … you introduced … [him] to P. Ramlee', which is over[whelming], for me … I never expected such a [broad reception].… It started as something fun … [and became] … something … big.[66]

Alongside the broad appeal and opportune self-promotion, the compilation also presented its contributors with a more intimate musical understanding of P. Ramlee's repertoire, demystifying misconceptions about the supposed simplicity of music from his era while bridging the musical aesthetics of the past and the present:

It was exciting as a whole because … for the bands themselves … most of them would come and tell me, 'Eh, I didn't know that P. Ramlee's music is actually that complex'. You know, the simplest song is actually very complex. A good example would be Hujan's [version

---

66 Interview with Adly Syairi Ramly, *Indiepretasi* Album (2010), 2013.

of] 'Tunggu Sekejap'.… At the first listen you'd say it's very simple, straightforward, 'ta ta tatata'. When you actually break down the music … [P. Ramlee's] original music, there's actually layers of complexity in terms of arrangement, what goes where and stuff and stuff, *kan* [right]? … I believe most of the bands who were involved had a good learning experience from the P. Ramlee [compilation].

For a Malaysian indie music habit that often looks outwards (predominantly to the West or Indonesia) for musical inspiration, *Indiepretasi* provided its contributors the opportunity to look inwards, to the local repertoire of the independence era. Music from the Malaysian indie scene is often regarded as 'not being "Malaysian" enough', in comparison to the commercial Malay-language repertoire that circulates in the local mass media.[67] This led Alif Omar Mahfix to question the 'accusatory baggage' that is often linked to non-mainstream artists:

Just ask any indie musicians out there about the kind of criticism they'd usually face from the mainstream—the Malay mainstream in particular—and there'd be a high probability that they'll tell you they were accused of not being 'Malaysian' enough. This creates a perpetual identity crisis—bands either forcefully incorporate traditional elements into their music or start singing in their native tongue. Some more successfully than others, some should have sung in their own language in the first place, but most importantly, it gets us questioning; can't local music stand on its own without having to sound 'Malaysian'?[68]

Alif Omar Mahfix's article in *Juice*, a local monthly magazine featuring international and local music,[69] sought the opinions of local indie musicians about what it means to be Malaysian in their music. The

---

[67] Alif Omar Mahfix, 'Pop Malaysiana: Soul searching of the music kind', *Juice*, 2012, p. 52.

[68] Ibid.

[69] The editor of *Juice*, Ben Liew, said that the magazine started out featuring the electronic dance music scene in Malaysia, focusing on parties held in local dance clubs. The demise of music magazines like *Tone* or periodicals that featured local indie music such as *KLue* allowed *Juice* to fill the void by reporting on the local indie music. Personal communication, 2012.

article was published in the August 2012 issue in anticipation of Malaysia's independence day (*merdeka*) on 31 August. Alif's interviews of individual artists garnered a range of responses. Most argue against traditionalist 'tokenism' in expressing Malaysian-ness in their music, while one of the interviewees expresses a more militant view on instilling local culture in music. The bandleader and guitarist LoQue, from the band MonoloQue, says:

> Have some sense of originality my fellow Malaysians, stop aping the West too much.... Not many bands are [using local traditional music] ... right now. You can't say a band that sounds 99 per cent like Kings of Leon or Gotye to be the new Malaysian sound without any traditional influences even though it's a band from Malaysia, right? That's plagiarism [laughs] ... Malaysians ... especially Malays ... are carbon copying the West and forgetting their roots. Perhaps 50 years from now Malaysian bands will sound Malaysian because they sound like Elvis instead of P. Ramlee.[70]

While some of LoQue's statements are tongue-in-cheek, he alludes to his own personal views on actively incorporating aspects of the traditional into his rock-influenced music. Ironically, his critical stand on 'plagiarism' and mimicking the West mirrors the outline of the National Culture Policy. However, his views are the most nationalistically chauvinist of the five artists interviewed.

Others, like the rapper Altimet (who is also on *Indiepretasi*), express a more nuanced and flexible view on Malaysian-ness in music:

> I just try to make good music, that perception [of being fake in performing Western musical genres] is shallow minded and the remedy for that perception is similarly shallow minded.... [P]ut some gamelan in your song and suddenly you're not 'copying the West' anymore? No it's deeper than that.... [The use of local languages and colloqualisms

---

70   Alif Omar Mahfix, 'Pop Malaysiana', p. 63. MonoloQue contributed an indiepretation of Ramlee's 'Tiada Kata Secantik Bahasa' (No Words as Beautiful as Language) in the *Indiepretasi* compilation.

in Malaysian hip-hop are] one of the steps in the evolution … [of the music].… It comes back to my belief that hip-hop is folk music. If you make music for your folks, it should be in a language that's accessible to them.… Is the *inang* uniquely ours? It's rooted in India. *Zapin*, the Arabs brought it here. *Joget*, the Portuguese … but they've all been transformed into something different once they're here.… These transformations don't happen overnight, maybe the new modern genre for us is in gestation.[71]

Altimet provides a more flexible outlook on musical identity in Malaysian music, one that is aware of the fluid cosmopolitan past of the region's musical practices while also accommodating the subjectivity of what it means to be local in music. He grounds this sense of localness in likening hip-hop, a seemingly global (or Western) style, to 'folk music'.[72] He suggests that new Western-sounding music that is locally produced and includes local content in 'a language that's accessible' can be considered 'folk' music for Malaysian 'folks'. He also highlights the 'transformations' of musical cultures over time emphasising a processual state of identity-making in local musical practices—a 'new modern genre … in gestation'. This is a view that can also be applied in observing cultural identity-making in film music of the 1950s and 1960s. Malay film music had always been fluidly cosmopolitan in its influences while also rooted in local practices. Unlike LoQue, who seems to be on a quest to salvage or safeguard 'tradition' in his music, Altimet is more aware of the changing contexts of localness in music.

One factor that escapes Altimet, however, is the impact of colonialism and the globalised industry of production and distribution on local music. In what ways are indie music and hip-hop products of a globalised and commercialised taste industry? While global or

---

[71] Alif, 'Pop Malaysiana', p. 61. Altimet's contribution was the only hip-hop song in the compilation. His backing track or beat samples from the chorus of P. Ramlee's 'Maafkan Kami' (Forgive Us) over which he raps original verses.

[72] For an important study on Malaysian hip-hop in Chinese and Indian languages see Shantini Pillai, 'Syncretic cultural multivocality and the Malaysian popular musical imagination', *Kajian Malaysia* 31, 1 (2013): 1–18.

cosmopolitan music cultures can be understood and experienced as unique to their spaces of production and consumption, such observations must be considered alongside critical analyses of postcolonial, global capitalist or neo-liberal industries of culture—the Western-based popular music industry—that dictate the fields of taste or genres of music that are reproduced in local contexts.[73] Altimet's view of a constantly transforming local industry overlooks the postcolonial cultural politics and economics of global musical industries of production, distribution and consumption that drive local consumers and music industries.

Another view expressed in Alif Omar Mahfix's article by Phang, the bandleader of Citizens of Ice Cream, perhaps consolidates the more sobering reality of identity politics and globalisation. He says that Malaysia is

> a post-colonial society in denial, too immature for the information age explosion and so obsessed with our hollow idea of 'identities' that we forgot how to just experience, learn, enjoy, respect and celebrate with each other.... Why do we constantly need to draw lines and say 'this is Malaysian, that is not very Malaysian'? The fact is, it's always been there without the need to shout it out, without the need to define the obvious.... [I]t's kinda like the half-arsed slogans we hear all the time; constantly crying it out loud makes it hollow.... [I]f traditional influences rock your socks, go ahead and do it, if not don't force it. Just be who you are.... If you're Malaysian, that's an identity you can't shake off and you can't deny, and if you're honest about it, it will always be there.... The Malaysian identity in music, if anything, is when we stop thinking and bickering about a Malaysian identity and just play ... this identity politics discourse in local music is really getting old.

---

73 See Louise Meintjes, 'Paul Simon's *Graceland*, South Africa, and the mediation of musical meaning', *Ethnomusicology* 34, 1 (1990): 37–73; Thomas Turino, *Nationalists, Cosmopolitans, and Popular Music in Zimbabwe*. Chicago: University of Chicago Press, 2000; Jan Fairley, 'The "local" and "global" in popular music', in *The Cambridge Companion to Pop and Rock*, ed. Simon Frith, Will Straw and John Street. Cambridge: Cambridge University Press, 2001, pp. 272–89; and Stokes, 'Music and the global order'.

The lived reality suggested by Phang involves local musicians simply producing and performing music that they are drawn to, without being overtly concerned with cultural identity. However, from his comments it is evident that there is a marked tension between musicians and consumers who seek a clearly defined Malaysian identity and musicians and consumers who are not concerned with it at all. What he emphasises is that Malaysian-ness in music will ultimately be expressed by any Malaysian individual making music of any kind or genre. It is the sociocultural experience of being a Malaysian that feeds into the musical expressions across genres and aesthetic intentions. It is, moreover, the inherent contestations, or emotionally frustrating internal discourses about identity, that define Malaysian musical culture. Indeed, many musicians are weary of the incessant 'identity politics discourse' that 'is really getting old'. Phang cannot seem to escape it either, as he actively positions himself against these discourses of 'localness'.

The comments cited here consider how referencing, appropriating and reinterpreting Malay film music from the independence and nation-making era to contemporary, globalised and commodified contexts of indie music production are connected with processes of national identity-making. Nation-making sentiments from the past, found in Malay film music of the 1950s and 1960s, are being reiterated in the musical practices of the present. National policies on culture in Malaysia form the framework for musical contestation in current musical practices followed by a new generation of artists. A parallel contestation for autonomous identity is evident in the creative output of an earlier generation of Malay film-writers, directors and composers who had to legitimise their art in the face of colonial rule and ideology. However, rigid notions of national identity can also be perpetuated by those who position themselves as against Western hegemony. Similarly, there are local musicians who resist the rigid definitions and discourses of identity politics. Ultimately, some artists generally accept that the history of musical practices are fluid and fall outside the purview of rigid classification. They consider their honest musical contributions to the experience of being Malaysian in spaces of production, performance and consumption as ample evidence of the genuine Malaysian-ness of their music. *Indiepretasi* is unique in its warm embrace of a diverse range of artists to articulate the music of an exemplary Malaysian icon. Such a messy plurality, expressed with emotional nostalgic potency, is perhaps *the* most accurate representation of Malaysian music culture.

Conclusion

The film music of the Malay Peninsula in the 1950s and 1960s continues to form a major part of the present-day discourse on nationalism in Singapore and Malaysia. Malay film music, through its most enduring icons P. Ramlee and Zubir Said, provides an affective discourse for Singaporean and Malaysian citizens to embrace their national identity and also challenge rigid or autocratic boundaries of citizenship. The notion of indiepretation captures how independence (that is, Malay film music of the independence era) is interpreted in the context of contemporary nation states and their citizens. Just as Malay film music was integral to nation-making in the 1950s and 1960s, the rearticulations of this music and its icons are pervasive to political, social and musical acts of remembering in Singapore and Malaysia.

Government-defined national cultural policies in both countries since the 1970s sought to delineate the boundaries of what would constitute national music through a discourse of refinement that, in effect, defined traditions of music. The music of composers like P. Ramlee and Zubir Said became emblematic of national music. They were both representative of Malay musical nationalism in a period of active nation-making. But P. Ramlee's and Zubir Said's omnipresence also complicates the notion of a shared nationhood beyond borders. While P. Ramlee is generously remembered, recontextualised and decontextualised by a younger generation of Malaysians, Zubir Said is remembered as an unsung hero, whose national presence is mostly limited to the Malay community of Singapore. Despite state-sponsored projects to remember Zubir Said that ignore his explicit Malay nationalist position in the 1950s, the Malay community of Singapore has mobilised his iconicity to claim legitimacy and a larger cultural stake in the nation state.

Across the border, P. Ramlee's iconicity is mobilised in divergent ways. Despite his eclectic and cosmopolitan life and music, the state promotes him to instil a rigid notion of Malay artistry and national culture. The affective narrative of his *irreplaceability* (fittingly, the theme of one of his most famous songs) is articulated in state-sponsored institutions like the P. Ramlee Memorial Museum and documentary films that dramatise his life as a tragedy. As such, the intimate trope of *kasihan* that is linked to his life narrative is employed as an allegory of underappreciated local traditions and state-sanctioned national cultures that are in need of safeguarding from decadent outsider cultures. Meanwhile, the *Indiepretasi* compilation, collectively produced by indie musicians, appropriated this rigid notion of national culture by embracing P. Ramlee's status as a national music icon through unorthodox interpretations of his songs. *Indiepretasi* represents one of many enduring and complex acts of nostalgia that demonstrate the relevance of Malay film music from the independence era to nation-making in the past and the present.

There has yet to be an indiepretation compilation of Zubir Said's film music involving Malaysian, Singaporean and Indonesian artists. Until then, the once cosmopolitan and transnational articulations of Malay film music remain confined to bounded national spaces of nostalgia—Zubir Said to Singapore and P. Ramlee to Malaysia. Beyond understanding the politics of cosmopolitan nation-making and cultural intimacy in Malay film music, contemporary cultures of musical production are closely intertwined in the national spaces of Malaysia and Singapore that are too often imagined as separate.[74]

---

[74] An important volume that attempts to bridge this divide and analyses the intertwined multiculturalism of Malaysia and Singapore is Daniel P.S. Goh, Matilda Gabrielpillai, Phillip Holden and Gaik Cheng Khoo, eds. *Race and Multiculturalism in Singapore*. Singapore: Routledge, 2009.

Chapter 7

Conclusion

Rampong ngising Semar tilem!
(Selepas buang air besar, Semar tidur [ke tilam]!
After relieving himself, Semar will now sleep!)
Phrase sung for closing the cave of riches in *Ali Baba Bujang Lapok* (1961)

Even when appropriated as part of nation-building projects, it seems that music can consistently provide hints, or perhaps better, *reminders*, of more complex notions of identity and belonging.[1]

Malay film music from the 1950s and 1960s expressed the cosmopolitan intimacies of nation-making. These, in turn, have articulated the postcolonial contestations and paradoxes of ethnonationalism. Malay film music was indeed constitutive of a homogeneous national identity, but it was also inherently hybrid, pluralistic and subversive—much like the Javanese phrase quoted above. These subversive ideas, that at times reinforce but also challenge ethnonational identity, are expressed through the intimate sentiments contained in Malay film music in narrative, lyrical or musical contexts. This is nowhere more evident than what an intertextual analysis reveals of music from the golden age of Malay film. As a consequence, this music, and the accompanying discourses and icons, continue to have an impact on current understandings and practices of national culture in Malaysia and Singapore.

Historical antecedents also matter. The musical practices of the Malay world were already hybrid and cosmopolitan prior to European

---

[1] David Hesmondhalgh, *Why Music Matters*. Chichester: Wiley-Blackwell, 2013, p. 164.

colonialism, and the colonial process further intensified pluralistic interactions and developments. Towards the end of British rule, aspirations for national independence were visually and sonically present in the medium of film. The rise of the vernacular film industry in the Malay Peninsula coincided with the emergence of modern popular culture and the commercially driven production and consumption of popular entertainment. These avenues for popular entertainment in the Malay world were, at the same time, also a means for articulating a postcolonial politics of self-determination and autonomy from colonial rule.[2]

Film was a particularly effective medium for expressing new ideas of postcolonial independence to a mass and largely illiterate audience. And the inclusion of locally produced music in this medium amplified a message, initially aspirational but later constitutive, of national autonomy. As national independence was achieved, music in film came to activate an aesthetic of nationhood through representations of tradition in modernity. It was the cosmopolitan intimacies of Malay film music that relayed this aspiration for a modern and postcolonial nationhood. The musical aesthetic frameworks and affective narratives developed in the 1950s and 1960s would eventually form the benchmark for Malay ethnonational culture in present-day Singapore and Malaysia. The historic formation of the two nations is closely intertwined, and the ethnomusicological history of film music illuminates this relationship even further. The films analysed in this book are limited to those made in Singapore in the 1950s and 1960s; but the music and personalities associated with them are iconic to Malaysian national culture. The Singaporean state has only recently started to associate the Malay film and musical past with its national identity. Yet the Malay community there has always referred to these films and this music as some of the most important cultural contributions to their nation.[3]

---

[2] See Tan Sooi Beng, 'Negotiating "His Master's Voice": Gramophone music and cosmopolitan modernity in British Malaya in the 1930s and early 1940s', *Bijdragen tot de Taal-, Land- en Volkenkunde* 169, 4 (2013): 457–94; and Peter Keppy, 'Southeast Asia in the age of jazz: Locating popular culture in the colonial Philippines and Indonesia', *Journal of Southeast Asian Studies* 44, 3 (2013): 444–64.

[3] Alfian Bin Sa'at, a prominent playwright, tracks the history of the Malay studio film era and links its palimpsestic continuity in Singaporean independent films made

To better understand these complex articulations of nationhood across the border, the films of the Singapore-based Malay film industry of the 1950s and 1960s are best analysed from a historically informed ethnomusicological perspective. The first chapter provided a theoretical framework for examining aesthetic agency and cultural intimacy in the musically cosmopolitan expressions of Malay films. I drew attention to the paradoxes that emerge from considering the enduring and contested impact of P. Ramlee on Malaysian and Singaporean national culture.

Chapter Two offered an intertextual analysis of film music in *Hang Tuah* (1956) and *Sergeant Hassan* (1958), revealing the divergent articulations of reinventing a precolonial past and projecting a postcolonial future. *Sergeant Hassan* portrays colonial rule in a positive light via a leitmotif of the defence of the Malayan nation against its communist enemy within. Although the film is set during the Japanese occupation, its overtly pro-British and Malay nationalist sentiments are none too subtle allegories for the tumultuous state of emergency and communist insurgency of the 1950s. The use of a Western-sounding monothematic theme score, featuring P. Ramlee's song 'Tunggu Sekejap', expresses a sentiment of passive decolonisation, thereby projecting an ambivalent future for Malayan independence. By contrast, *Hang Tuah* melodramatically portrays precolonial Malay feudal excess as the justification for resisting dominant powers such as European colonialists. The film is set in the precolonial Melakan sultanate, featuring music that is deceptively ahistorical but evocative of a Malay folk music tradition. The music in *Hang Tuah* represents a reinvention of the precolonial past in ways that tie the music to the cosmopolitan environment and

---

after 2000. He argues that while the legacy of Malay films produced in Singapore has been claimed by the Malaysian film industry and linked to the national imaginary of Malaysian film history, clear connections can be discerned through Singaporean narratives about the contemporary suburban, lower-class 'heartland' in opposition to the urban, upper-class cosmopolis. This modern iteration of the once referenced 'hinterland' that is now Malaysia is part of a continuity of Malay film narratives that reference the tensions and conflicts between the modern city and the idyllic *kampung*, the social anxieties of immoral urbanity encroaching on traditional values (*adat* for Malays). See Alfian Bin Sa'at, 'Hinterland, heartland, home: Affective topography in Singapore films', in *Southeast Asian Independent Cinema: Essays, Documents, Interviews*, ed. Tilman Baumgärtel. Singapore: NUS Press, 2012, pp. 33–50.

commercial goals of the Malay film industry. Nonetheless, the music greatly amplifies the anti-colonial subtext of the film, particularly through the theme of sacrifice embodied in the 'sacrificial maiden' Melur and the song 'Berkorban Apa Saja'.[4] Counter-intuitively, this more subversive narrative of resistance was intimated a year before Malayan independence in 1957, while *Sergeant Hassan*'s more ambivalent message of decolonisation was expressed a year after. The Malay films of the mid-1950s reflected the cosmopolitan, commercial and late colonial context of capitalist production in the Singaporean film industry. However, these films also provided a platform for the aesthetic agency of producers to articulate subtexts of Malay nationalism in their film music. Looking beyond the social-structural limitations of late colonialism and a profit-driven film industry, these articulations of aesthetic agency reveal a politics of decolonisation and resistance that could not be expressed overtly on the silver screen. The emotional narrative of resistance, passive or active, would solidify into more self-determining modes of musical expression in the early 1960s.

The new decade saw a rise in politically radical Malay films set in precolonial times. Chapter Three showed how Zubir Said's film music in *Dang Anom* (1962), reflecting as it did the ideology of cosmopolitan Malay nationalists, sounds a subversive postcolonial critique of unequal power relations between lustful men and victimised women, autocratic rulers and subjects aspiring to freedom, British paternalism and Malay nationalism, colonialism and independence. This socially conscious film provided Zubir Said—in collaboration with the directorial vision of Hussein Haniff—with a platform to construct a *traditionalised* musical aesthetic that was constitutive of Malay nationhood. This was a paradoxical process that involved the incorporation of 'traditional' musical elements with modern Western forms and structures that were suited to the medium of film. In tandem with the cosmopolitan milieu of the Malay film industry in Singapore, this process of actively fashioning a musical tradition highlights the aesthetic agency of Zubir

---

4   I borrow 'sacrificial maiden' from M. Elise Marubbio, *Killing the Indian Maiden: Images of Native American Women in Film*. Lexington: University Press of Kentucky, 2006.

Said's film music. As one of the first film composers for the post-war film industry who was also a vocal nationalist, Zubir Said initiated a musical aesthetic discourse of a traditionalised nationalism that resonated in many Malay films of the early 1960s. In contrast to this traditionalised musical aesthetic were the musical mediations of modernity present in P. Ramlee's social films.

In Chapter Four the analysis of P. Ramlee's social films of the early 1960s unravelled the musical mediations of Malay modernity through technologies and affectations of *classiness* and narratives of *class*. These films, unlike the historical ones, are set in contemporary urban contexts, featuring Western cosmopolitan musical technologies in the form of instruments, modes of production, reproduction, distribution and reception (microphones, recording studios, nightclubs, records and radio) as part of a favourable—that is, 'classy'—aesthetic of Malay modernity. The interactive relationship between music, musicians and social class in *Antara Dua Darjat* (1960) illuminates a narrative that challenges the antiquated and divisive structures of inequality in Malay society. In the film, the intimate musical interactions between a working-class musician hero and an upper-class heroine articulate a social narrative of mutual dependence between the classes in Malay society in the 1960s. The theme of a mutually dependent gendered and power-laden relationship is expressed in the lyrics of the film's feature song 'Getaran Jiwa' that employs a musical metaphor in its lyrics about the inseparability of rhythm (*irama*) and melody (*lagu*). My musical reading of *Ibu Mertua-ku* (1962) challenges existing interpretations of the film as a cautionary tale about the excesses of modern immorality in Malay society. Such interpretations do not consider how musical discourses, practices and aesthetics in social films actually portray an embodied cosmopolitan modernity. Music was an integral aesthetic space in which modernity and supposedly exogenous practices and affectations were embraced as a rooted cosmopolitan Malay culture. Social films in the early 1960s intimated the ethical aspirations of a modern Malay nation-in-the-making and the musical technologies, discourses and aesthetics in these films mediated and reconciled an acceptable modernity for Malay society.

If the early 1960s represented a conciliatory embrace of modern Malay (musical) identity in cinema, the period from the mid-1960s to early 1970s was far more contested. At the centre of these contestations over musical aesthetics and national culture was the new youth music culture of the rock 'n' roll era. In Chapter Five I examined the Singaporean and Malaysian state authorities' concerns about the counter-cultural 'degeneracy' they discerned in the vibrant *pop yeh yeh* and beat culture. The authorities and conservative ideologues were vigilant in their policing of youths' bodily practices, for example dances, young women wearing miniskirts and young men growing their hair. These embodied practices of self-fashioning incited a moral panic and were seen as antithetical to the states' conception of decency for their young citizens. Strongly advocating a sense of national identity in music in the midst of this new musical culture were Zubir Said and P. Ramlee. The latter was especially reactionary in his opinions of the youth music cultures that were quickly overtaking the popularity of Malay films and musical styles from the 1950s and 1960s. Nonetheless, a symbiotic relationship existed between the newly emerging Malay youth culture and the film industry. P. Ramlee was in fact the first Malay film director and composer to introduce a rock 'n' roll-style song of his own creation, 'Bunyi Gitar' in the film *Tiga Abdul* (1964). Films such as *Muda Mudi* (1965) feature youth and *pop yeh yeh* music, albeit from the narrative perspective of an ageing film star. *A Go Go '67* (1967) provides an even greater emphasis on youth music, featuring numerous young bands, singers and dancers. More importantly, unlike its predecessors, the film attempts to narrate from the youths' perspective, even though this is done in a patronising way by emphasising the potential of youth to contribute to society. The prevalence of the disquieting youth culture of the mid-1960s to early 1970s marked the final phase of the Malay studio film industry in Singapore. While *A Go Go '67* was one of the last films to be produced at Shaw Brothers' Malay Film Productions' studio in Jalan Ampas, Singapore, the film's music director Kassim Masdor would move on to become a successful music producer for EMI Singapore's Malay music division.[5] Even though the film industry in Singapore had shut

---

5   The last two films made in the Jalan Ampas studio were *A Go Go '67* and *Raja Bersiong* (Vampire King, 1968, dir. Jamil Sulong).

down, the legacy of Malay film music endured in individuals such as Kassim Masdor, who had already gained a wealth of musical experience and skills under the tutelage of P. Ramlee. Moreover, after the 1980s there would be a resurgence in popularity of Malay films of the 1950s and 1960s, and especially the film songs composed by P. Ramlee.

The music of films made in Singapore during the nation-making period continue to resonate in present-day practices and discourses about national identity in both Malaysia and Singapore. In Chapter Six I analysed how the divergent acts of remembering Zubir Said in Singapore and P. Ramlee in Malaysia perpetuate the homogeneous and rigid national cultural policies of both nations. Conversely, such acts of nostalgia also challenge the hegemonic cultural policies of the state. In Singapore, state-sponsored events to commemorate Zubir Said, such as the 'Majulah!' festival organised by the National Museum, paralleled other concurrent events in which his national iconicity was mobilised by the Malay minority to claim legitimacy in a state that marginalises Malay culture. In Malaysia, by contrast, P. Ramlee's iconicity is synonymous with Malay(sian) national culture. Despite his vibrantly cosmopolitan music and films, his life is interpreted as a tragic, melodramatic allegory that employs a narrative of *kasihan* to safeguard Malay musical culture and tradition from the threat of exogenous cultures.

Even though P. Ramlee is an omnipresent icon of a homogeneous national culture in Malaysia, he is also mobilised by culturally marginal groups to legitimate their own Malaysian identity. In examining the production of the P. Ramlee tribute album *Indiepretasi* (2010), which involved indie musicians, I disclosed the paradoxical discourses of what it means to have a Malaysian musical identity today. The *Indiepretasi* album challenges the hegemonic boundaries of Malaysian national culture while embracing P. Ramlee's omnipresent national iconicity. As the album's musicians were asked by the producer Adly Syairi Ramly to *interpret*—as opposed to covering or reproducing—P. Ramlee's music in their own indie styles (such as rock, punk and hip-hop), the *Indiepretasi* project was a nuanced act of nostalgia, an act of *interpreting independence* that highlights the enduring nation-making impact of earlier film music on national musical identity in the present. While Singapore has only recently begun to remember Zubir Said's musical contributions, Malaysia cannot escape the memory and music of P. Ramlee as a recurring leitmotif of its national culture.

The music of the golden age of Malay films produced in Singapore's studio film industry articulated the cosmopolitan intimacies of nation-making that continue to unravel the contestations and paradoxes of Malay ethnonationalism. The cosmopolitan music of independence-era films, while emblematic of a supposedly homogeneous Malay national culture, is also remembered and reinterpreted in counter-hegemonic ways by citizens of Malaysia and Singapore. These societies are inescapably and unforgettably intertwined, just like rhythm (*irama*) is to melody (*lagu*).

Appendices

A. Film Song Lyrics

1. 'Melaka', music by P. Ramlee, lyrics by P. Ramlee

Negeri Melaka yang mewah	Melaka is a land of affluence
Tempat lahirnya Datuk Hang Tuah	The birthplace of Datuk Hang Tuah
Banyak berjasa dalam sejarah	Many good deeds are in its history
Sangat terbilang tiap daerah	Countless in every province
Negeri Melaka negeri mulia	The state of Melaka is noble
Sudah terkenal dalam dunia	Well known throughout the world
Negeri Melaka aman dan makmur	The state of Melaka is peaceful and prosperous
Sejak dahulu sudah termasyur	Illustrious since its beginnings
Negeri Melaka negeri yang asal	The state of Melaka is the state of origin
Negeri Melayu memang terkenal	A Malay state that is well known
Tempat pahlawan gagah dan handal	A place of gallant and consummate warriors
Dagang senteri datang berjual	Numerous foreigners come to trade
Negeri Melaka aman dan makmur	The state of Melaka is peaceful and prosperous
Sejak dahulu sudah termasyur	Illustrious since its beginnings

2. 'Berkorban Apa Saja' (To Sacrifice Anything At All), music by P. Ramlee, lyrics by Jamil Sulong

Berkorban apa saja	To sacrifice anything at all
Harta ataupun nyawa	Material possessions or your life
Itulah kasih mesra	That is a joyous love
Sejati dan mulia	Genuine and noble

Kepentingan sendiri	Personal importance
Tidak diingini	Is not desirable
Bahagia kekasih	The happiness of your lover
Saja yang diharapi	Is all you should wish for
Berkorban apa saja	To sacrifice anything at all
Harta ataupun nyawa	Material possessions or your life
Itulah kasih mesra	That is a joyous love
Sejati dan mulia	Genuine and noble
Untuk menjadi bukti	To find evidence
Kasih yang sejati	Of a love that is genuine
Itulah tandanya	That is the sign
Jika mahu diuji	If one wants to be tested
Berkorban apa saja	To sacrifice anything at all
Harta ataupun nyawa	Material possessions or your life
Itulah kasih mesra	That is a joyous love
Sejati dan mulia	Genuine and noble

3. 'Tunggu Sekejap' (Wait for a While), music by P. Ramlee, lyrics by S. Sudarmaji

Tunggu sekejap wahai kasih	Wait for a while my love
Kerana hujan masih renyai	Because the rain is still pouring
Tunggu sekejap	Just wait for a while
Dalam pelukan asmaraku	In my passionate embrace
Jangan bimbang	Don't worry
Walaupun siang akan menjelma	Even though the sun will rise
Malam ini	Tonight
Belum puas ku bercumbu dengan dinda	I am not satisfied flirting with you
Tunggu sekejap wahai kasih	Wait for a while my love
Tunggulah sampai hujan teduh	Wait for the rain to subside
Mari ku dendang	Let me serenade you
Jangan mengenang orang jauh	Don't long for those who are far away
Jangan pulang	Don't return
Jangan tinggalkan daku seorang	Don't leave me all by myself
Tunggu sekejap kasih	Wait for a while my love
Tunggu	Wait

4. 'Saat demi Saat' (Second after Second), music and lyrics by Zubir Said

Dang Anom:
Saat demi saat telah berlalu
Ingatan daku hanya padamu
Tika berjuang menentang seteru
Menentang seteru

Aku menabuh hati nan rindu
Saat sangat genting luas terbentang
Debaran hati bertambah kencang
Cemat gelisah semakin bergoncang
Semakin bergoncang
Mudah-mudahan dikau selamat pulang

Saat demi saat pulang berulang
Permata hati terlalu terpandang

Malang:
Janganlah asyik memuja bayang
Memuja bayang

Malang and Dang Anom:
Kita yang suci tak akan terhalang

Dang Anom:
Second after second have passed
My thoughts are only of you
As you confront our enemies
Confront our enemies

I possess a heart in longing
A second so perilous and spread wide open
My heart beats with increasing turbulence
My anxieties increasingly shaken
Increasingly shaken
With hopes that you may return safely

Second after second return and repeat
The jewel of my heart gazes intently

Malang:
Don't always idolise shadows
Idolise shadows

Malang and Dang Anom:
We, who are pure, cannot be restrained

5. 'Getaran Jiwa' (Vibrations of the Soul), music by P. Ramlee, lyrics by S. Sudarmaji

Getaran jiwa melanda hatiku,
Tersusun nada irama dan lagu

Walau hanya sederhana
Tetapi tak mengapa
Moga dapat membangkitkan
Sedarlah kamu wahai insan

Tak mungkin hilang irama dan lagu
Bagaikan kumbang sentiasa bermadu
Andai dipisah lagu dan irama
Lemah tiada berjiwa
Hampa

Vibrations of the soul envelop my heart
My pulsations are arranged like a rhythm to
a melody

Even if the vibrations are faint
It does not matter
As long as it can awaken
My awareness of your existence

The rhythm and melody cannot be lost
Like a bee always making honey
If the melody and rhythm are separated
My soul will be weakened
Disappointed

Tak mungkin hilang irama dan lagu	The rhythm and melody cannot be lost
Bagaikan kumbang sentiasa bermadu,	Like a bee always making honey
Andai dipisah lagu dan irama	If the melody and rhythm are separated
Lemah tiada berjiwa	My soul will be weakened
Hampa	Disappointed

6. 'Jeritan Batin' (Wailing Soul), music by P. Ramlee, lyrics by S. Sudarmaji

Dengar oh jeritan batinku	Hear, oh the wailing of my soul
Memekik-mekik, memanggil-manggil namamu slalu	It cries and calls for your name always
Sehari rasa sebulan	A day feels like a month
Hatiku tiada tertahan	My heart cannot stand it
Ku pandang kiri, ku pandang kanan	I look to the left, I look to the right
Ji-kau tiada	If you are not present
Risau batinku nangis risau	Constantly my soul cries with worry
Makin kau jauh, makin hatiku bertambah kacau	The further you are, the more my heart is uneasy
Mengapa kita berbisa tak sanggup nahan asmara	Why could we not bear to resist our romance
Oh dengarlah, jeritan batinku	Oh hear it, the wailing of my soul

7. 'Bunyi Gitar' (Sound of the Guitar), music by P. Ramlee, lyrics by S. Sudarmaji

Oh bunyi gitar irama twist	Oh the sound of the guitar in the melody of twist
Tidak sabar si gadis manis	The young ladies are impatient
Dengar lagu rancak gembira	To listen to an upbeat and happy song
Hatinya rindu tergoda	Their hearts aroused with longing
Ingin dapat teman	To find a partner
Menari suka ria	Dance and party
Sungguh merdu lagu ini	This song is so melodious
Siapa mahu boleh menari	Anyone who wants can dance
Pilih satu teman sendiri	Find your own partner
Ataukah si hitam manis	Or a dark sultry beauty
Kalau sudi mari	If you feel like coming
Kita menari twist	We will dance the twist

Oh gitar berbunyi	Oh the guitar sounds
Menawan hati sedang berahi	Attracting hearts in passion
Oh rancaknya irama	Oh how lively this rhythm is
Dapat mikat sukma	Able to attract youths
Gadis dan teruna	Young ladies and bachelors
Mari cari teman gembira	Let's find a happy partner
Gitar solo dan melodi	The guitar plays the solo and melody
Ikut tempo kalau menari	Following the tempo of your dancing
Sila adik sila cik abang	Young ladies and gents
Marilah kita berdendang	Let us sing together
Irama gembira hati jadi riang	A happy melody begets a joyful heart

B. Malay Texts Cited with Translations

Chapter 2

An interview with P. Ramlee in *Utusan Zaman*, n.d., in Ahmad Sarji, *P. Ramlee: Erti Yang Sakti* [P. Ramlee: The Sacred Reality]. 2nd ed., Petaling Jaya: MPH, 2011, pp. 276–77

Lagu dan muzik pop yang tidak bermutu akan melahirkan generasi yang liar pada masa hadapan. Anak-anak muda yang menyanyi ikut suka hati, bermain muzik ikut suka hati, berpakaian ikut suka hati akan menjadi terdedah kepada unsur-unsur yang tidak baik dan dengan sendirinya lahir angkatan yang tidak berdisiplin.

Pop songs and music that are not of quality will give birth to a wild generation in the future. Youths that sing self-indulgently, play music self-indulgently, dress self-indulgently, will be exposed to qualities that are disagreeable and out of that will be born a generation that is without discipline.

*

Yusnor Ef, *Muzik Melayu Sejak 1940-an*. Kuala Lumpur: YKNA Network, 2011, p. xix.

Lagu Melayu adalah sebahagian jati diri orang Melayu, pengaruh luar boleh diterima tetapi harus berteraskan Melayunya, seperti muzik atau lagu-lagu P. Ramlee asasnya Melayu, tetapi unsur barat, latin [sic] dan India diserapkan tanpa disedari. Elemen-elemen jazz, bassanova [sic], mambo dan cha-cha terdapat di lagu-lagunya, tetapi jiwanya tetap jiwa Melayu.

Malay songs are an integral part of a Malay person's identity, in which external influences can be accepted while Malayness must be central, just like the music or songs of P. Ramlee; the foundations are Malay, but Western, latin [sic] and Indian elements are absorbed subconsciously [internalised]. Elements from jazz, bossa nova, mambo and cha-cha are found in his songs, but his soul [enduringly] remains a Malay soul.

Chapter 3

Dialogue from *Hang Tuah* (1956, dir. Phani Majumdar)

Jika saya mengeluarkan semua air mata saya sekalipun, takkan dapat membasuh lumuran darah pada tubuh si Melur dan Jebat. Mereka telah mengorbankan nyawa mereka kerana kematian saya. Padahal saya masih hidup.

If I release all my tears for but once, it would not be able to wash away the flow of blood from the bodies of Melur and Jebat. They have sacrificed their lives because of my death. In truth, I was alive.

Chapter 4

P. Ramlee, 'Kata sambutan dari P. Ramlee' [The speeches of P. Ramlee], *Majallah Filem*, April 1960, p. 4.

'MAJALLAH FILEM' berkembang biak di-dalam masharakt [sic] sabagai 'jurusan' yang membimbing pembacha2-nya meredas di-Dunia Filem; juga menjadi sabagai salah satu daripada alat2 penting untuk meninggikan darjat Bahasa Kebangsaan.

Kerana majallah ini, di-terbitkan di-dalam bahasa dan ejaan Kebangsaan, tidak salah kalau saya katakan, 'MAJALLAH FILEM', ada-lah satu majallah yang berani. Berani berjuang di-tengah2 gelanggang yang sedang di-bena.

Hendak-nya keberanian 'MAJALLAH FILEM', dalam memulakan langkah-nya ini, akan berkekalan dan makin bertambah subur sa-hingga chita2-nya— Majallah Bahasa Kebangsaan Kebanggaan Kita—akan terlaksana.

'MAJALLAH FILEM' will expand widely in [our] society as a 'benchmark' to guide its readers in their foray into the world of films; also as an important instrument to raise the standard of the National Language.

As this magazine is published in the National Language and its [official] spelling, it is not wrong for me to say 'MAJALLAH FILEM' is a courageous magazine. Courageous to strive in the midst of an arena that is in the process of being built.

The courageousness of 'MAJALLAH FILEM' that is needed in initiating this process will endure and be ever fertile until its goal—[to be the] Magazine of Our National Language—is achieved.

*

Kassim Masdor, Oral History Interviews, Reel/Disc 7, Accession Number 002141, National Archives of Singapore, 13 May 1999 (my emphasis).

Kebanyakan lagu-lagu (filem) Cathay-Keris ini terlampau ke-Melayuan sangat. Jadi tak dapat diterima oleh masyarakat kerana mungkin lagunya, sorry to say, tak begitu menarik tapi filem-filem Shaw Brothers walaupun tidak mempunyai itu, satu, apa kata orang; lagu yang very typical Malay tapi dia mempunyai commercial touch.

A lot of the film songs from Cathay-Keris were too excessively Malay. So, they were not accepted by society possibly because, sorry to say, they weren't that exciting but despite the Shaw Brothers' films not having any, what people call very typical Malay songs … [Shaw Brothers' film songs] have a *commercial touch.*

*

Dialogue from *Dang Anom* (1962, dir. Hussein Haniff)

Malang: *Datuk, tiap-tiap sesuatu di dunia ini, ada batasnya. Begitu jugalah sabra…. Kalau Sultan bebas melakukan kehendak hawa nafsunya saya juga selaku manusia bebas mengeluarkan kata-kata hati saya yang benar.*

Rajuna Tapa: *Memang benar kata-katamu itu tetapi kita rakyat tidak boleh menderhaka kepada Sultan. Lagipun salah di sisi adat.*

Malang: *Ah! Adat! Bukankah adat itu ciptaan nafsu untuk meluaskan kezaliman? Sedangkan Sultan bebas merampaskan anak-isteri orang untuk memuaskan hawa nafsu tetapi rakyat; rakyat diikat dengan adat-adat kejam. Di manakah keadilan, Datuk?*

Rajuna Tapa: *Malang, jangan terlalu melayan perasaan darah mudamu. Kelak binasa badanmu.*

Malang: *Tidak, tidak. Demi untuk keselamatan Anom dan kebenaran saya rela berkorban apa saja untuk menghancurkan adat-adat yang kejam ini.*

Malang:	Sir, everything in this world has its limits. The same goes with patience…. If the sultan is free to appease his lustful desires then I too as a free human being should be free to express the words from my heart that are true.
Rajuna Tapa:	Your words are true but the citizens cannot be treasonous to the sultan. Moreover, it is wrong on the side of our customs.
Malang:	Ah! Customs! Are not customs a manifestation of desire to spread cruelty? Meanwhile, the sultan is free to abduct people's children and wives to fulfil his lustful desires, but the citizens, the citizens are bound to ruthless customs. Where is the justice, sir?
Rajuna Tapa:	Malang, do not give in to your the feelings of your young blood. It will destroy your body.
Malang:	Never, never. For the safety of Anom and the truth I am willing to sacrifice anything at all to demolish these ruthless customs.

Chapter 5

Dialogue from *Antara Dua Darjat* (1960, dir. P. Ramlee)

Zaleha: *Ghazali, mengapakah irama dan lagu tak boleh dipisahkan?*
Ghazali: *Kalau dipisahkan, pincanglah lagu dan rosaklah seni.*
Zaleha: *Kalaulah aku dan kamu dipisahkan?*
Ghazali: *Pincanglah asmara dan rosaklah penghidupan.*

Zaleha: Ghazali, why can't rhythm and melody be separated?
Ghazali: If they are separated, song will be disordered and art will be ruined.
Zaleha: What if you and I are separated?
Ghazali: Our romance will be disordered and our lives will be ruined.

Chapter 6

Zubir Said, 'Menuju tahun 1967' [Towards 1967], *Filem Malaysia*, June 1967, p. 20.

Akibat perubahan2 dalam susunan masharakat menimbulkan perubahan2 pula dalam perkembangan seni nyanyian Melayu. Biduan2 dan ahli2 pantun tidak lagi mendapat pemeliharaan yang baik dan dalam masharakat lahirlah-lah seniman2 yang tidak bertanggong jawab dalam nilai chiptan-nya. Perubahan2 telah membawa kerosakkan pada lagu dan bahasa yang di-pakai dalam nyanyian akibat kemasokan unsor2 asing.

The result of changes in the organisation of society leads to changes in the development of Malay sung arts. Singers [artists] and poets do not receive adequate patronage and there are artists born in society that do not take responsibility in the value of their creations. These changes have brought detriment to the songs and language used in songs due to the intrusion of foreign elements.

Unsor2 kebangsaan hendak-lah di-tanamkan sa-banyak mungkin ka-dalam nyanyian Melayu bagi memelihara keperibadian-nya.

Unsor2 asing yang merosakkan hendak-lah di-hapuskan dan yang membawa kebaikan boleh-lah diterima.

Penggubah2 lagu serta biduan2 hendak-lah mempunyai pengetahuan yang se-layak-nya tentang bahasa dan jalan bahasa.

Sistem pengajaran (kebangsaan) nyanyian dengan tulisan musik hendak-lah di-adakan di-sekolah2.

National elements need to be implanted as much as possible into Malay songs to preserve its uniqueness.

Foreign elements that are destructive must be eliminated and [those that are] that are beneficial should be accepted.

Songwriters and singers [artists] must possess adequate knowledge of [Malay] language [vocabulary] and language usage [grammar].

A [nationalised] system for teaching singing and writing should be implemented in schools.

*

P. Ramlee, 'Cara-cara meninggikan mutu dan memperkayakan muzik jenis asli dan tradisional Malaysia demi kepentingan negara' [Ways to elevate and enrich the original and traditional music of Malaysia for the benefit of the nation], in *Asas Kebudayaan Kebangsaan*, 1st ed. Kuala Lumpur: Kementerian Kebudayaan Belia dan Sukan Malaysia, 1973, p. 205.

... secara lekas dapat mempengaruhi jiwa muda-mudi kita Malaysia, sehingga pemuda-pemudi tidak sedar pula berambut panjang (ala Beattle [sic]), berpakaian 'Groovy' yang tidak ketentuan, menghisap ganja dan lain-lain. Pemuda-pemudi pula berpakaian 'mini-skirt' yang singkat, kerana terpengaruh dengan pemain-pemain muzik pop.

... rapidly influenced the souls of our [Malaysian] youths to the point that these youths are unaware of their long hair (like the Beatles), dress in 'groovy' styles that are unfamiliar, smoke ganja [marijuana] and other things. There are also young women that wear short 'miniskirts' due to the influence of pop musicians.

*

N. Hanis, 'Untok mengembalikan kesedaran' [To restore awareness], *Bintang dan Lagu*, July 1967, p. 51.

Mini-skirt ialah suatu pakaian yang mendedahkan betis kita kapada umum. Adakah ini dikatakan kemajuan? Kemajuan akan terchapai dengan tidak payah memakai mini-skirt. Dan dengan memakai baju kurong kita dapat menarek hati lelaki, tak payahlah dengan memakai mini-skirt.... Kalau benar2 kita hendak memakai pakaian2 yang pendek, pakai sahaja chelana dalam, bukankah lebeh pendek?

Miniskirts are a type of clothing that exposes [a woman's] calves to the public. Is this what is called progress? Progress can be achieved without having to wear miniskirts. And, by wearing *baju kurong* [traditional Malay dress] we are able to attract males; we don't need to wear miniskirts for this.... If we really want to wear short [revealing] clothes, wear underwear, isn't that even shorter [more revealing]?

Mengapakah kita mesti meniru2 akan pakaian yang datangnya dari negeri lain, saperti negeri2 dari Barat. Tidakkah chukup pakaian yang ada pada negeri kita? Sedangkan negeri2 Barat tidak pernah bahkan tidak mahu manggunakan pakaian2 kita, mengapa pula kita mesti mempertinggikan lagi pakaian yang datang dari Barat yang tidak sesuai dengan kita.

Why must we copy the clothes that come from other countries, like Western countries[?] Aren't there enough clothes in our own country? While Western countries have never ever wanted to use our clothes, why then must we favour clothes that come from the West that are not suitable for us.

*

A. Anis Sabirin, 'Jangan pakai baju langsong' [Don't wear clothes at all], *Bintang dan Lagu*, September 1967, p. 51.

Buat saya miniskirt itu saolah2 saperti sarong nangka. Diatas tutup rapi, sedangkan betis dan peha ditunjok2kan dikhalayak ramai. Rasa saya dari memakai miniskirt itu lebeh baik jangan memakai langsong, itu lebeh menawan hati lelaki.

For me miniskirts are like jackfruit covers. The top is wrapped tightly, while the calves and thighs are shown to the general public. I feel that instead of wearing miniskirts it is better not to wear anything at all; that is even more attractive for men.

*

A. Zainy Nawawi, 'Pakaian lelaki perempuan tak berbedza' [Women's clothing is different], *Bintang dan Lagu*, November 1967, p. 48.

Kalau sipemudi bergaya dengan miniskirtnya yang menonjolkan sabahagian pehanya, maka kapada sipemuda, mereka beraksi pula dengan baju dan seluar yang ketat2 atau 'fensi', kata muda-mudi dewasa ini. Biar apa jua pakaian yang mereka gayakan, tidak saorang pun boleh menegor-sapa mereka kerana pasti mendapat jawapan yang tidak bagitu menyenangkan.

While young women are stylish with their miniskirts that reveal parts of their thighs, young males show off their shirts and trousers that are tight or 'fancy', as these young adults like to say. No matter what clothes they wear, no one can tell them otherwise because they will reply with an answer that is unsettling [rude or inappropriate].

*

An interview with P. Ramlee in Noor As Ahmad, 'Nasihat P. Ramlee', *Mastika Filem*, August 1967, p. 31.

Satu hal yang sangat menduka-chitakan, ia-lah menurut yang saya tau, kebanyakan dari penyanyi2 dan pemain2 muzik pop itu tidak boleh membacha note lagu. Bagi saya ini ada-lah satu kelemahan yang mesti segera diperbaiki.... Kerana kalau tidak ... saya khuatir hari depan penyanyi2 pop itu tidak-lah dapat di-bawa ka-tengah dan ka-tepi, saperti perahu yang berlayar manggunakan layar burok saja.

One matter that is disappointing is that, based on what I know, many pop singers and musicians cannot read musical notes. For me, this is a weakness that needs to be fixed.... Because if it is not [addressed] ... I worry that the future of pop singers cannot be brought to the centre or to the side [as in lacking direction], like a ship sailing with a ruined sail.

*

Dialogue from *Muda Mudi* (1965, dir. M. Amin)

Ana, kau baru dalam dunia ini. Lagu atau rekod pertama tidak ada erti. Hari ini, orang suka dengan suara kau. Esok, orang tak dengar lagi. Aku suka kau mashyur dan aku tahu kau boleh menyanyi disukai ramai. Tapi, aku suka beri kau nasihat. Kau terima atau buang, anak.... Ana, aku sudah mengalami segala-galanya.

Ana, you are new to this world. A debut single or record has no meaning. Today, everyone likes your voice. Tomorrow, people won't listen to you anymore. I want you to be successful and I know your singing is widely appreciated. However, I like to give you advice. You can accept it or not.... Ana, I have experienced everything.

*

Dialogue from *A Go Go '67* (1967, dir. Omar Rojik)

Bukan semua pemudi begini tak bermoral dan jahat, ayah. Juga tak semua orang yang alim baik, ayah. Saya dah besar. Saya tahu buruk-baiknya. Ayah tahu, kebanyakkan dari mereka itu tak mempunyai pekerjaan yang tetap, ayah. Jadi, dengan menumpuhkan minat mereka terhadap muzik, mereka dapat mengisi kekosongan hidup dan terelak dari perkara-perkara jenayah.... Ayah suka mendegar pemuda-pemuda kita mencuri, merompak, menyamun kerana kekosongan hidup mereka?

Not all youth are immoral and delinquent, father. Also, not all people who are religious are good, father. I am an adult. I know right from wrong. You know father, a lot of them [youths] do not have permanent jobs. So, by directing their interest towards music, they are able to fill the emptiness of their lives and avoid criminal activities.... Father, do you like hearing of our youths stealing, thieving, extorting because of the emptiness in their lives?

Ayah selalu menuduh bahawa pemuda-pemuda dan pemudi-pemudi seperti kita ini adalah sampah masyarakat yang sudah tak berguna langsung. Yah [Fauziah] mahu Joe [Johari] buktikan pada masyarakat terutama pada ayah Yah sendiri bahawa kita dapat digunakan untuk sesuatu tujuan yang baik asalkan seseorang itu tahu menggunakannya.

My father always accuses that youth like us are the trash of society that are absolutely useless. I want you [Johari] to prove to society, especially my father, that we can be used for a good cause as long as people know how to make use of us.

*

Interview with Kassim Masdor, Experience in the Malay Film and Popular Music Industry, 2013.

Bila Uncle cipta lagu-lagu filem, Uncle taruk kat filem, Uncle rekod kat EMI. So become promotion [untuk filem]. So, one day, the manager of Malay Film Production [Kwek Chip Jian], dia stop Uncle.... Stop-kan Uncle [supaya] jangan rekod-kan ke EMI. Dia panggil Uncle, dia bilang, 'From today onward, you punya lagu tak boleh rekod kat EMI.' I said, 'Why?' [To which he replied], 'Because, we pay you, already … You [should] pay me (untuk lagu-lagu yang direkod untuk EMI).' [Tapi, kebetulan] you [Malay Film Productions] pinjam lagu I untuk filem…. [Kwek kata]: 'You [should] pay me, that means the song(s) … belongs to us [Malay Film Productions].' Pasal dia dah jealous Uncle punya [lagu] dah make money juga, kan?…. No such thing … [Saya balas balik]: 'You must remember Mr Kwek, I working in Malay Film Productions. I work with you not as a composer, you must remember that … I am working with you as a continuity clerk…. If the lawyer [dari EMI] come to see you don't blame me.' [Balas Mr. Kwek]: 'Why lawyer?' [Uncle jawab]: 'Because whatever song I write is belong to EMI. I signed the [song-writing] contract with EMI.' … Jadi, lagu-lagu filem … Yusof B. dan Osman Ahmad … [mereka] memang bekerja di Jalan Ampas [Malay Film Productions] sebagai composer and their song is belong to Malay Film Productions. Uncle dengan P. Ramlee—P. Ramlee kerja sebagai actor. Uncle sebagai continuity clerk. Kita dua orang punya lagu, bebas. Dia boleh recording kat mana-mana. They have no right to stop my songs.

When I wrote songs for film, I would use them on the films as well as record them for EMI. So such recorded songs would be promotional for the film. So, one day the manager of Malay Film Productions [Kwek Chip Jian], he stopped me…. He [tried] to stop me from recording [my film songs] for EMI. He called me and said, 'From today onward, your songs cannot be recorded for EMI.' I said, 'Why?' To which he replied, 'Because we pay you, already … You [should] pay me [for your EMI recordings].' [In reality] you [Malay Film Productions] borrowed my songs for the films … [Kwek then responded]: 'You [should] pay me, that means the song(s) … belong to us [Malay Film Productions].' The reason … [Kwek] said this was because he was jealous as my songs were already making money, as well, right? … No such thing … [I replied]: 'You must remember Mr Kwek, I work in Malay Film Productions. I work with you not as a composer, you must remember that … I am working with you as a continuity clerk…. If the lawyer [from EMI] comes to see you don't blame me.' [Kwek responded]: 'Why [would a] lawyer [come to see me]?' I answered: 'Because whatever song I write belongs to EMI. I signed the [song-writing] contract with EMI.' … As such, the film songs of … Yusof B. and Osman Ahmad … they were actually working in Jalan Ampas [Malay Film Productions] as composers [by contract] and their songs belonged to Malay Film Productions. Myself and P. Ramlee—P. Ramlee was hired as an actor. I was a continuity clerk. Both of our songs were free [to use in whatever way we wanted]. They could be recorded anywhere. They [Malay Film Productions] have no right to stop [the recording and distribution of] my songs.

Dalam masa Uncle bekerja [di Malay Film Productions], Uncle juga as a part-time producer for EMI ... as a talent-scout ... rakam artis kasi EMI, bikin lagu kasi EMI.... Lama-lama mereka sukakan Uncle.... So, satu hari Malay Filem Production nak bikin satu filem, A Go Go '67.... Jadi, music directornya, Uncle and Yusof B. So kita publish kat (news)paper ... [untuk panggil] semua kita punya kugiran datang untuk audition.... Siapa layak, bagus, timbullah [dalam filem].... Di situ, Uncle banyak bikin lagu and di situ Uncle dapat banyak talent. Seperti, Sanisah Huri belum penyanyi. Dia adalah [seorang] dancers dalam kumpulan Terwellos.... So, Uncle ... [sebagai] talent scout ... Uncle tengok dia ... cute, cantik.... Uncle ambil dia ... dia tak boleh menyanyi. Uncle kasi dia menyanyi dalam filem A Go Go '67 itu.... Dari situ dia yanyi, Uncle ambil dia taruk kat EMI. Terus EMI. Pass.

When I worked [in Malay Film Productions], I was also a part-time producer for EMI ... as a talent scout ... I recorded artists for EMI and made songs for EMI.... In time, they took a liking to me.... So one day Malay Film Productions wanted to make a film, *A Go Go '67*.... So the musical directors for the film were Yusof B. and myself. So we published an advertisement in the newspaper ... to call all the *kugiran* to come to [Malay Film Productions] for an audition.... Whoever was eligible, good, would appear [in the film].... From there I wrote many songs and from there I found many talents. For example, Sanisah Huri was not yet a singer. She was one of the dancers from the Terwellos band.... So, I ... [as] a talent scout ... I saw her ... [she was] cute, pretty.... So I featured her ... she could not sing. I made her sing in the film *A Go Go '67*.... From there, she [started] singing, and I brought her to EMI. Straight to EMI. Pass.

Chapter 7

Ministry of Culture, Youth and Sports [Kementerian Kebudayaan, Belia dan Sukan Malaysia], *Asas Kebudayaan Kebangsaan* [Basis of National Culture], Kuala Lumpur: KBBS, 1973, p. vii.

1. *Kebudayaan Kebangsaan Malaysia haruslah berasaskan kebudayaan asli rakyat rantau ini;*
2. *Unsur-unsur kebudayaan lain yang sesuai dan wajar boleh diterima menjadi unsur kebudayaan kebangsaan; dan*
3. *Islam menjadi unsur yang penting dalam pembentukan kebudayaan kebangsaan itu.*

1. Malaysian national culture must be based on the indigenous culture(s) of the citizens of this region;
2. Cultural elements of other cultures that are appropriate and reasonable may be accepted as an element of national culture; and
3. Islam is an important element in the shaping of this national culture.

*

Ariff Ahmad, 'Muzik Malaysia jenis barat (seriosa) dan kedudukannya dalam masyarakat Malaysia baru' [Western (seriosa) Malaysian music and its place in new Malaysian society], in *Asas Kebudayaan Kebangsaan*. Kementerian Kebudayaan Belia dan Sukan Malaysia, 1973, p. 210.

Masyarakat Melayu khasnya sukar menerima seni muzik bercorak berat sedikit oleh kerana pengertian seni yang bercorak berat tidak ada. Muzik yang berbentuk asli yang mempunyai form atau structure di masyarakat Melayu adalah primitif dan melebih-beratkan rhythm sahaja. Oleh itu tidaklah dapat dinafikan bahawa jika masyarakat Melayu dikehendaki menikmati seni muzik jenis berat ini, konsep seni muziknya terpaksa ditambah dengan konsep Barat.

Malay society, especially, finds it quite difficult to accept serious styles of music because there is no understanding of serious styles of music. Indigenous types of music that have form and structure in Malay society are primitive and only emphasise rhythms. Because of this, it cannot be denied that if Malay society is required to appreciate these serious musical arts, their own musical concepts need to be added with Western concepts.

*

Interview with Ramli Kecik in *P. Ramlee* (2010, dir. Shuhaimi Baba)

P. Ramlee pernah kena 'boo' di stage. Di Dewan Bahasa [dan] Pustaka [Kuala Lumpur]. Waktu itu 'Malam Tiga Ramlee': P. Ramlee, A. Ramlie, L. Ramli. Saya cameraman. Jadi, bila P. Ramlee nak keluar menyanyi, semua orang 'boo'. Saya tengok … [konsert] pop di stadium, penyanyi Singapore and Malaysia, bila penyanyi Malaysia keluar, mesti orang 'boo'. Jadi orang [Malaysia] tak suka waktu itu penyanyi tempatan.

P. Ramlee has been 'booed' on stage. At the Malaysian Institute of Language and Literature [Kuala Lumpur]. It was the 'Night of Three Ramlees': P. Ramlee, A. Ramlie and L. Ramli. I was the cameraman. So, when P. Ramlee came out to sing, everyone 'booed'. I noticed … [in] pop [concerts] held in stadiums that had singers from Singapore and Malaysia, when Malaysian singers come out, people had to 'boo'. So, at the time, [Malaysian] people did not like local singers.

*

Interview with P. Ramlee in *P. Ramlee* (2010, dir. Shuhaimi Baba)

Lagu-lagu macam lagu joget, orkes-orkes combo … lagu-lagu asli, ghazal, dan … dendang sayang tidak pernah dipertandingkan atau dipertunjukkan. Kalau lagu-lagu ini tidak diberi galakkan, maka nescaya lagi sepuluh dua puluh tahun akan datang lagu ini akan dilupa terus dan muzik-muzik dari Barat … akan mewakili muzik kita.

Songs [or musical styles] such as *joget*, *orkes-orkes combo* [small Malay orchestras] … *asli* songs, *ghazal* and … *dondang sayang* have never been put on competitions or presented. If these songs are not encouraged, hence in less than 10 or 20 years to come these songs will be fully forgotten and music from the West ... will be representative of our music.

*

Interview with Aziz Sattar in *P. Ramlee* (2010, dir. Shuhaimi Baba)

Hidup dia melarat, lah. Kasihan. Last saya pergi rumah dia [di Kuala Lumpur]. Saya tengok [tears welling up in his eyes and looking down], dia makan nasi dengan telur [holding back sobs]. Nama dia besar. Orang tahu P. Ramlee siapa. Tapi hidup dia melarat.

His life was burdensome. [I felt much] pity [for him]. The last time I went to his home [in Kuala Lumpur]. I saw [*tears welling up in his eyes and looking down*], he was eating rice with egg [*holding back sobs*]. His name was big. People [used to] know who P. Ramlee was. But his life was burdensome.

*

Interview with Ahmad Nawab Khan, Malay Film Music and P. Ramlee, 2013.

[Dokumentari] Shuhaimi Baba tu, ada ... banyak yang tak berapa perfect. Saya pun dia ada interview juga.... Interview tu saya tak berapa puas hati, pasal apa, ada orang-orang ... especially Aziz [Sattar]; saya bukan nak jatuh dia. Dia cerita benda yang tak betul. Dia (ber)cerita. Jadi, bila jumpa dia, dia nak nama. Dia nak dapat macam kedudukan yang 'tu everything kalau nak (tahu) tentang P. Ramlee, 'you must come to me'. Ah, macam 'tu. Orang dia. Tapi ada orang-orang lain yang tahu tentang P. Ramlee itu dia orang tak ... [pergi] jumpa. And then bila dia jumpa dia, dia cerita. Dia create the story.... Today different. Tomorrow different. Kalau tidak dia akan cerita yang sama. Dia kenal P. Ramlee dekat Jalan Ampas saja. Bila P. Ramlee datang Kuala Lumpur [selepas 1964] dah tak ada lagi dah.

[In the] Shuhaimi Baba [documentary] there are ... many things that are not that perfect. She interviewed me, too.... [In] that interview, I was not very satisfied because there are [certain] people ... especially Aziz [Sattar]; I don't want to defame him. He said a story that was not right. He [tells] stories. So, when you seek him [for information], he wants to make a name of himself. It is like he wants to occupy a position whereby everything that you want to know about P. Ramlee, 'you must come to me'. Ah, it's like that. People like him. However, there are other people that are knowledgeable about P. Ramlee that they [the film-makers] do not … go to meet [and interview]. And then, [the people] they [do] meet; they create a story. Today [the story is] different. Tomorrow [the story is] different. If [they were] not [fabricating stories] they would say the same story. They only know P. Ramlee at Jalan Ampas. When P. Ramlee came to Kuala Lumpur [after 1964] they were not around anymore.

*

Interview with P. Ramlee in *P. Ramlee* (2010, dir. Shuhaimi Baba)

Kalau kita tidak semaikan muzik-muzik traditional, asli ini ke dalam dada anak-anak kita, anak muda kita … satu hari muzik lain akan mengambil tempat kerana di dalam dada mereka itu kosong. Tidak ada apa-apa. Sama juga macam kita mengajar anak kita pergi belajar ugama. Walaubagaimanapun dia pergi berapa tinggi pun dia jarang hendak menukar ugama kerana ugama yang telah diajar ibu-bapanya telah tersimpan dalam dadanya. Itu juga [dengan] muzik … supaya muzik lain tak boleh mempenuhi jiwanya.

If we do not cultivate traditional and *asli* music into the chests of our children, our young children … one day other musics will occupy that space because the inside of their chests are empty. There is nothing. The same goes for when we teach our children to learn religion. However far s/he goes, s/he will rarely change religion because the religion that is taught by her/his parents are kept in the chest. It is the same [with] music … so that other musics cannot fill their soul.

C. Musical Transcriptions

1. Partial transcription of Saloma's playback vocal performance for Saadiah performing 'Tunggu Sekejap' in *Sergeant Hassan* (1958, dir. Lamberto V. Avellana). This transcription notes the musical transition from the child Salmah to the adult Salmah.

2. Transcription of P. Ramlee performing 'Tunggu Sekejap' in *Sergeant Hassan*. Music and arrangement by P. Ramlee, with lyrics by S. Sudarmaji.

3. Transcription of title theme music from *Dang Anom* (1962, dir. Hussein Haniff), composed by Zubir Said.

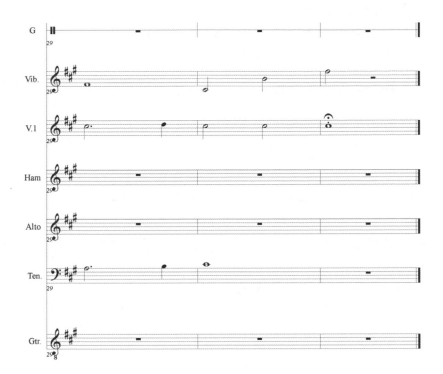

4. Second performance of 'Jeritan Batin' (Wailing Soul) from *Ibu Mertua-ku* (1962, dir. P. Ramlee). Music and arrangement by P. Ramlee, with lyrics by S. Sudarmaji.

ngar- lah   je-ri-tan ba- ti- in ku...

Glossary of Non-English Terms

adat	custom
ahli muzik	musician
angkatan liar	wild youth movements
angklung	musical instrument made from bamboo tubes
asli	rhythmic pattern, or style of song, which is slow and rich with ornamentation, lit. original, indigenous
awok-awok	chorus of singers
baju kurong	traditional Malay dress
bangsa	race
bangsawan	form of musical theatre which had its heyday in the Malay Archipelago in the early twentieth century
bendahara	viceroy or representative of a sultan
berat	serious, heavy
biduan	female court singer
boria	form of music theatre
bunyi	sound
caklempong	gong chime
canang	small knobbed gong
cemat	rope that ties a boat to a dock
datuk	deity or ancestral spirit (also a Malay honorific title)
dikir barat	musical form involving singing in groups
ding galung	bamboo idiophone
dondang sayang	form of love song based on *pantun*, usually accompanied by a violin, drums and a gong, lit. love song
filem masharakat	social film
gambus	short-necked lute

gedumbak	single-headed drum
gendang	double-headed frame drum
ghazal	type of love poem or ode
goh	bamboo idiophone
inang	rhythmic pattern or style of song
irama	rhythm, tempo, musical style
Jawa halus	refined Javanese
Jawi	Arabic script of the Malay language
joget	dance, thought to be of Portuguese origin, or a *social* occasion where dancing is enjoyed
kacukan	mixed
kampung	village
kasihan	sympathy, compassion
Kempetai	Japanese military police
kerajaan	government, state, lit. condition of having a raja
kerambit	small curved dagger
kereb	bamboo, plucked, two-stringed tube zither
keroncong	continuously evolving form of music in which plucked instruments form a filigree of delicate sounds, over which the melody is sung
ketua penyamun	chief thief
kompang	frame drum
kumpulan gitar rancak	upbeat guitar group
lagu	melody, song
laksamana	admiral
mak inang	nursemaid
manja	indulgent, spoilt, lenient, pampered
maqam	modes
masri	rhythmic pattern or style of song
Melayu	Malay
Melayu Baru	New Malays
merdeka	independence
mudah dinyanyikan	singability
nasyid	vocal music that is either sung a cappella or accompanied by percussion instruments
negara	nation

nenek-moyang	ancestral spirit
nobat	drum used in royal ceremonies
Orang Asli	indigenous person/people
orkes Melayu	Malay music ensembles
orkes-orkes combo	small Malay orchestras
pantun	poetic form consisting of a rhyming quatrain
perempuan darat	woman of the hinterlands
pontianak	vampire
pop yeh yeh	guitar and drum music influenced by the Beatles
rakyat	subjects, citizens
rebab	bowed string instrument
rebana	single-headed frame drum or tambourine
rentak	rhythmic stylings
ronggeng	dance or a social occasion where dancing is enjoyed
Rumi	romanised script of the Malay language
sedih	melancholy
selendang	shawl
seruling	bamboo flute
serunai	reed wind instrument
sesuai	appropriate
silat	form of martial art
sirih jampi	magical betel quid
songkok	traditional Malay headpiece
suara	voice
syair	poetic form of storytelling
tanah air	homeland
telor Arab	Arabic accent
tetawak	large, hanging knobbed gong
togunggak (*togunggu*)	bamboo idiophone
tok juara	lead singer
tokoh	deity
wajar	reasonable
wayang kulit	shadow puppet theatre
zapin	dance form introduced to Malay Peninsula by Arabs

Bibliography

I. Primary Sources

National Archives of Singapore
Ismail Haron, Oral History Interviews, Interview with Ismail Haron by Joseph C. Pereira, Accession Number 003001, National Archives of Singapore, 31 December 2005.
Kassim Masdor, Oral History Interviews, Reel/Disc 6, Accession Number 002141, National Archives of Singapore, 1 May 1999.
Kassim Masdor, Oral History Interviews, Reel/Disc 7, Accession Number 002141, National Archives of Singapore, 13 May 1999.
Zubir bin Said, Oral History Interviews, Reel 12, Accession Number 000293, National Archives of Singapore, 7 September 1984.
Zubir bin Said, Oral History Interviews, Reel 13, Accession Number 000293, National Archives of Singapore, 13 September 1984.

Newspapers and Periodicals
Berita Harian (Singapore)
Bintang (Singapore)
Bintang dan Lagu (Singapore)
Bulanan Gelanggang Film (Singapore)
Filem Malaysia (Malaysia)
Film Melayu (Singapore)
Juice (Malaysia)
Majallah Filem (Singapore)
Malay Mail Online (Malaysia)
Mastika Filem (Singapore)
Sinar Harian (Malaysia)
Star, The (Malaysia)
Straits Times (Singapore)

II. Interviews

Though some of the interviews are not cited in the text, they are nonetheless important to the ideas and arguments advanced in the book.
Adly Syairi Ramly, *Indiepretasi* Album (2010), 11 July 2013.
Ahmad Merican, Malay Music and the History of Malaysian Broadcasting, 8 June 2013.
Ahmad Nawab Khan, Malay Film Music and P. Ramlee, 12 June 2013.
Alif Omar Mahfix and Ben Liew, *Juice* Magazine: Indie Music, 29 October 2012.
Azlan Mohamed Said and Juffri Supa'at, *Musika* Book, 16 August 2013.
Farizam Mustapha, P. Ramlee Memorial Museum, 9 July 2013.
Kassim Masdor, Experience in the Malay Film and Popular Music Industry, 6 September 2013.
Khoo, Eddin, Music, Tradition and National Culture, 5 August 2013.
Low Zu Boon, 'Majulah!' Film music of Zubir Said, 19 October 2012.
Pereira, Joseph C., Beat Music Bands in 1960s Singapore, 21 October 2012.
Peters, Joe, Zubir Said's Music, 16 August 2013.

III. Secondary Sources

A. Anis Sabirin, 'Jangan pakai baju langsong' [Don't wear clothes at all], *Bintang dan Lagu*, September 1967.
A. Zainy Nawawi, 'Pakaian lelaki perempuan tak berbedza' [Women's clothing is different], *Bintang dan Lagu*, November 1967.
Abdullah Hussain, *Kisah Hidup Seniman Agung P. Ramlee* [The Story of the Great Artist P. Ramlee]. Kuala Lumpur: Dewan Bahasa dan Pustaka, 2016.
Adil Johan, 'Disquieting degeneracy: Policing Malaysian and Singaporean popular music culture from the mid-1960s to early-1970s', in *Sonic Modernities in the Malay World: A History of Popular Music, Social Distinction and Novel Lifestyles (1930s–2000s)*, ed. Bart Barendregt. Leiden: Brill, 2014, pp. 135–61.
———, 'Scoring tradition, making nation: Zubir Said's traditionalised film music for *Dang Anom*', *Malaysian Music Journal* 6, 1 (2017): 50–72.
Adorno, Theodor and Hanns Eisler, *Composing for the Films*. New York: Oxford University Press, 1947.
Ahmad Sarji, *P. Ramlee: Erti Yang Sakti* [P. Ramlee: The Sacred Reality]. 2nd ed., Petaling Jaya: MPH, 2011.
Alatas, Syed Hussein, *The Myth of the Lazy Native: A Study of the Image of the Malays, Filipinos and Javanese from the 16th to the 20th Century and Its Function in the Ideology of Colonial Capitalism*. London: Frank Cass, 1977.
Alfian Bin Sa'at, 'Hinterland, heartland, home: Affective topography in Singapore films', in *Southeast Asian Independent Cinema: Essays, Documents, Interviews*, ed. Tilman Baumgärtel. Singapore: NUS Press, 2012, pp. 33–50.
'AliBaba', W.E. Chronicles, 23 December 2010. Available at https://niwtode. wordpress.com/2010/12/23/e-lol-alibaba/ [accessed 18 December 2017].

Alicia Izharuddin, 'Anis Sabirin: Suara feminis lantang yang terkubur' [Anis Sabirin: An articulate feminist voice buried], *Malay Mail Online*, 9 March 2015.

———, 'Pain and pleasures of the look: The female gaze in Malaysian horror film', *Asian Cinema* 26, 2 (2015): 135–52.

Alif Omar Mahfix, 'Pop Malaysiana: Soul searching of the music kind', *Juice*, 2012.

Aljunied, Syed Muhd Khairudin, 'A theory of colonialism in the Malay world', *Postcolonial Studies* 14, 1 (2011): 7–21.

Amir Muhammad, *120 Malay Movies*. Petaling Jaya: Matahari Books, 2010.

Andaya, Barbara Watson, 'Distant drums and thunderous cannon: Sounding authority in traditional Malay society', *International Journal of Asia Pacific Studies* 7, 2 (2011): 19–35.

Andaya, Barbara Watson and Leonard Andaya, *A History of Malaysia*. 2nd ed., Honolulu: University of Hawai'i Press, 2001.

Anderson, Benedict, *Imagined Communities: Reflections on the Origins and Spread of Nationalism*. Rev. ed., London: Verso, 2006.

———, 'Colonial cosmopolitanism', in *Social Science and Knowledge in a Globalising World*, ed. Zawawi Ibrahim. Kajang: Malaysian Social Science Association and Petaling Jaya: Strategic Information and Research Development Centre, 2012, pp. 371–88.

Appiah, Kwame Anthony, *Cosmopolitanism: Ethics in a World of Strangers*. London: Penguin, 2006.

Ariff Ahmad, 'Muzik Malaysia jenis barat (seriosa) dan kedudukannya dalam masyarakat Malaysia baru' [Western (seriosa) Malaysian music and its place in new Malaysian society], in *Asas Kebudayaan Kebangsaan*. Kementerian Kebudayaan Belia dan Sukan Malaysia, 1973, pp. 208–14.

Arkib Negara Malaysia, *Senandung Warisan* [Song Legacy]. 2nd ed., Kuala Lumpur: Arkib Negara Malaysia, 2008 (Orig. publ. 2004).

Arnold, Alison E., 'Aspects of production and consumption in the popular Hindi film song industry', *Asian Music* 24, 1 (1992): 122–36.

———, 'Popular film music in India: A case of mass-market musical eclecticism', *Popular Music* 7, 2 (1988): 177–88.

Asby, H., 'Kalau dia menyanyi menyuroh orang teringat kapada Bing Crosby' [When he sings he asks people to remember Bing Crosby], *Bulanan Gelanggang Film*, April 1961.

Azlan Mohamed Said, *Musika: Malaya's Early Music Scene (Arena Muzik Silam Di Malaya)*, ed. Juffri Supa'at. Singapore: Stamford Printing, 2013.

Azmyl Md Yusof, 'Facing the music: Music subcultures and "morality" in Malaysia', in *Media, Culture and Society in Malaysia*, ed. Yeoh Seng Guan. London: Routledge, 2010, pp. 179–96.

Bakhle, Janaki, *Two Men and Music: Nationalism in the Making of an Indian Classical Tradition*. Oxford: Oxford University Press, 2005.

Barendregt, Bart, 'Cyber-*nasyid*: Transnational soundscapes in Muslim Southeast Asia', in *Medi@sia: Global Media/tion in and out of Context*, ed. Todd Joseph Miles Holden and Timothy Scrase. London: Routledge, 2006, pp. 170–87.

————, 'The art of no-seduction: Muslim boy-band music in Southeast Asia and the fear of the female voice', *IIAS Newsletter* 40 (2006): 10.

————, 'Pop, politics and piety: *Nasyid* boy band music in Muslim Southeast Asia', in *Islam and Popular Culture in Indonesia and Malaysia*, ed. Andrew N. Weintraub. London: Routledge, 2011, pp. 235–56.

————, 'Sonic discourses on Muslim Malay modernity: The Arqam sound', *Contemporary Islam* 6, 3 (2012): 315–40.

————, ed. *Sonic Modernities in the Malay World: A History of Popular Music, Social Distinction and Novel Lifestyles (1930s–2000s)*. Leiden: Brill, 2014.

Barendregt, Bart and Wim van Zanten, 'Popular music in Indonesia since 1998, in particular fusion, indie and Islamic music on video compact discs and the internet', *Yearbook for Traditional Music* 34 (2002): 67–113.

Barlow, H.S., 'Bibliography of Tan Sri Dato Dr Haji Mubin Sheppard', *Journal of the Malaysian Branch of the Royal Asiatic Society* 68, 2 (1995): 59–66.

Barnard, Rohayati Paseng and Timothy P. Barnard, 'The ambivalence of P. Ramlee: *Penarek Beca* and *Bujang Lapok* in perspective', *Asian Cinema* 13, 2 (2002): 9–23.

Barnard, Timothy P., 'Vampires, heroes and jesters: A history of Cathay Keris', in *The Cathay Story*, ed. Ain-ling Wong. Hong Kong: Hong Kong Film Archives, 2002, pp. 124–41.

————, '*Sedih sampai buta*: Blindness, modernity and tradition in Malay films of the 1950s and 1960s', *Bijdragen Tot de Taal-, Land- en Volkenkunde* 161, 4 (2005): 433–53.

————, 'Decolonization and the nation in Malay film, 1955–1965'. *South East Asia Research* 17, 1 (2009): 65–86.

————, 'Film Melayu: Nationalism, modernity and film in a pre-World War Two Malay magazine', *Journal of Southeast Asian Studies* 41, 1 (2010): 47–70.

————, 'Gelanggang Film', *Cinemas of Asia* 1 (2012).

————, ed. *Contesting Malayness: Malay Identity across Boundaries*. Singapore: Singapore University Press, 2004.

Barnard, Timothy P. and Jan van der Putten, 'Malay cosmopolitan activism in post-war Singapore', in *Paths Not Taken: Political Pluralism in Post-War Singapore*, ed. Michael D. Barr and Carl A. Trocki. Singapore: NUS Press, 2008, pp. 132–53.

Basapa, Lawrence, 'Hippism does not start or end with pot and long hair', *Straits Times*, 20 September 1970.

Baumgärtel, Tilman, '"I want you to forget about the race of the protagonists half an hour into the film". Interview with Yasmin Ahmad', in *Southeast Asian Independent Cinema: Essays, Documents, Interviews*, ed. Tilman Baumgärtel. Singapore: NUS Press, 2012, pp. 245–52.

Beck, Ulrich and Natan Sznaider, 'Unpacking cosmopolitanism for the social sciences: A research agenda', *British Journal of Sociology* 57, 1 (2006): 1–23.

Booth, Gregory D., 'Making a woman from a *Tawaif*: Courtesans as heroes in Hindi cinema', *New Zealand Journal of Asian Studies* 9, 2 (2007): 1–26.

————, 'Religion, gossip, narrative conventions and the construction of meaning in Hindi film songs', *Popular Music* 19, 2 (2000): 125–45.

———, *Behind the Curtain: Making Music in Mumbai's Film Studios*. New York: Oxford University Press, 2008.

Born, Georgina and David Hesmondhalgh, *Western Music and Its Others: Difference, Representation, and Appropriation and Music*. Berkeley: University of California Press, 2000.

Brown, C.C., trans. *Sejarah Melayu, or, The Malay Annals*. Kuala Lumpur: Oxford University Press, 1970 (Orig. publ. 1953).

Brown, Katherine Butler, 'The social liminality of musicians: Case studies from Mughal India and beyond', *Twentieth-century Music* 3, 1 (2007): 13–46.

Campbell, Felicia, 'Silver screen, shadow play: The tradition of the wayang kulit in *The Year of Living Dangerously*', *Journal of Popular Culture* 28, 1 (1994): 163–69.

Chan, Clare Suet Ching, 'P. Ramlee's music: An expression of local identity in Malaya during the mid-twentieth century', *Malaysian Music Journal* 1, 1 (2012): 16–32.

Cheah Boon Kheng, 'Power behind the throne: The role of queens and court ladies in Malay history', *Journal of the Malaysian Branch of the Royal Asiatic Society* 66, 1 (1993): 1–21.

Cheah Pheng, 'Cosmopolitanism', *Theory, Culture & Society* 23, 2/3 (2006): 486–96.

Chong, Terence, 'A return to normal politics: Singapore general elections 2011', in *Southeast Asian Affairs 2012*, ed. Daljit Singh and Pushpa Thambipillai. Singapore: ISEAS–Yusof Ishak Institute, 2012, pp. 283–98.

Christianto, Wisma Nugraha, 'Peran dan fungsi tokoh Semar-Bagong dalam pergelaran lakon wayang kulit gaya Jawa Timuran', *Humaniora* 15, 3 (2003): 285–301.

Chua, Henry, *Call It Shanty: The Story of the Quests*. Singapore: BigO Books, 2001.

Chua, Juliana and Hawazi Daipi, *Zubir Said: His Songs*. Singapore: Singapore Cultural Foundation, 1990.

Cohen, Matthew Isaac, *The Komedie Stamboel: Popular Theatre in Colonial Indonesia, 1891–1903*. Leiden: KITLV Press, 2006.

Cohen, Stanley, *Folk Devils and Moral Panic: The Creation of the Mods and Rockers*. London: MacGibbon and Kee, 1972.

Comber, Leon, *13 May 1969: The Darkest Day in Malaysian History*. 2nd ed., Singapore: Marshall Cavendish, 2009.

Dissanayake, Wimal, 'Nationhood, history, and cinema: reflections on the Asian scene', in *Colonialism and Nationalism in Asian Cinema*, ed. Wimal Dissanayake. Bloomington: Indiana University Press, 1994, pp. ix–xxix.

Fairley, Jan, 'The "local" and "global" in popular music', in *The Cambridge Companion to Pop and Rock*, ed. Simon Frith, Will Straw and John Street. Cambridge: Cambridge University Press, 2001, pp. 272–89.

Foucault, Michel, 'What is an author?' in *The Foucault Reader*, ed. Paul Rabinow. New York: Pantheon, 1984, pp. 101–20.

Fuziah Kartini Hassan Basri, 'Representations of gender in Malaysian Malay cinema: Implications for human security', *Asian Cinema* 19, 2 (2008): 135–49.

Ghosh, Bishnupriya, *Global Icons: Apertures to the Popular*. Durham, NC: Duke University Press, 2011.

Gilroy, Paul, 'Great games: Film, history and working-through Britain's colonial legacy', in *Film and the End of Empire*, ed. Lee Grieveson and Colin MacCabe. London: British Film Institute, 2011, pp. 13–32.

Gledhill, Christine, 'Dialogue: Christine Gledhill on "Stella Dallas" and feminist theory', *Cinema Journal* 25, 4 (1986): 44–48.

———, 'The melodramatic field: An investigation', in *Home Is Where the Heart Is: Studies in Melodrama and the Woman's Film*, ed. Christine Gledhill. London: BFI Publishing, 1987, pp. 5–39.

Goh, Daniel P.S., Matilda Gabrielpillai, Phillip Holden and Gaik Cheng Khoo, eds. *Race and Multiculturalism in Singapore*. Singapore: Routledge, 2009.

Goh, Daryl, 'P. Ramlee goes indie', *The Star*, 22 October 2010.

———, 'Dreamtime with Zee Avi's lullaby album', *The Star*, 25 February 2014.

Gomez, Edmund Terence and Johan Saravanamuttu, eds. *The New Economic Policy in Malaysia: Affirmative Action, Ethnic Inequalities and Social Justice*. Singapore: NUS Press, 2012.

Grant, Catherine, 'Rethinking safeguarding: Objections and responses to protecting and promoting endangered musical heritage', *Ethnomusicology Forum* 21, 1 (2012): 31–51.

Grieveson, Lee and Colin MacCabe, eds. *Film and the End of Empire*. London: British Film Institute, 2011.

Guilbault, Jocelyne, *Governing Sound: The Cultural Politics of Trinidad's Carnival Music*. Chicago: University of Chicago Press, 2007.

Guneratne, Anthony R., 'The urban and the urbane: Modernization, modernism and the rebirth of Singaporean cinema', in *Theorizing the Southeast Asian City as Text: Urban Landscapes, Cultural Documents, and Interpretive Experiences*, ed. Robbie B.H. Goh and Brenda S.A. Goh. Singapore: World Scientific, 2003, pp. 159–90.

Hamzah Hussin, 'Zubir Said: Man of music', in *Majulah! The Film Music of Zubir Said*. Singapore: National Museum of Singapore, 2012, pp. 62–72.

Harding, James and Ahmad Sarji, P. *Ramlee: The Bright Star*. 2nd ed., Petaling Jaya: MPH, 2011.

Harper, T.N., *The End of Empire and the Making of Malaya*. 2nd ed., Cambridge: Cambridge University Press, 2001.

Hassan Abdul Muthalib, '"Winning hearts and minds": Representations of Malays and their milieu in the films of British Malaya', *South East Asia Research* 17, 1 (2009): 47–63.

———, 'The end of empire: The films of the Malayan Film Unit in 1950s British Malaya', in *Film and the End of Empire*, ed. Lee Grieveson and Colin MacCabe. London: British Film Institute, 2011, pp. 177–96.

———, *Malaysian Cinema in a Bottle: A Century (and a Bit More) of Wayang*. Petaling Jaya: Merpati Jingga, 2013.

Heide, William van der, *Malaysian Cinema, Asian Film: Border Crossings and National Cultures*. Amsterdam: Amsterdam University Press, 2002.

Hennion, Antoine, 'Music and mediation: Toward a new sociology of music', in *The Cultural Study of Music: A Critical Introduction*, ed. Martin Clayton, Trevor Herbert and Richard Middleton. London: Routledge, 2003, pp. 80–91.

Herzfeld, Michael, *Cultural Intimacy: Social Poetics and the Real Life of States, Societies, and Institutions*. 3rd ed., London: Routledge, 2016.

Hesmondhalgh, David, 'Indie: The institutional politics and aesthetics of a popular music genre', *Cultural Studies* 13, 1 (1999): 34–61.

———, *Why Music Matters*. Chichester: Wiley-Blackwell, 2013.

Hibbett, Ryan, 'What is indie rock?' *Popular Music and Society* 28, 1 (2005): 55–77.

Hobsbawm, Eric J., *Nations and Nationalism Since 1780: Programme, Myth, Reality*. 2nd ed., Cambridge: Cambridge University Press, 1992.

Jamil Sulong, *Kaca Permata: Memoir Seorang Pengarah*. Kuala Lumpur: Dewan Bahasa dan Pustaka, 1990.

Jones, Andrew F., *Yellow Music: Media Culture and Colonial Modernity in the Chinese Jazz Age*. Durham, NC: Duke University Press, 2001.

Kahn, Joel S., *Other Malays: Nationalism and Cosmopolitanism in the Modern Malay World*. Singapore: Singapore University Press, 2006.

Kalinak, Kathryn, *Settling the Score: Music and the Classical Hollywood Film*. Madison, WI: University of Wisconsin Press, 1992.

———, *How the West Was Sung: Music in the Westerns of John Ford*. Berkeley: University of California Press, 2007.

———, *Film Music: A Very Short Introduction*. Oxford: Oxford University Press, 2010.

Kamus Dewan. 4th ed., Kuala Lumpur: Dewan Bahasa dan Pustaka, 2007.

Kanda, Tamaki Matsuoka, 'Indian film directors in Malaya', in *Frames of Mind: Reflections on Indian Cinema*, ed. Aruna Vasudev. New Delhi: Indian Council for Public Relations, 1995, pp. 43–50.

Kartomi, Margaret, 'Kapri: A synthesis of Malay and Portuguese music on the west coast of North Sumatra', in *Cultures and Societies of North Sumatra*, ed. Rainer Carle. Berlin: Dietrich Reimer, 1987, pp. 351–93.

Keppy, Peter, 'Southeast Asia in the age of jazz: Locating popular culture in the colonial Philippines and Indonesia', *Journal of Southeast Asian Studies* 44, 3 (2013): 444–64.

Kertesz, Elizabeth and Michael Christofordis, 'Confronting *Carmen* beyond the Pyrenees: Bizet's opera in Madrid, 1887–1888', *Cambridge Opera Journal* 20, 1 (2009): 79–110.

Khoo Boo Teik, 'Ethnic structure, inequality and governance in the public sector: Malaysian experiences', Democracy, Governance and Human Rights Programme Paper Number 20, 2005, pp. 1–45.

Khoo Gaik Cheng, *Reclaiming Adat: Contemporary Malaysian Film and Literature*. Singapore: NUS Press, 2006.

King, Barry, 'Idol in a small country: *New Zealand Idol* as the commoditization of cosmopolitan intimacy', in *TV Formats Worldwide: Localizing Global Programs*, ed. Albert Moran. Bristol: Intellect, 2007, pp. 271–89.

Kong, Lily, 'Music and cultural politics: Ideology and resistance in Singapore', *Transactions of the Institute of British Geographers* 20, 4 (1995): 447–59.

Lee Chor Lin, 'Foreword', in *Majulah! The Film Music of Zubir Said*. Singapore: National Museum of Singapore, 2012, pp. 12–13.

Leyden, John, trans. *Sejarah Melayu: The Malay Annals*. Kuala Lumpur: Silverfish Books, 2012 (Orig. publ. 1821).

Lim, Juliana, 'Tribute to national anthem composer Zubir Said on the 25th anniversary of his demise', 2012. Available at http://julianalim.wordpress.com/2012/10/18/tribute-month/ [accessed 18 December 2017].

Lim, Serene, 'Audience turns misty-eyed at tribute to Zubir', *Straits Times*, 10 March 1990.

Lim Teck Ghee, 'British colonial administration and the "ethnic division of labour" in Malaya', *Kajian Malaysia* 2, 2 (1984): 28–66.

'Lim warns of flower people, yellow culture', *Straits Times*, 13 January 1968.

Littrup, Lisbeth, 'Development in Malay criticism', in *The Canon in Southeast Asian Literatures: Literatures of Burma, Cambodia, Indonesia, Laos, Malaysia, the Philippines, Thailand and Vietnam*, ed. David Smyth. Richmond: Curzon, 2000, pp. 76–87.

Lockard, Craig A., 'From folk to computer Songs: The evolution of Malaysian popular music, 1930–1990', *Journal of Popular Culture* 30, 3 (1996): 1–26.

———, *Dance of Life: Popular Music and Politics in Southeast Asia*. Honolulu: University of Hawai'i Press, 1998.

Locke, Ralph P., 'Constructing the oriental "other": Saint-Saëns's "Samson et Dalila"', *Cambridge Opera Journal* 3, 3 (1991): 261–302.

———, 'Cutthroats and casbah dancers, muezzins and timeless sands: Musical images of the Middle East', *19th-Century Music* 22, 1 (1998): 20–53.

———, *Musical Exoticism: Images and Reflections*. Cambridge: Cambridge University Press, 2009.

'Long hair ban on grant holders', *Straits Times*, 17 November 1975.

Luvaas, Brent, *DIY Style: Fashion, Music and Global Digital Cultures*. London: Berg, 2012.

Mahyuddin Ahmad and Yuen Beng Lee, 'Negotiating class, ethnicity and modernity: The "Malaynisation" of P. Ramlee and his films', *Asian Journal of Communication* 25, 4 (2015): 408–21.

Maier, Henk, '"We are playing relatives": Riau, the cradle of reality and hybridity', *Bijdragen Tot de Taal-, Land- En Volkenkunde* 153, 4 (1997): 672–98.

Malay Heritage Centre Singapore, *Malam Pesta Muda Mudi* Exhibition, Library@Esplanade, October 2012.

'Malaysian singer-songwriter sensation Yuna blazes US trail', ABC Radio Australia, 12 September 2013. Available at http://www.radioaustralia.net.au/international/radio/program/asia-pacific/malaysian-singersongwriter-sensation-yuna-blazes-us-trail/1189557 [accessed 2 February 2018].

Manuel, Peter, *Popular Music of the Non-Western World*. Oxford: Oxford University Press, 1988.

———, *Cassette Culture: Popular Music and Technology in North India*. Chicago: University of Chicago Press, 1993.

Marubbio, M. Elise, *Killing the Indian Maiden: Images of Native American Women in Film*. Lexington: University Press of Kentucky, 2006.

Matusky, Patricia, *Malaysian Shadow Play and Music: Continuity of an Oral Tradition*. Kuala Lumpur: The Asian Centre, 1997.

Matusky, Patricia and Tan Sooi Beng, *The Music of Malaysia: The Classical, Folk and Syncretic Traditions*. Aldershot: Ashgate, 2004.

Maznah Mohamad and Syed Muhd Khairudin Aljunied, eds. *Melayu: Politics, Poetics and Paradoxes of Malayness*. Singapore: NUS Press, 2011.

McClary, Susan, *George Bizet: Carmen*. Cambridge: Cambridge University Press, 1992.

McGraw, Andrew Clay, 'Music and meaning in the independence-era Malaysian films of P. Ramlee', *Asian Cinema* 20, 1 (2009): 35–59.

Meintjes, Louise, 'Paul Simon's *Graceland*, South Africa, and the mediation of musical meaning', *Ethnomusicology* 34, 1 (1990): 37–73.

Mera, Miguel and Anna Morcom, 'Introduction: Screened music, trans-contextualisation and ethnomusicological approaches', *Ethnomusicology Forum* 18, 1 (2009): 3–19.

'Merekam lagu filem' [Recording film song], *Majallah Filem*, May 1960.

Merriam, Alan, *The Anthropology of Music*. Evanston, IL: Northwestern University Press, 1964.

Milner, Anthony C., *The Invention of Politics in Colonial Malaya: Contesting Nationalism and the Expansion of the Public Sphere*. Cambridge: Cambridge University Press, 1995.

———, *The Malays*. Chichester: Wiley-Blackwell, 2008.

'Miniskirt: Apa salahnya gadis2 Melayu memakai miniskirt?' [Miniskirts: What is the harm in Malay women wearing miniskirts?], *Bintang dan Lagu*, November 1967.

Ministry of Culture, Youth and Sports [Kementerian Kebudayaan, Belia dan Sukan Malaysia], *Asas Kebudayaan Kebangsaan* [Basis of National Culture], Kuala Lumpur: KBBS, 1973.

Ministry of Information [Kementerian Penerangan Malaysia], 'Dasar Kebudayaan Kebangsaan', 2018. Available at http://pmr.penerangan.gov.my/index.php/component/content/article/88-dasar-dasar-negara/238-dasar-kebudayaan-kebangsaan.html [accessed 28 January 2018].

Mitchell, Katharyne, 'Geographies of identity: The intimate cosmopolitan', *Progress in Human Geography* 31, 5 (2007): 706–20.

Mohd Anis Md Nor, *Zapin: Folk Dance of the Malay World*. Singapore: Oxford University Press, 1993.

Mohd Raman Daud, ed. *7 Magnificient [sic] Composers: 7 Tokoh Muzik*. Singapore: Perkamus, 2002.

Monson, Ingrid, *Freedom Sounds: Civil Rights Call Out to Jazz and Africa*. Oxford: Oxford University Press, 2007.

Morcom, Anna, 'An understanding between Bollywood and Hollywood? The meaning of Hollywood-style music in Hindi films, *Ethnomusicology Forum* 10, 1 (2001): 63–84.

——, *Hindi Film Songs and the Cinema*. Aldershot: Ashgate, 2007.

Moro, Pamela, 'Constructions of nation and the classicisation of music: Comparative perspectives from Southeast and South Asia', *Journal of Southeast Asian Studies* 35, 2 (2004): 187–211.

Mulaika Hijjas, *Victorious Wives: The Disguised Heroine in 19th-Century Malay Syair*. Singapore: NUS Press, 2011.

Mustafar Abdul Rahim and Aziz Sattar, *Filem-Filem P. Ramlee* [The Films of P. Ramlee]. Senawang: MZA Terbit Enterprise, 2008.

N. Hanis, 'Untok mengembalikan kesedaran' [To restore awareness], *Bintang dan Lagu*, July 1967.

Naficy, Hamid, 'Phobic spaces and liminal panics: Independent transnational film genre', in *Multiculturalism, Postcoloniality, and Transnational Media*, ed. Ella Shohat and Robert Stam. New Brunswick, NJ: Rutgers University Press, 2003, pp. 203–26.

Nagata, Judith, 'Boundaries of Malayness: "We have made Malaysia: now it is time to (re)make the Malays but who interprets the history?"', in *Melayu: Politics, Poetics and Paradoxes of Malayness*, ed. Maznah Mohamad and Syed Muhd Khairudin Aljunied. Singapore: NUS Press, 2011, pp. 3–33.

National Heritage Board, 'About us—National Heritage Board', 2018. Available at https://www.nhb.gov.sg/who-we-are/about-us/mission-and-vision [accessed 2 February 2018].

National Museum of Singapore, *Majulah! The Film Music of Zubir Said*. Singapore: National Museum of Singapore, 2012.

Nazeri Nong Samah, 'Allahyarham P. Ramlee: Tetap seniman misteri', *Utusan Online*, 29 May 2003. Available at http://ww1.utusan.com.my/utusan/info. asp?y=2003&dt=0529&pub=utusan_malaysia&sec=Hiburan&pg=hi_02.htm [accessed 5 March 2018].

Nazry Bahrawi, 'A thousand and one rewrites: Translating modernity in the *Arabian Nights*', *Journal of World Literature* 1, 3 (2016): 357–70.

'Need to play down "hippie trend" on TV', *Straits Times*, 18 May 1970.

Noor As Ahmad, 'Nasihat P. Ramlee', *Mastika Filem*, August 1967.

Nordin Selat, *Renungan*. Kuala Lumpur: Utusan, 1978.

Nureza Ahmad and Nor-Afidah A. Rahman, 'Lieutenant Adnan Saidi', Singapore Infopedia, Singapore Library Board, 2005. Available at http://eresources.nlb.gov.sg/infopedia/articles/SIP_456_2005-01-18.html [accessed 18 December 2017].

Ong Soh Chin, 'Who are you? Where do you live?' *Straits Times*, 19 August 2006.

Ortmann, Stephan, 'Singapore: Authoritarian but newly competitive', *Journal of Democracy* 22, 4 (2011): 153–64.

P. Ramlee, 'Kata sambutan dari P. Ramlee' [The speeches of P. Ramlee], *Majallah Filem*, April 1960.

——, 'Cara-cara meninggikan mutu dan memperkayakan muzik jenis asli dan tradisional Malaysia demi kepentingan negara' [Ways to elevate and enrich the original and traditional music of Malaysia for the benefit of the nation], in *Asas Kebudayaan Kebangsaan*, 1st ed. Kuala Lumpur: Kementerian Kebudayaan Belia dan Sukan Malaysia, 1973, pp. 205–7.

Parakilas, James, 'The soldier and the exotic: Operatic variations on a theme of racial encounter', *Opera Quarterly* 10, 3 (1994): 43–69.

Pasha, Prem K., *The Krishnan Odyssey: A Pictorial Biography of Dato' L. Krishnan*. Kuala Lumpur: NASARRE, 2003.

Pereira, Joseph C., *Legends of the Golden Venus: Bands That Rocked Singapore from the '60s to the '90s*. Singapore: Times Editions, 1999.

——, *The Story of Singapore Sixties Music*. Vol. 1: *Apache Over Singapore*. Singapore: Select Publishing, 2011.

——, *The Story of Singapore Sixties Music*. Vol. 2: *Beyond the Tea Dance*. Singapore: Select Publishing, 2014.

Peters, Joe, 'Zubir Said and his music for film', in *Majulah! The Film Music of Zubir Said*. Singapore: National Museum of Singapore, 2012, pp. 74–90.

Pillai, Shantini, 'Syncretic cultural multivocality and the Malaysian popular musical imagination', *Kajian Malaysia* 31, 1 (2013): 1–18.

Proudfoot, Ian, *Early Malay Printed Books: A Provisional Account of Materials Published in the Singapore-Malaysia Area up to 1920, Noting Holdings in Major Public Collections*. Kuala Lumpur: Academy of Malay Studies and the Library, University of Malaya, 1993.

Putten, Jan van der, 'Negotiating the Great Depression: The rise of popular culture and consumerism in early-1930s Malaya', *Journal of Southeast Asian Studies* 41, 1 (2010): 21–45.

——, '"Dirty dancing" and Malay anxieties: The changing context of Malay ronggeng in the first half of the twentieth century', in *Sonic Modernities in the Malay World: A History of Popular Music, Social Distinction and Novel Lifestyles (1930s–2000s)*, ed. Bart Barendregt. Leiden: Brill, 2014, pp. 113–34.

Putten, Jan van der and Timothy P. Barnard, 'Old Malay heroes never die: The story of Hang Tuah in films and comics', in *Film and Comic Books*, ed. Ian Gordon, Mark Jancovich and Matthew P. McAllister. Jackson: University Press of Mississippi, 2007, pp. 246–67.

Rahim, Lily Zubaidah, *Singapore in the Malay World: Building and Breaching Regional Bridges*. London: Routledge, 2009.

Rahmah Bujang, *Sejarah Perkembangan Drama Bangsawan di Tanah Melayu dan Singapura* [The History of the Development of *Bangsawan* Drama in Malaya and Singapore]. Kuala Lumpur: Dewan Bahasa dan Pustaka, 1975.

Razha Rashid, 'Martial arts and the Malay superman', in *Emotions of Culture: A Malay Perspective*, ed. Wazir Jahan Karim. Singapore: Oxford University Press, 1990, pp. 64–95.

Regev, Motti, 'Cultural uniqueness and aesthetic cosmopolitanism', *European Journal of Social Theory* 10, 1 (2007): 123–38.

Reid, Anthony, 'Understanding *Melayu* (Malay) as a source of diverse modern identities', in *Contesting Malayness: Malay Identity Across Boundaries*, ed. Timothy P. Barnard. Singapore: Singapore University Press, 2004, pp. 1–24.

Richards, Arthur, 'Singapore censors ban pop colour film Woodstock', *Straits Times*, 29 December 1970.

Rohana Zubir, *Zubir Said, the Composer of Majulah Singapura*. Singapore: ISEAS Publishing, 2012.

Saidah Rastam, *Rosalie and Other Love Songs*. 2nd ed., Petaling Jaya: Strategic Information and Research Development Centre, 2017.

Saiful Bahari, 'Perkembangan muzik Malaysia dan matlamatnya' [The growth of Malaysian music and its objectives], in *Asas Kebudayaan Kebangsaan*. Kuala Lumpur: Kementerian Kebudayaan Belia dan Sukan Malaysia, 1973, pp. 215–21.

'Salamah Basiron: Penggubah muda yang berjiwa gelora' [Salamah Basiron: The young composer who is so turbulent], *Bintang dan Lagu*, November 1966.

Sarkissian, Margaret, *D'Albuquerque's Children: Performing Tradition in Malaysia's Portuguese Settlement*. London: University of Chicago Press, 2000.

———, 'Playing Portuguese: Constructing identity in Malaysia's Portuguese community', *Diaspora: A Journal of Transnational Studies* 11, 2 (2002): 215–32.

———, '"Religion never had it so good": Contemporary *nasyid* and the growth of Islamic popular music in Malaysia', in *Yearbook for Traditional Music* 37 (2005): 124–52.

Schofield (née Brown), Katherine Butler, 'Reviving the golden age again: "Classicization", Hindustani music, and the Mughals', *Ethnomusicology* 54, 3 (2010): 484–517.

———, 'The courtesan tale: Female musicians and dancers in Mughal historical chronicles, c.1556–1748', *Gender & History* 24, 1 (2012): 150–71.

Scott, Derek B., 'Orientalism and musical style', *Musical Quarterly* 82, 2 (1998): 309–35.

Seckinelgin, Hakan, 'Cosmopolitan intimacies and sexual politics in global civil society', in *Bottom-up Politics: An Agency-Centred Approach to Globalization*, ed. Denisa Kostovicova and Marlies Glasius. London: Palgrave Macmillan, 2011, pp. 61–74.

Shamsul A.B., 'A history of an identity, an identity of a history: The idea and practice of "Malayness" in Malaysia reconsidered', in *Contesting Malayness: Malay Identity Across Boundaries*, ed. Timothy P. Barnard. Singapore: Singapore University Press, 2004, pp. 125–48.

Shennan, Margaret, *Our Man in Malaya: John Davis, CBE, DSO, Force 136 SOE and Post-War Counter-Insurgency*. Singapore: Monsoon Books, 2014.

Sheppard, Mubin, *Malay Courtesy: A Narrative Account of Malay Manners and Customs in Everyday Use*. Singapore: Eastern Universities Press, 1959.

——, *Taman Indera: A Royal Pleasure Ground: Malay Decorative Arts and Pastimes*. Kuala Lumpur: Oxford University Press, 1972.

——, *Living Crafts of Malaysia*. Singapore: Times Books International, 1978.

——, *Taman Budiman: Memoirs of an Unorthodox Civil Servant*. Kuala Lumpur: Heinemann Educational Books, 1979.

——, *Taman Saujana: Dance, Drama, Music and Magic in Malaya, Long and Not-so-Long Ago*. Petaling Jaya: International Book Service, 1983.

'Singapura kongsi arkib warisan sejarah' [Singapore shares historical heritage archives], *Sinar Harian*, 21 October 2012.

Slobin, Mark, 'The Steiner superculture', in *Global Soundtracks: Worlds of Film Music*, ed. Mark Slobin. Middletown, CT: Wesleyan University Press, 2008, pp. 3–35.

——, 'The superculture beyond Steiner', in *Global Soundtracks: Worlds of Film Music*, ed. Mark Slobin. Middletown, CT: Wesleyan University Press, 2008, pp. 36–62.

——, ed. *Global Soundtracks: Worlds of Film Music*. Middletown, CT: Wesleyan University Press, 2008.

Srivastava, Sanjay, 'Voice, gender and space in time of five-year plans: The idea of Lata Mangeshkar', *Economic and Political Weekly* 39, 20 (2004): 2019–28.

Stivens, Maila, 'The youth, modernity and morality in Malaysia', in *Questioning Modernity in Indonesia and Malaysia*, ed. Wendy Mee and Joel S. Kahn. Singapore: NUS Press, 2012, pp. 169–200.

Stokes, Martin, 'Music and the global order', *Annual Review of Anthropology* 33 (2004): 47–72.

——, 'On musical cosmopolitanism', *The Macalester International Roundtable 2007*, Paper 3, 2007. Available at http://digitalcommons.macalester.edu/intlrdtable/3 [accessed 18 December 2017].

——, 'Listening to Abd Al-Halim Hafiz', in *Global Soundtracks: Worlds of Film Music*, ed. Mark Slobin. Middletown, CT: Wesleyan University Press, 2008, pp. 309–33.

——, "Abd Al-Halim's microphone', in *Music and the Play of Power in the Middle East, North Africa and Central Asia*, ed. Laudan Nooshin. Aldershot: Ashgate, 2009, pp. 55–73.

——, *The Republic of Love: Cultural Intimacy in Turkish Popular Music*. Chicago: University of Chicago Press, 2010.

Subramanian, Lakshmi, 'The reinvention of tradition: Nationalism, Carnatic music and the Madras Music Academy, 1900–1947', *Indian Economic and Social History Review* 36, 2 (1999): 131–63.

——, 'Culture and consumption: Classical music in contemporary India and the diaspora', *Transforming Cultures* 3, 1 (2008): 75–92.

————, *From the Tanjore Court to the Madras Music Academy: A Social History of Music in South India*. 2nd ed., Oxford: Oxford University Press, 2011.

Sumarsam, 'Music in Indonesian "historical" films: Reading *Nopember 1828*', in *Global Soundtracks: Worlds of Film Music*, ed. Mark Slobin. Middletown, CT: Wesleyan University Press, 2008, pp. 217–40.

Sunshine, Jane, 'My language is mine: Ya in sing mata kaji', The Splendid Chronicles, 30 August 2005. Available at http://splenderfulchronicles.blogspot.my/2005/08/my-language-is-mine-ya-in-sing-mata.html [accessed 18 December 2017].

Tan Chong Tee, *Force 136: Story of a WWII Resistance Fighter*. Singapore: Asiapac, 1994.

Tan Sooi Beng, 'The performing arts in Malaysia: state and society', *Asian Music* 21, 1 (1989): 137–71.

————, 'From popular to "traditional" theater: The dynamics of change in *bangsawan* of Malaysia', *Ethnomusicology* 33, 2 (1989): 229–74.

————, 'Counterpoints in the performing arts of Malaysia', in *Fragmented Vision: Culture and Politics in Contemporary Malaysia*, ed. Joel S. Kahn and Francis Kok Wah Loh. Honolulu: University of Hawai'i Press, 1992, pp. 282–305.

————, *Bangsawan: A Social and Stylistic History of Popular Malay Opera*. Singapore: Oxford University Press, 1993.

————, 'The 78 RPM record industry in Malaya prior to World War II', *Asian Music* 28, 1 (1996/97): 1–41.

————, 'Negotiating identities: Reconstructing the 'local' in Malaysia through "world beat"', *Perfect Beat* 5, 4 (2002): 3–20.

————, 'From folk to national popular music: Recreating *ronggeng* in Malaysia', *Journal of Musicological Research* 24, 3 (2005): 287–307.

————, 'Dissonant voices: Contesting control through alternative media in Malaysia', 2006. Available at http://geekrawk.wordpress.com/2006/01/21/dissonant-voices-contesting-control-through-alternative-media-in-malaysia/ [accessed 29 January 2018].

————, 'Negotiating "His Master's Voice": Gramophone music and cosmopolitan modernity in British Malaya in the 1930s and early 1940s', *Bijdragen tot de Taal-, Land- en Volkenkunde* 169, 4 (2013): 457–94.

Tan, Joanna, 'Popular music in the 1960s', *Singapore Infopedia*. Singapore: National Library of Singapore, 2010. Available at http://eresources.nlb.gov.sg/infopedia/articles/SIP_1658_2010-04-15.html [accessed 29 January 2018].

————, 'Popular music in 1960s Singapore', *Biblio Asia* 7, 1 (2011): 10–14.

Tan, Karen J., Faridah Stephens and Najua Ismail, *Behind the Scenes at P. Ramlee—The Musical*. Petaling Jaya: MPH, 2008.

Taruskin, Richard, *Text and Act: Essays on Music and Performance*. New York: Oxford University Press, 1995.

Taylor, C.G., *The Forgotten Ones of 'South East Asia Command' and 'Force 136'*. Ilfracombe: Stockwell, 1989.

Théberge, Paul, '"Plugged in": Technology and popular music', in *The Cambridge Companion to Pop and Rock*, ed. Simon Frith, Will Straw and John Street. Cambridge: Cambridge University Press, pp. 1–25.

'Tiga Ramlee di malam amal banjir '71' [Three Ramlees in the night flood '71], *Berita Harian*, 10 March 1971.

Trenowden, Ian, *Malayan Operations Most Secret: Force 136*. Singapore: Heinemann Asia, 1983.

Turino, Thomas, *Nationalists, Cosmopolitans, and Popular Music in Zimbabwe*. Chicago: University of Chicago Press, 2000.

Turner, Victor, 'Liminality and communitas', in *The Ritual Process: Structure and Anti-Structure*. New Jersey: Transaction Publishers, 1969, pp. 94–130.

U-Wei Haji Saari, 'Zubir Said, semoga bahagia' [Zubir Said, may you achieve happiness], in *Majulah! The Film Music of Zubir Said*. Singapore: National Museum of Singapore, 2012, pp. 54–61.

Uhde, Jan and Yvonne Ng Uhde, *Latent Images: Film in Singapore*. 2nd ed., Singapore: NUS Press, 2010.

Vasudevan, Ravi, 'Addressing the spectator of a "Third World" national cinema: The Bombay "social" film of the 1940s and 1950s', *Screen* 36, 4 (1995): 305–24.

——, 'Shifting codes, dissolving identities: The Hindi social film of the 1950s as popular culture', *Third Text* 10, 34 (1996): 59–77.

Vaughan Williams, Ralph, *National Music and Other Essays*. 2nd ed., Oxford: Oxford University Press, 1987.

Vickers, Adrian, '"Malay identity": Modernity, invented tradition and forms of knowledge', in *Contesting Malayness: Malay Identity Across Boundaries*, ed. Timothy P. Barnard. Singapore: Singapore University Press, 2004, pp. 25–55.

Wade, Geoff, 'The origins and evolution of ethnocracy in Malaysia', Asia Research Institute Working Paper, no. 112 (2009): 1–39.

Waterman, Christopher A., '"Our tradition is a very modern tradition": Popular music and the construction of a pan-Yoruba identity', *Ethnomusicology* 34, 3 (1990): 367–79.

Wazir Jahan Karim, 'Introduction: Emotions in perspective', in *Emotions of Culture: A Malay Perspective*, ed. Wazir Jahan Karim. Singapore: Oxford University Press, 1990, pp. 1–20.

——, 'Prelude to madness: The language of emotion in courtship and early marriage', in *Emotions of Culture: A Malay Perspective*, ed. Wazir Jahan Karim. Singapore: Oxford University Press, 1990, pp. 21–63.

Weidman, Amanda J., *Singing the Classical, Voicing the Modern: The Postcolonial Politics of Music in South India*. London: Duke University Press, 2006.

Weintraub, Andrew N., *Dangdut Stories: A Social and Musical History of Indonesia's Most Popular Music*. New York: Oxford University Press, 2010.

White, Timothy, 'Historical poetics, Malaysian cinema and the Japanese occupation', *Kinema* 6 (1996): 5–27.

Whittall, Arnold, 'Leitmotif', *Grove Music Online*, Oxford Music Online, 2012. Available at https://doi.org/10.1093/gmo/9781561592630.article.16360 [accessed 18 December 2017].

Winstedt, R.O., *The Malay Annals, or, Sejarah Melayu: The Earliest Recension from Ms. No. 18 of the Raffles Collection in the Library of the Royal Asiatic Society, London*, Singapore: Malayan Branch of the Royal Asiatic Society, 1938.

Young, Jock, *The Drugtakers: The Social Meaning of Drug Use.* London: Paladin, 1971.

Yusnor Ef, *Muzik Melayu Sejak 1940-An.* Kuala Lumpur: YKNA Network, 2011.

Zizi Azah Bte Abdul Majid and Amri Amin, '*Bintang Hati—Malam Kenangan Zubir Said*' [Star of the Heart—Remembering Zubir Said], Concert Programme Booklet, 12 October 2012.

Zubillaga-Pow, Jun and Ho Chee Kong, eds. *Singapore Soundscape: Musical Renaissance of a Global City.* Singapore: National Library Board Singapore, 2014.

Zubir Said, 'Bahasa Melayu dalam nyanyian' [The Malay language in song], Paper presented at the Third Congress on Malay Language and Literature, Singapore and Johor Bahru, 1956/1957.

———, 'Menuju tahun 1967' [Towards 1967], *Filem Malaysia*, June 1967.

———, 'Music in the age of Merdeka', in *Majulah! The Film Music of Zubir Said.* Singapore: National Museum of Singapore, 2012, pp. 94–97.

———, 'The development of Malay music', in *Majulah! The Film Music of Zubir Said.* Singapore: National Museum of Singapore, 2012, pp. 98–103.

IV. Theses and Dissertations

Arnold, Alison E., 'Hindi Filmigit: On the History of Commercial Indian Popular Music'. PhD thesis, University of Illinois, 1991.

Burhanuddin Bin Buang, 'Pop Yeh Yeh Music in Singapore: 1963–1971'. BA Honours thesis, National University of Singapore, 2000.

D'Cruz, Marion F., 'Joget Gamelan: A Study of Its Contemporary Practice'. MA thesis, Universiti Sains Malaysia, 1979.

Gray, Gordon T., 'Malaysian Cinema and Negotiations with Modernity: Film and Anthropology'. PhD thesis, Napier University, 2002.

Raja Iskandar bin Raja Halid, 'Malay Nobat: A History of Encounters, Accommodation and Development'. PhD thesis, King's College London, 2015.

Filmography

A Go-Go '67. Malay Film Productions, dir. Omar Rojik, 1967. Available at: https://www.youtube.com/watch?v=boX_n2AZWoA.

Ali Baba Bujang Lapok [Ne'er Do Well Bachelors Ali Baba]. Malay Film Productions, dir. P. Ramlee, 1961. Available at: https://www.youtube.com/watch?v=hPQwkUxLqcg.

Aloha. Malay Film Productions, dir. B.S. Rajhans, 1950.

Anak Bapak [Father's Son]. Merdeka Film Studio, dir. P. Ramlee, 1968. Available at: https://www.youtube.com/watch?v=Plqf0BVMJ_8.

Anak Pontianak [Vampire's Child]. Cathay-Keris, dir. Ramon A. Estella, 1958. Available at: https://www.youtube.com/watch?v=zBZzpDS83Dw.

Anak-ku Sazali [My Son Sazali]. Malay Film Productions, dir. Phani Majumdar. 1956. Available at: https://www.youtube.com/watch?v=FhdAnjH92ko.

Antara Dua Darjat [Between Two Classes]. Malay Film Productions, dir. P. Ramlee, 1960. Available at: https://www.youtube.com/watch?v=FlMFn2iZ18E.

Bawang Puteh Bawang Merah [Garlic and Onions]. Cathay-Keris, dir. S. Roomai Noor. 1959. Available at: https://www.youtube.com/watch?v=SJAmdnT68jc.

Bujang Lapok [Ne'er Do Well Bachelors]. Malay Film Productions, dir. P. Ramlee, 1957. Available at: https://www.youtube.com/watch?v=JN-MxHTYhHo.

Buloh Perindu [Bamboo of Longing]. Cathay-Keris, dir. B.S. Rajhans, 1953.

Chinta [Love]. Malay Film Productions, dir. B.S. Rajhans, 1948.

Dang Anom. Cathay-Keris, dir. Hussein Haniff, 1962. Available at: https://www.youtube.com/watch?v=pGZbFFmQAdw.

Hanchor Hati [Broken Heart]. Shaw Brothers, dir. Wan Hai Ling, 1941.

Hang Jebat. Cathay-Keris, dir. Hussein Haniff, 1961. Available at: https://www.youtube.com/watch?v=wsC6p3poLYw.

Hang Tuah. Malay Film Productions, dir. Phani Majumdar, 1956. Available at: https://www.youtube.com/watch?v=Ko-adGo5Log.

Hantu Gangster [Gangster Ghost]. UB Prodigee Entertainment, dir. Wee Meng Chee, 2012.

Ibu [Mother]. Malay Film Productions, dir. S. Ramanathan, 1953. Available at: https://www.youtube.com/watch?v=lpLmOWAGgM0.

Ibu Mertua-ku [My Mother-in-law]. Malay Film Productions, dir. P. Ramlee, 1962. Available at: https://www.youtube.com/watch?v=cmsWBBneRqw.

339

Jula Juli Bintang Tiga [The Magical Tale of the Three Stars]. Cathay-Keris, dir. B.N. Rao, 1959. Available at: https://www.youtube.com/watch?v=o1Dbs262zYw.

Kami [Us]. Indra Film, dir. Patrick Yeoh, 1982. Available at: https://www.youtube.com/watch?v=VIOgAAKa-sY.

Labu Labi. Malay Film Productions, dir. P. Ramlee, 1962. Available at: https://www.youtube.com/watch?v=Ia74Rzb3prE.

Leftenan Adnan [Lieutenant Adnan]. Paradigmfilm and Grand Brilliance, dir. Aziz M. Osman, 2000. Available at: https://www.youtube.com/watch?v=FVeryOrYdd4.

Leila Majnun. Motilal Chemical Company, dir. B.S. Rajhans, 1934.

Love Parade. Shaw Brothers, dir. Doe Ching, 1961.

Masam Masam Manis [Sweet and Sour]. Merdeka Film Studio, dir. P. Ramlee, 1965. Available at: https://www.youtube.com/watch?v=e-9xTKOD-wI.

Mata Syaitan [Devil's Eyes]. Cathay-Keris, dir. Hussein Haniff, 1962. Available at: https://www.youtube.com/watch?v=DKd4YapHDSw.

Muda Mudi [The Youths]. Cathay-Keris, dir. M. Amin, 1965. Available at: https://www.youtube.com/watch?v=_MLPuVwMpzg.

Nasi Lemak 2.0 [Coconut Rice 2.0]. Prodigee Media, dir. Wee Meng Chee, 2011.

P. Ramlee. Persona Pictures, dir. Shuhaimi Baba. 2010. Available at: https://www.youtube.com/watch?v=3GNKBkeDDlg&t=188s.

Penarak Beca [Trishaw Puller]. Malay Film Productions, dir. P. Ramlee, 1955. Available at: https://www.youtube.com/watch?v=TXbKphDt8L8.

Pendekar Bujang Lapok [Ne'er Do Well Bachelor Warriors]. Malay Film Productions, dir. P. Ramlee, 1959. Available at: https://www.youtube.com/watch?v=e_8qt88Z3NQ.

Pontianak [Vampire]. Cathay-Keris, dir. B.N. Rao, 1957.

Rachun Dunia [Poison of the World]. Malay Film Productions, dir. B.S. Rajhans, 1950. Available at: https://www.youtube.com/watch?v=KnZs4WqG3-A.

Raja Bersiong [Vampire King]. Malay Film Productions, dir. Jamil Sulong, 1968. Available at: https://www.youtube.com/watch?v=dEvjR0Mxk8g.

Semerah Padi [As Red As Paddy], Malay Film Productions, dir. P. Ramlee, 1956. Available at: https://www.youtube.com/watch?v=SOFOH5NuE8w.

Seniman Bujang Lapok [Ne'er Do Well Bachelors Artists]. Malay Film Productions, dir. P. Ramlee, 1961. Available at: https://www.youtube.com/watch?v=PTOYXNpMNUo.

Sergeant Hassan [Sergeant Hassan]. Malay Film Productions, dir. Lamberto V. Avellana, 1958. Available at: https://www.youtube.com/watch?v=rH9wadsELuE.

Sri Mersing. Cathay-Keris, dir. Salleh Ghani. 1961. Available at: https://www.youtube.com/watch?v=i_kd-tOil9w.

Sumpah Pontianak [Curse of the Vampire]. Cathay-Keris, dir. B.N. Rao, 1958. Available at: https://www.youtube.com/watch?v=T7Q03AvOAS8.

Talentime. Grand Brilliance, dir. Yasmin Ahmad. 2009.

Terang Bulan Di-Malaya. Cathay-Keris, dir. B.S. Rajhans, 1941.

The Last Communist. Red Films, dir. Amir Muhammad, 2002.

Tiga Abdul [The Three Abduls]. Malay Film Productions, dir. P. Ramlee, 1964. Available at: https://www.youtube.com/watch?v=XEVORFxHMSM.

Picture Credits

I would like to acknowledge all those who have supplied the photographs appearing in this book. Every effort has been made to identify and contact those who hold the copyright of the illustrations. If there are instances where the copyright holder has not been acknowledged, then, if notified, the publisher will be pleased to rectify errors or omissions at the earliest opportunity.

My own photos: Figures 5.1 (with kind permission of Singapore Esplanade Library), 5.9, 6.1, 6.2 and 6.3. Courtesy of the Shaw Organisation: Figures 2.1, 2.4, 4.1, 4.2, 4.3, 4.4, 4.5, 4.6, 4.7, 4.8 and 4.9. Photographer unknown, with kind permission of Rohana Zubir: Figure 3.8. With kind permission of Joseph C. Pereira: Figures 5.2, 5.3, 5.4, 5.5, 5.6, 5.7 and 5.8. Album design by Rewan Ishak, with kind permission of Jeffrey Little for Laguna Music: Figure 6.4.

Index